Foreword

To say that "Fril - Fuzzy and Evidential Reasoning in AI" is a truly outstanding work is an understatement. What it is, in effect, is a comprehensive exposition of a far-reaching theory developed over the past two decades principally by Professor James Baldwin in co-operation with a group of talented associates.

The theory addresses a key issue in the conception, design and application of knowledge-based systems - the issue of uncertainty and imprecision.

It is a truism that the real world is pervasively uncertain and imprecise. And yet, most commercially available expert systems do not provide ways of handling data which are uncertain and/or imprecise. Why? In part, the reason is that certainty and precision carry a cost. But, most importantly, the reason was -- and still is -- that our understanding of how to deal with uncertainty and imprecision has not reached a point where we can feel assured that the results yielded by any theory are verifiably correct.

Historically, the first uncertainty management system was developed by Shortliffe and Buchanan in their seminal work on the medical expert system MYCIN. The sticky points in any uncertainty management system are the rules of combination of evidence. The rules used in MYCIN employed certainty factors in an intuitively appealing but ad hoc way. Experience has shown that the rules yield reasonably good results even though their validity is in question. A serious shortcoming of MYCIN is that it makes no provision for if-then rules with fuzzy consequents and/or fuzzy antecedents.

A fundamental problem which arises in any system which employs numerical probabilities for inference from uncertain evidence is the following. If H is a hypothesis and E1 and E2 are items of evidence, then nothing can be inferred concerning the probability of H given E1 and E2 from the knowledge of the probabilities of H given E1 and H given E2. Similarly, nothing can be inferred concerning the probability of H given E from the knowledge of the probability of H given E2 and the probability of E2 given E1. Thus, to be able to infer something it is necessary to make some assumptions concerning independence. Whether such assumptions are justified or not is frequently hard to assess.

During the past few years, Bayesian belief networks have attracted considerable attention as a basis for evidential reasoning under uncertainty. In my view, there are three basic problems with the Bayesian belief network approach. First, validation of the structure of a belief network presupposes a knowledge of causal dependencies which may be unavailable or hard to substantiate. Second, the conditional probabilities linking the nodes must represent crisp rather than fuzzy events. These problems call into question the reliability of precise numerical probabilities which are yielded by the Bayesian belief network approaches.

Professor Baldwin's theory is far more complete and far less ad hoc than alternative theories of uncertainty management in expert systems. It grew out of his earlier work on support logic programming and FRIL (Fuzzy Relational Inference Language), which was basically a Prolog-based system in which rules are allowed to be probability qualified, with probabilities assumed to lie in a specified interval. The original system was capable of handling fuzzy predicates but at a cost of inconvenience and loss of transparency. Reflecting the extensive experience acquired in the use of the original version, the system described in the volume is substantially more complete, more capable, more easy to use and more satisfying intellectually. Particularly noteworthy are the improved treatments of mass assignment and voting models, the expositions of fuzzy relations and possibility measures, and the application of mass assignment theory to control, case-based reasoning, data-browsing and search problems, meaning representation, and deductive databases. The exposition is capped in the final chapter with illustrative applications to practical problems which make it clearer how the theory can be employed in real-world settings.

Professor Baldwin's work and that of his associates may be viewed as a highly skilful, competent and imaginative fusion of the knowledge-representation and inferential power of Prolog with a system of uncertainty management based on propagation of fuzzy constraints. The overall system is as complete and as effective as any uncertainty management system can be. To say this does not mean that the uncertainty management problem has been solved. There are still many basic issues which elude understanding and may continue to do so in the foreseeable future. But what can be said is that Professor Baldwin's work is a major advance toward a better understanding of the complex interplay between knowledge, reasoning and decision analysis under uncertainty. The magnitude of the advance is such that no one who has a serious interest in uncertainty management in any setting can afford not to have "Fril - Fuzzy and Evidential Reasoning in AI" on his or her desk.

Lotfi A. Zadeh
Berkeley, CA
November 25, 1994

Editorial Preface

In 1965 Lotfi Zadeh published a paper called "Fuzzy Sets" and later stated the principle of incompatibility:

"As the complexity of a system increases, our ability to make precise and significant statements about its behaviour diminishes until a threshold is reached beyond which precision and significance become almost mutually exclusive characteristics."

Other scientists and mathematicians, stimulated by Zadeh's vision for new ways of looking at complex systems, joined forces with him and a new body of researchers was born.

Uncertainty theory plays an important part in the modelling of knowledge based systems for real applications. Applications of Artificial Intelligence methods in such areas as engineering, medicine, economics, business and law must cope with missing information, corrupted data, incompleteness of definition of concepts and vagueness of various forms. Model simplification and data summarisation is also relevant to avoid excessive computational complexity. Generalisation from specific cases and case-based reasoning play an equally important role to that of logical deduction. Both probability and fuzzy set theories therefore play an essential part in the basic development of knowledge based systems methods and modelling.

Probability theory is adequate to deal with missing information and can be useful for generalisation and simplification in certain cases but does not naturally help in the representation of vagueness of definition or for some essential forms of generalisation. These are the province of fuzzy set theory. These theories should not be thought to be in competition but as complementary to one another. The two theories should also be consistent with each other. One provides constraints on possibilities, the other on chances of events occurring. Possibilities constrain chances so the theories are linked. The books in this series will emphasise such an integration of these theories and provide methods for combining the various forms of uncertainty.

Knowledge representation necessarily plays an essential role. If we are dealing with pure deterministic knowledge systems then we can use first order predicate logic or some variant or extension of it for modelling purposes. What forms of knowledge representation should we use when allowing both probability and fuzzy types of uncertainty to occur? For a given form of representation what inference methods should be used? These are important questions and there are several partial solutions. This series will be concerned with such problems.

The Knowledge Engineer requires modelling paradigms and associative inference methods which can be used for software development of practical applications. Such is contained within the AI computer language - Fril. Different theories of how to represent and handle the two forms of uncertainty can be programmed in Fril. This book describes the Fril language, provides a general theory of uncertainty for knowledge based applications providing methods for the management of both fuzzy and probabilistic uncertainties and provides models for fuzzy control, data bases containing imperfect information, case-based reasoning, causal nets, evidential logic, intelligent manuals, data browsers and Zadeh's PRUF language. It provides a software tool kit for the Knowledge Engineer which can be used to quickly develop Artificial Intelligence applications for real systems.

Professor J. F. Baldwin

University of Bristol,

August 1994.

Acknowledgements

The authors would like to thank Mark Coyne, Richard Gooch, Hilary Hynam, Jonathan Lawry, Mark Swabey, and Zhou Yiming for their invaluable help in proof-reading the book, and testing the demonstration software.

Contents

CHAPTER 1

Introduction

1.1 AIMS OF THE BOOK

The aims of the book are
> (1) to present a theory of uncertainty relevant to knowledge engineering which is consistent with and brings together the theories of probability and fuzzy sets
> (2) to extend the logic programming form of knowledge representation and method of inference to allow for the inclusion of uncertainties of various forms including probabilistic knowledge and fuzzy incompleteness
> (3) to show the application to general areas of knowledge engineering such as
> > expert and decision support systems
> > evidential and case based reasoning
> > probabilistic and fuzzy causal nets
> > fuzzy control
> > fuzzy databases
> > intelligent manuals
> (4) to present the artificial intelligence language FRIL which implements this theory of uncertainty in the style of logic programming and contains modules for the various applications.

1.2 THE IMPORTANCE OF UNCERTAINTY IN MODELLING APPLICATIONS

It is generally recognised that models of practical applications will contain uncertainties and incomplete information. Model parameters, model structures, input data, interpretation of concepts can all be uncertain in some respect. Model variability can be represented using probability and fuzzy set theories.

A value of a parameter may not be known for certain, and the best that one can do is specify a probability distribution over the set of possible values the parameter can take. A conditional probability required for some model may only be known to be contained in a certain interval. In some cases it may be the probability distribution over the power set of the set of possible values the variable can take which is known. An everyday concept can rarely be given a precise definition in terms of necessary and sufficient conditions. We often interpolate between known similar cases and the concept 'similar' has no precise definition. We may only have partial belief that a particular model is

1

relevant to a given situation. Even if we have a complete model it may be too complicated to work with. Under different special circumstances more simple models can be used from which we can gain valuable judgment. A new circumstance may not fit precisely any of these cases. Nevertheless the engineer is often able to draw valuable conclusions using these documented cases.

An often dangerous procedure is to attempt to complete the incompleteness of the types mentioned by using average or typical values etc. This will ignore any sensitivity in the conclusions with respect to the variability discussed and lead to erroneous decisions being made.

1.3 THE TREATMENT OF UNCERTAINTY

In the main, ad hoc or controversial theories have been used to represent uncertainties in the field of AI. While probability theory is accepted, it is difficult to apply in practice since most practical applications cannot provide the complete information required for such a theory to be applied.

The mass assignment theory developed in this book is consistent with probability theory but allows for incomplete data concerning probabilities. The mass assignment is equivalent to a family of probability distributions although, in general, the converse is not true. We assume that we can specify such a family or a linear combination of orthogonal families for any variable. A special case of a mass assignment is the support pair which defines an interval containing the unknown probability. The support pair plays a fundamental role in the theory of Fril.

The mass assignment is not the same as the basic probability assignment in the Shafer Dempster theory of evidential reasoning. An algebra of mass assignments is defined whose meet is not equivalent with the Shafer Dempster method of combining evidences. The algebra is obtained by introducing a restriction relation. A mass assignment is a restriction of another mass assignment if the family of probability distributions corresponding to the first is a subset of the other. This is used to construct a lattice of mass assignments.

The theory of fuzzy sets is presented since the modelling of incompletely specified concepts is important in knowledge engineering which purports to be relevant to real world problems. The instantiation of a variable to a fuzzy set is interpreted as defining a possibility distribution for the variable which is equivalent to a family of probability distributions and hence to a mass assignment. The mass assignment algebra applied to fuzzy sets provides a justification for the rules of intersection, complementation and union used in Fuzzy Set Theory. This approach to interpreting fuzzy sets should prevent the conflict which often arises between probabilists and fuzzy set enthusiasts. In practice it is often easier to prescribe a possibility distribution than a probability distribution. There is no point in making assumptions in order to choose a unique probability distribution from the family of distributions resulting from the possibility distribution.

1.4 THE FRIL LANGUAGE

Fril is an Artificial Intelligence logic programming language which allows both probabilistic uncertainties and fuzzy sets to be included. The probabilistic uncertainties can be in the form of support pairs. Both continuous and discrete fuzzy sets can be used. If no uncertainties are used then Fril is equivalent to Prolog. A different syntax is used from standard Prolog.

Fril is written in "C" and is commercially available. It will run on a wide range of workstations and under various operating systems. It is in use for many applications including expert systems for aircraft design, command and control, vision understanding, evidential reasoning and decision support systems.

Two Fril demonstration disks are provided in the book. One is for the Macintosh computer and will run on any Macintosh under System 7 or later. The other is for the IBM PC or clone and will work under Windows 3.1 or later. Installing and running the demonstration software is straightforward and is described in the "Read Me" file on each of the disks.

The version of Fril provided in the book is a demonstration version and will only run the problems discussed. A full version without this restriction can be obtained from Fril Systems Ltd at the following address:

> Fril Systems Ltd
> Bristol Business Centre
> Maggs House
> 78, Queens Road, Clifton
> Bristol BS8 1QX, UK

Full versions of Fril are available to run on many different hardware platforms and operating systems. For example, Fril runs on Unix workstations under X-windows, on PC's under Windows 3.1, and on Apple Macintosh series machines under System 7. Single user and multi-user network licences are available. A Fril application generator is also available on all platforms supported; so that programs can be converted to stand-alone applications, such as the Fril demonstration system provided on the accompanying disks.

3

1.5 RULES IN FRIL

Fril programs consist basically of facts and rules. In addition to the Fril Prolog rule, three types of uncertainty rules can be represented in Fril:

(1) Basic Rule

(2) Extended Rule

(3) Evidential Logic Rule

Strictly speaking, the basic rule is a special case of the extended rule and was the only rule in the previous versions of the Fril language.

The extended rule is important for fuzzy causal net type applications. Both the second and third rules can be simulated using programs written in terms of only the basic rule but it is more efficient to have them in the core Fril.

The evidential logic rule can be used for those types of problem for which neural nets are applicable. The theory of the evidential logic rule does not correspond directly to a neural net, but the motivation for the rule came from connectionist theory. This type of rule can be used for case-based and analogical reasoning.

The unification of Prolog is extended in Fril to allow for a form of semantic unification. The theory of this comes from the mass assignment theory and provides a partial matching of terms in which the degree of this partial matching is contained in a support pair.

1.6 CONTENTS OF THE BOOK

The second chapter introduces Fril in a tutorial style of presentation. It only describes the Prolog aspects of Fril and is a simple introduction to logic programming. More advanced and meta- programming are covered in Chapter 5.

The uncertainty theory which forms the basis for the inference methods of Fril under uncertainty is described in Chapters 3 and 4. A tutorial style rather than a formal approach is used to present the main ideas and relate them to Fril.

Chapters 6 and 7 provides modules for the various application areas mentioned above, namely

Fuzzy Databases

Fuzzy Control

Intelligent Manuals

Fuzzy Causal Nets

Pruf

Evidential Logic

The Pruf module introduces a discussion of Zadeh's PRUF and shows how it can be represented in Fril.

The final chapter describes briefly some of the applications that Fril has been used for in industry.

1.7 RELEVANCE TO RESEARCHERS

The book describes a theory of uncertainty which has many application in such fields as

> Expert systems, knowledge-based systems, decision support systems
> Maintenance and diagnostic systems
> Control of complex systems using an AI approach
> Case-Based Reasoning
> Fuzzy Causal Net Modelling
> Engineering design using an AI approach
> Data Fusion
> Soft Computing
> Human / Computer Interfaces
> Mathematical Modelling of Engineering Systems
> Vision Understanding
> Speech Recognition
> Fuzzy Neural Nets

and a language which can be used to program these applications.

There is much work to be done in showing exactly how the theory can be used for any given application. For example, causal net modelling can result in computationally intensive models, especially when variables which can be instantiated to many possible values are used rather than binary valued variables. A fuzzy causal net can reduce the complexity of the model in a similar manner to the reduction of complexity of control models using fuzzy control. Decomposition theorems can be used to decompose a model into sub-models. There are many questions to be answered before we have a practical approach for this.

The fuzzy control indicates how the methods given in this book can be used for a more sophisticated type of control application than those which at present use fuzzy set methods. How can we use and extend the theory for control of complex systems?

Only the rudiments of case-based reasoning are given here. How can we develop a theory of generalisation relevant to case base reasoning based on the theory of uncertainty and the evidential logic rule given here? What other forms of evidential logic

5

rules should we consider?

The intelligent manual shows a pleasing user interface for investigating technical documentation. What further intelligence can we build into this system? The system should be able to interpret the intention of the user in requesting information, and supply appropriate answers to questions.

High level vision understanding is only at a beginning. How can we integrate the low level and high level capabilities? A similar question can be asked of speech recognition. The evidential logic rule has been used for handwritten character recognition. To interpret general handwriting we require rules which will allow context to be identified and used to help the recognition.

Knowledge acquisition in the form of knowledge revision is an important area of research. Some work to date has used Prolog as the representation language. The Fril language could prove to be more relevant for this task. For example, statements like

most tall persons wear large shoes

are more appropriate than

all tall persons wear large shoes.

How can we extract such a statement from the relevant data of persons? How do we decide what are the important statements, in the form of probabilistic / fuzzy type rules, to extract from data?

In this general area of uncertainty management and its application to real problems there are a wealth of difficult questions to be answered, large chunks of theory to be developed and interesting new areas of applicablity to be discovered. The field presents the researcher with many challenging problems.

In this book we provide both a theory and a computer language to tackle such problems. New theories and extensions of that presented here can easily be coded in Fril and tested for their scientific value. We hope that young researchers will take up the challenge and provide new pathways and new insights into how to model applications in which uncertainties of various forms play an important role.

CHAPTER 2

Logic Programming in Fril

2.1 INTRODUCTION

This chapter introduces the essential concepts needed to understand and write Fril programs. Fril is similar to another logic programming language, Prolog, but it is more powerful for many Artificial Intelligence applications as it has built-in features for handling uncertainty. Later in the book, these additional features of Fril are used and described extensively, but for the purposes of this chapter we will be treating Fril mostly as a dialect of Prolog.

In a procedural language, a program is written in terms of operations which are directly related to the underlying machine instructions, e.g. X=3 would store the value 3 in a particular memory location. The program is compiled and then run. Logic programming offers a different approach to computing, where a program can be viewed either as a set of logical statements defining a problem or as an algorithm describing in high-level terms how a problem may be solved. Logic programs are executed by means of queries - this is analogous to the problem of proving a theorem from a set of axioms in logic. The query can be viewed as a theorem to be deduced from the knowledge base. This chapter describes the way in which data are stored in Fril, how to run programs by executing queries, and how to use the built-in predicates, which are necessary for "nonlogical" programming tasks. The style is tutorial in nature, with many worked examples.

2.2 OUTLINE OF THE LANGUAGE

The data types of Fril are simple but expressive. Everything in the Fril language is known as a term, which can either be a variable, a constant, a number, a fuzzy set, or a list. These are described informally below - a comprehensive syntax definition is given in the Fril manual.

2.2.1 Variables

A *variable* is used to represent an unknown value. A variable symbol can be a single capital letter, a capital letter followed by one or more digits, two capital letters followed by zero or more characters, or an underscore followed by anything. Examples of variables are

  X X1 M32 VARIABLE VAriabLe _123

The following are not variables:

x Variable Xone Bristol

An underscore on its own, i.e. the symbol _ is known as the *anonymous variable*. It is important to understand that a variable in Fril is more like a mathematical variable than a variable in a conventional programming language. In Fril, a variable is used to stand for an unknown value. Once a value is found for the variable, it cannot be overwritten later. In contrast, a variable in a conventional programming language represents a machine location and its contents can be changed at any time.

2.2.2 Numbers

A *number* is a string of digits with an optional + or - preceding it and an optional decimal point embedded in it, e.g.

10   −30   +21.2

Fril also allows numbers in "exponent" form, such as

2.5e3 or 2.5E3 or even 25000e-1

all of which represent the floating point number 2500.0.

2.2.3 Constants

A *constant* is an alphanumeric string not covered by the two definitions above, or any character string enclosed in single or double quotes. Examples of constants are

c c1 constant cONSTANT "QUOTED" '123'

'I contain spaces
and a new line'

Note that the last constant extends over two lines because the carriage-return is read as part of the string. It is quite common for programmers in Fril (as in many other languages) to link separate words by underscores to form a single constant symbol e.g.

long_Fril_name

no_spaces_in_me

rather than the quoted forms "long Fril name" and "no spaces in me". This is a matter of personal taste, although the form linked by underscores is probably more common.

2.2.4 Fuzzy Sets

A fuzzy set in Fril is a sequence of element-membership pairs separated by spaces or commas and enclosed in square or curly brackets. A fuzzy set enclosed in square brackets, such as

[0:0 1:1 2:0]

is a continuous fuzzy set. Each element must be a either a variable or a number, and its associated membership must be a variable or a number in the range 0 to 1. The elements must be in ascending order, and the membership of any element not explicitly listed is

8

found by interpolation between the given points. For this reason, a continuous fuzzy set is often referred to as an *i-type*, the *i* standing for interpolation.

A fuzzy set enclosed in curly brackets is a discrete fuzzy set, whose only members are those explicitly listed. The elements of a discrete fuzzy set may be numbers, constants, or variables. As in the continuous case, the membership of each element can be a variable or a number in the range 0 to 1. Examples of discrete fuzzy sets are:

{a:0.2 b:1 c:0.3 d:0.1}

{99:0.8, 100:1, 101:0.9, 102:0.3}

Fuzzy sets are described in later chapters, and are mentioned here for completeness only. They are not used in this chapter.

2.2.5 Lists

A list is an ordered sequence of one or more terms enclosed in parentheses "(" and ")". Each opening bracket must have a matching closing bracket, and the terms can be separated by spaces or commas. Examples of lists are

(list of constants)

(LIST OF VARIABLES)

((embedded) ((lists)))

(Mixture of terms [1:0.1,2:1,3:1,4:0] (and lists) 2.3 X –8)

The list is the fundamental data structure in Fril, and is given special attention later in this chapter. Since a list is defined simply as a sequence of terms and a term can be a list, it is possible to nest lists to an arbitrary depth.

2.2.6 Comments

A comment is a sequence of symbols enclosed in /* and */, or any text between the symbol % and the end of a line. Each /* must have a closing */, so that it is possible to nest comments. This makes it easy to comment out a section of program which may already contain comments.

2.2.7 Clauses

A Fril program can be viewed as a set of statements defining a problem. The individual statements are known as *clauses*. Each clause expresses a relationship between terms related to the problem. For instance, we might wish to represent the knowledge that a certain person Oscar has a logical mind. In Fril, we could write this as

((mind of Oscar is logical))

Alternatively, we could express this in the more concise but perhaps less clear form:

((mind_of Oscar logical))

It is common practice in Fril to adopt the second (more Spartan) style, although it might be argued that this is less clear. The choice of one style or the other is largely a matter of

9

taste, but as we shall see later it is necessary to be consistent throughout a program.

In logic programming, the relationship *mind_of* is known as a *predicate*, and the terms *Oscar* and *logical* are its *arguments*. The clause

((mind_of Oscar logical))

expresses an unconditional relationship between its arguments, and is known as a *fact*. Similarly, the clause

((parent_of John Bill))

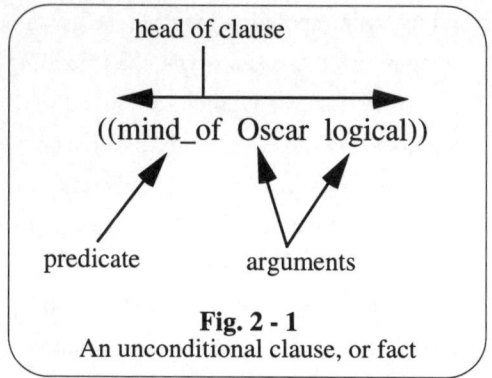

Fig. 2 - 1
An unconditional clause, or fact

expresses the proposition that Bill is a parent of John. Note that we have used names that suggest this meaning - an equally valid clause would have been

((pa a1 a2))

In practice, the correspondence between the symbols in a program and the problem being modelled should be obvious and unambiguous.

A fact is nothing more than a list containing a single term. That term is also a list, whose first element is the predicate being defined and whose remaining elements are the arguments of the predicate. This observation is important when considering *metaprogramming*, i.e. writing programs which use other programs as data, as discussed in more detail in Chapter 5. More complex clauses are known as rules, which contain one or more conditions. The rule in Fig. 2 - 2 is read as

"X is capable of Fril if X has a logical mind",

where X is understood to be a variable that can stand for anything. If we can find some value of X for which it is true to say that X has a logical mind, then we can conclude that X is capable of Fril. The term *(capable_of Fril X)* is known as the head of the clause, and *(mind_of X logical)* forms the body of the clause.

In general there can be more than one term in the body of a clause - for instance we could write

((grandparent_of X Y) (parent_of X Z) (parent_of Z Y))

which has two terms in its body and states that for any X and Y, the grandparent of X is Y if the parent of X is some person Z and the parent of Z is Y. The terms in the body of a clause are known as *goals*.

We can see that a fact is simply a special case of a rule, in which there is no body. A rule is a list

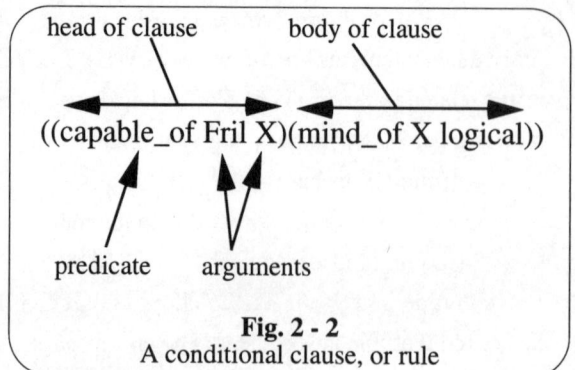

Fig. 2 - 2
A conditional clause, or rule

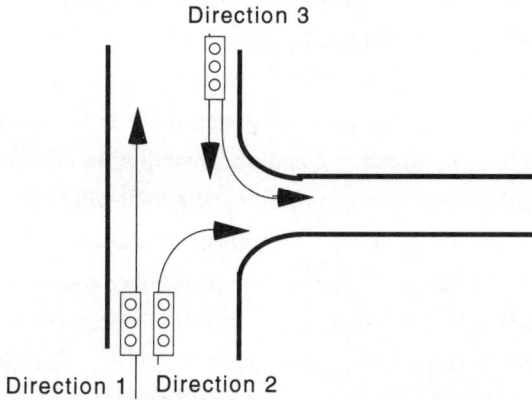

Fig. 2 - 3

A junction consisting of a main road and a small side road. Traffic in direction 1 is controlled by one set of lights and continues on the main road, traffic in direction 3 is controlled by another set of lights and either turns left into the side road or continues on the main road, and traffic in direction 2 is controlled by a third set of lights and turns right into the side road (across the traffic moving in direction 3)

of two or more terms, the first being the head of the rule and the remainder being the body of the rule, or conditions. The variables used in a clause are local to that clause. Thus in the clause

((grandparent_of X Y) (parent_of X Z) (parent_of Z Y))   ①

the X in the head *(grandparent_of X Y)* is the same as the X in the first goal of the body, *(parent_of X Z)*. We could change X to any other variable name (except Y and Z which are already used in the clause) without changing the meaning or behaviour of the clause in any way. Similarly, the X in the head of the rule

((capable_of Fril X) (mind_of X logical))   ②

is the same as the X in the body of this rule. However, the occurrences of X in clause ① are completely independent of the occurrences of X in clause ②; thus we consider the variables to be local variables.

Finally, we define a *procedure* to be a sequence of clauses, all of which have the same predicate.

2.3 PROGRAM EXECUTION - QUERIES

A Fril program consists of a set of clauses known as the *knowledge base*. Executing the program is the process of checking whether a particular piece of information is in the knowledge base, either explicitly or implicitly, i.e. whether it can be derived by a process of deduction using the facts and rules in the knowledge base. This is known as querying the knowledge base.

We will take a very simple example to illustrate this principle. Consider a road junction that is controlled by traffic lights, as shown in Fig. 2 - 3. For simplicity, we take the lights to be set to either red or green. Clearly some combinations of light settings will be potentially hazardous, e.g. if all lights are green, there is a possibility of collision between a vehicle travelling in direction 2 and one travelling in direction 3. It would be relatively straightforward to devise an algorithm to determine which settings of the lights are safe and which are unsafe. However, we will adopt the more direct approach and write out a table of light settings and judgments as to whether each setting is safe or not. We will use a set of facts where the first three arguments represent the settings of lights in directions 1, 2, and 3 respectively, and the the fourth argument represents the judgment. Thus the first Fril clause below should be read as *"the junction with light 1 set to green, light 2 set to green, and light 3 set to green is unsafe"*. The full table is:

```
((junction green  green  green  unsafe))
((junction red    red    red    safe))
((junction green  red    green  safe))
((junction red    green  green  unsafe))
((junction green  green  red    safe))
((junction red    red    green  safe))
((junction red    green  red    safe))
((junction green  red    red    safe))
```

This is a simple Fril program, or knowledge base. Unlike a program in a procedural language, this program can be executed in a number of ways. In order to check that a particular setting for the lights is safe, we could use the query:

> ?((junction green red green safe))

The '?' indicates that we are asking whether the information *"is safe the correct judgment when the lights 1, 2, and 3 are green, red, and green respectively ?"* can be derived from the knowledge base

Fril will respond

> yes

because this information is present in the third row of the table above. If we had asked the query

> ?((junction red green green safe))

Fril would respond

> no

because this information is not present in the table. The information that this setting is unsafe is present, but this is not relevant to our query. Anyone given the information in the table would answer no to the query because the fourth clause states that this

12

combination is unsafe, not because there are no clauses stating that it is safe; however, we must always bear in mind that Fril is not intelligent and does not understand the meaning of the symbols. If we changed the program to use just the initial letters of the constants so that the fourth clause became

((j r g g u))

then the meaning would be far less obvious to the human observer, but Fril would use the same process to reach its conclusion.

The queries above simply *check* whether a particular piece of information is present in the knowledge base or not. How can we find out the correct judgment without having to guess *safe* or *unsafe* and see whether we get yes or no? Recall that a variable is used to stand for an unknown value, so that we can use a variable in place of the last argument:

?((junction green red green X))

This query can be read as asking *"is there some value X which is the correct judgment when lights 1 2 and 3 are green, red, and green respectively?"*. The Fril response to this query is

yes

since there is indeed a value of X which is the correct judgment in this case. However, this is not as helpful as we might have expected - we are interested in knowing what the value for X is, not just whether there is a value or not. To accomplish this, we must also tell Fril to print the value it finds for X:

?((junction green red green X) (p X))

p is a built-in predicate that is part of the Fril system. It prints out its argument on the screen. In response to the above query, Fril would print

unsafe

and then respond

yes

Thus we can determine the setting for any combination of lights.

We can execute the program in a different way by using a query to find a combination that is safe :

?((junction X Y Z safe) (p X Y Z))

Fril would print

red red red

yes

These queries *generate* values that satisfy a particular relation (in this case, the relation defined by the predicate *junction*). As in the case of queries which check that the relation holds for specified arguments, the query either succeeds (and Fril answers *yes*) or it fails (and Fril responds *no*).

It is important to note that the program can be used in many different ways, and that the arguments to a particular predicate do not have to be classified as program "inputs" or "outputs" - this is defined by the query used. This is in marked contrast to the situation in a conventional language, where it is necessary to specify in advance which arguments are inputs, which are outputs and possibly also the type of each argument.

In order to explain the execution of Fril programs we must first define the process of *unification*, and then examine the way in which queries are solved by Fril.

2.3.1 Pattern Matching - Unification

The basic operation of Fril execution is unification, which is essentially a pattern-matching process. At the moment, we are interested in syntactic unification, which is derived from the resolution principle in predicate calculus theorem proving. In later chapters we will consider the more general case of semantic unification, which involves fuzzy sets. The process of syntactic unification succeeds if two terms are the same or can be made the same by a suitable choice of value for some or all of the variables in the terms. It can be summarised as follows:

• a variable will match any term, and in the process it will become *bound* or *instantiated* to that term. Any other occurrences of the variable also become bound to the term.

• a constant matches an identical constant

• a number matches an identical number

• a list matches another list, if corresponding elements match. If variables are contained in a list, e.g. X in (John X X), then instantiating one occurrence of the variable instantiates all occurrences of that variable. (The exception to this is the anonymous variable, _ , where each occurrence is taken to be separate, as illustrated in example 11.)

2.3.2 Examples of Unification

1. *X* and *green* match with the variable *X* instantiated to the constant *green*. We can write this as (X=green).

2. *green* and *red* do not match - they are both constants, but are not identical.

3. *one* and *1* do not match - *one* is a constant, whereas 1 is a number.

4. *1* and *1.0* match - both are numbers and their values are the same.

5. *PI* and *3.14159* match, with the instantiation (PI=3.14159) - *PI* is a variable, and so will match anything.

6. *X* and *Y* match with (X =Y).

7. *(John Y Y)* and *X* match with (X = (John Y Y)) - the variable X becomes instantiated to a list of terms.

8. *(mind_of Oscar is logical)* and *(mind_of Oscar logical)* do not match, as the third elements of the lists are different.

9. *(John X X)* and *(Y Bill Z)* match with (Y=John, Z=Bill, X=Bill) - we take corresponding elements from each list and unify them until either the end of both lists is reached or

14

we encounter a pair of elements that cannot be unified.

10. *(John X X)* and *(Y Bill Y)* do not match - taking the first elements from each list we obtain the instantiation (Y=John), and the second elements lead to (X=Bill). Under these instantiations, the two lists are

> *(John Bill Bill)* and *(John Bill John)*

which clearly do not match because the third elements are different. Thus it is not possible to make the two lists identical, and they do not match.

11. *(John _ _)* and *(Y Bill Y)* match with (Y=John) - the anonymous variable is used to represent cases where the binding is irrelevant, and is treated specially in that each occurrence is taken to be a separate variable. Thus the first list above is treated as if it were (John X1 X2), which matches the list (Y Bill Y) with (Y=John, X1=Bill, X2=John). Since anonymous variables are used, their bindings are ignored and the instantiation (Y=John) is all that is needed to make these two terms identical.

We will return to the unification of lists later in the chapter. The set of instantiations which makes two terms identical is said to be a unifier for the two terms. If two terms can be unified, there is a single most general unifier for them. A most general unifier is one which makes no "unnecessary" variable bindings - to illustrate this, consider example 6 above. The set of instantiations (X=Apple, Y=Apple) makes both terms the same and is therefore a unifier for them. However, it is not the most general unifier, since it is only necessary to make the instantiation (X =Y) to make them the same - any other unifier can be obtained from the most general case by additional instantiations.

2.3.3 Execution

Consider the simple knowledge base shown in Fig. 2 - 4. These facts represent information on flights between various cities, showing the origin, destination, and flight number, e.g. the first clause should be read as stating *"there is a flight from London to Dublin with flight number ba172"*. The knowledge base is illustrative only. In order to extract information, we use a query that

((flight London Dublin ba172))

((flight London Paris ba345))

((flight Paris Amsterdam af271))

((flight Edinburgh London ba215))

((flight London Frankfurt lf419))

((flight Amsterdam Frankfurt ba119))

Fig. 2 - 4
A simple knowledge base

will match a fact in the knowledge base. Thus to determine whether there is a flight from Edinburgh to London and print its flight number, we would use the query:

> ?((flight Edinburgh London X)(p X))

to which Fril responds:

> ba215

> yes

The query consists of a list of *goals*, treated as an ordered conjunction, in which the goals are considered from left to right and all of the goals must be satisfied for the query to be satisfied . The first goal is *(flight Edinburgh London X)* and the second is *(p X)*. In order to answer this query, Fril tries to satisfy the first goal, then the second. To satisfy the first goal, Fril attempts to match the term

> *(flight Edinburgh London X)*

with the head of a clause in the knowledge base. This matching process starts by looking at the first clause in the knowledge base, and works through the clauses sequentially. Thus Fril initially attempts to match the terms

> *(flight Edinburgh London X)* and *(flight London Dublin ba172)*.

These will not match because the second elements in the lists are not identical, and cannot be made identical. Similarly the second and third clauses will not match,because neither has a head which can be made identical to the goal. However, the head of the fourth clause will match the goal, with the instantiation X=ba215. Having found a solution to the first goal in the query, Fril moves on to the second goal, *(p X)*. This is a built-in predicate and causes the current binding of X to be printed on the screen, i.e. *ba215* is printed. Finally, as the query has been completed successfully, Fril prints *yes*

A query such as

> ?((flight London Edinburgh X)(p X))

would yield the response

> no

as there is no clause in the knowledge base whose head matches the first goal of this query. The search starts with the first clause for *flight* and checks all clauses before finding that there is no match. Because the first goal cannot be solved, Fril does not look at the second goal, and responds *no*. This does not mean that there is no flight from London to Edinburgh, just that this information is not in the knowledge base. If we had a knowledge base containing an exhaustive list of all flights, then we could be sure that Fril's *no* definitely means there is no such flight. If, however, our knowledge base might be incomplete, i.e. it is possible that there are flights which are not recorded in the knowledge base, we can only conclude that Fril's *no* means "unknown". The first case is known as a closed world, where all relevant information is held in the knowledge base, and the second case is known as an open world, where it is possible that some information is not recorded in the knowledge base.

2.3.4 Compound Queries

The query

> ?((flight London Amsterdam X)(p X))

would fail because it does not match any clause. However, anyone with a little knowledge would realise that it is possible to get from London to Amsterdam using two flights, from London to Paris, and then from Paris to Amsterdam (remember this knowledge base is an illustrative example only!). A query to find these two flights would be

> ?((flight London X F1)(flight X Amsterdam F2) (p X F1 F2))

which can be translated as *"is there a flight F1 from London to some city X, and a flight F2 from the city X to Amsterdam"*. Fril would respond

> Paris ba345 af271
>
> yes

The query consists of three goals. In order to find a solution, Fril starts with the first goal *(flight London X F1)* and searches the knowledge base for a clause whose head matches. The first clause matches, giving X=Dublin and F1=ba172. Under these bindings, the second goal is *(flight Dublin Amsterdam F2)*. This goal does not match any clause in the knowledge base. Thus the goal fails, but the overall query has not failed yet because there are alternative ways of solving the first goal. Instead of matching with the first clause, we can use the second clause with the bindings X=Paris and F1=ba345 and a second goal *(flight Paris Amsterdam F2)*. This matches the third clause in the knowledge base and therefore succeeds, and the answer is printed by the final goal in the query. This strategy of finding the first matching clause, and then looking for alternatives if a subsequent goal fails is known as *backtracking*. We can represent the process using an execution tree, as shown in Fig. 2 - 5. The root of the tree is the query that must be solved; below that are individual goals in the query. Each goal has a number of descendants representing clauses that possibly match in the knowledge base. Fril solves a query by finding the first solution to each goal; if a goal has no solution then Fril goes back to the most recent goal where there is an alternative, and tries again.

2.3.5 Finding more Solutions

Suppose that we wish to find a flight from London to anywhere. The query to do this would be

> ?((flight London X Y)(p X Y))

giving the response

> Dublin ba172
>
> yes

Looking at the knowledge base, it is clear why this solution is produced - it is the first matching clause. However, there are other matching clauses, and we might like to know that there are alternatives to the solution produced. In other words, we want to force Fril to backtrack and find alternative solutions, even though the query has succeeded. One way to do this is to use the built-in predicate *fail*, which never succeeds. It can be thought of as a goal which never matches a clause in the knowledge base. When Fril reaches this goal, it always backtracks and will thus step through all solutions to the query. Note however that including the *fail* goal ensures there is no solution to the whole query (although

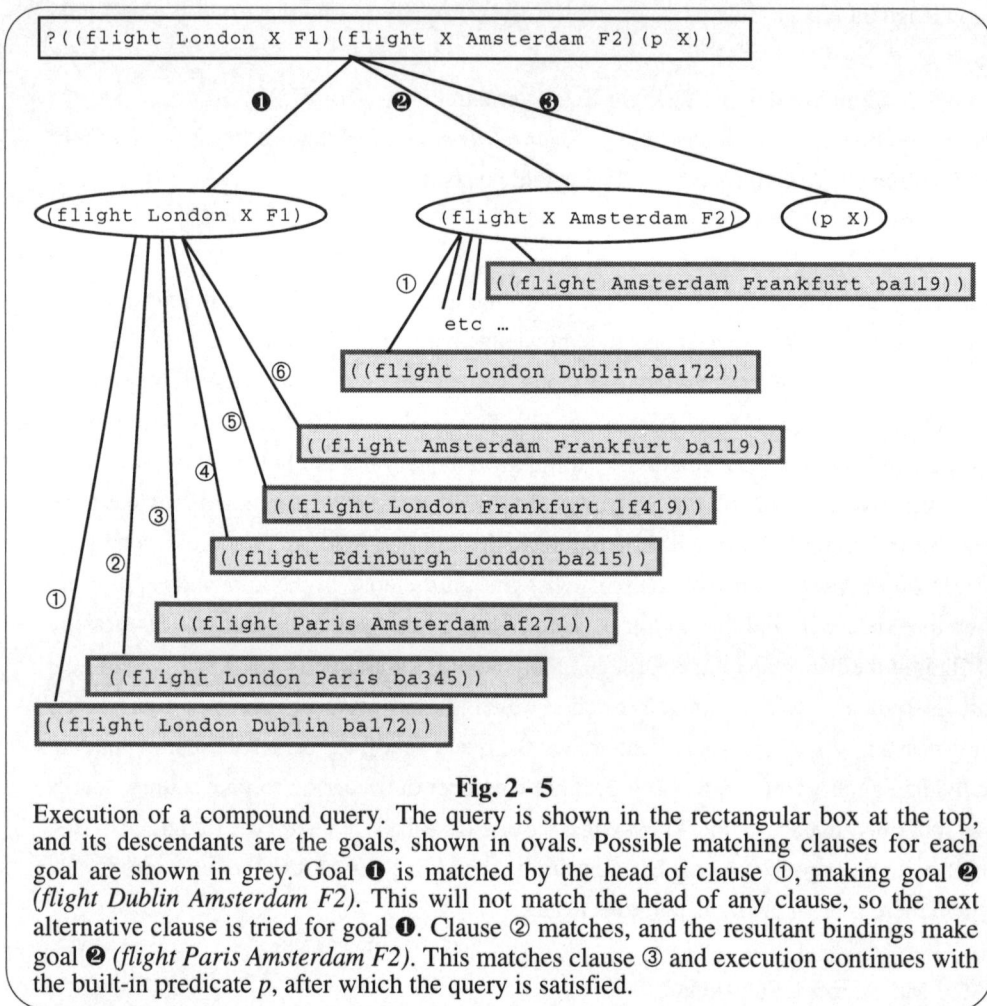

Fig. 2 - 5
Execution of a compound query. The query is shown in the rectangular box at the top, and its descendants are the goals, shown in ovals. Possible matching clauses for each goal are shown in grey. Goal ❶ is matched by the head of clause ①, making goal ❷ *(flight Dublin Amsterdam F2)*. This will not match the head of any clause, so the next alternative clause is tried for goal ❶. Clause ② matches, and the resultant bindings make goal ❷ *(flight Paris Amsterdam F2)*. This matches clause ③ and execution continues with the built-in predicate *p*, after which the query is satisfied.

there may be solutions to the earlier goals), and hence the query eventually fails and Fril responds

> no

The query is

> ?((flight London X Y)(p X Y)(pp)(fail))

giving the response

> Dublin ba172
>
> Paris ba345
>
> Frankfurt lf419
>
> no

The built-in predicate *pp* is similar to *p*, but prints its arguments on separate lines; if it has no arguments, as in this case, it just prints a new line. The method above is the most fundamental way of finding all solutions - there are other built-in predicates which can be used instead of the ? ((…) (fail)) combination, namely *qh*, *oh*, or *wh*. The *q*, *o*, and *w* can be thought of as standing for *query*, *one*, and *which* respectively, and the *h* as standing for *Horn* (as we are using Horn-clause logic). Their behaviour is illustrated below.

qh((flight London X Y))

((flight London Dublin ba172))
((flight London Paris ba345))
((flight London Frankfurt lf419))
no (more) solutions
yes

oh((flight London X Y)) % prints solutions one at a time

((flight London Dublin ba172))
more y/n? y
((flight London Paris ba345))
more y/n?n
no (more) solutions
yes

wh(X (flight London X Y)) % prints X for each solution.

Dublin
Paris
Frankfurt
no (more) solutions
yes

2.3.6 Rules

The previous section illustrated the use of a compound query to determine whether there is a two stage journey between two cities, stopping at an intermediate city. More frequently in Fril we would define a *rule* for this case

((two_stage X Y) (flight X Z F1)(flight Z Y F2))

which we can read as

"there is a two stage journey between any two cities X and Y if there is a flight from X to some intermediate city Z and a flight from Z to Y"

This is a logical definition of what we mean by a two stage journey. It can also be viewed as a procedure for finding a two stage route between two cities X and Y - first find a flight from X to some intermediate city Z, and then find a flight from that Z to the city Y. This second viewpoint implicitly includes the idea of searching and backtracking - if the first choice for Z is inappropriate, try another and see whether that has a flight to city Y. Notice that in this rule, the values found for variables F1 and F2 are unimportant, i.e. they

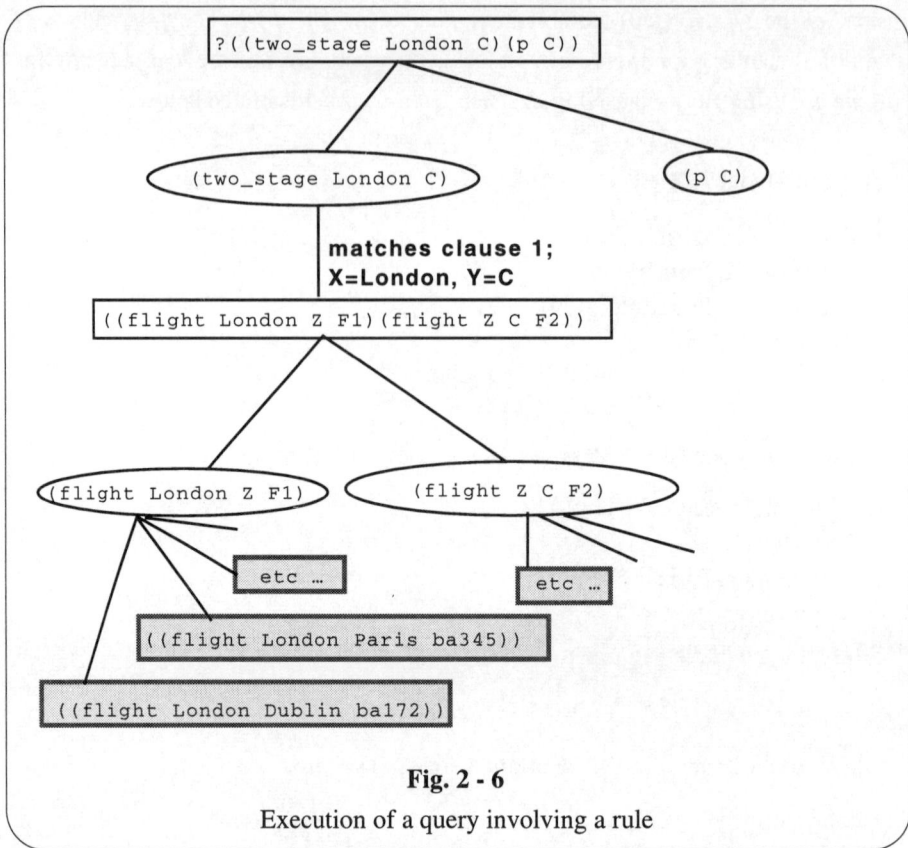

Fig. 2 - 6

Execution of a query involving a rule

are not used anywhere else in the clause. These variables could therefore be replaced by anonymous variables.

Having defined a rule, we can use it in queries or in other rules. For example, we could ask

?((two_stage London C) (p C))

printing

Amsterdam

yes

The execution tree for this is shown in Fig. 2 - 6.

When a goal matches the head of a rule, Fril executes the goals in the rule body. If these are satisfied, Fril continues with the remaining goals in the query. A fact is a special case in which there are no goals to be solved in the body. In this case, Fril can simply continue with the next goal in the query. This execution strategy allows us to nest rules to any depth - for example, we could use the definition for *two_stage* to define a rule for three stage journeys, such as

((three_stage X Y) (flight X Z F1)(two_stage Z Y))

The first goal in the body matches a fact in the knowledge base; the second matches a rule, which causes further goals to be executed. The tree representation can be helpful in understanding this process.

2.3.7 Where is the Logic?

The knowledge base and queries shown above may appear to be fairly straightforward and not bear much relation to logic. However, the process of extracting an answer to a query is equivalent to a logical inference procedure - the knowledge base corresponds to a set of *axioms*, and the query to a *theorem* to be proved from the axioms.

2.4 SOME USEFUL BUILT-IN PREDICATES

Before looking further at techniques for writing programs in Fril, we will consider some predicates which are built-in to the system. Most built-in predicates are used for tasks that are either non-logical, meta-logical, or inconvenient to program in the usual way. We will defer consideration of meta-logical predicates to Chapter 5. Non-logical built-in predicates allow us to perform operations which have no logical meaning, but which are essential in order to make logic programming systems practical. Examples include predicates for input and output, and control of execution. We have already seen the built-in predicates *p* and *pp*, which take any number of arguments (up to 31 on most hardware platforms) and print them on the screen. *p* separates the arguments by spaces, whereas *pp* prints each argument on a separate line. The built-in predicate *fail* is used to control execution, by forcing backtracking.

Sometimes predicates could theoretically be written in Fril, but are more convenient as built-in predicates. For example, to perform addition on the integers we could define a large set of facts

((sum 0 0 0))

((sum 0 1 1)) etc,

where the third argument gives the sum of the first two. This would require a very large number of facts to be entered - the exact number being dependent on the machine being used and the maximum values which could be represented on it. Instead, "sum" is provided as a built-in predicate which is logically equivalent to the set of facts in many ways, but is much more compact. The built-in version is not quite as versatile as the set of facts would be - we can use it to check that the relation *sum* holds between three given numbers, or to generate any one of the three numbers, given the other two. We cannot use it, for example, to generate three numbers X, Y, Z such that X + Y = Z, i.e. *(sum X Y Z)* holds. This is mainly because there are so many solutions that it is unlikely ever to be useful in a program.

The Fril Technical Reference Manual describes all of the built-in predicates of the system, and these descriptions are also available via Fril's on-line help system. In order to illustrate various points, brief descriptions of some useful built-in predicates for arithmetic are given below.

2.4.1 Addition and Subtraction - Sum

Fril provides various arithmetic predicates which can be thought of as (infinitely) large sets of facts defining the appropriate relations. For example, *sum* takes three arguments and succeeds if the third argument is equal to the sum of the other two. For example

?((sum 1 2 3)) would succeed, whereas

?((sum 1 2 4)) would fail. This built-in predicate can also be used to perform addition and subtraction, by leaving different arguments uninstantiated:

    ?((sum 1 2 X)(p X))   % addition X = 1+2

    3
    yes

    ?((sum 1 X 3)(p X))   % subtraction 1+X=3 or X=3-1

    2
    yes

Note however that only one argument can be left uninstantiated - the query

    ?((sum 1 Y X)(p Y X))

would cause an error message to be generated.

2.4.2 Multiplication and Division - Times

times takes three arguments and succeeds either if the product of the first two arguments is equal to the third argument, or if the instantiation of one argument makes this the case. For example the following queries produce the output shown

    ?((times 2.3 6 X)(p X))   % multiplication X = 2.3×6

    13.8
    yes

    ?((times X 1.2 12)(p X))   % division $1.2 \times X=12$ or X=12/1.2

    10
    yes

    ?((times 12 1.2 1.44))

    yes

    ?((times 12 1.2 1.43))

    no

2.4.3 Less

less succeeds if its first argument is numerically less than its second argument. It can only be used to check that this relation holds between its arguments, e.g.

    ?((less 42 12))
    no
    ?((less 12 42))
    yes

Attempting to use a query such as *?((less X 12))* to generate a value for X would cause an error. *less* can also be used to compare character strings, using alphabetic order.

2.4.4 Square

square succeeds if its second argument is the square of its first argument, or if it can be made so by the instantiation of one argument, e.g.

    ?((square 12 144))
    yes
    ?((square 12 43))
    no
    ?((square 4.2 X)(p X))
    17.64
    yes
    ?((square X 2)(p X))
    1.41421
    yes

Notice that, in the latter case, only the positive square root is given as a solution.

2.5 RECURSIVE RULES

In Section 2.3.6, we defined rules *two_stage* and *three_stage* to cover methods of getting from place to place without needing a direct flight. In principle, if we wanted to travel from one place to another, we could first try a query for a direct flight, then for a two stage journey, then a three stage journey, etc. Alternatively, we could define a rule which would check each of these possibilities:

    ((travel X Y) (flight X Y F))
    ((travel X Y) (two_stage X Y))
    ((travel X Y) (three_stage X Y))
    ((travel X Y) (four_stage X Y))

where we assume the previous definitions for *flight*, *two_stage*, and appropriate definitions for *three_stage, four_stage*.

This would succeed whenever it was possible to travel from X to Y by up to four flights. However, it is not an elegant definition and it is also potentially incomplete - if for example we expanded our set of flights so that journeys of longer than four stages were possible, these would not be found as solutions to the predicate *travel*. We need to generalise the definition so that it covers journeys involving *any* number of flights. This can be done using a *recursive* definition. Essentially, we define the predicate in terms of itself; however, this is not a circular definition as the recursive goal is actually a simpler problem to solve than the original. In our example, we know we can travel from X to Y if there is a direct flight between them; alternatively, if there is a flight from X to Z, and we can travel from Z to Y, then we can travel from X to Y. We can represent the flights

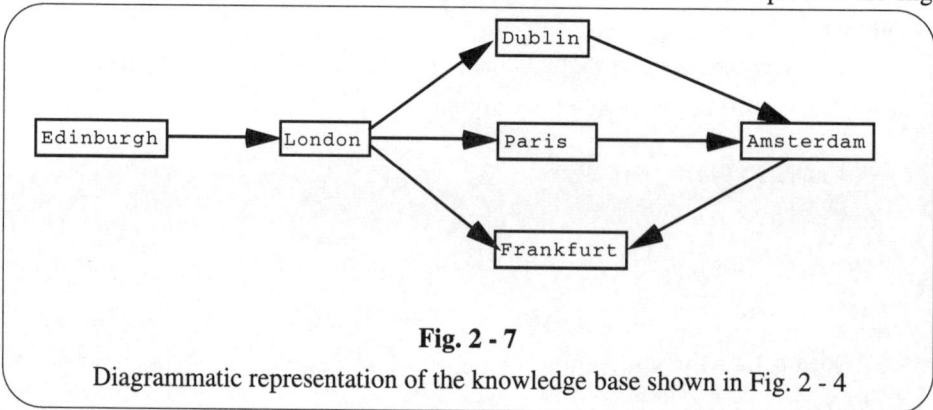

Fig. 2 - 7

Diagrammatic representation of the knowledge base shown in Fig. 2 - 4

using the directed graph shown in Fig. 2 - 7. The recursive rule allows us to break down the problem of getting from A to B into the easier task of getting from A to an intermediate location C, and then a smaller problem of getting from C to B. The intermediate location C is closer to B than A is to B, where we define closeness as the number of arcs that must be traversed in order to get from one node to the other. The definition is

((travel X Y) (flight X Y F))

((travel X Y) (flight X Z F) (travel Z Y))

Unlike the previous definition, this one will handle any number of steps.

2.5.1 Execution of Recursive Rules

Let us consider the steps taken by Fril using this recursive definition in order to find a route from Edinburgh to Frankfurt, i.e. to solve the goal

?((travel Edinburgh Frankfurt))

Rule 1 states that it is possible to travel from A to B if there is a direct flight between cities A and B. The head of this rule matches the query, making the body of the rule (flight Edinburgh Frankfurt F).

As this does not match any clauses, the goal fails and the second clause for travel is tried. This has two goals in its body,

(flight Edinburgh Z F) (travel Z Frankfurt)

The first goal matches the fact

((flight Edinburgh London ba215))

leaving the goal

(travel London Frankfurt)

This is the recursive goal, and we can see that this is easier to solve than the original as there is only one step to go from London to Frankfurt. Thus the recursive definition breaks the problem down into easier sub-problems.

There are two complications that are apparent when we consider the pictorial representation of the search space. In the first place, suppose that we add information on flights from Edinburgh to Dublin and from Dublin to Amsterdam to the beginning of the

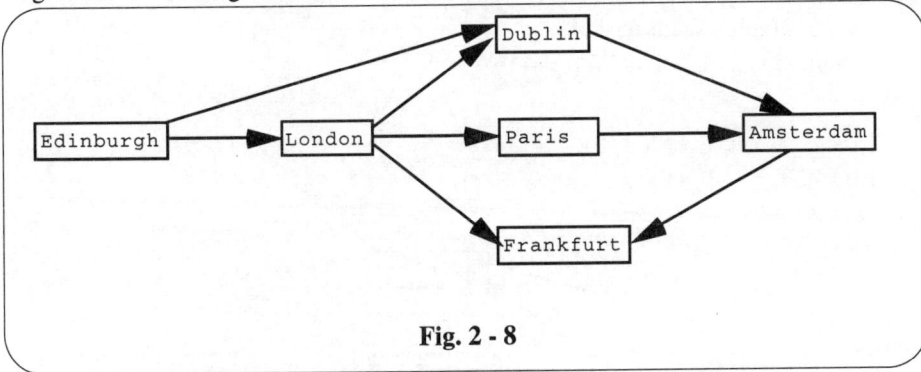

Fig. 2 - 8

knowledge base (see Fig. 2 - 8). Then execution of the query

?((travel Edinburgh Frankfurt))

would build up a route as follows:

(i)   travel Edinburgh-Frankfurt

(ii) flight Edinburgh-Dublin
      travel Dublin-Frankfurt

(iii) flight Edinburgh-Dublin
      flight Dublin-Amsterdam
      travel Amsterdam-Frankfurt

(iv) flight Edinburgh-Dublin
      flight Dublin-Amsterdam
      flight Amsterdam-Frankfurt

where the second clause for travel was used in going from (i) to (ii) and (ii) to (iii), and the first clause for travel took us from (iii) to (iv). This gives a means of travelling from

25

Edinburgh to Frankfurt, but clearly there is a shorter route, i.e. Edinburgh-London-Frankfurt. Fril finds the other route because of the order in which clauses are searched. The problem in this particular case is that we have no means of ensuring that the recursive sub-problem is actually an easier problem than the original problem. In practice it is usually possible to ensure that the recursive problem is simpler, as we shall see in later examples.

The other problem arises from the possibility of loops in the graph. Consider adding a flight from Dublin to Edinburgh, at the beginning of the knowledge base so that the modified knowledge base is:

((flight Dublin Edinburgh ei231))
((flight London Dublin ba172))
((flight London Paris ba345))
((flight Paris Amsterdam af271))
((flight Edinburgh London ba215))
((flight London Frankfurt lf419))
((flight Amsterdam Frankfurt ba119))

((travel X Y) (flight X Y F))
((travel X Y) (flight X Z F)(travel Z Y))

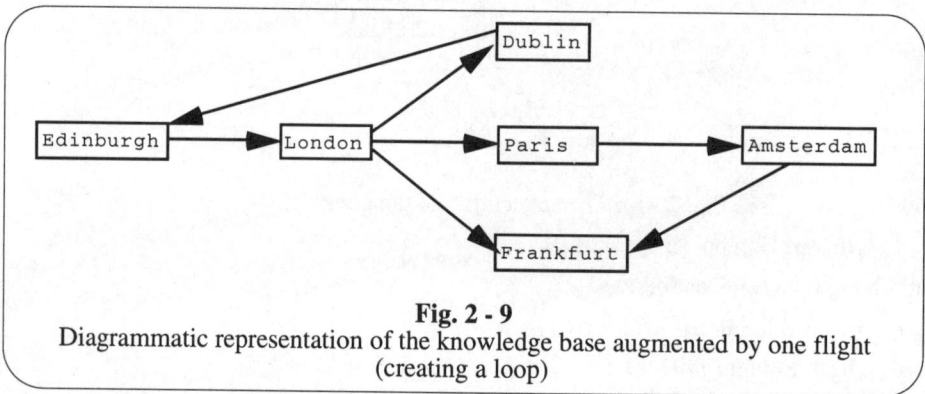

Fig. 2 - 9
Diagrammatic representation of the knowledge base augmented by one flight
(creating a loop)

The query
        ?((travel Edinburgh Frankfurt))
would then develop as follows:
 (i)   travel Edinburgh-Frankfurt
 (ii)   flight Edinburgh-London
        travel London-Frankfurt
 (iii) flight Edinburgh-London
        flight London-Dublin
        travel Dublin-Frankfurt

(iv) flight Edinburgh-London
      flight London-Dublin
      flight Dublin-Edinburgh
      travel Edinburgh-Frankfurt

This brings us to the original query again, and clearly this will be solved in exactly the same way, yielding the same query again after another four stages. This will continue for an infinite time in theory, although in practice it will probably terminate with an error. The problem again arises because it is not possible to ensure that the recursive sub-problem is simpler than the original. We will return to the specific problem of searching a graph in Chapter 5.

2.5.2 Factorial Example

Examples from integer arithmetic provide some easily understood cases where recursive definitions are appropriate.

We recall that the factorial function N! = N (N-1) (N-2) ...3 2 1

with the special case 0! =1

More formally, we can say that

factorial(N)   = 1 if N=0
                = N factorial(N-1) if N> 0

In a conventional language, this would probably be programmed iteratively. Fril allows us to write a program that is much closer to the mathematical definition:

    ((factorial 0 1))
    ((factorial N FACTN)
        (less 0 N)
        (sum NMINUS1 1 N)
        (factorial NMINUS1 FNM1)
        (times N FNM1 FACTN))

The first clause states that the factorial of 0 is 1. This is a fact, and is known as the terminating condition - if a goal is satisfied using this clause, the recursion is terminated. The second clause is recursive and splits the problem of finding N! into the sub-problems of finding (N-1)! and multiplying it by N. Although we still have to find a factorial, the problem is now simpler as we are calculating the factorial of N-1 rather than the factorial of N. The new calculation will be split into sub-problems of finding (N-2)! and multiplying it by (N-1); this process continues until we reach the terminating condition, i.e. calculating 0!. This has no recursive calls, and hence execution of the query continues with solution of the outstanding *times* goals. Each recursive call takes us slightly closer to the terminating condition

Note that this clause can be used to

(i) check that the factorial of a given number is a particular value e.g.

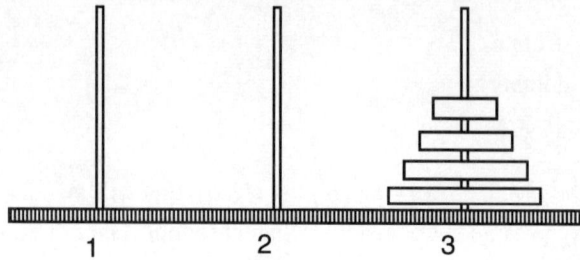

Fig. 2 - 10

The Towers of Hanoi. The puzzle consists of a set of discs (4 in this case), each of which can be placed on one of the three poles. No disc may be placed on top of a disc smaller than itself, and each move is accomplished by moving a disc from the top of one stack to the top of another. The aim is to move all discs from their starting location (pole 3 in this case) to a destination, say pole 1

```
?((factorial 6 720))
yes


?((factorial 3 720))
no
```

(ii) find the factorial of a given number

```
?((factorial 6 X)(pp X))
720
yes
```

However, the definition cannot be used to find a number whose factorial is a specified value, i.e. the query

```
?((factorial X 24))
```

will cause an error rather than printing 4. The reason for this is that built-in predicates are used in the definition and they are less flexible than the normal Fril definitions we have seen so far. In this case, the first goal in the body of the rule

```
(less 0 N)
```

will only work if both of its arguments are instantiated. The query

```
?((factorial X 24))
```

causes the first goal to be (less 0 X) which cannot be satisfied by Fril.

2.5.3 Thinking Recursively

Readers who have experience of programming in conventional languages such as C, Pascal, Fortran may find that some adjustment is necessary before getting up to full speed in Fril. For example, given the task of finding the sum of the positive square roots of the first N integers, a procedural programmer tends to think immediately in terms of an iterative loop with a counter and test for termination, temporary variables to store intermediate results, etc. The logic programming approach to the problem is recursive (as is the formal mathematical specification of the problem). Recursion is actually a far more natural way of thinking about the problem, although those who have had long exposure to procedural programming languages tend to think of iterative constructs as being the natural components of a solution. Recursion is frequently the natural programming style in Fril, as it is in many problem solving activities. Many problems can be arranged so that solving a simpler but similar problem can lead to the solution of the original problem. A classic example of this is the so-called *Tower of Hanoi* problem in which a number of discs of decreasing size are stacked on a pole as shown in Fig. 2 - 10.

The problem can be neatly solved by observing that if it were possible to move three discs, we can solve the problem involving four discs (see Fig. 2 - 11). Thus the problem of moving four discs is reduced to two simpler problems involving three discs, and the straightforward task of moving one disc. Similarly , the problem of moving three discs is reduced to the sub-problems of moving two discs and one disc. This is the key feature of recursive thinking - a problem is broken down into simpler but similar problems, which can be solved by the same approach, breaking them down into still simpler problems until some elementary case (in this case, moving a single disc) is reached.

2.6 LISTS

We have seen how logic programs can represent simple pieces of information, and how we can make deductions from this knowledge by means of rules. Powerful programs can be written compactly using the concept of recursion, provided that the execution order imposed by the Fril system is taken into account. So far we have not seen any method of imposing more structure on data, or how to represent pieces of information that are more complex than the examples seen until now. For example, in the program of Section 2.5, which checked the possibility of travelling between two cities, it might have been convenient to know the route rather than simply get a yes or no answer according to whether the journey was possible or not. We could modify the program to print intermediate steps, but this might not be very helpful due to the backtracking search mechanism, as once a message has been printed it cannot be 'unprinted' by backtracking (e.g. consider *?((travel Edinburgh Frankfurt))*). Additionally, we might not want to simply print the route - we might want to embed this code in a larger program, and call the *travel* predicate from there. With the knowledge of Fril gained so far, we cannot easily modify the program to return the intermediate cities as arguments because we do not know how many intermediate cities there will be. We need to store an unknown number of intermediate cities.

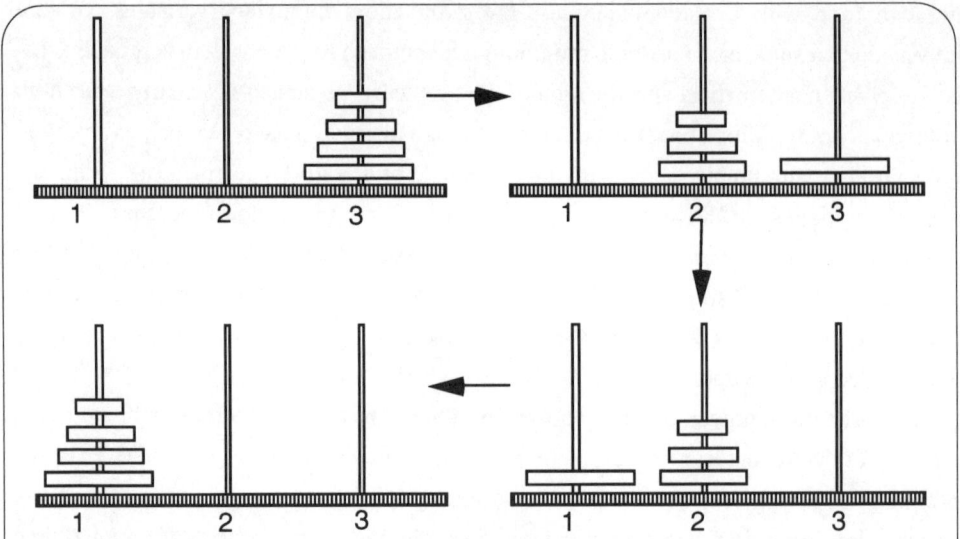

Fig. 2 - 11
Recursive solution to the Towers of Hanoi puzzle. Assume we know how to move three discs from one pole to another. In order to move the four discs legally to pole 1, we must first move the three top discs to pole 2. Once this is accomplished, we can move the large disc from pole 3 to pole 1, and then the three remaining discs from pole 2 to pole 1

This capability is given by *lists*. A list is an ordered sequence of terms enclosed in parentheses (remember that a term is a constant, a variable, a number, a fuzzy set, or another list). We can use lists to group together related pieces of information - for example, to represent a point in the plane, we might give its x and y coordinates

(point 2 3.4)

and to represent a triangle we could use three points

((point 0 0) (point 3 1) (point 2.5 2.5))

In order to write programs that work with lists, we must first consider how the matching process (unification) treats lists.

2.6.1 Unification of Lists

As we have already seen, a list in Fril consists of an ordered sequence of one or more terms known as the elements of the list. Alternatively we can think of a list as being made up of a first element and the rest of the list. We call the first element the *head* of the list, and the remaining elements the *tail*. We can emphasise this split into head and tail by using a slightly different notation for lists, where we would write the list (a b c) as

(a | (b c)) - that is, a head *a* and a tail *(b c)*. Note that the tail of a list is itself a list. Because of this, it too can be represented using the head and tail notation (see Fig. 2 - 12). This leads to the question of what happens when we reach the end of the

30

list, i.e. how do we split the list (c) into head and tail? There is a special list, the *empty list*, which is written (). This is the counterpart of the empty set in set theory. Strictly speaking, the empty list is not a list at all, as it does not contain at least one element. From the system's point of view, the empty list is

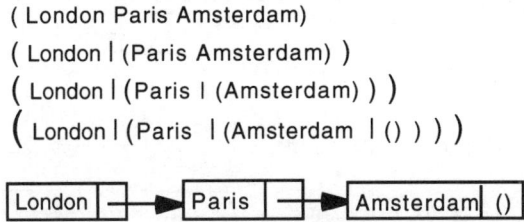

(London Paris Amsterdam)
(London I (Paris Amsterdam))
(London I (Paris I (Amsterdam)))
(London I (Paris I (Amsterdam I ())))

London ⟶ Paris ⟶ Amsterdam ()

Fig. 2 - 12
Alternative representations of the list
(London Paris Amsterdam)

actually a constant; however, it is often convenient to think of it as a list. The empty list is the tail of any list containing just one element, i.e. (c) could be written (c I ()). The head and tail structure of a list can be represented pictorially by drawing a "list cell" for each element. Each list cell contains two boxes - one contains the element itself and the other contains an arrow pointing to the cells representing the remainder of the list. In the case of the last list cell, the second box contains the empty list (see Fig. 2 - 13). Complicated structures with nested lists can be visualised quite easily using this approach (see Fig. 2 - 14).

These alternative ways of visualising lists would be no more than a curiosity except for the impact on unification. As we have already seen, a variable will match a list, and in the process become instantiated to that list. Two lists match if corresponding elements match - for example, the lists (a b c) and (X Y Z) will match with instantiations (X=a, Y=b, Z=c). The head and tail notation allows a more general statement to be made - two lists match if their heads match and their tails match. The most general list we can write is one whose head is unknown and whose tail is also unknown. This list, (HIT) will match *any* other list (see Fig. 2 - 13). In many cases when we are writing programs that manipulate lists, we do not know in advance how many elements there will be in a list and we must use a list of the form (HIT). This immediately gives us a very powerful way of writing recursive list processing programs as we shall see later in this section.

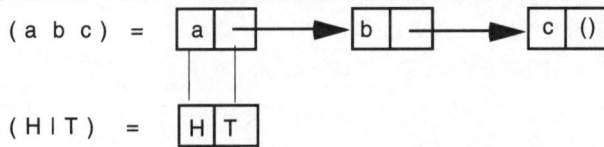

(a b c) = a ⟶ b ⟶ c ()

(H I T) = H T

Fig. 2 - 13
(HIT) matches (a b c) with H=a, T=(b c)

Note that lists are the *only* complex data structures in Fril, i.e. the only terms that can be decomposed into constituent terms. Fuzzy sets are treated as simple entities, and cannot be split into components in the way lists can.

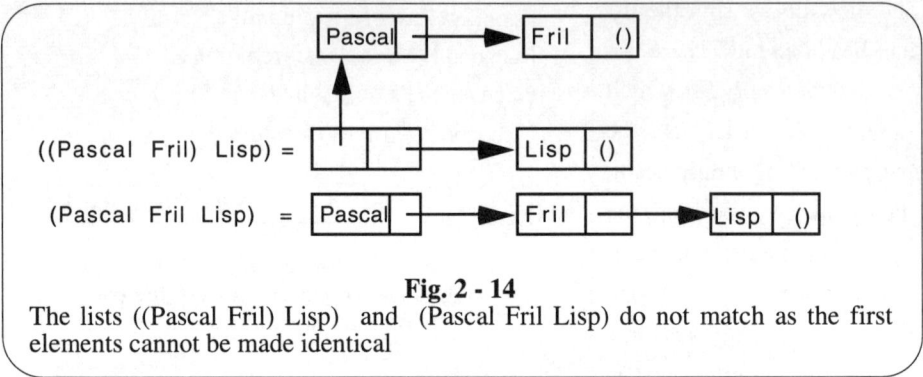

Fig. 2 - 14
The lists ((Pascal Fril) Lisp) and (Pascal Fril Lisp) do not match as the first elements cannot be made identical

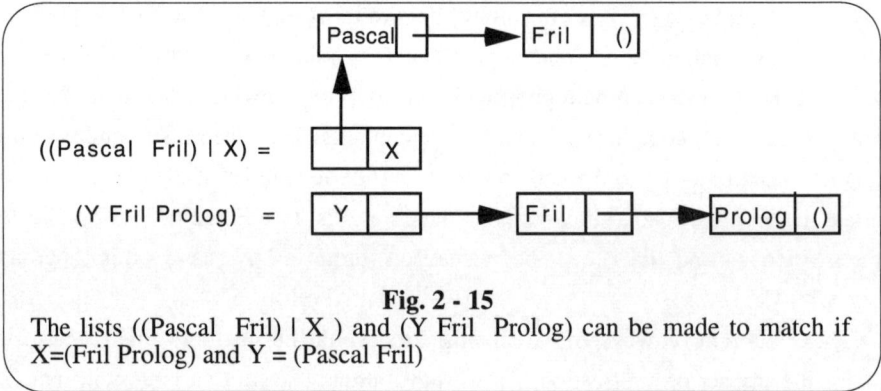

Fig. 2 - 15
The lists ((Pascal Fril) | X) and (Y Fril Prolog) can be made to match if X=(Fril Prolog) and Y = (Pascal Fril)

2.6.2 Examples of List Unification

1. *(a b X)* and *(a b c d)* do not match -the lists do not have equal numbers of elements.

2. *(a | X)* and *(a b c d)* match with X = (b c d).

3. *(H | T)* and *(Fred)* match with H=Fred.

4. *((Pascal Fril) Lisp)* and *(Pascal Fril Lisp)* do not match - the first element of list 1 is itself a list *(Pascal Fril)*, whereas the first element of list 2 is a constant, *Pascal*. Since a constant does not match a list, there is no match in this case.

5. *((Pascal Fril) | X)* and *(Y Fril Prolog)* match with the substitutions X=(Fril Prolog) and Y = (Pascal Fril). This is illustrated in Fig. 2 - 15.

2.6.3 List Processing

We define the length of a list to be the number of elements contained in that list. Let us consider how to find the length of a list. Clearly one way to do it (up to a given maximum) would be to use a set of clauses:

((length () 0))
((length (A) 1))
((length (A B) 2))
((length (A B C) 3)) ... etc.

where these clauses are read as
"the length of the list ( ) is 0"
"the length of list (A) is 1"... etc.
Thus the query

?((length (Fred John Bill) X))

would match the fourth clause, with (A=Fred, B=John, C=Bill, X=3). This solution is both inelegant and incomplete as it is possible that many clauses will not be used, and we must anticipate the maximum length of a list in advance.

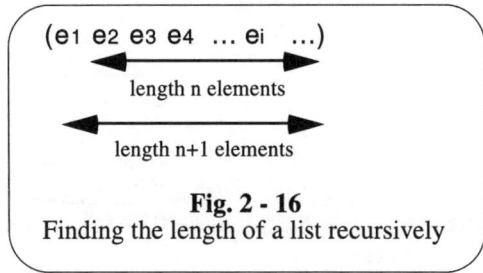

(e1 e2 e3 e4 ... ei ...)

length n elements

length n+1 elements

Fig. 2 - 16
Finding the length of a list recursively

A more elegant solution would be to use a recursive definition (see Fig. 2-16). As in previous recursive definitions, we must consider two cases:
(i) the simplest case (the terminating condition)
(ii) the recursive case, which breaks down a problem into a similar one closer to the terminating condition.

For the length of a list, this is straightforward. The easiest case is that of an empty list, which we define to have a length of zero. The recursive part rests on splitting a list into head and tail. If we can find the length of the tail, we need only add one to this to give the length of our list. Although this may look initially like a circular definition, notice that the recursive call actually finds the length of a shorter list; thus after sufficient time we will reach the empty list and hence the terminating condition. The program is

((length ( ) 0))

((length (H|T) N) (length T M) (sum M 1 N))

Notice that the terminating condition comes first. This may not be necessary, but is good practice as Fril always checks this clause first and so will detect when the terminating condition has been reached.

Let us consider the execution of this program, for example using the query

?((length (a b c) X)(pp X))

The first goal *(length (a b c) X)* will match the second clause in the knowledge base, giving two further goals to be solved, *(length (b c) M)* and *(sum M 1 X)*. If we ignore the internal workings of *(length (b c) M)* and assume it succeeds and binds M to 2, we must then solve *(sum 2 1 X)*. This is a built-in predicate, and will succeed binding X to 3; we have now solved the first goal in the query and the second one succeeds, printing 3. It is often a good approach to program development to "black-box" a recursive call, i.e. assume that it works as required and then simply concentrate on the rest of the clause. This may seem like cheating as we are assuming that the predicate works properly while we are still designing it to ensure that it does work properly, but adopting this approach can simplify matters. Readers familiar with inductive proof in mathematics should have no problem with this.

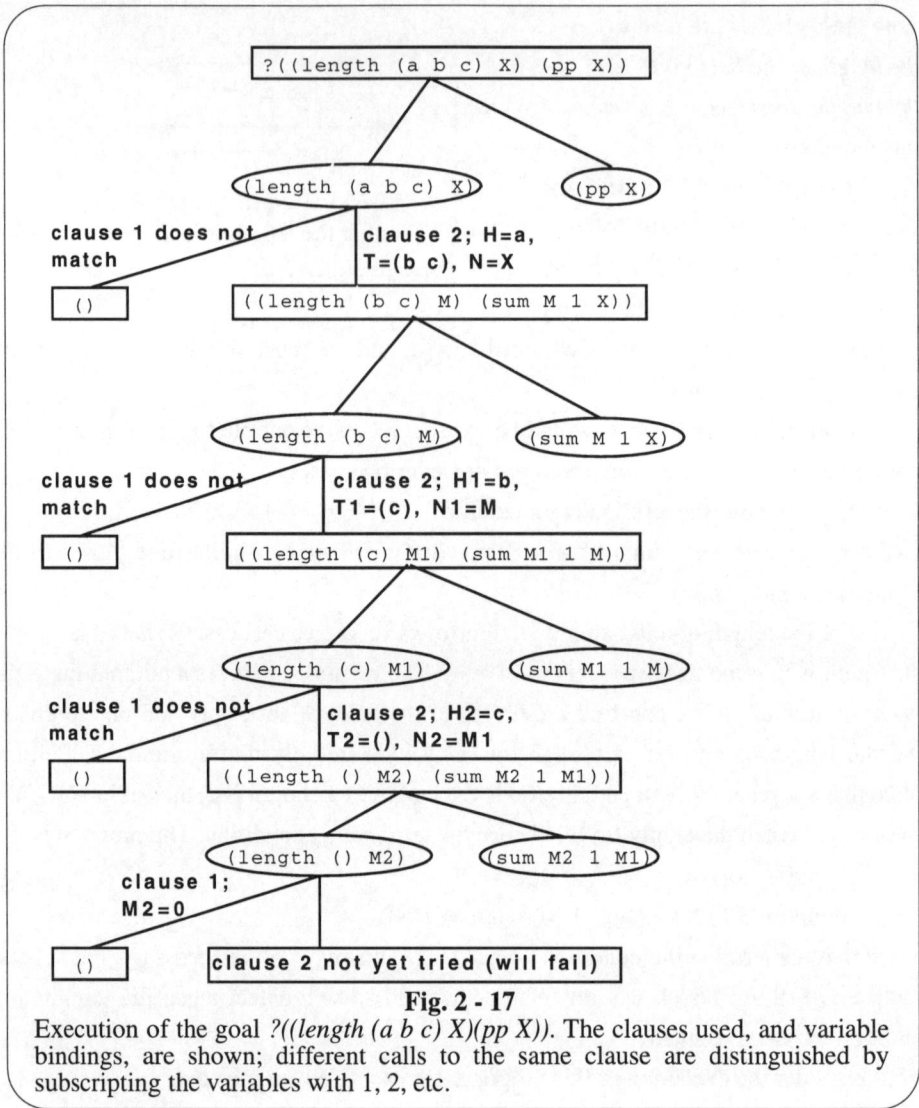

?((length (a b c) X) (pp X))

(length (a b c) X)   (pp X)

clause 1 does not match   clause 2; H=a, T=(b c), N=X

()   ((length (b c) M) (sum M 1 X))

(length (b c) M)   (sum M 1 X)

clause 1 does not match   clause 2; H1=b, T1=(c), N1=M

()   ((length (c) M1) (sum M1 1 M))

(length (c) M1)   (sum M1 1 M)

clause 1 does not match   clause 2; H2=c, T2=(), N2=M1

()   ((length () M2) (sum M2 1 M1))

(length () M2)   (sum M2 1 M1)

clause 1; M2=0

()   clause 2 not yet tried (will fail)

Fig. 2 - 17

Execution of the goal *?((length (a b c) X)(pp X))*. The clauses used, and variable bindings, are shown; different calls to the same clause are distinguished by subscripting the variables with 1, 2, etc.

For illustrative purposes in this case, let us consider the whole of the query execution. It is worthwhile examining this program closely to ensure understanding, as many other list processing programs follow a similar pattern. The execution is shown more fully in Fig. 2 - 17. Note that recursive calls which use the same clause have distinct variables - in the diagram, this has been shown by numbering the different occurrences e.g. H, H1, H2, etc. Each time Fril has to solve a goal of the form

    (length (...) X)

it attempts to match the first clause with the goal, and if this fails moves on to the second clause. Once the recursion has terminated, the various calls to *sum* are executed, eventually binding X to 3.

In common with most programs that we have already seen, *length* can be used in more than one way. We have seen above that the program can be used to find the length of a list, using a query such as

　　　?((length (a b c) X)(pp X))

It can also be used to check the length of a list, e.g.

　　　?((length (a b c) 3))

would succeed and

　　　?((length (a b c) 4))

would fail. Finally, the program could be used to generate lists of a given length, using the query

　　　?((length L 3)(pp L))

This succeeds and binds L to (A B C), which is the most general list containing 3 elements.

It is in this last usage that the ordering of clauses is important, i.e. putting the terminating condition first followed by the recursive case. In the other usages, the two clauses are mutually exclusive as the first argument of a goal is either a list or it is the empty list, and the goal will only match one clause. If however the first argument is a variable, as it is in the goal *(length L 3)* then the goal will match the head of either clause. If the order of clauses is reversed, the recursive case will always be used and Fril will never reach the terminating condition. We should also note that in general, list processing programs are written with a specific use in mind and may be inefficient or not terminate if we attempt to use them in different ways.

2.6.4 List Membership

One of the most fundamental things we can do with a list of elements is to check whether or not a particular value is contained in the list. For example, suppose we find a route in list form from Edinburgh to Amsterdam using the knowledge base shown in Fig. 2 - 4 , i.e. (Edinburgh London Paris Amsterdam). How could we get Fril to check whether or not London is in the list? More generally, we want to check whether a given term is in a list or not. Recall that the simplest operation we can perform on a list is to split it into head and tail. Clearly if the element we are looking for is the same as the first element in the list, we know it is a member of that list. Alternatively, if it is not the first element, we must look in the tail to see if it is there. These two alternatives define the predicate:

　　　((member E (E|T)))

　　　((member E (H|T)) (member E T))

The first clause states that an element E is a member of a list if it is the first element of that list. The second states that E is a member of the list if it is a member of the tail. Notice that the recursive case considers a simpler list, which has one element fewer than the original. The program can be used in three ways:

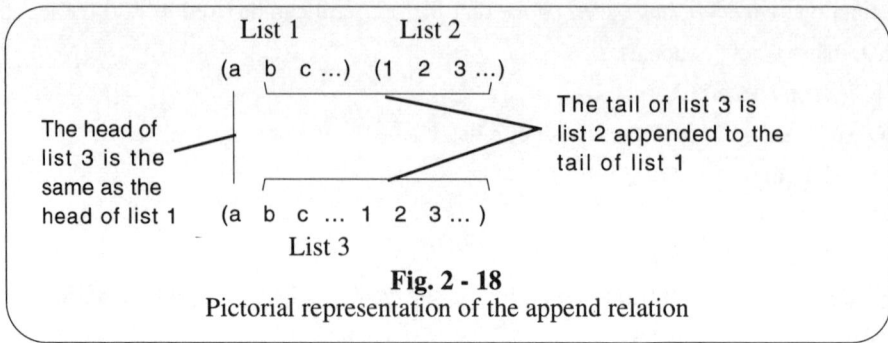

Fig. 2 - 18
Pictorial representation of the append relation

• to check that an item is contained in a list, e.g.

> ?((member b (a b c)))
>
> yes

> ?((member d (a b c)))
>
> no

• to generate an element that is on a list, e.g.

> ?((member X (f r i l)) (member X (p r o l o g)) (pp X))
>
> r
>
> yes

The first goal initially succeeds with X=f, and the second goal becomes

> (member f (p r o l o g)

This fails, and the first goal is resatisfied with X=r. This time, the second goal is

> (member r (p r o l o g))

which succeeds, and the third goal succeeds, printing r.

• to generate a list containing a specified element, e.g.

> ?((member a L)(pp L))
>
> (a | _1)
>
> yes

where _1 is an internally generated variable.

2.6.5 Appending Two Lists

The following program concatenates two lists, giving a third - for example the two lists (a b c) and (1 2 3) would yield (a b c 1 2 3) when concatenated. The predicate is given the name *append*, since the second list is appended to the first to yield the third. It may not be immediately clear how to write this, since we can only split a list into a head and a tail, and here we want to add elements to the end of the first list. If we call the two lists list1 and list2 and the result list3, looking at Fig. 2 - 18 we notice that the first

36

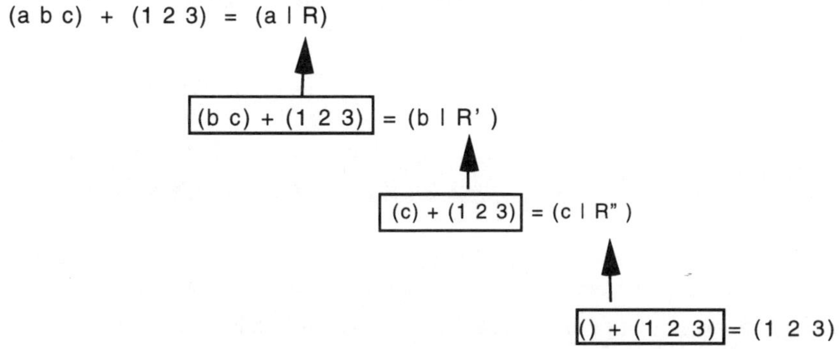

Fig. 2 - 19
Illustration of appending the lists (a b c) and (1 2 3). The symbol + is used to represent the append operation, and the result is (a | (b | (c | (1 2 3)))) which is identical to (a b c 1 2 3)

element of list1 is the same as the first element of list3. The remainder of list3 is the result of appending list2 to the tail of list1. Thus one part of our definition must be

$$((append\ (H|T)\ L\ (H|R))\ (append\ T\ L\ R))$$

We must also include a terminating condition. The recursive call above is simpler than the original in the sense that it is appending list2 to the tail of list1. The limit of this process will occur when list1 is an empty list. Thus the terminating condition is

$$((append\ ()\ L\ L))$$

As before, we write the definition with terminating condition first. The program is:

$$((append\ ()\ L\ L))$$
$$((append\ (H|T)\ L\ (H|R))\ (append\ T\ L\ R))$$

The first clause states that the result of appending any list L to an empty list is just the list L, and the second clause states that if we are appending a list L to any non-empty list (H|T) then the result will have the same first element H, and a tail formed by appending L to T. It is perhaps more difficult to see what is happening in the second clause, as there does not seem to be anywhere where the answer is produced. In fact, the answer is built up slowly, piece by piece as the second clause is used (see Fig. 2 - 19). Each use of the second clause adds a little more to the answer until the terminating condition is reached and first clause is used, when the remainder of the answer is filled in. This process of partially specifying an answer is a very common technique in list processing programs.

In addition to finding the result of concatenating two lists, the *append* definition can also be used to generate pairs of lists which concatenate to give a specified third list. Thus the query

$$?((append\ \ X\ Y\ (a\ b\ c))\ (p\ X\ Y)(pp)(fail))$$

37

will generate solutions for X and Y such that Y appended to X gives (a b c). Fril responds

() (a b c)

(a) (b c)

(a b) (c)

(a b c) ()

no

These are the four possible pairs of lists that satisfy the condition Y appended to X gives (a b c). They are generated in the order shown because of the Fril execution strategy. The first goal is

(append X Y (a b c))

This matches the head of the first clause in the knowledge base, with the bindings (X=(), Y=L=(a b c)), giving the first solution (since the clause is a fact, there are no conditions to satisfy, and execution continues with the next goal in the top level query). On backtracking, the first goal matches the second clause with the bindings (H=a, R=(b c), X=(a|T), Y=L) and the body of this clause becomes

(append T Y (b c))

This matches the head of clause 1 with (T=(), L' =Y=(b c)), giving the overall solution X=(a) and Y=(b c). Subsequent backtracking follows a similar pattern, and the details are left as an exercise for the reader.

The reader who is used to procedural programming in a conventional language may be uneasy about this definition. What if the second list is empty ? Would it not lead to faster execution if a special clause were used to cover this case? Where are the sizes calculated so that we know how much space to allocate for the result list?

Questions such as these arise from trying to think too much in terms of the constructs of conventional languages. It requires a certain amount of effort to shake off the constraints imposed by using a programming language whose design was dictated largely by the underlying hardware. To answer the questions above, it is certainly possible to add the clause

((append L () L))

as a second terminating condition. Whether or not this leads to faster execution is very dependent on the way the program is used, and also on matters such as internal optimisations carried out by the Fril compiler. However, we can definitely state that adding this clause would lead to redundancy during execution. For example, the goal

(append X Y ())

matches the head of clause 1 in the existing definition, giving the solution X=() Y=(). If the system is forced to backtrack, this goal will also match the head of the new clause, again giving the solution X=(), Y=(). Whilst this is not strictly incorrect, it is not efficient and may give misleading results if embedded in a larger program.

In answer to the other question, there is no need to calculate how much space is required for the result, or to allocate space for the result, as this is done automatically within the definition as the result is built up by repeated use of the second clause.

2.6.6 Splitting a List into Sublists

We can combine *length* and *append* to split a list into sublists of specified lengths. For example, given the lists (a b c d e f g h) and (3 2 1 2), we would split the first list into (a b c) (d e) (f) (g h). We know that *append* can be used to split a list into pairs of lists, and that *length* can be used to check that a list has a specified number of elements. The required program is

```
((split () () ()))
((split L (N|T) (S|R))
     (append S  LREM  L)
     (length S  N)
     (split LREM  T  R))
```

Note that this program is designed to have arguments one and two specified. We have seen above that simple list processing programs will often work in more than one way. In this case, calling the predicate with either of the first two arguments unspecified will lead to an non-terminating query e.g. consider execution of

```
?((split  (a b c d e) LN LS))
```

To be robust, some checking of arguments should be carried out first, and this is discussed in Chapter 5.

2.6.7 Reversing a List

A simple program to reverse the order of elements in a list is

```
((reverse () ()))
((reverse (H|T) R) (reverse T RT) (append RT (H) R))
```

where *append* was defined in Section 2.6.4. In order to reverse a non-empty list, we must first reverse its tail and then insert the head element at the end of the reversed tail. For example, reversing *(a b c)* gives a head *a* and reversed tail *(c b)*. We must add the *a* to the end of *(c b)* giving *(c b a)*. One way of doing this is to use the list *(a)* rather than the element *a*, and then use the *append* relation already defined to join the two lists together.

Note that this program can also be interpreted as a logical definition of the *reverse* relation, just as *append* is a logical definition of concatenating two lists. The program given for *reverse* has been written with the intention that the first argument will be specified, and the second argument will be either a variable or a list, e.g.

```
?((reverse (a b c) X) (pp X))
```

(c b a)

yes

?((reverse (1 2 3) (3 2 1))

yes

?((reverse (1 2 3) (3 1 2))

no

The program can also be used with a variable as the first argument and a list as second argument e.g.

?((reverse X (1 2 3))(pp X))

prints (3 2 1). However, this query may take a lot longer than using the program in the intended fashion.

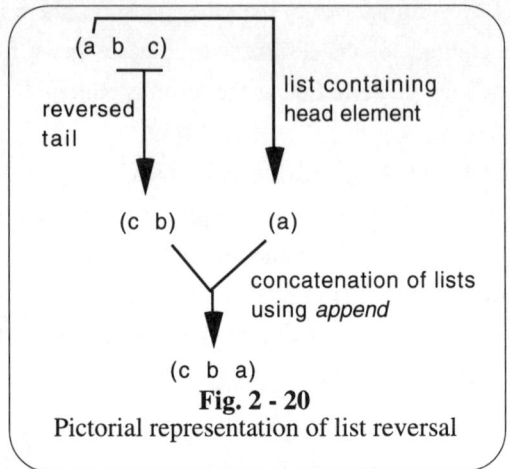

(a b c)

reversed tail

list containing head element

(c b)   (a)

concatenation of lists using *append*

(c b a)

Fig. 2 - 20

Pictorial representation of list reversal

2.6.8 More General Use of the | Notation in Lists

So far we have used the bar to separate the first element of a list (the head) from the remainder of the list (the tail). This is the most common usage but in fact we can generalise this notion, and write any number of elements before the bar, e.g. (a b | (c)). For example, we might write a predicate to check that the elements of a list are in ascending order. The easiest way to achieve this is to consider the first two elements in the list; if these are correctly ordered, then consider the second and third element, etc. until the end of the list is reached. The terminating condition is when there is only one element in the list. The program is

((ascending (E)))
((ascending (E1 E2|T)) (less E1 E2) (ascending (E2|T)))

Note that in order to be robust, this definition should also check that the list elements can be compared using the built-in predicate *less*.

2.7 NEGATION, THE CUT, AND CONTROL ISSUES

We have seen how Fril executes programs using a simple pattern matching strategy, searching the knowledge base from the top when looking for a match and backtracking on failure. This can be visualised as a tree search, where branches of the tree correspond to different clauses. Fril allows a certain degree of control over the backtracking process, and enables the programmer to avoid unnecessary computation in cases where this can be detected in advance.

2.7.1 Controlling Execution - the Cut

Occasionally when writing programs we wish clauses to cover mutually exclusive cases - for example, we could define factorial as

((factorial 0 1))
((factorial N FN)
　　(sum M 1 N)(factorial M FM)(times N FM FN))

The first clause covers the case when we are looking for the factorial of 0, and the second clause covers all numbers greater than 0. Thus we can say that if the first clause is used, then the second should not be, and vice versa. One way to enforce this is to add a condition to the body of the second clause:

((factorial N FN)
　　(less 0 N)(sum M 1 N)(factorial M FM)(times N FM FN))

and this gives a mathematically correct definition, which was used in Section 2.5. An alternative is to use a built-in predicate known as the *cut*, written !. This has the effect of preventing backtracking to any goals between the cut and the head of the clause in which it appears. In the example shown (see Fig. 2 - 21), the goal

(factorial 0 FM)

is solved using the first clause, and an answer is printed. If we then cause the program to backtrack and look for further solutions - in this case by means of the *(fail)* goal - execution returns to the most recent point at which there was a choice, i.e. the goal *(factorial 0 FM)*. This will match the second clause, and execution will continue. In fact execution will continue for a long time as the program will now try to calculate the factorial of -1, -2, -3, …. One way to avoid this is to use an explicit check in the second clause, as mentioned above; the alternative is to use the *cut* to prevent this unwanted backtracking. If we rewrite the first clause as

((factorial 0 1) (!))

the cut removes the additional choice(s) for solving any goal which matches the head. Thus in the example the empty list of goals would be replaced by a list containing a single goal ((!)); when this is executed, it discards all resatisfiable goals between it and its parent node, including the parent. Backtracking would then not find any resatisfiable goals in the example above.

We can think of the cut as enforcing exclusivity of clauses - if the head of a clause matches a goal (and possibly satisfies some goals in the body also), a cut can make this clause the only applicable one. Another example is the *max* program which finds (or checks) the maximum of two numbers:

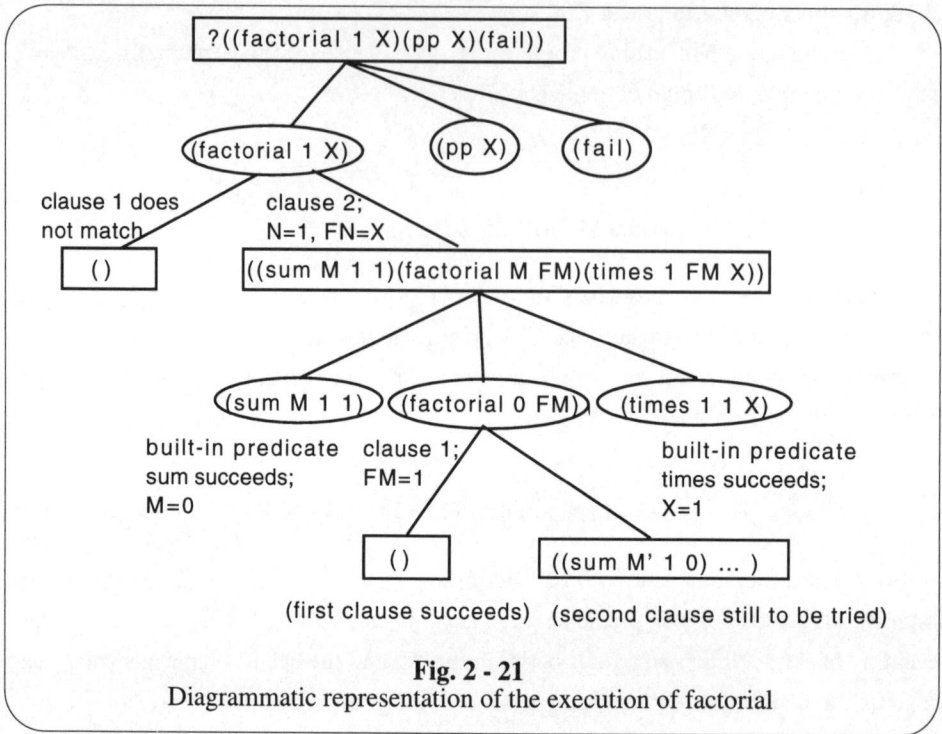

Fig. 2 - 21
Diagrammatic representation of the execution of factorial

((max X Y X)(less Y X))	% maximum of X and Y is X if Y < X
((max X Y Y)(less X Y))	% maximum of X and Y is Y if X < Y
((max Y Y Y))	% both numbers are the same

We can say that if X and Y values match the first clause and satisfy the condition X<Y then they will not satisfy either of the other two clauses. Backtracking in this case will not be as disastrous as in *factorial* but is nevertheless redundant. We can rewrite the program as

        ((max X Y X)(less Y X) (!))
        ((max X Y Y))

which states that X is the maximum of X and Y if Y<X; if this condition is not satisfied then Y is the maximum of X and Y. Note that this will work without the cut if no backtracking is involved, i.e.

        ((max X Y X)(less Y X))
        ((max X Y Y))

will correctly answer the query

        ?((max 3 2 Z)(pp Z))

but would give two answers to the query

42

?((max 3 2 Z)(pp Z)(fail))

The program involving the cut will work correctly in both cases.

We can therefore view the cut as an "efficiency hack" which can be justified only in certain cases. From a logical point of view, it destroys the meaning of a program - we can read the *max* program as stating that for any values of X and Y

1. X is the maximum if $Y < X$
2. Y is the maximum if $X < Y$
3. Y is the maximum if $Y = X$

As the cut has no logical meaning, the second version simply states that for all X, Y

1. X is the maximum if $Y < X$
2. Y is the maximum

This is clearly nonsense from a logical point of view.

2.7.2 Negation

It is often convenient to check that a condition doesn't hold, e.g. in the *max* example above, we wrote clauses for each of the three cases $Y<X$, $Y>X$, $Y=X$. In fact we know that if $X<Y$ is false then one of the other two conditions must hold. Fril allows this to be expressed using the *negg* built-in predicate. This implements *negation as failure* - if a goal fails, its negation is assumed to be true, i.e. it assumes that the information in the knowledge base is complete, and anything that is not in the knowledge base is therefore false. We could write the *max* program as

((max X Y X) (less Y X))
((max X Y Y) (negg less Y X))

The second clause covers the case where $X \leq Y$. This is a valid use of negation as failure, since our "knowledge base" is complete with respect to the relation *less* defined on numbers.

Negation can only be used to *check* that a relation does not hold between arguments - it cannot be used to generate values for which a relation does not hold. As an example, in the *flight* knowledge base (Fig. 2 - 4), we could use the query

?((negg flight Amsterdam London af215))
which would succeed; however we could not use

?((negg flight Amsterdam X F)(pp X))
to generate a value of X satisfying this condition. In practice this restriction is easy to work with. There is a syntactic variant of negation as failure, the predicate *neg* which takes the form

?((neg (flight Amsterdam X F)))
The two differ only in their syntax, not in any features of execution.

2.7.3 Negation vs Cut - Clarity vs Efficiency

The following program assumes that lists represent sets, and finds the intersection of two sets. Note that some care is needed in representing sets by lists as a set is unordered and does not contain duplicate elements, whereas a list is ordered and can contain duplicate elements. For example, the lists (a b c) and (c b a) are not identical from Fril's point of view; however, regarded as sets they are identical.

With these reservations, we will write a program to find the intersection of two "sets". The predicate will have the form (intersect *set1 set2 set3*), which holds if *set3* is the intersection of *set1* and *set2*. We can treat *set1* element by element, and distinguish three cases:

1. *set1* is empty; in which case the intersection is also empty.

2. The selected element of *set1* is also an element of *set2*, in which case the element should be in the intersection; the remainder of the intersection is the result of intersecting the rest of *set1* with *set2*.

3. The selected element of *set1* is not an element of *set2*, in which case it is not in the intersection; the intersection is the result of intersecting the rest of *set1* with *set2*.

This is represented diagrammatically in Fig. 2 - 22. Each of the three cases gives rise to a clause, and the resulting definition is:

```
((intersect ()  S2 ()))
((intersect (E|T) S2 (E|R))
    (member E S2) (intersect T S2 R))
((intersect (E|T) S2 R)
    (negg member E S2) (intersect T S2 R))
```

This program for intersection is logically correct and will solve goals where the first two arguments are lists. It will give a single answer, with no further solutions produced by backtracking.

However, we can question its efficiency. Consider the case where *set1* is given by the list (a b c) and *set2* is given by (c d e). The first element of (a b c) is not in (c d e) and hence is not in the intersection. The second clause will try the goal

(member a (c d e))

This goal fails, so that the second clause fails and Fril moves on to the third clause. This requires the goal

(negg member a (c d e))

to be executed; however, we know that this goal will succeed since

(member a (c d e))

has already failed. It might be thought that the goal

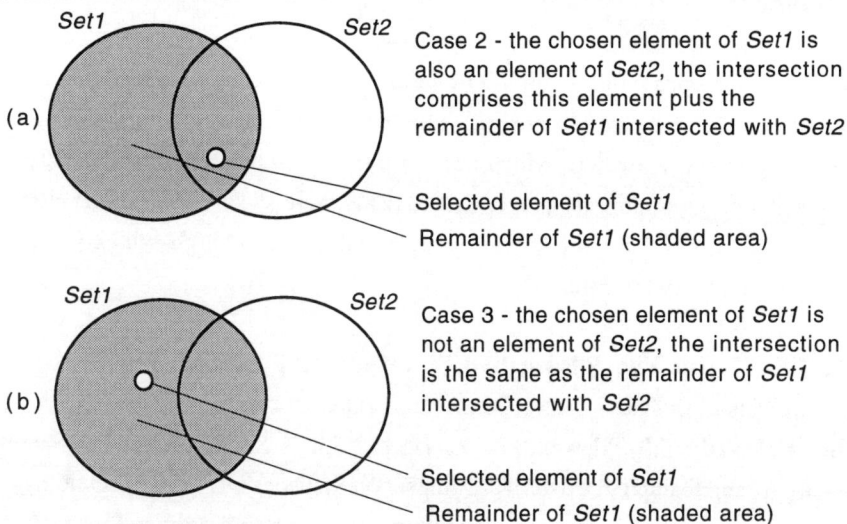

Fig. 2 - 22
Illustration of the intersection program by considering a selected element in the intersection of two sets *(set1* is assumed to be non-empty)
(a) the selected element is a member of both sets
(b) the selected element is a member only of the first set

(negg member a (c d e))

is therefore redundant; however, removing it causes the definition of intersection to be incorrect since it will return multiple solutions on backtracking. The point is that clauses 2 and 3 are mutually exclusive cases. We can be sure that if clause 2 is applicable, i.e. if the goal *(member E S2)* succeeds, then clause 3 is not applicable. Rather than enforcing this by repeating the test and negating the result, we can add a cut after the test:

```
((intersect () S2 ()))
((intersect (E|T) S2 (E|R))
    (member E S2) (!) (intersect T S2 R))
((intersect (E|T) S2 R)
    (intersect T S2 R))
```

If the *member* test succeeds, the cut removes the third clause as an option. We can guarantee that the third clause will only be used in cases where the goal *(member E S2)* has failed, and hence we do not need to include the negated test in the third clause. This leads to a more efficient implementation at the expense of making the definition less clear, and logically incorrect.

45

2.8 BIBLIOGRAPHY

The Fril manual contains a full definition of the language, together with a comprehensive listing of all built-in predicates. There are a number of texts on logic programming, such as those by Lloyd and Kowalski, which deal with the theoretical and practical issues of using logic as a programming language. Bratko deals more specifically with Prolog, and his book is a good introduction although it deals with the Edinburgh syntax rather than the list-based syntax used in Fril.

Baldwin J.F, Martin T.P, Pilsworth B.W, (1988), "Fril Manual, version 4.0", Fril Systems Ltd, Bristol Business Centre, Bristol BS8 1QX, UK.

Baldwin J.F, Martin T.P, Pilsworth B.W, (1991), "Fril: A Support Logic Programming System" in "AI and Computer Power: The Impact on Statistics", Unicom Technology Transfer Series, pp 159-172; also in "Expert Systems and Optimisation in Process Control" (same series, pp 225-238) and "AI and Computer Power: The Impact on Statistics", ed D. Hand, Chapman and Hall.

Baldwin J.F, Martin T.P, Pilsworth B.W, (1994), "Fril Manual, version 5.0", Fril Systems Ltd, Bristol Business Centre, Bristol BS8 1QX, UK.

Bratko I, (1986), Prolog Programming for Artificial Intelligence, Addison Wesley.

Lloyd J.W, (1984), Foundations of Logic Programming, Springer-Verlag.

Kowalski R, (1979), Logic for Problem Solving, Elsevier Science Publishing Co.

CHAPTER 3

A Theory of Uncertainty

3.1 TYPES OF UNCERTAINTY

Two types of uncertainty are important in the modelling of applications, namely those depicted by probability and fuzzy set theories. Fuzzy set theory is not an alternative to probability theory and the two theories are not competing. These two theories are in fact related. A normalised fuzzy set on X induces a possibility distribution over X which defines a family of probability distributions over X. This family of probability distributions can be represented as a mass assignment which is a probability distribution over the power set of X. Modification to this understanding must be made in the case of un-normalised fuzzy sets in which a degree of inconsistency is present.

In this chapter we will therefore develop the required theory of fuzzy sets, possibility theory, mass assignments and probability theory to understand the treatment of uncertainty in Fril.

3.2 PROBABILITY DISTRIBUTIONS

3.2.1 Probability Measure

The probability of a proposition, $Pr(P)$, measures the degree of belief in the truth of that proposition P while $1 - Pr(P)$ measures the belief that P is false. This measure can be subjective or based on relative frequency calculations.

A probability measure on a finite power set $P(X)$
is a function

$$Pr : P(X) \rightarrow [0, 1]$$

which satisfies the axioms

$$Pr(A) \geq 0 \text{ for any } A \, \varepsilon \, P(X)$$

$$Pr(X) = 1 \, ; \; Pr(\emptyset) = 0$$

$$Pr(A \cup B) = Pr(A) + Pr(B) \text{ if } A \cap B = \emptyset \text{ for any } A, B \, \varepsilon \, P(X)$$

Therefore for an exhaustive and exclusive set of propositions $\{P1, ..., Pn\}$ we have

(1) $Pr(Pi) \geq 0 \, ; \; i = 1, ..., n$

(2) $Pr(P1 \vee P2 \vee ... \vee Pn) = 1$

(3) $Pr(Pi \vee Pj) = Pr(Pi) + Pr(Pj) \, ; \; i = 1, ..., n \, ; \; j = 1, ..., n, i \neq j$

For this uncertainty model propositions can only be true or false.

The set of probabilities, {Pr(Pi)}, represents a probability distribution over the set of propositions {Pi}.

One can also be uncertain about the actual values of {Pr(Pi)}. Suppose that all we know is that $\alpha_i \leq Pr(Pi) \leq \beta_i$ and the constraint $Pr(P1) + ... + Pr(Pn) = 1$

We are therefore given a family of probability distributions, namely,

$$\{Pr(Pi) = x_i \mid \alpha_i \leq x_i \leq \beta_i, \text{all } i, ; x1 + ... + xn = 1\}$$

3. 2. 2 Support Pairs

Suppose we want to determine $Pr(Pi \vee Pj \vee Pk)$ for some i, j and k. We can only determine an interval which will contain this probability. Let $z1 \leq Pr(Pi \vee Pj \vee Pk) \leq z2$. Then

$z1 = MIN\{x_i + x_j + x_k\}$
subject to

$\alpha_r \leq x_r \leq \beta_r$; r = 1, ..., n
$x1 + ... + xn = 1$

$z2 = MAX\{x_i + x_j + x_k\}$
subject to

$\alpha_r \leq x_r \leq \beta_r$; r = 1, ..., n
$x1 + ... + xn = 1$

These optimisation problems are trivial to solve. We will call z1 the necessary support for $Pi \vee Pj \vee Pk$, written as $Sn(Pi \vee Pj \vee Pk)$, and z2 the possible support for $Pi \vee Pj \vee Pk$, written as $Sp(Pi \vee Pj \vee Pk)$. Alternatively we can call the necessary support the Belief for $Pi \vee Pj \vee Pk$ written as $Bel(Pi \vee Pj \vee Pk)$ and the possible support the plausibility for $Pi \vee Pj \vee Pk$, written as $Pl(Pi \vee Pj \vee Pk)$. [z1, z2] is also called a support pair and defines an interval containing the required probability. We can then write

$Pi \vee Pj \vee Pk : [z1, z2]$

Example

Given

P1 : [0.2, 0.3]
P2 : [0.4, 0.6]
P3 : [0.1, 0.3]

the support pair for $P1 \vee P2$ is given by

$P1 \vee P2 : [0.7, 0.9]$

since

$$z1 = \text{MIN}\{x1 + x2\}$$

subject to

$$0.2 \le x1 \le 0.3$$

$$0.4 \le x2 \le 0.6$$

$$0.1 \le x3 \le 0.3$$

$$x1 + x2 + x3 = 1$$

$$z2 = \text{MAX}\{x1 + x2\}$$

subject to

$$0.2 \le x1 \le 0.3$$

$$0.4 \le x2 \le 0.6$$

$$0.1 \le x3 \le 0.3$$

$$x1 + x2 + x3 = 1$$

3. 2. 3 Mass Assignments

Suppose the support pair for a proposition P is given by

$$P : [z1, z2]$$

then we can interpret this as

$$m(P) = z1, m(\neg P) = 1 - z2, m(\{P, \neg P\}) = z2 - z1$$

which we can write as

$$m = P : z1, \neg P : 1 - z2, \{P, \neg P\} : z2 - z1$$

where m is a probability distribution over the power set of $\{P, \neg P\}$. m is called a mass assignment. $m(A)$, for any subset A of the power set of $\{P, \neg P\}$, is the mass associated with exactly A. The necessary support for A is therefore the sum of masses associated with all the subsets of A.

More generally, suppose that the relevant variables to be considered in answering a query are X, Y, Z, ... with possible instantiations $\{x1, ...\}$, $\{y1, ...\}$ ... respectively. Let XYZ... be the label variable and S the set of all labels, i.e. all possible instantiations of the label variable.

A mass assignment over the set of label instantiations S is given by the probability distribution over the power set of S, i.e.

$$m(A) \ge 0 \text{ for all } A \varepsilon\, P(S) \text{ such that } \sum_{A\,\varepsilon\, P(S)} m(A) = 1$$

We **do not require** that $m(\emptyset) = 0$ but if $m(\emptyset) \ne 0$ then the mass assignment is not strictly a probability distribution over the power set of S. It can be interpreted as an unnormalised probability distribution.

A mass assignment can be denoted by $\{Li : mi\}$ where Li is a subset of $P(S)$ and mi is the mass associated with Li. Only those Li with positive masses are included.

The **complement** of this mass assignment is formed by allocating each mass to the complement w.r.t. S of the set it is associated with.

If $m(\emptyset) = 0$ then the mass assignment is said to be **complete**, otherwise it is **incomplete**. A complete mass assignment over S corresponds to a family of probability distributions for S.

Example

The witnesses A and B speak the truth with probability p and q respectively. The probability that they disagree in a statement is r. What is the probability that they will both tell the truth on the same occasion?

Let a represent that A tells the truth and b that B tells the truth on some occasion. We can express this problem in terms of mass assignments. To answer the query, namely the probability of $a \wedge b$, we must combine these. This is dealt with in Section 3.6.3.

For this problem S = {ab, a¬b, ¬ab, ¬a¬b} where xy represents the conjunction $x \wedge y$. S represents the set of labels which are the various possible instantiations of the Boolean variables A, B in the conjunction $A \wedge B$ where A is a or ¬a and B is b or ¬b. The statements given can be represented by the three mass assignments

Mass Assignment m1 = {a¬b, ¬ab} : r, {ab, ¬a¬b} : 1 - r

Mass Assignment m2 = {a _} : p, {¬a _} : 1 - p

Mass Assignment m3 = {_ b} : q, {_ ¬b} : 1 - q

where we use the underscore _ to represent any value from the appropriate set of values, ie {a, ¬a} in first position and {b, ¬b} in second position.

The complement of m3 is given by $\overline{m3}$ = {_ ¬b} : q, {_ b} : 1 - q.

The mass assignments m1, m2 and m3 are all complete. They represent families of probability distributions over S. For example, the mass assignment m3 corresponds to the family of distributions given by

$$Pr(ab) = x1, Pr(a¬b) = x2, Pr(¬ab) = x3, Pr(¬a¬b) = x4$$

where

$$x1 + x3 = q \; ; \; x2 + x4 = 1 - q \; ; \; x1 + x2 + x3 + x4 = 1$$

It should be noted that not every family of probability distributions can be represented by a mass assignment. Combining mass assignments will be dealt with later.

Example

Three horses enter a race and experts judge that no horse has a greater than evens chance of winning the race. Let Ei represent horse i wins. S = {E1, E2, E3} and the statement is represented by the linear combination

$$\sum_i \alpha_i m_i \; ; \; \sum_i \alpha_i = 1$$

where the mass assignments m_i are

m_1 = E1: 0.5, {E2, E3}: 0.5 ; m_2 = E2: 0.5, {E1, E3}: 0.5 ; m_3 = E3: 0.5, {E1, E2}: 0.5

This illustrates the need for linear combinations of **orthogonal** mass assignments. The definition of an orthogonal mass assignment is given later.

3. 3 POSSIBILITY DISTRIBUTIONS

3. 3. 1 Possibility Distribution

In real life, concepts are rarely defined in terms of necessary and sufficient conditions. There is no precise range of heights which defines the concept of tall for a man of a certain nationality. Anyone who is over 6ft could be said to be tall for sure and anyone who is less than 5ft 10 ins could be said to be NOT tall for sure. For heights between 5ft 10 ins and 6 ft the possibility of accepting a given height as representing tall increases as the height increases. We therefore allow possibility values in the range [0, 1] and we can introduce the concept of a possibility distribution. This can be defined on a continuous or discrete space.

Thus we might represent the concept tall by the possibility distribution

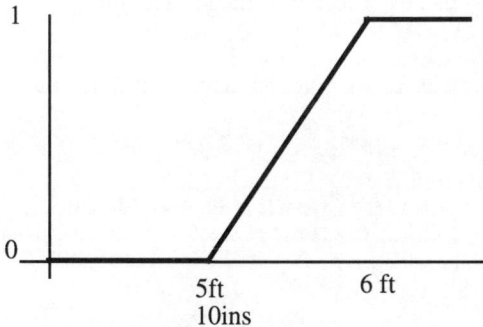

Fig 3.1

Possibility distribution for the height of a tall man, denoted by $\Pi(h)$.

We accept that the possibility measure can take values in the unit interval [0, 1].

We can state this as a proposition

height of John is **tall**

where **tall** is a fuzzy set defined on the height space by means of the membership function

$$\chi_{\textbf{tall}}(h) = \begin{cases} 0 \text{ for } h \leq 5 \text{ ft 10ins} \\ \dfrac{h}{2} - 35 \text{ for 5ft 10 ins} \leq h \leq 6\text{ft} \\ 1 \text{ for } h \geq 6 \text{ ft} \end{cases}$$

The fuzzy set **tall** induces a possibility distribution on the height space for the height of John.

3. 3. 2 Possibility Measure

Let the universal set be X and suppose we have a possibility distribution $\{\Pi(x) ; x \in X\}$ then a possibility measure on $P(X)$, the power set of X, is defined by

$$\Pi(A) = \underset{x \in A}{MAX} \; \Pi(x) \; \text{ for any } A \in P(X)$$

with

$\Pi(X) = 1$ for a normalised possibility distribution.

We do allow non-normalised possibility distributions in which $\Pi(X) < 1$. This will correspond to some form of inconsistency.

3. 3. 3 A Fuzzy Set

A formal definition of a fuzzy set is now given. Let X define a universal set. Then the fuzzy set **f**, written in bold, is defined by means of its membership function

$$\chi_f : X \to [0, 1].$$

Fuzzy sets can be defined on a continuous space as for **tall** above, or a discrete space as in the next example.

In the discrete case, for which $X = \{x1, ..., xn\}$ say, then we write the fuzzy set as

$$\mathbf{f} = x1 / \chi_f(x1) + ... + xn / \chi_f(xn)$$

Example

Consider X = {house_1, house_2, house_3, house_4, house_5}

suitable_house = house_1 / 1 + house_2 / 0.7 + house_3 / 0.4 + house_4 / 0.1

Any element in the universal set not included in this sum has the membership value of 0.

The concept suitable_house is not well defined. The buyer may have examples in mind of suitable houses. The membership value $\chi_{\textbf{suitable\_house}}(\text{house\_i})$ is the degree to which the buyer thinks that house_i satisfies his concept of suitable house from his example set. The buyer performs a mental match of house_i with each of the houses in his example set of suitable houses. This mental match depends on how well certain features are satisfied. We will return to this later. Here we accept that the buyer is able to give the required membership values. The important point is that the acceptability of a given house being suitable is not binary, i.e. it does not take a value of 0 or 1, but can have degrees in the interval [0, 1].

A fuzzy set is normal if its maximum membership value is 1, otherwise it is non-normalised.

3. 3. 4 Why should we use Fuzzy Sets?

We have defined a fuzzy set in terms of membership values, but what are these values and how can we estimate them? These are important questions and are equivalent to asking how can we interpret a fuzzy set. In the next Section we introduce the idea of a voting model to interpret a fuzzy set.

Consider that we are told the fact

John is **tall**

where **tall** is a fuzzy set.

We understand this statement to give a possibility distribution over the height space for the height of John. An example of this is given in 3.3.1 How did we arrive at this particular distribution or, equivalently, how did we interpret the fuzzy set **tall**.

One could argue that the world is not fuzzy so that everything that is real is precise. John, for example, has a precise height even if we cannot measure it precisely. The inaccuracy in our measuring instrument induces a probability distribution over the height space. The use of fuzzy sets as a description could compensate for measurement inaccuracy but we will not pursue this particular line of interpretation.

Why do we use such terms as **tall** in everyday language? Why do we not choose to define the term **tall** precisely? The word **tall** represents a concept and is therefore a label we can put on objects, but why do we allow it to have a fuzzy definition? Most concepts we use are in fact fuzzy, for example, car, large vehicle, dangerous bend, unstable stand, democratic society, moral judgment, inflationary, hot, good student, hardworking, dissonant, well orchestrated, pretty, etc. All these words represent labels which we can apply to different objects, situations etc. Each of us has our own way of assessing the degree to which a particular label applies. We do not understand the method by which we do this assessment. We will assume that the method in some way compares a given case with other cases learned from experience and stored in the brain. Some form of matching takes place and some calculation is performed to give a possibility for the applicability of the label.

Given that most labels we use, most concepts we understand, are in fact fuzzy and therefore have a personal interpretation based on our experience, it may appear rather surprising that we manage to communicate with one another. Of course, truthfully we should admit that we often do not communicate particularly well and if there are cultural differences we can misinterpret what is said even concerning quite simple concepts. A certain musical harmonisation can be acceptable in one culture and not another. A certain person can be tall if of one nationality and not tall if of another. The more precise sort of person might despair over this confusing state of affairs. Too much fuzziness could even lead to madness. A band must have a limit to the fuzziness of its playing or it will not be "tight enough". On the other hand, if everything were precisely defined, assuming it could be, the band would be accused of poor creativity. English law is defined by cases and a person can be guilty because his behaviour matches closely that of the behaviour of another case for which a guilty verdict was decided.

We can appreciate the need for fuzziness even though we do not understand it. Fuzziness is a human phenomenon and has little, if anything, to do with the real world. Humans need to label objects, give description to situations, generalise from one situation to similar ones. If we defined a car precisely we would require to update the definition each year a new model came out. A fuzzy understanding of the concept "car" allows us to appreciate that an object which is similar in the most important respects is a car. Fuzziness is necessary for generalisation and most inferences made by people are inductive rather than deductive. Understanding the concept of a car does not mean giving a precise specification and functionality of each and every part. We choose a set of generalised features and relations between these features which are important for giving the name 'car' to several examples. These features and relations will apply to other cases of 'car' and the differences will be lost in the abstractions of the semantics of the features and relations. There will nevertheless be difficult cases for which a decision seems borderline. In these cases we may wish to simply say we cannot make a decision. Fuzzy set theory expects one to be able to give a degree of applicability and therefore have some measure of closeness of match. This assumption accepts that there can be degrees of possibility and not simply possible and not possible.

Another reason why we use fuzzy labels is one of complexity. We simplify our understanding of the relationship between several concepts by using fuzzy labels. We might from experience conclude that "most tall people wear large shoes". This description is very economic and easy to handle. We could replace it with numerous more precise statements but would probably find the more complex description too difficult to handle. This is the reason for the success of fuzzy control. A few fuzzy rules give the required breadth of description without losing the accuracy required to make reasonable decisions.

We will accept that the need for fuzzy set theory arises because our natural language contains words that cannot be given precise definition. We need to classify, to divide reality into parts, to partition the set of values a variable can take into broad categories. This necessarily introduces fuzzy boundaries and we use fuzzy sets for the classifications.

3. 3. 5 A Voting Model for Interpreting a Fuzzy Set

Let f be a fuzzy set, defined on the space X, with membership function χ_f. Let P be a representative population of persons. For a given $x \in X$, each member of P is asked to accept or reject x as satisfying f. A binary decision must be made. Let $\mu(x)$ be the proportion of members of P who accept x as satisfying **f**. Then we interpret the value of the membership function for argument x as this proportion, i.e.

$$\chi_{\mathbf{f}}(x) = \mu(x)$$

This is repeated for all x ε X.

We also make the assumption that any member of P who accepts an x ε X with a membership value $\chi_{\mathbf{f}}(x)$ will accept all elements y ε X which have a higher membership value, i.e. a member of P accepts any y ε X for which $\chi_{\mathbf{f}}(y) \geq \chi_{\mathbf{f}}(x)$ if the member accepts x. This we call the constant threshold assumption.

Example

Let **f** = a / 1 + b / 0.7 + c / 0.5 + d / 0.2 ; X = {a, b, c, d, e, f, g}
The voting pattern for a group of 10 persons would then be
PERSONS

1	2	3	4	5	6	7	8	9	10
a	a	a	a	a	a	a	a	a	a
b	b	b	b	b	b	b			
c	c	c	c	c					
d	d								

Without the constant threshold assumption we would not have a unique voting pattern from simply knowing the proportional acceptance for each element of X. We could, for example, have the voting pattern

1	2	3	4	5	6	7	8	9	10
a	a	a	a	a	a	a	a	a	a
b	b	b	b	b	b			b	
c	c	c				c			c
d							d		

The constant threshold assumption provides a unique voting pattern and it is intuitively appealing. The more optimistic members of P with regard to accepting when given only the binary choice remains more optimistic for all elements of the set X.

3. 4 POSSIBILITY VS PROBABILITY

3. 4. 1 Relationship between Possibility and Probability

Suppose that you are told that the variable X can take any value in the set {x1, ..., xn}. Let the probability distribution of X be {Pr(xi)} and the possibility distribution for X be {Π(xi), both defined over {x1, ..., xn}. Is there any relationship between the probability distribution and the possibility distribution? Your belief that X = xi is Pr(xi) and your acceptance that X could take the value xi is Π(xi).

Example

Suppose X = {a, b, c, d} and

Y is **f**

where

$$f = a / 1 + b / 0.7 + c / 0.5 + d / 0.1 ; \ f \subseteq X$$

The fuzzy set **f** induces a possibility distribution on X for Y, namely

$$\Pi(a) = 1 , \Pi(b) = 0.7, \Pi(c) = 0.5, \Pi(d) = 0.1$$

Let the probability distribution over X for Y be

$$Pr(a) = p1, Pr(b) = p2, Pr(c) = p3, Pr(d) = p4$$

then

$$p1 + p2 + p3 + p4 = 1$$

From the definition of possibility measure we can also determine that

$$\Pi(\{a, b, c, d\}) = 1, \Pi(\{b, c, d\}) = 0.7, \Pi(\{c, d\}) = 0.5, \Pi(\{d\}) = 0.1$$

We will now make the assumption that $Pr(A) \leq \Pi(A)$ for any $A \ \varepsilon \ P(X)$

so that

$$p1 + p2 + p3 + p4 = 1$$
$$p2 + p3 + p4 \leq 0.7$$
$$p3 + p4 \leq 0.5$$
$$p4 \leq 0.1$$

so that

$$0.3 \leq p1 \leq 1 \ ; \ 0 \leq p2 \leq 0.7 \ ; \ 0 \leq p3 \leq 0.5 \ ; \ 0 \leq p4 \leq 0.1$$

which is a family of probability distributions given by the mass assignment

$$m = a : 0.3, \{a, b\} : 0.2, \{a, b, c\} : 0.4, \{a, b, c, d\} : 0.1$$

This mass distribution can be determined directly from the membership values of the fuzzy set. The fuzzy set summation is written in descending order of membership values. The mass assignment is then a nested set, defined from left to right, with mass allocations given by the differences of the membership levels.

Thus the statement that Y is **f** is equivalent to saying that the value of Y is given by the mass assignment m which is equivalent to saying that

a : [0.3, 1], b : [0, 0.7], c : [0, 0.5], d : [0, 0.1].

3. 4. 2 General Case of Mass Assignments from Possibility Distributions

We can easily generalise the derivation of the mass assignment corresponding to any possibility distribution.

Suppose that

V is **f**

where **f** is a fuzzy set defined on the discrete space $X = \{x1, ..., xn\}$, namely

$$\mathbf{f} = \sum_{i=1}^{n} xi / \chi_i$$

then the fuzzy set **f** induces a possibility distribution over X for the variable V, namely

$$\Pi(xi) = \chi_i$$

Suppose **f** is a normalised fuzzy set whose elements are ordered such that

$$\chi_1 = 1, \chi_i \geq \chi_j \text{ if } i < j$$

then

$$\Pi(\{xi, ..., xn\}) = \chi_i$$

so that with the assumption that $Pr(A) \leq \Pi(A)$ for any $A \varepsilon P(X)$ we have

$$\sum_{k=i}^{n} p_k \leq \chi_i \text{ for } i = 2, ..., n \text{ where } p_k = Pr(xk) \text{ and } \sum_{k=1}^{n} p_k = 1$$

so that

$$1 - \chi_2 \leq p_1 \leq 1, \ 0 \leq p_i \leq \chi_i \ (i = 2, ..., n)$$

so that the mass assignment corresponding to the fuzzy set **f** is

$$m_{\mathbf{f}} = \{ \ \{x1, ..., xi\} : \chi_i - \chi_{i+1}; i = 1, ..., n \ \} \text{ with } \chi_{n+1} = 0.$$

3. 4. 3 Mass Assignments for Non-normalised Fuzzy Sets

Suppose that

V is **f**

where **f** is a fuzzy set defined on the discrete space $X = \{x1, ..., xn\}$, namely

$$f = \sum_{i=1}^{n} xi / \chi_i$$

whose elements are ordered such that

$$\chi_1 < 1, \chi_i \geq \chi_j \text{ if } i < j$$

then

$$m_{\mathbf{f}} = \{ \ \{x1, ..., xi\} : \chi_i - \chi_{i+1}, \emptyset : 1 - \chi_1 \ \} \text{ with } \chi_{n+1} = 0.$$

Example

If $\mathbf{f} = a / 0.8 + b / 0.6 + d / 0.2$; $X = \{a, b, c, d\}$
then

$$m_{\mathbf{f}} = a : 0.2, \{a, b\} : 0.4, \{a, b, c\} : 0.2, \emptyset : 0.2$$

This is an incomplete mass assignment and does not correspond to a family of probability distributions. We can think of the mass assignment as generating a family of distributions in which

$$Pr(x1) + ... + Pr(xn) = \chi_1$$

We will call such a family a non-normalised family of probability distributions.

Alternatively we can renormalise the mass assignment by equating the mass associated with $\emptyset$ to 0 and then renormalising the other masses so they sum to 1. The normalised mass assignment will correspond to the fuzzy set obtained by normalising $\mathbf{f}$ according to

$$\chi_{\mathbf{f} \text{ normalised}}^{(xi)} = \chi_{\mathbf{f}}(xi) / \chi_{\mathbf{f}}(x1)$$

Example

For the above example, the normalised mass assignment is

$$(m_{\mathbf{f}})\text{normalised} = a : 0.2 / 0.8, \{a, b\} : 0.4 / 0.8, \{a, b, c\} : 0.2 / 0.8$$

$$= a : 0.25, \{a, b\} : 0.5, \{a, b, c\} : 0.25$$

which corresponds to the fuzzy set

$$\mathbf{f}^* = a / 1 + b / 0.75 + c / 0.25$$

and

$$\mathbf{f}^* = \mathbf{f} \text{ normalised}$$

using the above formula.

It is interesting to note that renormalising a non-normalised fuzzy set using the above membership value modification is equivalent to the Dempster's renormalisation for mass assignments.

3. 4. 4 The Voting Model and Mass Assignments

The voting model interpretation is consistent with the mass assignment interpretation of a fuzzy set given above. Consider that we are told

V is **f**

Then for any A ε $P(X)$, let the proportion of members of P who accept A, i.e. accept all members of A as satisfying **f**, be m(A).

Example

Let

$\mathbf{f} = a/1 + b/0.7 + c/0.5 + d/0.2$; X = {a, b, c, d, e, f, g}

The voting pattern for a group of 10 persons would then be

PERSONS

1	2	3	4	5	6	7	8	9	10
a	a	a	a	a	a	a	a	a	a
b	b	b	b	b	b	b			
c	c	c	c	c					
d	d								

Therefore

m({a, b, c, d} = 0.2, m({a, b, c}) = 0.3, m({a, b}) = 0.2, m({a}) = 0.3

Suppose we wish to derive a probability distribution over X for V when given V is **f**. We will interpret Pr(x) as the probability that a person chosen at random from the population P will say that V is x. Therefore

0.3 ≤ Pr(a) ≤ 1 since persons 8, 9, and 10 only accept a

0 ≤ Pr(b) ≤ 0.7 since persons 1 to 7 could choose b but could choose alternatives

0 ≤ Pr(c) ≤ 0.5 since persons 1 to 5 could choose c but could choose alternatives

0 ≤ Pr(d) ≤ 0.2 since persons 1 to 2 could choose d but could choose alternatives

Pr(e) = Pr(f) = Pr(g) = 0 since no one would choose any of the values e, f, g.

Therefore m given here is the mass assignment $m_{\mathbf{f}}$ as defined above.

We might note that if we were asked to choose a unique probability distribution then we would choose

Pr(a) = 0.3 + 1/2(0.2) + 1/3(0.3) + 1/4(0.2) = 0.55

Pr(b) = 1/2(0.2) + 1/3(0.3) + 1/4(0.2) = 0.25

Pr(c) = 1/3(0.3) + 1/4(0.2) = 0.15

Pr(d) = 1/4(0.2) = 0.05

since when a person chosen at random has a choice of values to choose from each one would be chosen as equally likely.

We can replace a fuzzy set or the possibility induced by that fuzzy set by a family of probability distributions defined by the associated mass assignment. If asked for a unique distribution we select this from the mass assignment by the equally likely distribution argument given above.

We will use the voting model to justify the use of the MIN and MAX rules for intersection and union of fuzzy sets in a later section.

3. 5 OPERATIONS ON FUZZY SETS

3. 5. 1 Complement, Intersection and Union

The **complement** of a fuzzy set f defined on X with membership function χ_f is $\bar{f}$ defined on X with membership function $\chi_{\bar{f}}$ where $\chi_{\bar{f}}(x) = 1 - \chi_f(x)$ for any $x \in X$.

The **intersection** of two fuzzy sets $f1$, with membership function χ_{f1}, and $f2$, with membership function χ_{f2}, both defined on X, is $f1 \cap f2$ defined on X with membership function $\chi_{f1 \cap f2}$ where $\chi_{f1 \cap f2}(x) = \chi_{f1}(x) \wedge \chi_{f2}(x)$. Note that $x \wedge y = MIN\{x, y\}$.

The **union** of two fuzzy sets $f1$, with membership function χ_{f1}, and $f2$, with membership function χ_{f2}, both defined on X, is $f1 \cup f2$ defined on X with membership function $\chi_{f1 \cup f2}$ where $\chi_{f1 \cup f2}(x) = \chi_{f1}(x) \vee \chi_{f2}(x)$. Note that $x \vee y = MAX\{x, y\}$.

3. 5. 2 Voting Model Interpretation

These definitions of intersection and union are consistent with the voting model interpretation of a fuzzy set provided the constant threshold assumption is extended to cover both $f1$ and $f2$. This is illustrated with a simple example given below.

Example
Let
$f1 = a / 1 + b / 0.7 + c / 0.5 + d / 0.2$; $X = \{a, b, c, d, e, f, g\}$
The voting pattern for a group of 10 persons would then be

1	2	3	4	5	6	7	8	9	10
a	a	a	a	a	a	a	a	a	a
b	b	b	b	b	b	b			
c	c	c	c	c					
d	d								

Let

$f2 = a/1 + c/0.7 + d/0.5 + e/0.3$; $X = \{a, b, c, d, e, f, g\}$

The voting pattern for a group of 10 persons would then be

1	2	3	4	5	6	7	8	9	10
a	a	a	a	a	a	a	a	a	a
c	c	c	c	c	c	c			
d	d	d	d	d					
e	e	e							

It is assumed that the more optimistic persons for **f1** are also the more optimistic for **f2**. This allows persons in each pattern to be labelled as given here.

The pattern for the intersection of **f1** and **f2** is given as

1	2	3	4	5	6	7	8	9	10
a	a	a	a	a	a	a	a	a	a
c	c	c	c	c					
d	d								

in which we record for a given person those elements which he accepts for **f1** and **f2**. This corresponds to the fuzzy set

$\qquad a/1 + c/0.5 + d/0.2$

which corresponds to **f1** $\cap$ **f2** using the MIN rule for intersection.

Similarly the pattern for the union of the two fuzzy sets is given as

1	2	3	4	5	6	7	8	9	10
a	a	a	a	a	a	a	a	a	a
b	b	b	b	b	b	b			
c	c	c	c	c	c	c			
d	d	d	d	d					
e	e	e							

in which we record for a given person those elements which are accepted for either **f1** or **f2** or both. This corresponds to the fuzzy set

$a/1 + b/0.7 + c/0.7 + d/0.5 + e/0.3$

which is equivalent to **f1** $\cup$ **f2** using the MAX rule for union.

3. 5. 3 Alternative Definitions

Not all researchers accept the min / max rule for intersection / union of fuzzy sets. We can interpret other definitions from consideration of the voting model. We will illustrate the multiplication rule for intersection for the example above by rejecting the extension of the constant threshold assumption.

Example

Let **f1** = a / 1 + b / 0.7 + c / 0.5 + d / 0.2 ; X = {a, b, c, d, e, f, g}

The voting pattern for a group of 10 persons would then be

1	2	3	4	5	6	7	8	9	10
a	a	a	a	a	a	a	a	a	a
b	b	b	b	b	b	b			
c	c	c	c	c					
d	d								

Let **f2** = a / 1 + c / 0.7 + d / 0.5 + e / 0.3 ; X = {a, b, c, d, e, f, g}

The voting pattern for a group of 10 persons would then be

P1	P2	P3	P4	P5	P6	P7	P8	P9	P10
a	a	a	a	a	a	a	a	a	a
c	c	c	c	c	c	c			
d	d	d	d	d					
e	e	e							

If {P1, ..., P10} corresponds to {1, ..., 10}, which corresponds to accepting the extension of the constant threshold principle, then this corresponds to the example above. Without this assumption we can choose {P1, ..., P10} to be any sequence of the digits 1 to 10. For example

3	7	2	5	8	10	1	4	9	6
a	a	a	a	a	a	a	a	a	a
c	c	c	c	c	c	c			
d	d	d	d	d					
e	e	e							

in which case the pattern corresponding to the intersection of the fuzzy sets would be

1	2	3	4	5	6	7	8	9	10
a	a	a	a	a	a	a	a	a	a
c	c	c		c					
d									

giving $f1 \cap f2 = a / 1 + c / 0.4 + d / 0.1$

Other choices for $\{P1, ..., P10\}$ would give different solutions for $f1 \cap f2$. No pattern is preferable to any other. We can say all patterns for $\{P1, ..., P10\}$ are equally likely and determine the expected fuzzy set for $f1 \cap f2$. This will give

$$f1 \cap f2 = a / 1 + c / 0.35 + d / 0.1$$

which corresponds to using a multiplication rule for fuzzy intersection, i.e.

$$\chi_{f1 \cap f2}(x) = \chi_{f1}(x) * \chi_{f2}(x)$$

3. 5. 4 t-norms and co-norms

More generally we can define a mapping t

$$t : [0, 1] \times [0, 1] \rightarrow [0, 1]$$

which satisfies the axioms

(1) $t(a, 1) = a$

(2) $t(a, b) = t(b, a)$

(3) $t(a, b) \geq t(c, d)$ if $a \geq c$ and $b \geq d$

(4) $t(a, t(b, c)) = t(t(a, b), c)$

t is called a t-norm and generalises the logic 'and' for conjunction. Thus

$$\chi_{f1 \cap f2}(x) = t(\chi_{f1}(x), \chi_{f2}(x))$$

A dual norm, called the t-conorm, s, exists which generalises disjunction. For any t-norm t there exists a dual norm s such that

$$s(a, b) = 1 - t((1 - a), (1 - b))$$

The mapping

$$s : [0, 1] \times [0, 1] \rightarrow [0, 1]$$

satisfies the axioms

(1) $s(a, 0) = a$

(2) $s(a, b) = s(b, a)$

(3) $s(a, b) \geq s(c, d)$ if $a \geq c$ and $b \geq d$

(4) $s(a, s(b, c)) = s(s(a, b), c)$

Examples

(1) $t(a, b) = \min\{a, b\}$; $s(a, b) = \max\{a, b\}$

(2) $t(a, b) = ab$; $s(a, b) = a + b - ab$

(3) $t(a, b) = \max\{a + b - 1, 0\}$; $s(a, b) = \min\{a + b, 1\}$

3.5.5 Properties of Fuzzy Operations

Let **f**, **f1**, **f2**, **f3** be fuzzy sets defined over X. The following idempotence, commutativity, associativity and absorption properties hold:

(1) $\mathbf{f} \cup \mathbf{f} = \mathbf{f}$; $\mathbf{f} \cap \mathbf{f} = \mathbf{f}$

(2) $\mathbf{f1} \cup \mathbf{f2} = \mathbf{f2} \cup \mathbf{f1}$; $\mathbf{f1} \cap \mathbf{f2} = \mathbf{f2} \cap \mathbf{f1}$

(3) $\mathbf{f1} \cup (\mathbf{f2} \cup \mathbf{f3}) = (\mathbf{f1} \cup \mathbf{f2}) \cup \mathbf{f3}$; $\mathbf{f1} \cap (\mathbf{f2} \cap \mathbf{f3}) = (\mathbf{f1} \cap \mathbf{f2}) \cap \mathbf{f3}$

(4) $\mathbf{f1} \cup (\mathbf{f1} \cap \mathbf{f2}) = \mathbf{f1} \cap (\mathbf{f1} \cup \mathbf{f2}) = \mathbf{f1}$

The fuzzy set **f1** is a subset of **f2**, denoted by **f1** $\subseteq$ **f2** if and only if

$$\chi_{\mathbf{f1}}(x) \leq \chi_{\mathbf{f2}}(x) \; ; \; \text{(all x)}$$

Also **f1** $\subseteq$ **f2** is equivalent to

$$\mathbf{f1} \cup \mathbf{f2} = \mathbf{f2} \quad \text{and} \quad \mathbf{f1} \cap \mathbf{f2} = \mathbf{f1}$$

Furthermore the following distributive properties hold

$$\mathbf{f1} \cup (\mathbf{f2} \cap \mathbf{f3}) = (\mathbf{f1} \cup \mathbf{f2}) \cap (\mathbf{f1} \cup \mathbf{f3})$$

$$\mathbf{f1} \cap (\mathbf{f2} \cup \mathbf{f3}) = (\mathbf{f1} \cap \mathbf{f2}) \cup (\mathbf{f1} \cap \mathbf{f3})$$

De Morgan's laws hold:

$$\mathbf{f1} \cap \mathbf{f2} = \overline{\mathbf{f1}} \cup \overline{\mathbf{f2}} \quad ; \quad \overline{\mathbf{f1} \cup \mathbf{f2}} = \overline{\mathbf{f1}} \cap \overline{\mathbf{f2}}$$

and the involution law holds:

$$\overline{\overline{\mathbf{f}}} = \mathbf{f}$$

Let **F** represent all fuzzy sets over X. $\langle \mathbf{F}, \cup, \cap, \overline{} \rangle$ is an algebra with idempotence, commutativity, associativity, absorption, distributivity and complementation properties given above. Full complementation properties are not satisfied. For example $\mathbf{f} \cup \overline{\mathbf{f}}$ is not necessarily equal to X. The algebra is a pseudo Boolean Algebra.

We can also view the structure in lattice terms. $\langle \mathbf{F}, \subseteq \rangle$ is a poset and further is a lattice since the union and intersection are defined everywhere. **f** with $\chi_{\mathbf{f}}(x) = 0$, all x, and **f** with $\chi_{\mathbf{f}}(x) = 1$, all x, are the universal bounds of the lattice. The lattice is distributive but not completely complemented.

$<F, \subseteq >$ is a pseudo complemented distributed lattice.

3. 6 OPERATIONS ON MASS ASSIGNMENTS

3.6.1 Restriction of a Mass Assignment

A mass assignment corresponds to a family of probability distributions. A restriction of a mass assignment corresponds to a subset of this family of probability distributions. It is necessary to define two types of restriction for mass assignments to validate this interpretation and connect sensibly with fuzzy set theory. A type 1 restriction corresponds to redistributing the mass associated with a focal element in the mass assignment to subsets of this focal element. A type 2 restriction is less intuitive but is necessary to show that some mass assignments correspond to a family of probability distributions which is a subset of that for a given mass assignment.

If m = {Li : mi} then

$$
m' = \begin{pmatrix}
\{Li : mi \mid Li \neq Lk, L'1, L'2\} \cup \{L'1 : m(L'1) + x\} \cup \{L'2 : m(L'2) + y\} \\
\text{if } x + y = mk \\[1em]
\{Li : mi \mid Li \neq Lk, L'1, L'2\} \cup \{L'1 : m(L'1) + x\} \cup \{L'2 : m(L'2) + y\} \\
\cup \{Lk : mk - x - y\} \\
\text{if } x + y < mk
\end{pmatrix}
$$

where $L'1 \subseteq Lk, L'2 \subseteq Lk, L'1 \neq L'2$

is a **restriction** of m and is denoted by m' $\leq$ m. We call this a restriction of type 1.

Example

If S = {a, b, c, d, e}

m = {a, b, c} : 0.3, {c, d, e} : 0.5, {a, b, c, d, e} : 0.2   then

m' = {a, b} : 0.2, {a, b, c} : 0.1, {c, d} : 0.2, {c} : 0.3, {a, b, c, d, e} : 0.2

is a restriction of m.

There is an additional form of restriction which we must define so that a restriction of a mass assignment corresponds to a subset of the family of probability distributions associated with that mass assignment. This additional restriction has other uses as will be seen later.

If m = {Li : mi} then if we replace

$Lk = \{\alpha \cup \beta\} : mk$

$Ls = \{\beta \cup \gamma\} : ms$

for some Lk, Ls belonging to m where α, β, γ are subsets of X, by

$$\{\alpha \cup \beta \cup \gamma\} : x$$

$$\{\alpha \cup \beta\} : mk - x$$

$$\{\beta \cup \gamma\} : ms - x$$

$$\beta : x$$

where $0 \le x \le mk$; $0 \le x \le ms$

then the modified mass assignment is also a restriction of m. We call this a restriction of type 2.

The family of probability distributions of the modified mass assignment is a subset of that for m.

Example

Let

$$m = a : 0.5, \{a, b\} : 0.2, \{a, c\} : 0.3$$
$$m' = a : 0.7, \{a, c\} : 0.1, \{a, b, c\} : 0.2$$

m' can be obtained from m using the above modification with $\{\alpha, \beta\} = \{a, b\}$, $\{\beta, \gamma\} = \{a, c\}$, $x = 0.2$.

The family of distributions for m is given by

$$Pr(a) = 1 - y - z, Pr(b) = y, Pr(c) = z \text{ where } 0 \le y \le 0.2 ; \ 0 \le z \le 0.3$$

The family of distributions for m' is given by

$$Pr(a) = 1 - y - z, Pr(b) = y, Pr(c) = z \text{ where } 0 \le y \le 0.2 ; 0 \le z \le 0.3 ;$$
$$0 \le y + z \le 0.3$$

This is a subset of the family for m since for the case of m $0 \le y + z \le 0.5$. For m' this is further restricted.

Mass assignments s1 and s2 are said to be **orthogonal** if one cannot be obtained from the other by restriction, i.e. $\neg (s1 \le s2) \wedge \neg (s2 \le s1)$.

3.6.2 Complements

The complement of a mass assignment m = {Li : mi} defined over X is given by

$$\overline{m} = \{\overline{Li} : mi\}$$

where $\overline{Li}$ is the complement of Li with respect to X.

If for m a mass is associated with X then this mass will be associated with Ø for $\overline{m}$ and the complement is an incomplete mass assignment. If m is an incomplete mass assignment then the mass associated with Ø is associated with X for $\overline{m}$.

3.6.3 Meet of two Mass Assignments

For mass assignments m and n defined on the power set $P(X)$ we can define analogous operations to intersection and union. We will call these the meet and join denoted by $\wedge$, $\vee$ respectively.

Let $m = \{Mi : mi\}$ and $n = \{Nj : nj\}$ where Mi and Nj are subsets of X.

A set of orthogonal solutions S for the meet of two mass assignments, m1 and m2, namely $m1 \wedge m2$, is complete if all solutions satisfying the constraints (1), (2) and (3) can be obtained as a restriction of a member of S or as a linear combination of members of S.

Then the meet $m1 \wedge m2$ can be defined as

$$m1 \wedge m2 = \sum_i \alpha_i s_i$$

where $\{s_i\}$ is a complete orthogonal set of $(m_1 \, \& \, m_2)$ satisfying

$m1 \, \& \, m2 = \{Lk : lk\}$ where $\{Lk\} = \{Lij\}$, $Lij = Mi \cap Nj$, lij is mass given to Lij and $\{lk\}$ must satisfy

$$lk = \sum_{\substack{i,j \\ Lk = Lij}} lij$$

$$Lk = Lij \tag{1}$$

$$\sum_j lij = mi \text{ for all } i \tag{2}$$

$$\sum_i lij = nj \text{ for all } j \tag{3}$$

The family of probability distributions of the meet $m_{f1} \wedge m_{f2}$ is equal to the intersection of the family of distributions for m_{f1} and that of m_{f2}. If this family does not correspond to a mass assignment then the meet is equal to a linear combination of orthogonal mass assignments.

Examples

We use the following examples to bring out some interesting points in the relationship of the meet of mass assignments. We leave the reader to generalise from these examples.

Ex 1.

$f1 = a / 1 + b / 0.8 + c / 0.3$ so that $m_{f1} = a : 0.2, \{a, b\} : 0.5, \{a, b, c\} : 0.3$

$f2 = a / 1 + b / 0.5 + c / 0.4$ so that $m_{f2} = a : 0.5, \{a, b\} : 0.1, \{a, b, c\} : 0.4$

The diagrams below give the mass assignments in the form of cell allocations. Each cell contains a set which is the intersection of the row set and column set associated with m_{f1}

and m_{f2} and a mass associated with the intersection. Constraints (2) and (3) above correspond to each of the row masses adding up to the corresponding row mass of m_{f1} and each of the column masses adding up to the column mass associated with m_{f2}.

	0.5 a	0.1 {a,b}	0.4 {a,b,c}
0.2 a	a 0.2	a 0	a 0
0.5 {a, b}	a 0.3	{a,b} 0.1	{a,b} 0.1
0.3 {a, b, c}	a 0	{a,b} 0	{a,b,c} 0.3

Fig 3.2

$m_{f1} \wedge m_{f2} =$

$a : 0.5, \{a, b\} : 0.2, \{a, b, c\} : 0.3$

Any other cell allocation satisfying the row and column constraints is a restriction of this solution.

This mass assignment corresponds to the fuzzy set $a / 1 + b / 0.5 + c / 0.3 = \mathbf{f1 \cap f2}$.

The family of probability distributions corresponding to $m_{f1} \wedge m_{f2}$ is that given by the intersection of the family of distributions corresponding to m_{f1} with that for m_{f2}.

Ex 2.

$\mathbf{f1} = a / 1 + b / 0.8 + c / 0.3$ so that $m_{f1} = a : 0.2, \{a, b\} : 0.5, \{a, b, c\} : 0.3$

$\mathbf{f2} = a / 1 + b / 0.2 + c / 0.7$ so that $m_{f2} = a : 0.3, \{a, c\} : 0.5, \{a, b, c\} : 0.2$

We have a unique cell allocation with the row and column constraints satisfied such that all other allocations satisfying row and column constraints are restrictions of it.

	0.3 a	0.5 {a,c}	0.2 {a,b,c}
0.2 a	a 0.2	a 0	a 0
0.5 {a, b}	a 0.1	a 0.2	{a,b} 0.2
0.3 {a, b, c}	a 0	{a,c} 0.3	{a,b,c} 0

Fig 3.3

$m_{f1} \wedge m_{f2} = m$

$m = a : 0.5, \{a, b\} : 0.2, \{a, c\} : 0.3$

The mass assignment m' which is obtained by maximising the mass in the cell corresponding to the largest set is given by

	0.3 a	0.5 {a,c}	0.2 {a,b,c}
0.2 a	a 0.2	a 0	a 0
0.5 {a, b}	a 0.1	a 0.4	{a,b} 0
0.3 {a, b, c}	a 0	{a,c} 0.1	{a,b,c} 0.2

Fig 3.4

$m' = a : 0.7, \{a, c\} : 0.1, \{a, b, c\} : 0.2$

This is a restriction of m since we can transform m to obtain this mass assignment as follows

a : 0.5		a : 0.7
{a, b} : 0.2	----->	{a, c} : 0.1
{a, c} : 0.3		{a, b, c} : 0.2

The family of probability distributions corresponding to $m_{f1} \wedge m_{f2}$ is that given by the intersection of the family of distributions corresponding to m_{f1} with that for m_{f2}.

The mass assignment m corresponds to this family of probability distributions of the meet. m does not correspond to a fuzzy set. If we impose the constraint that the meet must correspond to a fuzzy set then we obtain the meet = m' which is the same solution as that given by fuzzy set theory using the min rule for intersection.

This solution gives a subset of the family of probability distributions of the meet. The subset is obtained by adding the constraint that the family of probability distributions must come from a possibility distribution corresponding to a fuzzy set.

Ex 3.

$f1 = a / 1 + b / 0.8 + c / 0.3$; $m_{f1} = a : 0.2, \{a, b\} : 0.5, \{a, b, c\} : 0.3$

$f2 = a / 0.8 + b / 1 + c / 1$; $m_{f2} = \{b, c\} : 0.2, \{a, b, c\} : 0.8$

The meet is given by

	0.2 {b,c}	0.8 {a,b,c}
0.2 a	∅ 0	a 0.2
0.5 {a, b}	b 0	{a,b} 0.5
0.3 {a, b, c}	{b, c} 0.2	{a,b,c} 0.1

Fig 3.5

The mass associated with ∅ is 0 if possible for consistency.

$m_{f1} \wedge m_{f2} = m$

$m = a : 0.2, \{a, b\} : 0.5, \{b, c\} : 0.2,$
    $\{a, b, c\} : 0.1$

The solution given by

	0.2 {b,c}	0.8 {a,b,c}
0.2 a	Ø 0	a 0.2
0.5 {a, b}	b 0.2	{a,b} 0.3
0.3 {a, b, c}	{b, c} 0	{a,b,c} 0.3

m' = a : 0.2, b : 0.2, {a,b} 0.3, {a, b, c} : 0.3

Fig 3.6

is a restriction of m since we can modify m to give m' using the restriction modification as follows:

a : 0.2   a : 0.2

{a, b} : 0.5   ------>   {a, b} : 0.3

{b, c} : 0.2   {a, b, c} : 0.3

{a, b, c} : 0.1   b : 0.2

If we want to restrict m so that we obtain a mass assignment, m", corresponding to a fuzzy set, then we use the modification

a : 0.2

{a, b} : 0.5   ------>   {a, b} : 0.5

{b, c} : 0.2   {a, b, c} : 0.3 = m"

{a, b, c} : 0.1   Ø : 0.2

This is the most general fuzzy set solution which we can obtain from m. In fact no other fuzzy set solution can be obtained from m by restriction. The mass assignment m" corresponds to the fuzzy set a / 0.8 + b / 0.8 + c / 0.3 which is equal to **f1** ∩ **f2** using the min rule for intersection.

Ex 4.

This example shows the need for a complete orthogonal set to give the required family of probability distributions for the meet.

Let

m1 = a : 0.2, {a, b} : 0.5, {b, c} : 0.3 ;   m2 = b : 0.3, {a, c} : 0.4, {a, b, c} : 0.3

To find the meet we must fill in the cell allocation diagram Fig. 3.7.

Giving max value to {a,b} will introduce other choices.

The complete set of solutions which cannot be obtained from others by restriction is given by

(1) s1 = a : 0.2, b : 0.3, c : 0.2, {a, b} : 0.3

(2) s2 = a : 0.4, b : 0.3, {b, c} : 0.3

(3) s3 = a : 0.2, b : 0.3, c : 0.2, {a, b} : 0.2, {b, c} : 0.1

(4) s4 = a : 0.4, b : 0.3, {a, b} : 0.3

(5) s5 = a : 0.6, b : 0.3, {b, c} : 0.1

	0.3 b	0.4 {a,c}	0.3 {a,b,c}
0.2 a	Ø 0	a	a
0.5 {a, b}	b	a	{a,b}
0.3 {b, c}	b	c	{b,c}

Fig 3.7

The top row will allocate 0.2 to a and the leftmost column will allocate 0.3 to b.

We can maximise the entries in each of the four lower right cells.

The meet is given as a linear combination of these orthogonal solutions

$$m1 \wedge m2 = \alpha1 s1 + \alpha2 s2 + \alpha3 s3 + \alpha4 s4 + \alpha5 s5$$

where $\alpha1 + \alpha2 + \alpha3 + \alpha4 + \alpha5 = 1$

This shows the complication and the impracticality of using this meet for practical problems.

Ex 5.

Let

m1 = a : 0.7, {a, c} : 0.1, {a, b, c} : 0.2 ; m2 = a : 0.5, {a, b} : 0.2, {a, c} : 0.3

In fact m1 is a restriction of type 2 of the mass assignment m2, i.e. m1 ≤ m2

Therefore

m1 ∧ m2 = m1

From the meet tableau

	0.5 a	0.2 {a, b}	0.3 {a, c}
0.7 a	a	a	a
0.1 {a, c}	a	a	{a, c}
0.2 {a, b, c}	b	{a, b}	{a, c}

Fig 3.8

The complete set of orthogonal solutions satisfying the meet row and column constraints is given by

71

$$t1 = a : 0.7, \{a, c\} : 0.3 \quad ; \quad t2 = a : 0.7, \{a, b\} : 0.2, \{a, c\} : 0.1$$

and the meet is therefore given by

$$m = m1 \wedge m2 = \alpha t1 + (1 - \alpha) t2$$

We now show that $m = m1$. Let F_m be the family of probability distributions for m.

$$F_{t1} = a : 1 - x, c : x \text{ where } 0 \le x \le 0.3$$

$$F_{t2} = a : 1 - y - z, b : y, c : z \text{ where } 0 \le y \le 0.2, 0 \le z \le 0.1$$

so that

$$F_m = a : \alpha(1 - x) + (1 - \alpha)(1 - y - z), b : (1 - \alpha)y, c : \alpha x + (1 - \alpha)z$$

Also

$$F_{m1} = a : 1 - x' - y' - z', b : y', c : x'+ z' \text{ where } 0 \le x' \le 0.1, 0 \le y' + z' \le 0.2$$

so that

$$F_m = F_{m1}$$

with

$$y' = (1 - \alpha)y, x' + z' = \alpha x + (1 - \alpha)z$$

This equality can be deduced directly from t1 and t2 since
the family of distributions of $\alpha[\{a, c\} : 0.2] + (1 - \alpha)[\{a, b\} : 0.2]$ -- all α
is equivalent to the family of distributions of $\{a, b, c\} : 0.2$.
Thus

$$\alpha t1 + (1 - \alpha)t2 = a : 0.7, \{a, c\} : 0.1, \{a, b, c\} : 0.2$$

3.6.4 Multiplication Meet for Mass Assignments

Consider mass assignments m and n defined on the power set $P(X)$. Let m = {Mi : mi} and n = {Nj, nj} where Mi and Nj are subsets of X. The multiplication meet of m and n, denoted by m $\wedge$. n, is given by

$$m \wedge. n = \{Lk : lk\} \text{ where } \{Lk\} = \{Lij\}, \ Lij = Mi \cap Nj, \ lij \text{ is mass given to Lij}$$

$$lk = \sum_{\substack{i, j \\ Lk = Lij}} lij$$

where

$$lij = mi \ nj$$

This solution satisfies the constraints:

$$\sum_j lij = mi \text{ for all i}$$

72

$$\sum_i \text{lij} = \text{nj} \quad \text{for all } j$$

We do not require $m(\emptyset)$ to be zero.

Examples

Ex 1.

$f1 = a / 1 + b / 0.8 + c / 0.3$ so that $m_{f1} = a : 0.2, \{a, b\} : 0.5, \{a, b, c\} : 0.3$

$f2 = a / 1 + b / 0.5 + c / 0.4$ so that $m_{f2} = a : 0.5, \{a, b\} : 0.1, \{a, b, c\} : 0.4$

	0.5 a	0.1 {a,b}	0.4 {a,b,c}
0.2 a	a 0.1	a 0.02	a 0.08
0.5 {a, b}	a 0.25	{a,b} 0.05	{a,b} 0.2
0.3 {a, b, c}	a 0.15	{a,b} 0.03	{a,b,c} 0.12

Fig 3.9

$m_{f1} \wedge . m_{f2} =$

$a : 0.6, \{a, b\} : 0.28, \{a, b, c\} : 0.12$

This mass assignment corresponds to the fuzzy set $a / 1 + b / 0.4 + c / 0.12 = f1 \cap f2$ using the multiplication intersection rule.

The family of probability distributions corresponding to this meet is a subset of that for the meet $m_{f1} \wedge m_{f2}$ obtained in the previous Section. It corresponds to using the multiplication intersection rule for fuzzy set intersection. This was shown to have a certain voting model interpretation, see 3.5.3.

Ex 2.

$f1 = a / 1 + b / 0.8 + c / 0.3$; $m_{f1} = a : 0.2, \{a, b\} : 0.5, \{a, b, c\} : 0.3$

$f2 = a / 0.8 + b / 1 + c / 1$; $m_{f2} = \{b, c\} : 0.2, \{a, b, c\} : 0.8$

The multiplication meet is given by

	0.2 {b,c}	0.8 {a,b,c}
0.2 a	∅ 0.04	a 0.16
0.5 {a, b}	b 0.1	{a,b} 0.4
0.3 {a, b, c}	{b, c} 0.06	{a,b,c} 0.24

Fig 3.10

$m_{f1} \wedge . m_{f2} = a : 0.16$

$b : 0.1$

$\{a, b\} : 0.4$

$\{b, c\} : 0.06$

$\{a, b, c\} : 0.24$

$\emptyset : 0.04$

This does not correspond to a fuzzy set. If we transform this using the restriction algorithm we can obtain

a : 0.16   a : 0.06

b : 0.1

{a, b} : 0.4   ------>   {a, b} : 0.5   ------> {a, b} : 0.5

{b, c} : 0.06   {b, c} : 0.06

{a, b, c} : 0.24   {a, b, c} : 0.24   {a, b, c} : 0.3

Ø : 0.04   Ø : 0.14   Ø : 0.2

which corresponds to the fuzzy set a / 0.8 + b / 0.8 + c / 0.3 which is equal to **f1** $\cap$ **f2** using the multiplication rule. No other fuzzy set can be obtained by transformations like this. It is therefore the most general fuzzy set corresponding to the multiplication meet.

Ex 3.

m1 = a : 0.2, {a, b} : 0.5, {b, c} : 0.3 ;   m2 = b : 0.3, {a, c} : 0.4, {a, b, c} : 0.3

	0.3 b	0.4 {a,c}	0.3 {a,b,c}
0.2 a	Ø 0.06	a 0.08	a 0.06
0.5 {a, b}	b 0.15	a 0.2	{a,b} 0.15
0.3 {b, c}	b 0.09	c 0.12	{b,c} 0.09

m1 ∧. m2 = a : 0.34

b : 0.24

c : 0.12

{a, b} : 0.15

{b, c} : 0.09

Ø : 0.06

Fig 3.11

3.6.5 Join of two Mass Assignments

For mass assignments m and n defined on the power set $P(X)$ we can define the join denoted by $\vee$. Let m1 = {Mi : mi} and m2 = {Nj, nj} where Mi and Nj are subsets of X.

Then the join m1 $\vee$ m2 can be defined as

$$m1 \vee m2 = \sum_i \alpha_i s_i$$

where {s_i} is a complete orthogonal set of ($m_1 \mid m_2$) satisfying

m1 | m2 = {Lk : lk} where {Lk} = {Lij}, Lij = Mi $\cup$ Nj, lij is mass given to Lij and {lk} must satisfy

$$lk = \sum_{\substack{i, j \\ Lk = Lij}} lij$$

$$\sum_j lij = mi \text{ for all } i$$

$$\sum_i lij = nj \text{ for all } j$$

The family of probability distributions of the join $m_{f1} \vee m_{f2}$ is equal to the family of distributions for a linear combination of m_{f1} and m_{f2}, $\alpha m_{f1} + (1 - \alpha) m_{f2}$

The multiplication join of m and n, denoted by m $\vee$. n, is given by

$$m \vee. n = \{Lk : lk\} \text{ where } \{Lk\} = \{Lij\}, \; Lij = Mi \cup Nj, \; lij \text{ is mass given to } Lij$$
$$lk = \sum_{\substack{i,j \\ Lk = Lij}} lij$$

where

$$lij = mi \, nj$$

This solution satisfies the constraints:

$$\sum_j lij = mi \text{ for all } i$$

$$\sum_i lij = nj \text{ for all } j$$

We do not require m(∅) to be zero.

3.6.6 Algebra of Mass Assignments

Let the frame of discernment be X and $\{s_1, ..., s_n\}$ be a set of orthogonal mass assignments defined over X. The linear form

$$\mathbf{m} = \sum_{i=1}^{n} \alpha_i s_i \; ; \; \sum_{i=1}^{n} \alpha_i = 1$$

represents a family of mass assignments parametrised by $\alpha = \{\alpha 1, ..., \alpha n\}$.

Let **m1**, **m2** be two such families of mass assignments over X

$$\mathbf{m}1 = \sum_{i=1}^{n} \alpha_i u_i \; ; \; \sum_{i=1}^{n} \alpha_i = 1 \; ; \; \mathbf{m}2 = \sum_{i=1}^{m} \beta_i v_i \; ; \; \sum_{i=1}^{m} \beta_i = 1$$

then $\mathbf{m1} \leq \mathbf{m2}$ iff ui $\leq$ vj for all i = 1, ..., n, j = 1, ..., m where $\leq$ is the restriction ordering relation defined above.

$$\mathbf{m}1 \wedge \mathbf{m}2 = \sum_{i=1}^{n} \sum_{j=1}^{m} \varphi_{ij}(u_i \wedge v_j) \; ; \quad \sum_{i=1}^{n} \sum_{j=1}^{m} \varphi_{ij} = 1 \; ;$$

where for any i, j $\varphi_{ij} = 0$ if $u_r \wedge v_s \leq u_i \wedge v_j$ for any r, s

$$\mathbf{m}1 \vee \mathbf{m}2 = \sum_{i=1}^{n} \sum_{j=1}^{m} \varphi_{ij}(u_i \vee v_j) \; ; \quad \sum_{i=1}^{n} \sum_{j=1}^{m} \varphi_{ij} = 1 \; ;$$

where for any i, j $\varphi_{ij} = 0$ if $u_r \vee v_s \leq u_i \vee v_j$ for any r, s

The following idempotence, commutativity, associativity and absorption properties hold.

(1) $\mathbf{m} \vee \mathbf{m} = \mathbf{m}$; $\mathbf{m} \wedge \mathbf{m} = \mathbf{m}$

(2) $\mathbf{m1} \vee \mathbf{m2} = \mathbf{m2} \vee \mathbf{m1}$; $\mathbf{m1} \wedge \mathbf{m2} = \mathbf{m2} \wedge \mathbf{m1}$

(3) $\mathbf{m1} \vee (\mathbf{m2} \vee \mathbf{m3}) = (\mathbf{m1} \vee \mathbf{m2}) \vee \mathbf{m3}$; $\mathbf{m1} \wedge (\mathbf{m2} \wedge \mathbf{m3}) = (\mathbf{m1} \wedge \mathbf{m2}) \wedge \mathbf{m3}$

(4) $\mathbf{m1} \vee (\mathbf{m1} \wedge \mathbf{m2}) = \mathbf{m1} \wedge (\mathbf{m1} \vee \mathbf{m2}) = \mathbf{m1}$

Also $\mathbf{m1} \leq \mathbf{m2}$ is equivalent to

$$\mathbf{m1} \vee \mathbf{m2} = \mathbf{m2} \quad \text{and} \quad \mathbf{m1} \wedge \mathbf{m2} = \mathbf{m1}$$

Furthermore, the following distributive properties hold.

$$\mathbf{m1} \vee (\mathbf{m2} \wedge \mathbf{m3}) = (\mathbf{m1} \vee \mathbf{m2}) \wedge (\mathbf{m1} \vee \mathbf{m3})$$

$$\mathbf{m1} \wedge (\mathbf{m2} \vee \mathbf{m3}) = (\mathbf{m1} \wedge \mathbf{m2}) \vee (\mathbf{m1} \wedge \mathbf{m3})$$

Let

$$\mathbf{m} = \sum_{i=1}^{n} \alpha_i s_i \; ; \quad \sum_{i=1}^{n} \alpha_i = 1$$

be a family of mass assignments defined over X; then the complement $\overline{\mathbf{m}}$ is defined as

$$\overline{\mathbf{m}} = \sum_{i=1}^{n} \alpha_i \overline{s_i} \; ; \quad \sum_{i=1}^{n} \alpha_i = 1$$

De Morgan's laws hold. For families of mass assignments $\mathbf{m}$, $\mathbf{m1}$, $\mathbf{m2}$ defined over X

$$\overline{\mathbf{m1} \wedge \mathbf{m2}} = \overline{\mathbf{m1}} \vee \overline{\mathbf{m2}} \quad ; \quad \overline{\mathbf{m1} \vee \mathbf{m2}} = \overline{\mathbf{m1}} \wedge \overline{\mathbf{m2}}$$

and the involution law holds:

$$\overline{\overline{\mathbf{m}}} = \mathbf{m}$$

Let $\mathbf{M}$ represent all the families of mass assignments over X. $<\mathbf{M}, \vee, \wedge, ->$ is an algebra with   idempotence, commutativity, associativity, absorption, distributivity and complementation properties given above. Full complementation properties are not satisfied. The algebra is a pseudo Boolean Algebra.

We can also view the structure in lattice terms. $\langle \mathbf{M}, \leq \rangle$ is a poset and further is a lattice since the join and meet are defined everywhere. $\emptyset : 1$ and $X : 1$ are the universal bounds of the lattice $\mathbf{M}$. The lattice is distributive but not completely complemented.

$\langle \mathbf{M}, \leq \rangle$ is a pseudo complemented distributed lattice.

This algebra also holds if the meet and join are replaced by the multiplication meet and join.

3.7 SEMANTIC UNIFICATION

3.7.1 Conditional Mass Assignment

Let $\mathbf{g}$ and $\mathbf{g}'$ be fuzzy sets defined on X. We wish to find the mass assignment associated with the truth set of $\mathbf{g}$ given $\mathbf{g}'$, denoted by $m_{(\mathbf{g} \mid \mathbf{g}')}$ defined over $\{t, f\}$ where t represents true and f represents false.

Let $m_{\mathbf{g}} = \{Li : li\}$ and $m_{\mathbf{g}'} = \{Mi : mi\}$ be mass assignments associated with the fuzzy sets $\mathbf{g}$ and $\mathbf{g}'$. Form the matrix

$$M = \{T(Li \mid Mj) : li.mj\} \quad \text{where } T(Li \mid Mj) = \left\{ \begin{array}{l} t \text{ if } Mj \subseteq Li \\ f \text{ if } Mj \cap Li = \emptyset \\ u \text{ otherwise} \end{array} \right\}$$

u stands for uncertain and represents $\{t, f\}$.

The mass assignment $m_{(\mathbf{g} \mid \mathbf{g}')}$ is then given by

$$m_{(\mathbf{g} \mid \mathbf{g}')} = t : \sum_{\substack{i,j \\ T(Li \mid Mj) = t}} li.mj, \quad f : \sum_{\substack{i,j \\ T(Li \mid Mj) = f}} li.mj, \quad u : \sum_{\substack{i,j \\ T(Li \mid Mj) = u}} li.mj$$

This is called the multiplication model for semantic unification since the mass entries in the matrix M are obtained by multiplying the corresponding row and column masses. Other semantic models can be defined and these will be discussed below.

We can rewrite the mass assignment for $\mathbf{g} \mid \mathbf{g}'$ over $\{t, f\}$ as a support pair for $\mathbf{g} \mid \mathbf{g}'$. The support pair for $\mathbf{g} \mid \mathbf{g}'$ is given by

$$\mathbf{g} \mid \mathbf{g}' = [\sum_{\substack{i,j \\ T(Li \mid Mj) = t}} li.mj, \quad \sum_{\substack{i,j \\ T(Li \mid Mj) = t}} li.mj + \sum_{\substack{i,j \\ T(Li \mid Mj) = u}} li.mj]$$

Example

Let $\mathbf{g} = a/1 + b/0.7 + c/0.2$; $\mathbf{g}' = a/0.2 + b/1 + c/0.7 + d/0.1$ defined on $X = \{a, b, c, d, e\}$ so that

$m_g = a : 0.3, \{a, b\} : 0.5, \{a, b, c\} : 0.2$

$m_{g'} = b : 0.3, \{b, c\} : 0.5, \{a, b, c\} : 0.1, \{a, b, c, d\} : 0.1$

giving matrix

	0.3 b	0.5 {b, c}	0.1 {a, b, c}	0.1 {a, b, c, d}	
0.3 a	f 0.09	f 0.15	u 0.03	u 0.03	
0.5 {a, b}	t 0.15	u 0.25	u 0.05	u 0.05	**Fig 3.12**
0.2 {a, b, c}	t 0.06	t 0.1	t 0.02	u 0.02	

t : 0.33
f : 0.24   giving $g \mid g' = [0.33, 0.76]$
u : 0.43

so that $m_{g \mid g'} = t : 0.33, f : 0.24, u : 0.43$ giving $g \mid g' = [0.33, 0.76]$.

3.7.2 An Important Theorem

Let $g1, g'1 \subseteq_f X1, g2, g'2 \subseteq_f X2$

then the following can be proved

$$m_{(g1 \wedge. g2 \mid g'1 \wedge. g'2)} = m_{(g1 \mid g'1) \wedge.} m_{(g2 \mid g'2)}$$

where $\wedge.$ is the multiplication meet.

Furthermore, if $g1 \wedge. g2 \mid g'1 \wedge. g'2 = [\alpha, \beta], g1 \mid g'1 = [\alpha1, \beta1], g2 \mid g'2 = [\alpha2, \beta2]$ then

$\alpha = \alpha1.\alpha2$; $\beta = \beta1.\beta2$

This theorem is important since it allows the determination of the semantic unification of a conjunction of terms given appropriate data to be decomposed into sub-problems involving the semantic unification of one fuzzy set given another. The fuzzy sets in each term will be defined on different universal sets.

3.7.3 Alternative Semantic Models

Let g and g' be fuzzy sets defined on X. We wish to find the mass assignment associated with the truth set of g given g', denoted by $m_{(g \mid g')}$ defined over $\{t, f\}$ where t represents true and f represents false.

Let $m_g = \{Li : li\}$ and $m_{g'} = \{Mi : mi\}$ be mass assignments associated with the fuzzy sets g and g'. Form the matrix

$$M = \{T(Li \mid Mj) : m_{ij}\} \quad \text{where } T(Li \mid Mj) = \begin{cases} t \text{ if } Mj \subseteq Li \\ f \text{ if } Mj \cap Li = \varnothing \\ u \text{ otherwise} \end{cases}$$

where

$$\sum_i m_{ij} = mj \; ; (\text{all } j)$$

$$\sum_j m_{ij} = mi \; ; (\text{all } i)$$

The constraints do not ensure a unique solution for M, so various additional constraints can be imposed to provide a unique solution. These additional constraints will define the semantic model.

Example

Let $\mathbf{g} = a/1 + b/0.7 + c/0.2 \quad ; \quad \mathbf{g'} = a/0.2 + b/1 + c/0.7 + d/0.1$

defined on $X = \{a, b, c, d, e\}$ so that

$m_{\mathbf{g}} = a : 0.3, \{a, b\} : 0.5, \{a, b, c\} : 0.2$

$m_{\mathbf{g'}} = b : 0.3, \{b, c\} : 0.5, \{a, b, c\} : 0.1, \{a, b, c, d\} : 0.1$

We can make the additional constraint of extended constant threshold assumption of the voting model. The voting patterns would then look like those shown below. The decision that each person would make for the truth of g given g' when making his own interpretation of g and g' is also given.

persons

u	t	u	u	u	u	u	f	f	f	$\mathbf{g} \mid \mathbf{g'}$
1	2	3	4	5	6	7	8	9	10	
a	a	a	a	a	a	a	a	a	a	$\mathbf{g}$
b	b	b	b	b	b	b				
c	c									

---

a	a									
b	b	b	b	b	b	b	b	b	b	$\mathbf{g'}$
c	c	c	c	c	c	c				-
d										

This provides the support pair [0.1, 0.7] for $\mathbf{g} \mid \mathbf{g'}$.

79

We can obtain this solution from M as

	0.3 b	0.5 {b, c}	0.1 {a, b, c}	0.1 {a, b, c, d}	
0.3 a	f 0.3	f 0	u 0	u 0	t : 0.1
0.5 {a, b}	t 0	u 0.5	u 0	u 0	f : 0.3
0.2 {a, b, c}	t 0	t 0	t 0.1	u 0.1	u : 0.6

Support Pair for **g\|g'** is [0.1, 0.7]

Fig 3.13

3.7.4 Point Value Semantic Unification

We modify the above algorithm for the semantic unification which provides a support pair for the truth of **g** I **g'** to a version which gives a point value for the truth of **g** I **g'**.

Let **g** and **g'** be fuzzy sets defined on X. We wish to find a probability for the truth of **g** given **g'**, denoted by Pr(**g** I **g'**).

Let m_g = {Li : li} and $m_{g'}$ = {Mi : mi} be mass assignments associated with the fuzzy sets **g** and **g'**. Form the matrix

$$M = \{m_{ij}\} = \left\{ \frac{card(Li \cap Mj)}{card\ Mj} \right\} li\ mj$$

The probability Pr(**g** I **g'**) is then given by

$$Pr(\mathbf{g} \mid \mathbf{g'}) = \sum_{i,\,j} m_{ij}$$

This is called the multiplication model for point semantic unification since the mass entries in the matrix M are obtained by taking a proportion of the result of multiplying the corresponding row and column masses. The proportion used is the proportion of elements of Mj which are contained in Li.

Example

Let g = a / 1 + b / 0.7 + c / 0.2   ;   g' = a / 0.2 + b / 1 + c / 0.7 + d / 0.1
defined on X = {a, b, c, d, e} so that

m_g = a : 0.3, {a, b} : 0.5, {a, b, c} : 0.2

$m_{g'}$ = b : 0.3, {b, c} : 0.5, {a, b, c} : 0.1, {a, b, c, d} : 0.1

giving matrix

	0.3 b	0.5 {b, c}	0.1 {a, b, c}	0.1 {a, b, c, d}
0.3 a	0	0	0.01	0.00075
0.5 {a, b}	0.15	0.125	0.03333	0.025
0.2 {a, b, c}	0.06	0.1	0.02	0.015

Fig 3.14

$$Pr(g \mid g') = 0.53908$$

3.7.5 Extensions to Non-normalised Fuzzy Sets

Let $m_g = \{Li : li, \emptyset : lo\}$ and $m_{g'} = \{Mi : mi, \emptyset : mo\}$ be mass assignments associated with the non-normalised fuzzy sets **g** and **g'**. The interval semantic unification **g | g'** is determined using the matrix

$$M = \{T(Li \mid Mj) : li.mj\} \quad \text{where } T(Li \mid Mj) = \left\{ \begin{array}{l} t \text{ if } Mj \subseteq Li, Mj \neq \emptyset \\ f \text{ if } Mj \cap Li = \emptyset, Mj \neq \emptyset \\ u \text{ otherwise} \end{array} \right\}$$

For the point semantic unification case any mass associated with u arising from $Mj = \emptyset$ is equally shared between t and f.

3.7.6 Conditional Possibility Measure

Let **g** and **g'** be fuzzy sets defined on X. The possibility of **g | g'** is defined as

$$\Pi(g \mid g') = \text{MAX} (g \cap g')$$

The necessity of **g | g'** is defined as

$$\pi(g \mid g') = 1 - \Pi(\overline{g} \mid g')$$

Thus a possibilistic support pair, $[\pi(g \mid g'), \Pi(g \mid g')]$, can be defined analogous to the probabilistic support pair given above.

Example

Let $g = a / 1 + b / 0.7 + c / 0.2 \quad ; \quad g' = a / 0.2 + b / 1 + c / 0.7 + d / 0.1$
defined on X = {a, b, c, d, e} so that

$$\Pi(g \mid g') = 0.7$$

$$\overline{g} = b / 0.3 + c / 0.8 + d / 1 \text{ so that } \overline{g} \cap g' = b / 0.3 + c / 0.7 + d / 0.1$$

so that

$$\pi(g \mid g') = 1 - \Pi(g \mid g') = 1 - 0.7 = 0.3$$

The possibilistic support pair for **g | g'** is therefore [0.3, 0.7]. This possibilistic support

81

pair can be obtained from M as

	0.3 b	0.5 {b, c}	0.1 {a, b, c}	0.1 {a, b, c,d}	
0.3 a	f 0.2	f 0.1	u 0	u 0	
0.5 {a, b}	t 0.1	u 0.2	u 0.1	u 0.1	**Fig 3.15**
0.2 {a, b, c}	t 0	t 0.2	t 0	u 0	

$$t : 0.3$$
$$f : 0.3 \qquad \text{giving} \quad \mathbf{g} \mid \mathbf{g'} = [0.3, 0.7]$$
$$u : 0.4$$

3.7.7 More on Semantic Unification

In this Section we discuss more generally the concepts of semantic and point semantic unifications. To keep the mathematics simple we will discuss the case of discrete fuzzy sets with examples. It will be demonstrated that point semantic unification satisfies

$$Pr(\mathbf{f} \mid \mathbf{g}) + Pr(\bar{\mathbf{f}} \mid \mathbf{g}) = 1$$

The mass assignment theory can be used to show, in fact, that the point semantic unification is a conditional probability. The relative cardinality of conditional possibility theory does not satisfy this equality relation.

Suppose we are given the fuzzy sets

$\mathbf{f} = a / 1 + b / 0.8 + c / 0.5 + d / 0.1$ defined on the universe $\{a, b, c, d, e\}$

$\mathbf{g} = a / 0.7 + b / 1 + c / 1 + d / 0.2$ defined on the universe $\{a, b, c, d, e\}$

then the mass assignments associated with $\mathbf{f}$ and $\mathbf{g}$ are given by

$m_{\mathbf{f}} = a : 0.2, \{a, b\} : 0.3, \{a, b, c\} : 0.4, \{a, b, c, d\} : 0.1$

$m_{\mathbf{g}} = \{b, c\} : 0.3, \{a, b, c\} : 0.5, \{a, b, c, d\} : 0.2$

We wish to determine the interval and point semantic unifications for $\mathbf{f} \mid \mathbf{g}$.

Consider the mass assignment matrix for $\mathbf{f} \mid \mathbf{g}$ for the case of interval semantic unification (Fig 3.16).

We require the masses mij to be chosen such that

$m11 + m12 + m13 = 0.2$

$m21 + m22 + m23 = 0.3$ row masses sum to corresponding   (A)

$m31 + m32 + m33 = 0.4$ row mass of $m_{\mathbf{f}}$

$m41 + m42 + m43 = 0.1$

$m11 + m21 + m31 + m41 = 0.3$

$m12 + m22 + m32 + m42 = 0.5$ column masses sum to corresponding   (B)

$m13 + m23 + m33 + m43 = 0.2$ column mass of $m_{\mathbf{g}}$

	0.3 {b, c}	0.5 {a, b, c}	0.2 {a, b, c, d}
0.2 a	f m11	u m12	u m13
0.3 {a, b}	u m21	u m22	u m23
0.4 {a, b, c}	t m31	t m32	u m33
0.1 {a,b,c,d}	t m41	t m42	t m43

Fig 3.16

The multiplication model provides one solution to this problem. This, of course, is only one of many solutions.

$$m31 + m32 + 0.1 \leq Pr(\mathbf{f} \mid \mathbf{g}) \leq m31 + m32 + 0.4 + m12 + m13 + m33 \qquad (C)$$

We have a similar matrix, Fig 3.17, for the semantic unification $\bar{\mathbf{f}} \mid \mathbf{g}$ where $\bar{\mathbf{f}}$ is the complement fuzzy set of $\mathbf{f}$:

$$\bar{\mathbf{f}} = b / 0.2 + c / 0.5 + d / 0.9 + e / 1$$

The following constraints must be satisfied:

$$m'11 + m'12 + m'13 = 0.1$$
$$m'21 + m'22 + m'23 = 0.4 \qquad \text{row masses sum to corresponding} \qquad (D)$$
$$m'31 + m'32 + m'33 = 0.3 \qquad \text{row mass of } m_{\bar{\mathbf{f}}}$$
$$m'41 + m'42 + m'43 = 0.2$$

$$m'11 + m'21 + m'31 + m'41 = 0.3$$
$$m'12 + m'22 + m'32 + m'42 = 0.5 \qquad \text{column masses sum to corresponding} \qquad (E)$$
$$m'13 + m'23 + m'33 + m'43 = 0.2 \qquad \text{column mass of } m_{\mathbf{g}}$$

	0.3 {b, c}	0.5 {a, b, c}	0.2 {a, b, c, d}
0.1 e	f m'11	f m'12	f m'13
0.4 {d, e}	f m'21	f m'22	u m'23
0.3 {c, d, e}	u m'31	u m'32	u m'33
0.2 {b,c,d,e}	t m'41	u m'42	u m'43

Fig 3.17

83

Also

$$m'41 \leq \Pr(\bar{\mathbf{f}} \mid \mathbf{g}) \leq m'41 + m'42 + m'42 + m'23 + 0.3$$

We also require the constraint that

$$\Pr(\mathbf{f} \mid \mathbf{g}) + \Pr(\bar{\mathbf{f}} \mid \mathbf{g}) = 1 \tag{F}$$

Any set of $\{mij\}$ and any set of $\{m'ij\}$ satisfying constraints (A), (B), (C), (D), (E), and (F) are valid. Use of the multiplication model is valid and is used by Fril. This can be further justified using entropy arguments with the voting model semantics for fuzzy sets but we will not discuss that in this book. Therefore in Fril

	0.3 {b, c}	0.5 {a, b, c}	0.2 {a, b, c, d}
0.2 a	f 0.06	u 0.1	u 0.04
0.3 {a, b}	u 0.09	u 0.15	u 0.06
0.4 {a, b, c}	t 0.12	t 0.2	u 0.08
0.1 {a,b,c,d}	t 0.03	t 0.05	t 0.02

Fig 3.18

$$\Pr(\mathbf{f} \mid \mathbf{g}) \; \varepsilon \; [0.42, 0.94]$$

	0.3 {b, c}	0.5 {a, b, c}	0.2 {a, b, c, d}
0.1 e	f 0.03	f 0.05	f 0.02
0.4 {d, e}	f 0.12	f 0.2	u 0.08
0.3 {c, d, e}	u 0.09	u 0.15	u 0.06
0.2 {b,c,d,e}	t 0.06	u 0.1	u 0.04

Fig 3.19

$$\Pr(\bar{\mathbf{f}} \mid \mathbf{g}) = [0.06, 0.64]$$

These intervals satisfy all the constraints.

	0.3 {b, c}	0.5 {a, b, c}	0.2 {a, b, c, d}
0.2 a	0 / 0	1/3 / 0.0333	1/4 / 0.01
0.3 {a, b}	1/2 / 0.045	2/3 / 0.1	1/2 / 0.03
0.4 {a, b, c}	1 / 0.12	1 / 0.2	3/4 / 0.06
0.1 {a,b,c,d}	1 / 0.03	1 / 0.05	1 / 0.02

The upper left number is the proportion of product to be used.

The lower number is the product times the proportion.

Fig 3.20

$$Pr(\mathbf{f} \mid \mathbf{g}) = 0.6983$$

In the case of point semantic unification we have the corresponding mass assignment matrix given in Fig 3.20 for $Pr(\mathbf{f} \mid \mathbf{g})$ and that in Fig 3.21 for $Pr(\bar{\mathbf{f}} \mid \mathbf{g})$.

All the constraints are satisfied. This result can be shown to generally true for both discrete and continuous fuzzy sets.

We cannot use the relative cardinality, $\Sigma\_Cardinality(\mathbf{f} \mid \mathbf{g})$, given by Zadeh for this purpose, since the constraint

$$\Sigma\_Cardinality(\mathbf{f} \mid \mathbf{g}) + \Sigma\_Cardinality(\bar{\mathbf{f}} \mid \mathbf{g}) \geq 1$$

where $\Sigma\_Cardinality(\mathbf{f} \mid \mathbf{g}) = \dfrac{\Sigma\_Cardinality(\mathbf{f} \cap \mathbf{g})}{\Sigma\_Cardinality(\mathbf{g})}$

and $\Sigma\_Cardinality(\mathbf{g}) = \Sigma$ membership values of $\mathbf{g}$ is satisfied rather than the equality constraint.

	0.3 {b, c}	0.5 {a, b, c}	0.2 {a, b, c, d}
0.1 e	0 / 0	0 / 0	0 / 0
0.4 {d, e}	0 / 0	0 / 0	1/4 / 0.02
0.3 {c, d, e}	1/2 / 0.045	1/3 / 0.05	1/2 / 0.03
0.2 {b,c,d,e}	1 / 0.06	2/3 / 0.0667	3/4 / 0.03

Fig 3.21

$$Pr(\bar{\mathbf{f}} \mid \mathbf{g}) = 0.3017$$

In the above example the equality constraint holds for the relative cardinality but in the example below it does not.

Example

$\mathbf{f} = a / 1 + b / 0.2$ defined on $\{a, b, c\}$

$\bar{\mathbf{f}} = b / 0.8 + c / 1$

$\mathbf{g} = a / 1 + b / 0.8$

Point semantic unification gives

	m_g	
	0.2 a	0.8 {a, b}
m_f 0.8 a	1 0.16	1/2 0.32
0.2 {a, b}	1 0.04	1 0.16

$\Pr(\mathbf{f} \mid \mathbf{g}) = 0.68$

Fig 3.22

	m_g	
	0.2 a	0.8 {a, b}
$m_{\bar{f}}$ 0.2 c	0 0	0 0
0.8 {b, c}	0 0	1/2 0.32

$\Pr(\bar{\mathbf{f}} \mid \mathbf{g}) = 0.32$

Fig 3.23

so that the equality constraint holds.

$$\Sigma\_\text{Cardinality}(\mathbf{f} \mid \mathbf{g}) = \frac{\Sigma\_\text{Cardinality}(\mathbf{f} \cap \mathbf{g})}{\Sigma\_\text{Cardinality}(\mathbf{g})} = 0.6667$$

$$\Sigma\_\text{Cardinality}(\bar{\mathbf{f}} \mid \mathbf{g}) = \frac{\Sigma\_\text{Cardinality}(\bar{\mathbf{f}} \cap \mathbf{g})}{\Sigma\_\text{Cardinality}(\mathbf{g})} = 0.4444$$

so that the equality constraint is not satisfied.

3.8 FUZZY RELATIONS

3.8.1 Definition

A fuzzy relation $R(X1, ..., Xn)$ among sets $X1, ..., Xn$ is a fuzzy set defined on the Cartesian cross product $X1 \times ... \times Xn$. We will only consider the case in which R is a discrete fuzzy set since this restriction is present in Fril. Fuzzy relations have a special representation in Fril.

Example

Consider the relation **near_to** for cities close in ease of travel.

Let X = {London, Brighton, Bristol, Glasgow Swindon, Reading, Ipswich} and Y = {London, Reading}.

The relation **near_to** is defined on X × Y and is given by

near_to	City in X	City in Y	χ value
	London	London	1
	Brighton	London	0.7
	Bristol	London	0.3
	Swindon	London	0.5
	Reading	London	0.8
	Ipswich	London	0.4
	London	Reading	0.8
	Brighton	Reading	0.6
	Bristol	Reading	0.5
	Swindon	Reading	0.8
	Reading	Reading	1
	Ipswich	Reading	0.3

This is the table form of representation. Any pair of cities, one from X and one from Y, not present in the table has a membership value of 0. In this table format the column labels represent attributes. These attributes take values from the appropriate set. This table representation is called a base relation.

We can also give a matrix form of representation as follows:

near_to	London	Reading
London	1	0.8
Brighton	0.7	0.6
Bristol	0.3	0.5
Glasgow	0	0
Swindon	0.5	0.8
Reading	0.8	0.8
Ipswich	0.4	0.3

Fril uses the table form of representation.

We can generalise this definition to allow the attribute values to be fuzzy sets defined on the appropriate set.

Example

Let physique be a fuzzy relation among the sets N = {names of persons}, H = Height Space, W = Weight Space then

physique	Name	Height	Weight
	John	**tall**	**fairly_heavy**
	Bill	**average**	**light**
	Mary	5ft 2ins	**medium**
	Sally	**fairly_tall**	8 1/2 stone

In this table **tall**, **average**, **fairly_tall** are fuzzy sets on H, **fairly_heavy**, **light, medium** are fuzzy sets on W. The values do not, of course, have to be fuzzy sets. They can be precise values or even a range of possible values. A range of values can be represented by means of a fuzzy set. In this table the χ values are 1.

An extension of this definition of a fuzzy relation is available in Fril. The χ value can be a support pair $[\chi_1, \chi_2]$ rather than a single number. Both χ_1 and χ_2 are numbers in [0, 1] with $\chi_1 \leq \chi_2$. If the equality holds then a single χ is used. χ_1 represents the necessary support for the tuple satisfying the relation and χ_2 represents the possible support of the tuple satisfying the relation.

3.8.2 Fuzzy Relational Operations

Two important operations are those of expansion and selection. The first concerns the expansion of a fuzzy relation containing fuzzy set entries to a standard form containing only elements from the appropriate attribute set of possible values, while the latter corresponds to selecting tuples from a relation which satisfies certain conditions.

If Xi, (all i) are finite sets for a given fuzzy relation R(X1, ..., Xn) then the fuzzy sets defined on Xi, (all i), will be discrete. The tuple t = (..., **g**, ...) belonging to R, where **g** is a fuzzy set on Xi and Xi = $\{x_1, ..., x_n\}$, can be expanded to give the set of tuples $\{t_k\}$ = $\{(..., x_k, ... | \chi_{\mathbf{g}}(x_k))\}$. If on expansion a repeated tuple results, duplicates are removed and only the one with the largest membership value is included. The χ value for an expanded tuple is the smallest of the membership values associated with the tuple containing the fuzzy set and the χ value of the element in the fuzzy set.

Several fuzzy set entries in the relation can be handled by expanding the relation by considering one fuzzy set at a time. We only allow the operation of expansion in the case of attribute values being discrete fuzzy sets which can be interpreted as a conjunction possibility distribution. This means that all values can occur together. This is not the normal interpretation of a fuzzy set. The fuzzy database module in Chapter 7 discusses this further.

For example if R(A, B) is given by

R	A	B	χ
	a1	**g**	0.9
	a2	b2	1
	a1	b1	0.7

Fig 3.24

where **g** = b1 / 1 + b2 / 0.8

then
expanding gives tuples
(a1 b1 | 0.9)
(a1 b2 | 0.8)
(a2 b2 | 1)
(a1 b1 | 0.7)

88

giving the relation {(a1 b1 | 0.9), (a1 b2 | 0.8), (a2 b2 | 1)}.

We can form the sub-relation Sub(R(X1, ..., Xn), ≥ 0.7) which contains all those tuples of R whose membership value is greater than or equal to 0.7. In place of ≥ we can use = or <, ≤, > with obvious meaning.

We can select the sub-relation R(X1, ..., Xi-1, **f**, Xi+1, ..., Xn) from R(X1, ..., Xn) whose ith attribute of each tuple satisfies **f** with a possibilistic support pair.

If a tuple in R(X1, ..., Xn) with support pair $[\chi_1, \chi_2]$ has the ith attribute equal to the fuzzy set **g**, defined on Xi, then the support pair for this tuple in

R(X1, ..., Xi-1, **f**, Xi+1, ..., Xn) will be $[\pi(\mathbf{f} \mid \mathbf{g}) \wedge \chi_1, \Pi(\mathbf{f} \mid \mathbf{g}) \wedge \chi_2]$.

We can represent this diagrammatically as

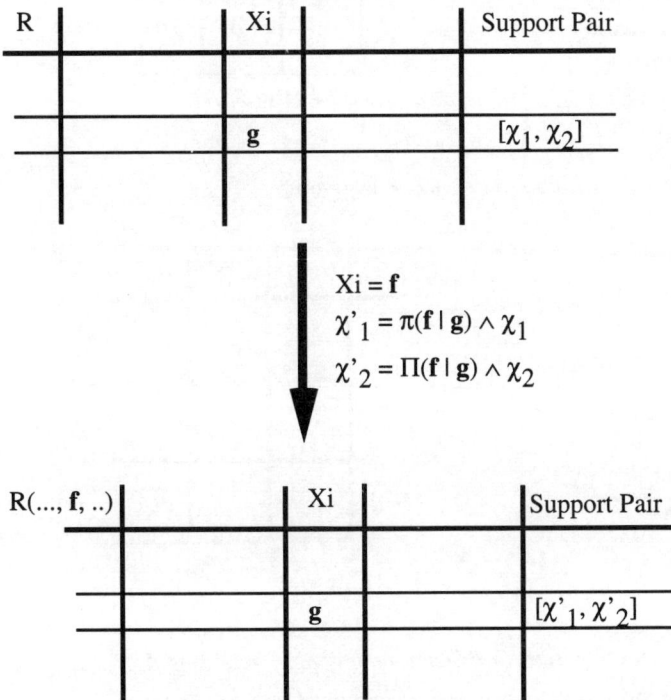

R		Xi		Support Pair
		g		$[\chi_1, \chi_2]$

$$Xi = \mathbf{f}$$
$$\chi'_1 = \pi(\mathbf{f} \mid \mathbf{g}) \wedge \chi_1$$
$$\chi'_2 = \Pi(\mathbf{f} \mid \mathbf{g}) \wedge \chi_2$$

R(..., **f**, ..)		Xi		Support Pair
		g		$[\chi'_1, \chi'_2]$

Fig 3.25

Examples

If **g** = 65 / 1 and **f** = 65 / 1 + 66 / 1 with $[\chi1, \chi2] = [1, 1]$ then $[\chi'_1, \chi'_2] = [1, 1]$.

If **g** = 65 / 1+ 66 / 1 and **f** = 65 / 1 with $[\chi1, \chi2] = [1, 1]$ then $[\chi'_1, \chi'_2] = [0, 1]$.

If **g** = 65 / 1+ 66 / 1 and **f** = 65 / 1 + 66 / 1 with $[\chi1, \chi2] = [1, 1]$ then $[\chi'_1, \chi'_2] = [1, 1]$.

89

If $g = 65 / 1 + 66 / 1$ and $f = 65 / 1$ with $[\chi1, \chi2] = [0.1, 0.1]$ then $[\chi'_1, \chi'_2] = [0, 0.1]$.

If $g = 65 / 0.2 + 66 / 1$ and $f = 65 / 0.9 + 66 / 1$ with $[\chi1, \chi2] = [0.1, 0.1]$

then $[\chi'_1, \chi'_2] = [0.1, 0.2]$.

If $f = b1 / 0.6 + b2 / 1$ and R is given by

R	A	B	χ
a1	b2	0.9
a2	b2	1
a1	b1	0.7

Fig 3.26

then

R(_, f)	A	B	χ
a1	b2	0.9
a2	b2	1
a1	b1	0.6

Fig 3.27

If $g = b1 / 1 + b2 / 0.8$ and $f = b1 / 0.6 + b2 / 1$ and R is given by

R	A	B	χ
a1	g	0.9
a2	b2	1
a1	b1	0.7

Fig 3.28

then

R(..., f, ...)	A	B	χ
a1	g	[0.6, 0.8]
a2	b2	1
a1	b1	0.7

Fig 3.29

Fuzzy relational algebra is a collection of operations on fuzzy relations. Each operation takes one or more fuzzy relations as its operand(s) and produces a new fuzzy relation as its result. Basic operations are union, difference, intersection, cross product, join, projection and truth functional modification. These take definitions as given below. The definitions are given for relations with a single membership value. If support pairs are given, the same operations are performed on both the lower and upper supports.

Union, difference and intersection. The union, difference and intersection of two compatible fuzzy relations A and B, denoted by $A \cup B$, $A - B$ and $A \cap B$ respectively, are sets of tuples t with the degree of compatibility $\chi(t)$ with which the tuple t satisfies the resulting relation:

$$\chi_{A \cup B}(t) = \chi_A(t) \vee \chi_B(t),$$

$$\chi_{A - B}(t) = \chi_A(t) \wedge (1 - \chi_B(t)),$$

$$\chi_{A \cap B}(t) = \chi_A(t) \wedge \chi_B(t).$$

Two relations A and B are compatible if they have the same arity, n say, and the ith attribute of them (i in the range 1 to n) must be drawn from the same domain, i.e. relation A and B are two subsets of the product space of domains $X1 \times ... \times Xn$.

Cross Product. The cross product of two fuzzy relations A and B, denoted by $A \times B$, is the set of all tuples t with the membership value $\chi(t)$ defined by

$$\chi_{A \times B}(t) = \chi_A(a) \wedge \chi_B(b), A \subseteq_f M, B \subseteq_f N, \forall a \in M, \forall b \in N, t = (a, b)$$

where

$X \subseteq_f Y$ signifies that X is a fuzzy subset of Y.

Join. The join of two fuzzy relations A and B with common attributes drawn from domains $C1, ..., Ck$, denoted by A & B, is a set of tuples t with the membership value $\chi(t)$ defined by

$$\chi_{A\&B}(t) = \chi_A(a) \wedge \chi_B(b)$$

where

$$A \subseteq_f C1 \times ... \times Ck \times AD1 \times ... ADm,$$
$$B \subseteq_f C1 \times ... \times Ck \times BD1 \times ... BDn,$$
$$a = (c, ad), \forall a \in A, \forall c \in C1 \times ... \times Ck,$$
$$\forall ad \in AD1 \times ... ADm,$$
$$b = (c, bd), \forall b \in B, \forall bd \in BD1 \times ... \times BDn,$$
$$t = (c, ad, bd).$$

If the relations have fuzzy sets as attribute values then the methods of selection associated with forming sub-relations are used in the join process.

Projection. The projection of a fuzzy relation $R(A1, A2) \subseteq_f X1 \times X2$ onto X2, denoted by $\text{Proj}_{A2} R$, is a set of tuples a2 with the membership value $\chi(a2)$ defined by

$$\chi_{\text{Proj}_{A2} R}(a2) = \bigvee\nolimits_{a1 \in D1} \chi_R(a1, a2).$$

This definition can easily be generalised to projections of n-ary relations on to compound spaces.

Truth Functional Modification.

Let A be a fuzzy relation and τ a fuzzy set, acting as a truth modifier, defined on the interval [0, 1]. The result of truth functional modification of A using τ, denoted by R_τ, is a relation such that each tuple t has the membership value given by $\chi_\tau(\chi_A(t))$.

A fuzzy set defined on the interval I = [d1, d2] can be defined as an I type fuzzy set by means of the list $((a1, \chi(a1)), ..., (aq, \chi(aq)))$ where all ai ε I. The membership value of the element x ε I is $\chi(x)$ if x is a member of this list, otherwise it is obtained by linear interpolation from its immediate neighbours in the list. For example, if

$$A = \{ (a, \alpha \mid 1), (b, \beta \mid 0.8), (c, \gamma \mid 0.4), (d, \delta \mid 0.2) \}$$

$$\tau = \{ (0.5, 0), (1, 1) \}, \text{an I type fuzzy set}$$

then

$$A_\tau = \{ (a, \alpha \mid 1), (b, \beta \mid 0.6) \}$$

Fuzzy sets can themselves be truth functionally modified, so that, for example, if

$$g = a / 1 + b / 0.8 + c / 0.4 + d / 0.2$$

then

$$g_\tau = a / 1 + b / 0.6$$

3.9 REPRESENTATION IN FRIL

3.9.1 Support Pairs

A support pair [Sn, Sp], where Sn and Sp are the necessary support and possible support respectively, is represented in Fril as a list of two numbers Sn and Sp, namely (Sn Sp). A Fril fact can be supported with a support pair. For example

((fault is hardware)) : (0.6 0.7)

which says that

$$0.6 \leq \text{Pr(fault is hardware)} \leq 0.7$$

and hence

$$0.3 \leq \text{Pr}(\neg \text{ fault is hardware}) \leq 0.4$$

3.9.2 Fuzzy Sets

Two types of fuzzy set can be defined in Fril, namely, a discrete fuzzy set and a continuous fuzzy set. The latter is called an i-type fuzzy set in Fril. Fuzzy sets must be defined prior to their use in Fril rules or facts.

A discrete fuzzy set is represented in Fril in the form

(<name> {<element> : <membership_value> ...})

where <name> is the name of the fuzzy set, <element> is an element from the universe of discourse, <membership_value> is a number in the interval [0, 1]. The three dots mean that any number of terms of the form <element : <membership_value> can be enclosed in the braces { and }. These terms can be separated by some delimiter, for example, a space or a comma.

Examples

(small_die_number {1 : 1, 2 : 1, 3 : 0.4, 4 : 0.1})

(small_die_number {1 : 1, 2 : 1, 3 : 0.4, 4 : 0.1})

(suitable_drink {coffee : 0.9, tea : 0.8, beer : 0.6, water : 0.2})

An i-type fuzzy set is defined by a list of pairs of the form $v : \chi_f(v)$, representing "value" : "membership of value", which are enclosed in square brackets. f is the name of the fuzzy set and is the first element of the list defining f. The complete form of definition is

$$(f\ [v : \chi_f(v)\ ...])$$

The values v are taken from a set of allowed values, and $\chi_f(v)$ is a number in the interval [0, 1]. The allowed values for i-type fuzzy sets are elements of the real line. $\chi_f(v)$ is the membership value of v for the fuzzy set, where v is one of the values in the definition. For values of v not contained in the definition $\chi_f(v)$ is obtained by linear interpolation of its neighbouring points.For values of v smaller than the smallest v value, v_s say, in the definition of f, $\chi_f(v)$ is $\chi_f(v_s)$. For values of v larger than the largest v value, v_l say, in the definition of f, $\chi_f(v)$ is $\chi_f(v_l)$.

Examples

(tall [67 : 0, 72 : 1])

(tall [67 : 0 72 : 1])

The fuzzy sets defined in these two examples are the same. A different delimiter is used to separate the pairs (comma in the first case, space in the second).

The fuzzy set can be represented graphically as

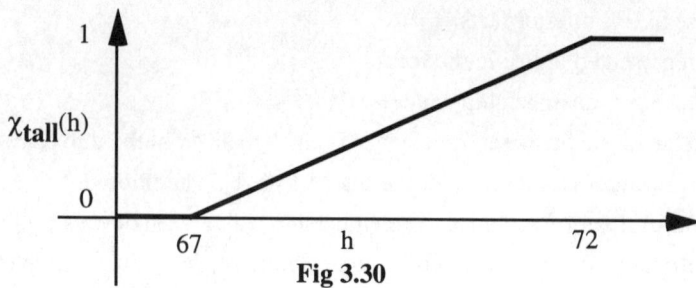

Fig 3.30

The fuzzy set

(my_fuzzy_set [1 : 0, 2 : 0.75, 3 : 0.5, 4 : 1, 5 : 0.75, 6 : 0.25, 7 : 0.5, 8 : 0])

has the graphical representation

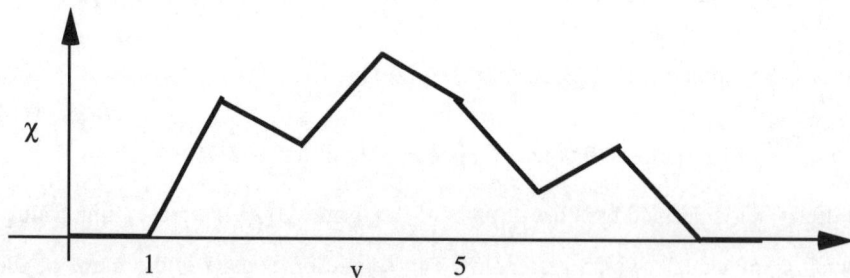

Fig 3.31

3.9.3 Fuzzy Relations

A fuzzy relation in Fril is of the form

(<name> (<tuple>) : <support> | <support pair> ...)

Examples

(free_date

(June	10):	0.2
(June	2)	: 0.9
(Oct	20):	0.4
(Oct	20):	0.5
(Nov	27):	0.9)

(g   {b1 : 1, b2 : 0.8})

(r	(a1	g)	: 0.2
	(a2	b2):	1
	(a1	b1):	0.7)

(rel (a1 g) : (0.2 0.3) (a2 b2) : (0.9 1) (a1 b1) : 0.7)

The fuzzy set **g** is defined prior to its use in a fuzzy relation.

3.10 BIBLIOGRAPHY

Further reading on Fuzzy Set theory can be found in the following references.

Baldwin J. F, (1979), "A new approach to Approximate Reasoning using Fuzzy Logic", Fuzzy Sets and Systems **2**, pp 309-325.

Baldwin J.F, Guild N.C.F, (1979), "Comparison of Fuzzy Sets on the same Decision Space", Fuzzy Sets and Systems **2**, pp 213-231.

Baldwin J.F, Pilsworth B.W, (1979), "A theory of Fuzzy Probability", Proc. 9th Int Symp. on Multi-Valued Logic, Bath, pp 53-61.

Baldwin J.F, Guild N.C.F, (1980), "The Resolution of Two Paradoxes by Approximate Reasoning using Fuzzy Logic", Synthese **44**, pp 397-420.

Baldwin J.F, Pilsworth B.W, (1982), "Dynamic Programming for Fuzzy Systems with Fuzzy Environment", J. Math. Anal. & App., vol 85, **1**, pp 1-23.

Baldwin J.F, Guild N.C.F, Pilsworth B.W, (1983), "A Group Voting Model for Fuzzy Logic", Int J. Measurement & Decision, vol 1, **2**, pp 1-11.

Baldwin J.F, (1992), "Fuzzy and Probabilisitic Uncertainties", in Encyclopedia of AI, 2nd edition, (Ed Shapiro), pp 528-537, Wiley.

Bandler W, Kohout L.J, (1980), "Semantics of Implication Operators and Fuzzy Relational Products", Int J. of Man-Machine Studies **22**, pp 347-353.

Bellman R, Giertz M, (1973), "On the Analytical Formalism of the Theory of Fuzzy Sets", Information Sciences **5**, pp 149-156.

Bellman R, Zadeh L.A, (1970), "Decision Making in a Fuzzy Environment", Management Science **17**, pp B-144 - B-164.

Bouchon-Meunier B, (1987), "Fuzzy Inferences and Conditional Possibility Distributions", Fuzzy Sets and Systems **23**, pp 33-41.

Buckles B.P, Petry F.E, (1982), "A Fuzzy Represention of Data for Relational Databases", Fuzzy Sets and Systems **7**, pp 213-226.

Dombi J, (1982), "A general class of Fuzzy Operators, the De Morgan class of Fuzzy Operators and fuzziness measures induced by Fuzzy Operators", Fuzzy Sets and Systems **9**, pp 149-163.

Dubois D, Prade H, (1980), Fuzzy Sets and Systems: Theory and Applications, Academic Press, New York.

Dubois D, Prade H, (1991), "Fuzzy Sets in Approximate Reasoning, Part 1 Inference and Possibility Distribtions", Fuzzy Sets and Systems **1**, pp 143-202.

Dubois D, Lang J, Prade H, (1991), "Fuzzy Sets in Approximate Reasoning, Part 2 Logical Approaches", Fuzzy Sets and Systems **1,** pp 203-244.

Gaines B.R, (1976), "Foundations of Fuzzy Reasoning", Int J. of Man-Machine Studies **8**, pp 623-668.

Gaines B.R, (1976), "Fuzzy and Probability Uncertainty Logics", Information and Control **38**, pp 154-169.

Klement E.P, (1984), "Operations on Fuzzy Sets: an Axiomatic Approach", Information Sciences **27**, pp 221-232.

Klir G.J, Folger T.A, (1988), Fuzzy Sets, Uncertainty, and Information, Prentice-Hall.

Negoita C.V, Ralescu D.A, (1975), Applications of Fuzzy Sets to Systems Analysis, Birkhauser, Basel and Stuttgart.

Ruspini E.H, (1982), "Recent developments in Fuzzy Clustering", in Fuzzy Sets and Possibility Theory, Ed Yager R.R, pp 191-200, Pergamon Press.

Yager R.R, (1982), "Measures of fuzziness based on t-norms", Stochastica **6,** pp 207-229.

Yager R.R, (1983) "Entropy and Specificity in a Mathematical Theory of Evidence", Int J. General Systems **9,** pp 249-260.

Yager R.R, (1985), "Inference in Multi-valued Logic System", Int J. of Man-Machine Studies **23**, pp 27-44.

Yager R.R, (1986), "Toward a General Theory of Reasoning with Uncertainty. 1: Non-specificity and Fuzziness", Int J. of Intelligent Systems **1,** (1), pp 45-67.

Zadeh L.A, (1965), "Fuzzy Sets", Information and Control **8**, pp 338-353.

Zadeh L.A, (1975), "Fuzzy Logic and Approximate Reasoning, Synthese **30**, pp 407-428.

Zadeh L.A, (1978), "Fuzzy Sets as a basis for a theory of Possibility", Fuzzy Sets and Systems **1,** pp 3-28.

Zadeh L.A, (1983), "The role of Fuzzy Logic in the Management of Uncertainty in Expert Systems", Fuzzy Sets and Systems **11,** pp 199-227.

Zadeh L.A, (1986), "A simple view of the Dempster-Shafer theory of evidence and its implication for the role of combination", AI Mag. **7**(2), pp 85-90.

Zimmermann H.J, Zysno P, (1980), "Latent connectives in human decision making", Fuzzy Sets and Systems **4,** pp 37-51.

Zimmermann H.J, (1987), Fuzzy Sets, Decision Making and Expert Systems, Kluwer Academic Publ., Boston.

Further reading in Mass Assignment theory and Belief function theory can be found in the following references.

Baldwin J.F, (1991), "Combining Evidences for Evidential Reasoning", Int J. of Intelligent Systems **6,** No 6, pp 569-616.

Baldwin J.F, (1991), "Towards a General Theory of Evidential Reasning", Uncertainty in Knowledge Bases (Eds Bouchon B, Yager R.R, Zadeh L.A.), Lecture Notes in Computer Science, Springer Verlag, 1991, pp 360-370.

Baldwin J.F, (1991), "A New Approach to Inference under Uncertainty for Knowledge-based Systems", Proc. European Conf. on Symbolic Quantitative Approaches for

Uncertainty - Marseille, Published in Lecture Notes of Computer Science, vol 548, (Eds Kruse R, Siegel P.), Springer Verlag, 1991.

Baldwin J.F, (1992), "Mass Assignments and Fuzzy Sets for Fuzzy Databases", in "Advances in the Dempster-Shafer Theory of Evidence", (Eds Fedrizzi M, Kacprzyk J, Yager R.R.), pp 577-595, John Wiley.

Baldwin J.F, (1991), "A Calculus for Mass Assignments in Evidential Reasoning", in "Advances in the Dempster-Shafer Theory of Evidence", pp 513-533, (Eds, Fedrizzi M, Kacprzyk J, Yager R.R.), 1992, John Wiley.

Baldwin J.F, (1991), "Approximate Reasoning, Fuzzy & Probabilistic Control using a theory of Mass Assignments", Proc. of IFES, Japan, 1991, pp 611-622.

Baldwin J.F, (1991), "A theory of Mass Assignments for Artificial Intelligence", Proc. IEEE AI Conference (Australia 1991), An invited paper, To be published in Lecture Notes of Computer Science, Springer Verlag, 1994.

Baldwin J.F, (1992), "A Mass Assignment theory for Uncertainty Reasoning", Proc. FUZZ-IEEE 92.

Baldwin J.F, (1992), "Evidential Reasoning under Probabilistic and Fuzzy Uncertainties", in An Introduction to Fuzzy Logic Applications in Intelligent Systems, (Eds Yager R.R, Zadeh L.A.), Dordrecht: Kluwer, pp 297-333.

Baldwin J.F, (1993), "Fuzzy, Probabilistic and Evidential Reasoning in Fril", IEEE Proc. Fuzzy Control, San Francisco, pp 1-10.

Dubois D, Prade H, (1986), "A set theory view of belief functions", Int J. of General Systems **12**, pp 193-226.

Shafer G, (1976), A Mathematical theory of Evidence, Princeton Univ. Press.

Shafer G, (1981), "Constructive Probability", Synthese **48**, pp 1-60.

Shenoy P.P, (1989), "A Valuation-based Language for Expert Systems", Int J. of Approx. Reasoning, Vol 3, **5**.

Shenoy P.P, Shafer G, (1990), "Axioms for Probability and Belief-function Propagation", in Uncertainty in Artificial Intelligence **4,** Eds Shachter et al, North Holland.

Smets P, (1988), "Belief Functions", in Non-Standard Logics for Automated Reasoning, Eds Smets P. et al, Academic Press, pp 253-286.

Smets P, (1990), "The Combination of Evidences in the Transferable Belief Model", IEEE Trans PAMI 12, pp 442-458.

CHAPTER 4

Rules in Fril – Fuzzy Control, Causal Nets and Evidential Reasoning

4.1 RULES IN FRIL

4.1.1 Discussion

Fril allows three different rules for knowledge representation involving uncertainty. We call these rules

the basic Fril rule

the extended Fril rule

the evidential logic rule.

The basic Fril rule is that found in the first version of the language and strictly speaking it is all that is necessary since the other Fril rules, with a slightly different syntax to that described here, can be defined in terms of it. The basic rule is a special case of the extended rule. These two rules use an inference procedure based on Jeffrey's rule. The basic rule can be used for fuzzy control. The extended rule can be used for modelling Bayesian causal nets and can extend the basic nets to fuzzy ones. This fuzzification can reduce the complexity of the net. The evidential logic rule uses a different inference procedure based on evidential logic. It can be used for case-based reasoning and has many applications to pattern recognition type problems and those problem areas for which neural nets are applicable.

4.1.2 Fril Representation of Rules

The Fril syntax for the three rules is as follows:

(h c1 c2 ... cn) : ((x y)(s t))

(h (b1 b2 ... bn)) : ((u1 v1)(u2 v2) ... (un vn))

(h (evlog **f** (c1 n1 c2 n2 ... cn nn))) : ((x y)(s t))

where

 h represents a head of the form (<pred> arguments), ci represents a goal of the form (<pred> arguments) and bi represents a list of goals of the form (c1 c2 ... cm)

For the first rule

c1 ... cn is the body of the rule, (x y) is an interval, called a support pair, containing $\Pr(h \mid c_1...c_n)$ and (s t) is an interval containing $\Pr(h \mid \neg \{c_1... c_n\})$. If only the support pair (x y) is put at the end of the rule then it is assumed that (s t) = (0 1). In this case the support clause ((x y)(s t)) is written as (x y). Each ci can contain a fuzzy set, discrete or continuous. If this fuzzy set is described by a name then the definition for this named fuzzy set must be given prior to its use.

For the second rule

(b1 ... bn) is the body of the rule and (ui vi) is an interval containing Pr(h I bi) where the list of goals bi is interpreted as a conjunction of goals.

It is also assumed that $\Sigma(Pr(bi)) = 1$. This means that the conditions in the body of the rule are mutually exclusive and exhaustive. Each bi can contain a fuzzy set in each of its goals. In this case Fril will still impose the summation constraint; exactly how this is done will be described later.

For the third rule

(c1 n1 ... cn nn) is the body of the rule, ci represent features and ni are importances of the features, $(0 \leq ni \leq 1)$. We choose $\Sigma ni = 1$. **f** is a fuzzy set on [0, 1] and (x y) is a support pair where x is the support for (h I body) and 1 - y is the support for ($\neg$ h I body). The second support pair (s t) has a similar interpretation for (h I $\neg$body) and ($\neg$h I $\neg$body).

Each ci can contain a fuzzy set which will represent the value for a feature.

This rule is implemented in Fril, and the user can modify the form of the rule to allow for positive and negative importances or weights. The summation constraint can also be modified. The inference mechanism can then be changed to simulate the behaviour of an artificial neuron, and the evidential logic rules used to implement a neural net which can be of various types.

The first rule is a special case of the second rule. It can be written as

(h ((c1 c2 ... cn) ($\neg$ (c1 c2 ... cn))) : ((x y)(s t))

Examples of rules of type 2 are

((illness of X is flu) (

        ((temp of X is high) (strength of X is weak) (throat of X is sore))

        ((temp of X is high) (strength of X is not_weak) (throat of X is sore))

        ((temp of X is high) (strength of X is weak) (throat of X is normal))

        ((temp of X is high) (strength of X is not_weak) (throat of X is normal))

        ((temp of X is not_high) (strength of X is weak) (throat of X is sore))

        ((temp of X is not_high) (strength of X is not_weak) (throat of X is sore))

        ((temp of X is not_high) (strength of X is weak) (throat of X is normal))

        ((temp of X is not_high) (strength of X is not_weak) (throat of X is normal))

)) : ((0.9 1)(0 0.1)(0.5 1)(0 0.1)(0 0)(0 0)(0 0)(0 0))

where

{high, not_high}, {weak, not_weak}, {sore, normal} are label sets. Elements of a label set can be defined by fuzzy sets. The label high is an example of this.

((illness of X is flu) (

    ((temp of X is high) (strength of X is weak) (throat of X is sore))

    ((not and (temp of X is high) (strength of X is weak) (throat of X is sore)))

        )) : ((0.9 1)(0 1))

which can also be written as a type 1 rule

    ((illness of X is flu)

        (temp of X is high) (strength of X is weak) (throat of X is sore)) : (0.9 1)

Applications which require rules of type 2 include causal net models using Bayesian methods. We will illustrate an example of this nature later in this chapter. Fril generalises causal net modelling to allow variables to take values which are fuzzy labels, probabilities to be partially specified and inputs to have probabilistic values. A Fril module for causal net modelling is described in another chapter.

    The rules of type 1 and 2 above represent general knowledge. The conditional probabilities can be thought of as arising from analysing a population of objects. Specific knowledge can also be represented in Fril as facts or by other rules. Specific knowledge belongs to one object taken from a population of objects. Examples of specific knowledge are

    ((temp of John is fairly_high))

    ((throat of John is sore)) : (0.9 1)

The first example says that the specific person John has a fairly high temperature where fairly high is a fuzzy set. The second example says that the probability that John has a sore throat is at least 0.9.

    Specific facts such as these can be used in conjunction with the general rules to infer a likeliness for John suffering from "flu". The inference rule used for types 1 and 2 rules is given in the next Section. In Fril rules can be nested so that the facts required to infer from a given rule can be inferred from other rules etc.

4.2 INFERENCE RULES IN FRIL

4.2.1 Inference for a Single Fril Rule with Point Probabilities

    Consider two variables H, which can take values $\{h, \neg h\}$, and B, which can take any value from the set of mutually exclusive and exhaustive values $\{b1, b2, ..., bn\}$. The Fril rule

    h IF $\{b1, b2, ..., bn\}$: u1, ..., un

is interpreted as $Pr(h \mid bi) = ui$; all i.

The Fril representation for this rule is

    ((h) (((b1))((b2))...((bn)))) : ((u1)(u2)...(un))

101

We will assume that the conditional probabilities $\{Pr(h \mid bi)\}$ are known. We will relax this assumption later. We will also relax the mutually exclusive condition for $\{bi\}$ and allow the variable B to take fuzzy sets as values. This rule corresponds to general knowledge. It can be thought of as applying to all objects of some population of objects P. In this sense $Pr(h \mid bi)$ is the proportion of objects of the population P satisfying bi for which h is satisfied.

Let an object from P, p say, be subject to experiments or tests to determine the value of the variable Bi for p. Suppose the test provides the specific knowledge

$$P'r(bi) = \alpha i, \; i = 1, ..., n.$$

These probabilities are specific to our knowledge about p drawn from the tests to determine the value of Bi for p. They are not necessarily related to the $\{Pr(bi)\}$ of the population P. $Pr(bi)$ is the apriori probability of bi and can be interpreted as the proportion of objects of P that satisfy bi. $P'r(bi)$ is simply the belief that object p satisfies bi. This belief comes from examining the object p.

Then Jeffrey's rule states that the specific probability $P'r(h)$ is given by

$$P'r(h) = Pr(h \mid b1)P'r(b1) + ... + Pr(h \mid bn)P'r(bn) = \sum_i \alpha_i u_i$$

This specific probability is interpreted as the belief that object p satisfies h. It is not necessarily related to the probability $Pr(h)$ interpreted as the proportion of objects in P that satisfy h. If we replaced $\{P'r(bi)\}$ with $\{Pr(bi)\}$ and $P'r(h)$ with $Pr(h)$ then the inference rule would simply be the theorem of total probabilities derivable from the axioms of probability theory.

The use of Jeffrey's rule is consistent with a special case of the mass assignment updating rule given developed by Baldwin in which the prior probability distribution $Pr(HB)$ is updated with the specific probability distribution $P'r(B)$ using the criterion of minimising the relative entropy of $P'r(HB)$ relative to $Pr(HB)$.

We therefore choose $P'r(HB)$ such that

$$\underset{\{\{P'r(hbi)\}, \{P'r(\neg hbi)\}\}}{\text{MIN}} \left\{ \sum_{i=1}^{n} P'r(hbi) \, Ln\left(\frac{P'r(hbi)}{Pr(hbi)}\right) + \sum_{i=1}^{n} P'r(\neg hbi) \, Ln\left(\frac{P'r(\neg hbi)}{Pr(\neg hbi)}\right) \right\}$$

subject to

$$Pr(hbi) \neq 0$$
$$Pr(\neg hbi) \neq 0$$
$$P'r(bi) = P'r(hbi) + P'r(\neg hbi) = \alpha i \; ; i = 1, ..., n$$
$$P'r(b1) + ... + P'r(bn) = \sum_{i=1}^{n} \{P'r(hbi) + P'(\neg hbi)\} = 1$$

If we write $xi = Pr(hbi)$, $yi = Pr(\neg hbi)$, $x'i = P'r(hbi)$ and $y'i = P'r(\neg hbi)$ for all i, then the optimisation problem is

$$\underset{\{x'i\}, \{y'i\}}{\text{MIN}} \left\{ \sum_{i=1}^{n} x'i \, Ln\left(\frac{x'i}{xi}\right) + \sum_{i=1}^{n} y'i \, Ln\left(\frac{y'i}{yi}\right) \right\}$$

subject to

$$x'_i + y'_i = \alpha_i \; ; \; \text{all } i$$

$$\sum_{i=1}^{n} (x'_i + y'_i) = 1$$

Optimisation is satisfied provided

$$x'_i = P'r(hb_i) = K_i \alpha_i x_i \; ; \quad y'_i = P'r(\neg hb_i) = K_i \alpha_i y_i$$

where $K_i = \dfrac{1}{x_i + y_i}$

so that

$$P'r(h) = \sum_{i=1}^{n} x'_i$$

We can represent the calculation in the following updating table

Pr(HB)	$\alpha 1$ b1	———	αn bn	Update = P'r(HB)
x1 : hb1	hb1 : K1x1α1 Ø : 0		Ø : 0	hb1 : K1x1α1
			Ø : 0	
xn : hbn	Ø : 0	———	hbn : Knxnαn	hbn : Knxnαn
y1 : ¬hb1	¬hb1 : K1y1α1 Ø : 0		Ø : 0	¬hb1 : K1y1α1
			Ø : 0	
yn : ¬hbn	Ø : 0	———	¬hb1 : Knynαn	¬hbn : Knynαn
	K1=1 / (x1+y1)	———	Kn=1 / (xn+yn)	

$$P'r(h) = \sum_i K_i x_i \alpha_i = \sum_i Pr(h \mid b_i) \alpha_i$$

since

$$Pr(h \mid b_i) = \frac{x_i}{x_i + y_i} = K_i x_i$$

In the following Section dealing with inference rules in Fril this updating rule will be generalised to allow the general knowledge conditional probabilities and the specific probabilities to be specified by support pairs.

4.2.2 Inference for Single Fril Rule with Support Pairs

Consider the inference for h when given the Fril rule

$$((h) (((b1))((b2)) \ldots ((bn)))) : ((u1 \; v1)(u2 \; v2) \ldots (un \; vn))$$

and facts

((bi)) : (αi βi)   ;   (all i)

The point probabilities ui and αi in the last Section are now replaced by the support pairs (ui vi) and (αi βi) where the support pair (x y) is an interval [x, y] containing the probability.

The inference is an interval version of that given for the point probability case. The inference is therefore

h : (z1 z2)

where

$$z1 = MIN \sum_i ui\ \theta i$$

$$\alpha i \leq \theta i \leq \beta i \quad (all\ i)$$

$$\sum_i \theta i = 1$$

$$z2 = MAX \sum_i vi\ \theta i$$

$$\alpha i \leq \theta i \leq \beta i \quad (all\ i)$$

$$\sum_i \theta i = 1$$

(z1 z2) is the support pair for the head h. z1 is the necessary support for the head and (1 - z2) is the necessary support for ¬h. Thus we find the smallest value of z1 and the largest value of z2 satisfying the given constraints.

These optimisation problems are trivial, requiring simple ordering of the {ui} and {vi} and an allocation algorithm for giving values to {θi} taking into account the sum equality constraint. We illustrate this algorithm for a given example. The generalisation from this example is obvious.

Example

((s) (((d1))((d2))((d3))((d4))) : ((0.5 0.7) (0.2 0.9) (0.3 0.5) (0.7 0.8))

((d1)) : (0.1 0.2)

((d2)) : (0.3 0.4)

((d3)) : (0 0.6)

((d4)) : (0 1)

((s)) : (z1 z2) = (0.28 0.83)

since

z1 = MIN{0.5(0.1≤θ1≤ 0.2) + 0.2 (0.3≤ θ2≤ 0.4) + 0.3(0≤ θ3≤ 0.6) + 0.7 (0≤ θ4≤ 1)

Ordering :   ui should be in ascending order

z1 = MIN{0.2 (0.3≤ θ2≤ 0.4) + 0.3(0≤ θ3≤ 0.6) + 0.5(0.1≤θ1≤ 0.2) + 0.7 (0≤ θ4≤ 1)

Standardise : constrain range of θ_i so that all lower supports can be satisfied

$z1 = MIN\{0.2 (0.3 \leq \theta2 \leq 0.4) + 0.3(0 \leq \theta3 \leq 0.6) + 0.5(0.1 \leq \theta1 \leq 0.2) + 0.7 (0 \leq \theta4 \leq 0.6)$

since sum of theta = 1, sum of alpha = 0.4, so that 0.6 can be added to each alpha

Allocation :   give max allocation to leftmost theta

$\theta2 = 0.4$

The processes of standardisation and allocation are repeated for remaining thetas

Standardisation :

$z1 = MIN\{0.3(0 \leq \theta3 \leq 0.5) + 0.5(0.1 \leq \theta1 \leq 0.2) + 0.7 (0 \leq \theta4 \leq 0.5)$

since sum theta = 0.6, sum alpha = 0.1, so that 0.5 can be added to each alpha

Allocation :

$\theta3 = 0.5$

Standardisation :

$z1 = MIN\{0.5(0.1 \leq \theta1 \leq 0.1) + 0.7 (0 \leq \theta4 \leq 0)$

since sum theta = 0.1, sum alpha = 0.1 so that 0 can be added to each alpha

Allocation :

$\theta1 = 0.1, \theta4 = 0$

In this case the allocation can be completed since there is no choice for theta values.
Therefore

$z1 = 0.2 \; 0.4 + 0.3 \; 0.5 + 0.5 \; 0.1 = 0.28$

The method for z2 is the same except that the ordering orders the v_i in descending order.

$z2 = MAX\{0.7(0.1 \leq \theta1 \leq 0.2) + 0.9 (0.3 \leq \theta2 \leq 0.4) + 0.5(0 \leq \theta3 \leq 0.6) + 0.8 (0 \leq \theta4 \leq 1)$

Ordering : v_i should be in descending order

$z2 = MAX\{0.9 (0.3 \leq \theta2 \leq 0.4) + 0.8 (0 \leq \theta4 \leq 1) + 0.7(0.1 \leq \theta1 \leq 0.2) + 0.5(0 \leq \theta3 \leq 0.6)$

Standardise :

$z2 = MAX\{0.9 (0.3 \leq \theta2 \leq 0.4) + 0.8 (0 \leq \theta4 \leq 0.6) + 0.7(0.1 \leq \theta1 \leq 0.2) + 0.5(0 \leq \theta3 \leq 0.6)$

since sum of theta = 1, sum of alpha = 0.4, so that 0.6 can be added to each alpha

Allocation :   give max allocation to leftmost theta

$\theta2 = 0.4$

Standardisation :

$z2 = MAX\{ 0.8 (0 \leq \theta4 \leq 0.5) + 0.7(0.1 \leq \theta1 \leq 0.2) + 0.5(0 \leq \theta3 \leq 0.5)$

since sum theta = 0.6, sum alpha = 0.1, so that 0.5 can be added to each alpha

Allocation :

$\theta4 = 0.5$

Standardisation :

$z2 = MAX\{\ 0.7(0.1 \leq \theta1 \leq 0.1) + 0.5(0 \leq \theta3 \leq 0)$

since sum theta = 0.1, sum alpha = 0.1 so that 0 can be added to each alpha

Allocation :

$\theta1 = 0.1, \theta3 = 0$

In this case the allocation can be completed since there is no choice for theta values.
Therefore

$z2 = 0.7\ 0.1 + 0.9\ 0.4 + 0.8\ 0.5 = 0.83$

4.2.3 Special Case

The following rule

$$(h\ (\ b \to b\ )\ ) : ((u1\ v1)(u2\ v2))$$

is a special case of the above rule. The variable B is allowed to have the mutual exclusive values b and $\neg b$.

It can be written in Fril as

$$((h)\ (b)) : ((u1\ v1)(u2\ v2))$$

The inference rule simplifies in this case. If we know

$$((b)) : (\alpha\ \beta)$$

then the inference is

$$((h)) :\ (z1\ z2)$$

where

$$z_1 = \begin{pmatrix} u1.\beta + u2.(1 - \beta)\ \text{if } u1 \leq u2 \\ u1.\alpha + u2.(1 - \alpha)\ \text{if } u1 > u2 \end{pmatrix} \qquad z_2 = \begin{pmatrix} v1.\alpha + v2.(1 - \alpha)\ \text{if } v1 \leq v2 \\ v1.\beta + v2.(1 - \beta)\ \text{if } v1 > v2 \end{pmatrix}$$

Example

The rule

((control is large) (((position is positive_small)(velocity is negative_medium))

 ((not and (position is positive_small)(velocity is negative_medium))))): ((1 1)(0 0))

can be written in Fril as

((control is large) (position is positive_small)(velocity is negative_medium)) : ((1 1)(0 0))

and defines an equivalence of the head and the body of the rule.

If (u2 v2) = (0 1) we need not include this support pair. Therefore from the rule

$$((h)\ (b)) : (u\ v)$$

and fact

$$((b)) : (\alpha \ \beta)$$

we can conclude

$$((h)) : (\alpha u \ \ \alpha v + (1 - \alpha))$$

The support pair $(\alpha \ \beta)$ for the body is determined from the support pairs for the terms of the body using the calculus discussed in the previous chapter.

For example, if the body of the rule is

$$((b1)(b2))$$

and

$$((b1)) : (\alpha 1 \ \beta 1)$$

$$((b2)) : (\alpha 2 \ \beta 2)$$

then

$$((b1)(b2)) : (z1 \ z2)$$

where $z1 = \alpha 1 \ \alpha 2$; $z2 = \beta 1 \ \beta 2$ if an independence conjunction is assumed

$$z1 = MAX \{\alpha 1 + \alpha 2 - 1, 0\} \ ; \ z2 = MIN \{\beta 1, \beta 2\} \ \text{if no assumption is made.}$$

If the body of the rule is the disjunction of (b1) and (b2) then the body will have the support pair (z1 z2) where

$$z1 = \alpha 1 + \alpha 2 - \alpha 1 \ \alpha 2 \ ; \ z2 = \beta 1 + \beta 2 - \beta 1 \ \beta 2$$

if independence is assumed

$$z1 = MAX \{\alpha 1, \alpha 2\} \ ; \ z2 = MIN \{\beta 1 + \beta 2, 1\}$$

if no assumption is made.

More generally a t-norm calculus can be assumed and the rules for conjunction and disjunction are interval versions of those discussed in the previous chapter.

These rules can be used to determine the support pair for any body made up of a mixture of conjunction and disjunctions of terms with known support pairs.

4.2.4 Use of Semantic Unification

The terms in the body of the rule can contain fuzzy sets, and the facts can also contain fuzzy sets. For example, the body can contain the term (variable X has value f) where f is a fuzzy set. A fact of the form (variable X has value f') can be given. Fril will automatically perform a semantic unification to obtain a support pair for $Pr(f \mid f')$. This is used as a fact by Fril for the probability of this term in the body of the rule, i.e. Fril uses the fact

$$((\text{variable X has value f})) : (x \ y)$$

where (x y) is the support pair obtained from the semantic unification $f \mid f'$.

The user can instruct Fril to use the point semantic unification instead of the default interval semantic unification.

Fril uses an efficient algorithm for semantic unification. Semantic unification for continuous fuzzy sets can be thought of as a limiting case of the discrete fuzzy set case in which the continuous fuzzy sets are replaced by n point approximate discrete fuzzy sets and n is allowed to tend to infinity.

4.2.5 Heads with Fuzzy Sets

The head of a Fril rule can contain a fuzzy set.

For example

((height of X is tall) (...)) : ((x y)(s t))

where ... denotes the body of the rule containing conditions to be satisfied for the head of the rule to be satisfied.

Facts will be used with the Fril inference rule to obtain a support pair for the head of the rule. For example

((height of John is tall)) : (α β)

We use this support pair to modify the fuzzy set in the head. This modification is equivalent to determining the expected fuzzy set using the mass assignment:

tall : α, $\overline{\text{tall}}$: 1 - β, Height Space : β - α

Suppose that we have an inference of the form

((variable Av is a)) : (x y)

where a is a fuzzy set on S

Suppose our query is of the form

qs((variable Av is b))

where b is a fuzzy set on S.

To answer the query, Fril automatically sets up a new rule of the form

((variable Av is b) (variable Av is a)) : ((x1 y1)(x2 y2))

where the support pairs (x1 y1) and (x2 y2) are calculated using the semantic unifications

b | a : [x1, y1] and b | $\overline{a}$: [x2, y2].

This rule is then used with the fact

((variable Av is a)) : (x y)

to deduce a support pair (γ1 γ2) for (variable Av is b) using the inference rule of Fril. The solution to the query is therefore

((variable Av is b)) : (γ1 γ2)

Suppose the query is

qs((variable Av is a))

Fril uses the inference ((variable Av is a)) : (x y) in the same way as just described to deduce the solution

((variable Av is a)) : (γ1 γ2)

In general (γ1 γ2) will not be the same as (x y) since we use this additional inference process. We will show an example to illustrate and justify this

4.2.6 An Example

In this example we will use discrete fuzzy sets so that all calculations can be performed by hand.

IF X is **f** THEN Y is **g**

X is **f1**

Therefore (Y is **g**) : [x, y]

Therefore (Y is **g1**) : [γ1, γ2]

where **f** = a / 1 + b / 0.7 + c / 0.3 ; F = {a, b, c, d} ; **f1** = a / 0.7 + b / 1 + c / 0.2

g = α / 1 + β / 0.5 + γ / 0.1 ; G = {α, β, γ} ; **g1** = α / 1 + β / 0.2

We will determine the inference using both the interval semantic unification and point semantic unification. The problem is to find a support pair for the statement that the variable takes the value **g1**.

The Fril program for this problem is:

set(univ1 (a b c d))
set(univ2 (α, β, γ))

(f {a : 1, b : 0.7, c : 0.3}univ1)
(f1 {a : 0.7, b : 1, c : 0.2}univ1)
(g {α : 1, β : 0.5, γ : 0.1}univ2)
(g1 {α : 1, β : 0.2}univ2)

((value of y is g) (value of x is f))
((value of x is f1))

qs((value of y is g1))

Fril Method with interval semantic unification

f | f1 : [0.62 0.91] since

	0.3 b	^{m}f1 0.5 {a, b}	0.2 {a, b, c}
0.3 a	f 0.09	u 0.15	u 0.06
^{m}f 0.4 {a, b}	t 0.12	t 0.2	u 0.08
0.3 {a, b, c}	t 0.09	t 0.15	t 0.06

t : 0.62
f : 0.09
u : 0.29

f | f1 : [0.62, 0.91]

Fig 4.1

Inference :

Y is **g** : [0.62, 1]

Also

Interval semantic unification of **g1 | g** = [0.58, 1] since

	0.5 α	0.4 {α, β}	0.1 {α, β, γ}
0.8 α	t	u 0.32	u
0.2 {α, β}	t	t 0.08	u

g1 | g : [0.58, 1]

Fig 4.2

Cell numerical entries for columns 1 and 3 not required since column 1 gives 0.5 to t and column 3 gives 0.1 to u.

t : 0.58
f : 0
u : 0.42

Interval semantic unification of **g1 | $\overline{g}$** = [0, 0.2] since

	0.4 γ	0.5 {β, γ}	0.1 Ø
0.8 α	f	f 0.4	u
0.2 {α, β}	f	u 0.1	u

g1 | $\overline{g}$: [0, 0.2]

t : 0
f : 0.8
u : 0.2

Fig 4.3

so that the additional rule generated by Fril is

((value of y is g1)(value of y is g)) : ((0.58 1)(0 0.2))

which it uses with the fact

((value of y is g)) : (0.62 1)

to give the final inference

((value of y is g1)) : (0.3596 1)

Fril Method with point semantic unification

f | f1 : 0.7683 since

	$^m\mathbf{f1}$ 0.3 b	0.5 {a, b}	0.2 {a, b, c}	
0.3 a	t : 0 0	t : 1/2 0.075	t : 1/3 0.02	t : 0.7683
$^m\mathbf{f}$ 0.4 {a, b}	t : 1 0.12	t: 1 0.2	t : 2/3 0.0533	f : 0.2317
0.3 {a, b, c}	t : 1 0.09	t : 1 0.15	t : 1 0.06	

f | f1 : 0.7683

Fig 4.4

Inference :

Y is **g** : [0.7683, 1]

Also point semantic unification of **g1 | g** = 0.8201 since

	0.5 α	0.4 {α, β}	0.1 {α, β, γ}
0.8 α	t	t : 1/2 0.16	t : 1/3 0.0267
0.2 {α, β}	t	t 0.08	t : 2/3 0.0534

g1 | g : 0.8201

Fig 4.5

Interval semantic unification of **g1 | g̅** = [0, 0.2] since

	0.4 γ	0.5 {β, γ}	0.1 Ø
0.8 α	t : 0	t : 0	t : 1/2 0.04
0.2 {α, β}	t : 0	t : 1/2 0.05	t : 1/2 0.01

g1 | g̅ : 0.1

Fig 4.6

so that the additional rule generated by Fril is

((value of y is g1)(value of y is g)) : ((0.8201 0.8201)(0.1 0.1))

which it uses with the fact

((value of y is g)) : (0.0.7683 1)

to give the final inference

((value of y is g1)) : (0.6532 0.8201)

4.2.7 Another Example

In this example we show how Fril answers queries which have the same fuzzy set as that contained in the head of the rule being used for inference.

We also justify the method by comparing it with alternative ways of performing the semantic unification.

Consider a Fril inference of the form

((solution is g)) : (0.8 1)

where **g** is a fuzzy set defined on {a, b, c}

Suppose we ask the query

qs((solution is g))

Fril determines

g | g : [0.68, 1] and **g | g̅** : [0.24, 0.72]

using interval semantic unification since

Fig 4.7

g | g : [0.68, 1]

and

Fig 4.8

g | g̅ : [0.24, 0.72]

112

Fril then uses the rule

((solution is g)(solution is g)) : ((0.68 1)(0.24 0.72))

with the fact

((solution is g)) : (0.8 1)

to provide the final solution to the query

((solution is g)) : (0.592 1)

The semantic unification uses the multiplication model to determine the masses in the cells of the conditional truth matrix. We can modify this multiplication model to provide the most optimistic solution and the most general solution.

The multiplication model gives an average solution based on the idea that various interpretations of the fuzzy sets can be given which are equally likely. This has been previously discussed.

To obtain the most optimistic solution to the query we should choose the support pairs (x1 y1) and (x2 y2) in the Fril generated rule

((solution is g)(solution is g)) : ((x1 y1)(x2 y2))

to be as close to ((1 1)(0 0)) as possible since the rule is then an equivalence and the support pair of the head is that of the body.

We can do this by maximising the masses in the t cells of the conditional matrix for $g \mid g$ and maximising the masses in the f cells of the conditional matrix for $g \mid \bar{g}$. This gives the results

$g \mid g$: [1, 1]   and $g \mid \bar{g}$: [0 0.4] as seen from Figs 4.9 and 4.10.

	0.2 a	m_g 0.4 {a, b}	0.4 {a, b, c}
0.2 a	t 0.2	u 0	u 0
m_g 0.4 {a, b}	t 0	t 0.4	u 0
0.4 {a, b, c}	t 0	t 0	t 0.4

Masses in t cells are maximised

Fig 4.9

$g \mid g$: [1, 1]

	0.4 c	$m_{\bar{g}}$ 0.2 {b, c}	0.4 Ø
0.2 a	f 0	f 0.2	u 0
m_g 0.4 {a, b}	f 0.4	u 0	u 0
0.4 {a, b, c}	t 0	t 0	u 0.4

Masses in f cells are maximised

Fig 4.10

$g \mid \bar{g}$: [0, 0.4]

The rule

((solution is g)(solution is g)) : ((1 1)(0 0.4))

with the fact

((solution is g)) : (0.8 1)

would then provide the solution to the query

((solution is g)) : (0.8 1)

To obtain the most general solution to the query we should choose the support pairs (x1 y1) and (x2 y2) in the Fril generated rule

((solution is g)(solution is g)) : ((x1 y1)(x2 y2))

to be as close to ((0 1)(0 1)) as possible. We can do this by maximising the masses in the u cells of the two conditional matrices for **g** I **g** and **g** I **ḡ**. This gives the results

g I **g** : [0.4, 1]   and   **g** I **ḡ** : [0 0.6] since

	0.2 a	m_g 0.4 {a, b}	0.4 {a, b, c}	
0.2 a	t 0	u 0.2	u 0	Masses in u cells are maximised
m_g 0.4 {a, b}	t 0	t 0	u 0.4	
0.4 {a, b, c}	t 0.2	t 0.2	t 0	

g I **g** : [0.4, 1]

Fig 4.11

and

	0.4 c	$m_{\bar g}$ 0.2 {b, c}	0.4 ∅	
0.2 a	f 0.2	f 0	u 0	Masses in u cells are maximised
m_g 0.4 {a, b}	f 0.2	u 0.2	u 0	
0.4 {a, b, c}	t 0	t 0	u 0.4	

g I **ḡ** : [0, 0.6]

Fig 4.12

The rule

((solution is g)(solution is g)) : ((0.4 1)(0 0.6))

with the fact

((solution is g)) : (0.8 1)

would then provide the solution to the query

((solution is g)) : (0.32 1)

114

4.3 MULTIPLE RULES

4.3.1 Combining Inferences from Various Rules using Intersection

Rules which contain the same head apart from a fuzzy set in the same position for each of the heads are called multiple rules for the same head.

Fril uses each rule separately to obtain an inference of the form

$$\text{<head i>} : (xi\ yi)$$

for the ith rule.

We must now combine these inferences. For this purpose we distinguish two cases.

Case 1:

Consider that the multiple rules contain exactly the same head, i.e. there is no fuzzy set in the head of the rules. Fril combines the inferences by taking the intersection of the support pairs associated with each of the rules. Therefore the final inference is

$$\text{<head>} : (x\ y)$$

where

$$(x\ y) = \bigcap_i (xi\ yi)$$

and the intersection operation is defined by

$$(x1\ y1) \cap (x2\ y2) = (a\ b) \text{ where } a = x1 \vee x2 \text{ and } b = y1 \wedge y2$$

Case 2:

Consider that the multiple rules contain the same head apart from a fuzzy set in the same position for each of the rules, i.e. of the form

$$((\text{<... fi ...>})) : (xi\ yi)$$

If a query of the form

$$qs((\text{<... g ...>}))$$

is asked, where g is a fuzzy set defined on the same space as {fi}, then Fril processes each rule in turn as shown below to obtain an inference for (<... g ...>) in the form of a support pair. Thus for the ith rule the inference will be

$$((\text{<... g ...>})) : (x'i\ y'i)$$

and these inferences are then combined by intersecting the support pairs {(x'i y'i)}. The final inference is therefore

$$((\text{<... g... >})) : (x\ y)$$

where

$$(x\ y) = \bigcap_i (x'i\ y'i)$$

The support pair for (x'i y'i) for ((<... g ...>)) of the ith rule is determined as follows. Fril determines

$$g \mid fi : (\alpha i \; \beta i) \quad \text{and} \quad g \mid \overline{fi} : (\gamma i \; \delta i)$$

using semantic unification.

It then uses the induced rule

$$((<... g ...>)(<... fi ...>)) : ((\alpha i \; \beta i)(\gamma i \; \delta i))$$

with the data

$$((<... fi ...>)) : (xi \; yi)$$

to obtain, using the standard Fril inference rule,

$$((<... g ...>)) : (x'i \; y'i).$$

This procedure is completely hidden from the user.

If a query of the form

$$qs((<... X ...>))$$

is asked, where X is a variable, then Fril simply returns the solutions

$$((<... f1 ...>)) : (x1 \; y1)$$
$$((<... f2 ...>)) : (x2 \; y2)$$

$$...............................$$

etc.

4.3.2 Example of Case 1

$$((\text{design of X is ok})$$
$$\quad (\text{performance of X is good})$$
$$\quad (\text{looks of X is modern})) : (0.9 \; 1)$$
$$((\text{design of X is ok})$$
$$\quad (\text{cost of X is expensive})) : (0 \; 0.05)$$
$$((\text{design of X is ok})$$
$$\quad (\text{not reliability of X is high})) : (0 \; 0.2)$$

$$((\text{performance of X is good})$$
$$\quad (\text{eng\_report of X is ok})$$
$$\quad (\text{reliability of X is high})) : (0.9 \; 1)$$

$$((\text{looks of d is modern})) : (0.8 \; 1)$$

$$((\text{reliability of d is high})) : (0.7 \; 0.8)$$

((eng_report of d is ok)) : (0.7 1)

((cost of d is expensive)) : (0.6 1)

qs ((design of X is Y))

Fril gives the solution
((design of d is ok)) : (0.31752 0.43)

The Fril calculations in determining this solution are as follows:
performance of d is good : [(0.9)(0.7)(0.7), 1] = [0.441, 1] using the first rule for the performance predicate.

head of rule 1 : [(0.441)(0.8)(0.9), 1] = [0.31752, 1]
head of rule 2 : [0, (0.05)(0.6) + 0.4] = [0, 0.43]
head of rule 3 : [0, (0.2)(0.2) + 0.8] = [0, 0.84]

Intersecting support pairs gives
head : [0.31752, 0.43]

4.3.3 Example of Case 2
We will use an extension of the example given in Section 4.2.6. The extension is in the form of an additional rule.

IF X is **f1** THEN Y is **g1**
IF X is **f2** THEN Y is **g2**
X is **fd**

Therefore (Y is **g**) : [$\gamma 1$ $\gamma 2$]

where **f1** = a / 1 + b / 0.7 + c / 0.3 ; F = {a, b, c, d} ; **fd** = a / 0.7 + b / 1 + c / 0.2
  f2 = a / 0.5 + b / 1 + c / 0.1

  g1 = α / 1 + β / 0.5 + γ / 0.1 ; G = {α, β, γ} ; **g** = α / 1 + β / 0.2

  g2 = α / 0.3 + β / 1

The problem is to find a support pair for the statement that the variable takes the value **g**. The Fril program for this problem is:

set(univ1 (a b c d))

set(univ2 (α, β, γ))

(f1{a : 1, b : 0.7, c : 0.3}univ1)

(f2 {a : 0.5, b : 1, c : 0.1} univ1)

(fd {a : 0.7, b : 1, c : 0.2}univ1)

(g1 {α : 1, β : 0.5, γ : 0.1}univ2)

(g2 {α : 0.3, β : 1} univ2)

(g {α : 1, β : 0.2}univ2)

((value of y is g1) (value of x is f1))

((value of y is g2) (value of x is f2))

((value of x is fd)

qs((value of y is g))

((value of y is g)) : (0.3596 0.5518)

since:

From Section 4.2.6 the inference from the first rule is

((value of y is g)) : (0.3596 1)

The second rule provides the inference

((value of y is g)) : (0.114 0.5518)

since

f2 | fd : [0.57, 1] since

^{m}**f2**		0.3 b	^{m}**fd** 0.5 {a, b}	0.2 {a, b, c}
0.5 b		t 0.15	u 0.25	u 0.1
0.4 {a, b}		t 0.12	t 0.2	u 0.08
0.1 {a, b, c}		t	t	t

f 2 | fd : [0.57, 1]

Fig 4.13

Also

g | g2 : [0.2, 0.44] and **g | $\overline{g2}$** : [0, 0.7] since

$\overline{g2}$ = α / 0.7 + γ / 1 and

118

Fig 4.14

	0.7 β	0.3 {α, β}
0.8 α	f 0.56	u 0.24
0.2 {α, β}	t	t

g | g2 : [0.2, 0.44]

Fig 4.15

	0.3 γ	0.7 {α, γ}
0.8 α	f	u
0.2 {α, β}	f	u

g | g2 : [0, 0.7]

so that the induced Fril rule is

((value of y is g)(value of y is g2)) : ((0.2 0.44)(0 0.7))

which is used with

((value of y is g2)) : (0.57 1)

to give the final inference for rule 2 of

((value of y is g)) : (0.114 0.5518)

The inferences for (value of y is g) from the two rules are then intersected to give

((value of y is g)) : (0.3596 0.5518)

4.3.4 Combining Inferences from various Rules with Dempster Rule of Combination

In this case we modify the last step in the combining method given in 4.3.1. Instead of using the intersection rule to combine the inferences from the various rules we use the Dempster rule of combination. Fril would use the Dempster method if the predicate in the head of the rules is defined to be a Dempster predicate.

In this case inferences are combined two at a time. Suppose inferences from two rules are

((h)) : (x1 x2)

((h)) : (y1 y2)

then we combine the corresponding mass assignments using the Dempster rule.

The mass assignments corresponding to these two inferences are given by

m1 = h : x1, ¬h : 1 - x2, {h, ¬h} : x2 - x1

m2 = h : y1, ¬h : 1 - y2, {h, ¬h} : y2 - y1

We combine these using a modified multiplication meet. The modification changes any mass associated with the null set Ø and redistributes this mass to the non-null cells of the meet matrix in proportion to the multiplication meet masses. This is illustrated pictorially as follows:

119

	$y1$ / h	$1-y2$ / $\neg h$	$y2-y1$ / $\{h,\neg h\}$
$h : x1$	h / $x1y1$	$\emptyset$ / $x1(1-y2)$	h / $x1(y2-y1)$
$\neg h : 1-x2$	$\emptyset$ / $(1-x2)y1$	$\neg h$ / $(1-x2)(1-y2)$	$\neg h$ / $(1-x2)(y2-y1)$
$\{h,\neg h\} : x2-x1$	h / $(x2-x1)y1$	$\neg h$ / $(x2-x1)(1-y2)$	$\{h,\neg h\}$ / $(x2-x1)(y2-y1)$

Multiplication Meet

Fig 4.16

Cell entries are the product of the corresponding row and column masses

The entries are modified to give a mass of 0 for any null entries, $\emptyset$. The other entries are then renormalised. This gives the modified meet shown pictorially below and corresponds to using the Dempster rule of combination.

The use of the multiplication assumes an independence of the conclusions of each of the rules. Each rule can be thought of as representing an independent viewpoint. The renormalisation is used to take account of the inconsistencies in the conclusions from the various rules. The multiplication meet with this renormalisation cannot be interpreted as equivalent to an intersection of families of probability distributions.

	$y1$ / h	$1-y2$ / $\neg h$	$y2-y1$ / $\{h,\neg h\}$
$h : x1$	h / $Kx1y1$	$\emptyset$ / 0	h / $Kx1(y2-y1)$
$\neg h : 1-x2$	$\emptyset$ / 0	$\neg h$ / $K(1-x2)(1-y2)$	$\neg h$ / $K(1-x2)(y2-y1)$
$\{h,\neg h\} : x2-x1$	h / $K(x2-x1)y1$	$\neg h$ / $K(x2-x1)(1-y2)$	$\{h,\neg h\}$ / $K(x2-x1)(y2-y1)$

$$K = \frac{1}{1 - x1(1-y2) - (1-x2)y1}$$

Fig 4.17

Masses of any $\emptyset$ entry put to zero.

Other masses renormalised so that they sum to 1

This meet corresponds to the mass assignment

$$m = h : K(x1y1 + x1(y2-y1) + (x2-x1)y1,$$
$$\neg h : K((1-x2)(1-y2) + (1-x2)(y2-y1) + (x2-x1)(1-y2))$$
$$\{h, \neg h\} : K(x2-x1)(y2-y1)$$

The combined inference is therefore
$$h : [K(x1y1 + x1(y2-y1) + (x2-x1)y1, \ 1-K((1-x2)(1-y2)+(1-x2)(y2-y1)+(x2-x1)(1-y2))]$$

120

For three rules, the first two are combined as given here. This result is then combined with the support pair from the third rule to give the final solution. This can be generalised to any number of rules.

4.3.5 Examples of Combining using Dempster's Rule of Combination
Example 1
The results of the example of 4.3.2 from each of the rules were

  head of rule 1 : [0.31752, 1]

  head of rule 2 : [0, 0.43]

  head of rule 3 : [0, 0.84]

giving the mass assignments

  m1 = h : 0.31752, {h, ¬h} : 0.68248 from rule 1

  m2 = ¬h : 0.57, {h, ¬h} : 0.43 from rule 2

  m3 = ¬h : 0.16, {h, ¬h} : 0.84 from rule 3

We now combine these using the Dempster rule.

Combining results from rules 1 and 2 gives

  h : 0.1667, ¬h : 0.475, {h, ¬h} : 0.3584 since

	0.57 ¬h	0.43 {h, ¬h}
0.31752 h	Ø 0.181 → 0	h .1365→.1667
0.68248 {h, ¬h}	¬h .389→.475	{h, ¬h} .2935→.3584

First numerical entries in each cell is the product of corresponding row and column masses

The entry in the cell with Ø is put to zero

Fig 4.18

Other entries x determined using x / (1 - 0.181) and combining this with m3 gives

  h : 0.1438, ¬h : 0.5469, {h, ¬h} : 0.3095 since

	0.16 ¬h	0.84 {h, ¬h}
0.1667 h	Ø 0.0267 → 0	h 0.14 → 0.1438
0.475 ¬h	¬h 0.076 → 0.0781	¬h 0.399 → 0.4099
0.3584 {h, ¬h}	¬h 0.0573 → 0.0589	{h, ¬h} 0.3011 → 0.3094

h : 0.1438

¬h : 0.5469

{h, ¬h} : 0.3095

Fig 4.19

so that

  ((design of d is ok)) : (0.1438 0.4533)

Example 2

The results of the example of 4.3.3 from each of the rules were

　　((value of y is g)) : (0.3596 1)

　　((value of y is g)) : (0.114 0.5518)

Using Dempster's rule we obtain

　　((value of y is g)) : (0.3236 0.6578)

since

	0.114 h	0.4482 ¬h	0.4378 {_}	
h : 0.3596	h 0.0489	Ø 0	h 0.1877	h : 0.3236
{_} : 0.6404	h 0.087	¬h 0.3422	{h, ¬h} 0.3342	¬h : 0.3422 {_} : 0.3342

$$K = \frac{1}{0.8388}$$　　h : [0.3236, 0.6578]

Fig 4.20

Example 3

Suppose in the last example, instead of being asked the query concerning **g**, we wanted to know which value from the list {α, β, γ} we should conclude given that we know only one of these values can be the correct one. We would ask Fril the three separate queries

　　qs((value of y is {α : 1}))

　　qs((value of y is {β : 1}))

　　qs((value of y is {γ : 1}))

The answers to these queries are

　　((value of y is {α : 1})) : (0.31 0.472)

　　((value of y is {β : 1})) : (0.399 0.538)

　　((value of y is {γ : 1})) : (0 0.43)

A decision making Fril program can be written to take the final decision from a knowledge of these results. One rule for such a decision making program would be that if a given result has a necessary support which is greater than the necessary supports for all other results, and a possible support which is greater than the possible supports for all other results, then we choose that result. Other rules must be devised to complete the decision making process. In this example we would then choose (value of y is β).

Example 4

In this example we repeat example 2 using point semantic unification rather than the interval version. The inferences from the two rules will be found to have a null intersection but we can still combine these inferences using the Dempster rule of combination. The use of point semantic unification for this example is questionable if the rules are not assumed to be independent viewpoints since it is only in the case of independent viewpoints that the Dempster rule can really be justified.

IF X is **f1** THEN Y is **g1**
IF X is **f2** THEN Y is **g2**
X is **fd**

Therefore (Y is **g**) : [$\gamma 1$ $\gamma 2$]

where **f1** = a / 1 + b / 0.7 + c / 0.3 ; F = {a, b, c, d} ; **fd** = a / 0.7 + b / 1 + c / 0.2

f2 = a / 0.5 + b / 1 + c / 0.1

g1 = α / 1 + β / 0.5 + γ / 0.1 ; G = {α, β, γ} ; **g** = α /1 + β / 0.2

g2 = α / 0.3 + β / 1

The results of the example of 4.3.3 from the first rule as determined in 4.2.6 are:
((value of y is g)) : (0.6532 0.8207)

The second rule provides the inference
((value of y is g)) : (0.32 0.3266)
since, using point semantic unification
f2 | fd : 0.7816 since

	0.3 b	^{m}**fd** 0.5 {a, b}	0.2 {a, b, c}

0.5
b
	t : 1
	  0.15
		t : 1/2
		  0.125
			t : 1/3
			  0.0333

^{m}**f2** 0.4
{a, b}
	t : 1
	  0.12
		t : 1
		  0.2
			t : 2/3
			  0.0533

0.1 {a, b, c}	t : 1	t : 1	t : 1

f 2 | fd : 0.7816   **Fig 4.21**

so that
((value of y is g2)) : (0.7816 1)

123

Also

$g \mid g2 : 0.32$ and $g \mid \overline{g2} : 0.35$ since

$\overline{g2} = \alpha / 0.7 + \gamma / 1$ and

	0.7 β	0.3 {α, β}
0.8 α	t : 0 0	t : 1/2 0.12
0.2 {α, β}	t : 1	t : 1

g | g2 : 0.32

Fig 4.22

	0.3 γ	0.7 {α, γ}
0.8 α	t : 0	t : 1/2
0.2 {α, β}	t : 0	t : 1/2

g | g2 : 0.35

Fig 4.23

so that the induced Fril rule is

((value of y is g)(value of y is g2)) : ((0.32 0.32)(0.35 0.35))

which is used with

((value of y is g2)) : (0.7816 1)

to give the final inference for rule 2 of

((value of y is g)) : (0.32 0.3266)

We must therefore combine the two inferences

((value of y is g)) : (0.6532 0.8201)

((value of y is g)) : (0.32 0.3266)

using Dempster's rule of combination to give

((value of y is g)) : (0.5308 0.533)

since

	0.32 h	0.6734 ¬h	0.0066 {h, ¬h}	
h :0.6532	h 0.4159	Ø 0	h 0.0086	h : 0.5308
¬h : 0.1799	Ø 0	¬h 0.2410	¬h 0.0024	¬h : 0.467
{h,¬h}:0.1669	h 0.1063	¬h 0.2236	{h, ¬h} 0.0022	{h, ¬h} : 0.0022

K = 0.5026

Fig 4.24

Therefore

h : [0.5308, 0.533]

124

4.3.6 Non-Monotonic Reasoning

Consider the following problem

      ((fly X) (bird X)) : (0.9 0.95)

      ((bird X) (penguin X))

      ((fly X) (penguin X)) : (0 0)

      ((penguin penny)) : 0.4

      ((bird penny)) : (0.9 1)

The query

      qs((fly penny))

will give no solution unless the predicate "fly" is treated as a Dempster predicate in which case Fril will combine the solutions from the two ways of determining the support pair for (fly penny) using Dempster's rule of combination. To force Fril to use the Dempster rule we declare

dempster fly

prior to defining the predicate fly.

The program

      dempster fly

      ((fly X)(bird X)) : (0.9 0.95)

      ((bird X)(penguin X))

      ((fly X)(penguin X)) : (0 0)

      ((penguin penny)) : 0.4

      ((bird penny)) : (0.9 1)

will give the solution

      ((fly penny)) : (0.7189 0.8476)

in answer to the query qs((fly X)).

We will now derive the solution using elementary probability theory.

The mass assignments for the facts over BP are

      {b _} : 0.9, {_ _} : 0.1   and   {_ p} : 0.4, {_ ¬p} : 0.6

These can be combined using the mass assignment theory as

	0.9 {b _}	0.1 {_ _}
0.4 {_ p}	{b p} 0.3 + x	{b p} 0.1 - x
0.6 {¬p _}	{b ¬p} 0.6 - x	{_ ¬p} x

$0 \leq x \leq 0.1$

Fig 4.25

The entry in top right cell is changed from {_ p} to {b p} since a penguin must be a bird.

The cell entries are chosen such that the cell entries for a given row add up to the row mass of the given mass assignment and the cell entries for a given column add up to the column mass of the given mass assignment.

Therefore the specific knowledge about penny is

bp : 0.4, b¬p : [0.5, 0.6], ¬b¬p : [0, 0.1], ¬bp : 0

i.e.

P'r(bp) = 0.4, 0.5 ≤ P'r(b¬p) ≤ 0.6, 0 ≤ P'r(¬b¬p) ≤ 0.1, P'r(¬bp) = 0

with the constraint

P'r(bp) + P'r(b¬p) + P'r(¬b¬p) + P'r(¬bp) = 1

We can also determine support pairs for Pr(f | bp), Pr(f | b¬p), Pr(f | ¬b¬p) from our general information, where f is the instantiation of the variable F to f. F can take values from {f, ¬f}. This gives

Pr(f | bp) = Pr(f | p) = 0

0.9 ≤ Pr(f | b¬p) ≤ 1

0 ≤ Pr(f | ¬b¬p) ≤ 1

We can now use an interval version of Jeffrey's rule in a similar way to that used by Fril, i.e.

P'r(f) = Pr(f | bp)P'r(bp) + Pr(f | b¬p)P'r(b¬p) + Pr(f | ¬b¬p)P'r(¬b¬p)

which gives the solution

0.45 ≤ P'r(f) ≤ 0.6

This shows that we should be careful in the use of the Dempster rule to try and avoid the non-monotonic problem. A theory for non-monotonic logic can be written in Fril. A fuller treatment of mass assignment theory with a relative entropy updating algorithm as given in [Baldwin 1991] can avoid the difficulties encountered here. This theory can be represented in Fril but we will not present it in this book.

4.4 EXTENDED FRIL RULE

4.4.1 The Use of the Extended Fril Rule for Causal Nets

The extended Fril rule, namely

(h (b1 b2 ... bn)) : ((u1 v1)(u2 v2) ... (un vn))

can be used to represent causal nets. We will show this using a simple example. A complete Fril module for causal nets is described in Chapter 6.

Here we wish to simply show how the extended rule can be used for this form of knowledge representation and inference. The required conditional probabilities are assumed. In the Fril module these are automatically calculated from the net.

In the extended rule above, the support pair (ui vi) represents the interval containing the probability $Pr(h | bi)$ where bi is the ith term in the body. This is discussed in 4.1.2. An easy way of interpreting this rule and providing an insight to its use is as follows. Consider a model of an application involving variables V_i ; $i = 1, ..., n$ and variable C such that the variables $V_1, ..., V_n$ influence the variable C. Each variable V_i can be instantiated to an element in the set $S_i = \{v_{i1}, ...\}$ for all i. The variable C can be instantiated to an element of $S = \{c_1, ...\}$. A rule of the form

((variable C has value ci)

(((variable V1 has value v1r))

...

((variable Vk has value vkt))

...

((variable Vn has value vns)))) : ((u1 v1)(u2 v2) ... (un vn))

says that

Pr(variable C takes value ci | variable Vk has value vkt) lies in the interval [uk vk].

It is assumed that the various instantiations in the body of the rule are exhaustive and mutually exclusive. By this we mean that for a given situation one and only one instantiation of each of the variables in the body of the rule is true so that one and only one conjunctive instantiation is true.

If we know support pairs for the each of the possible instantiations of each variable in the body then Fril, as given in 4.2.1, will derive a support pair for the head of the rule. For multiple rules Fril will derive a support for each head. If we have a rule for each possible instantiation of the variable in the head of the rule then we can combine these results by taking into account that the values of the variable in the head are exhaustive and mutually exclusive.

Below we give an example of a simple causal net. The required conditional probabilities to set up the rules are determined from the given data using Bayes theorem and the normal conditional independence assumptions used in causal net theory.

Specific information can be uncertain for the example below since the inference rule of Fril allows for this by using an interval version of Jeffrey's rule. In this case we have an extension of the normal Bayesian causal nets in which the specific information is assumed to be known with certainty. We illustrate both cases below.

The treatment given here can be extended to the fuzzy case in which the variables are instantiated to fuzzy labels rather than precise values. This will not be treated in any detail but it is important for applications since it can greatly reduce the complexity of the problem. In the same way that fuzzy control uses a reduced number of fuzzy rules the modelling of causal nets can also use a reduced number of fuzzy rules.

4.4.2 Example

Consider the example given by Pearl

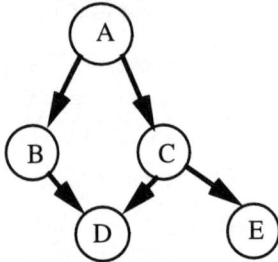

Fig 4.26

where the following conditional probabilities are given

Pr(A) : Pr(a) = 0.2

Pr(B | A) : Pr(b | a) = 0.8 ; Pr(b | ¬a) = 0.2

Pr(C | A) : Pr(c | a) = 0.2 ; Pr(c | ¬ a) = 0.05

Pr(D | BC) :

Pr(d | bc) = 0.8 ; Pr(d | ¬bc) = 0.8

Pr(d | b ¬c) = 0.8 ; Pr(d | ¬b¬c) = 0.05

Pr(E | C) : Pr(e | c) = 0.8 ; Pr(e | ¬c) = 0.6

and we know that for a given specific instance the probability distributions or mass assignments for P'r(D) and P'r(E) are given. We wish to determine the specific probability P'r(A) assuming the given specific information.

We can decompose the problem into two phases, phase 1 and phase 2, shown below.

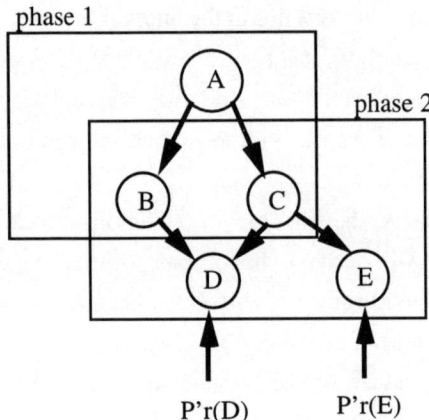

Fig 4.27

From the conditional probabilities and priors of the general knowledge statements given above we can calculate the distributions

Pr(BC | DE), Pr(A | BC)

to provide the required conditional probabilities for the Fril rules. In the Fril module these are calculated automatically.

We have the following Fril rules for both phases :

Phase 1

((a) (((bc)) ((b¬c)) ((¬ bc)) ((¬ b¬c)))) : ((0.8) (0.4571) (0.2) (0.05))

Phase 2

((bc)

(((d)(e)) ((d)(not e)) ((not d)(e)) ((not d)(not e)))) :

((0.125) (0.0556) (0.0156) (0.006))

128

((b→c)

    ((((d)(e)) ((d)(not e)) ((not d)(e)) ((not d)(not e)))) :

                        ((0.6562) (0.7778) (0.0817) (0.0833))

((¬bc)

    ((((d)(e)) ((d)(not e)) ((not d)(e)) ((not d)(not e)))) :

                        ((0.125) (0.0556) (0.0156) (0.006))

((¬b→c)

    ((((d)(e)) ((d)(not e)) ((not d)(e)) ((not d)(not e)))) :

                        ((0.0937) (0.1111) (0.8872) (0.9048))

Let the specific information be :

    ((d)) : P'r(d)

    ((e)) : P'r(e)

These rules assume that the specific inputs P'r(D) and P'r(E) are independent. If this assumption cannot be made then we replace all terms like

    ((d)(e))

by

    (conj (d) (e)).

Fril will then calculate the conjunction as the support pair

    $(0 \vee (P'r(d) + P'r(e) - 1)$ $P'r(d) \wedge P'r(e))$

The following results were obtained from Fril

For inputs	For inputs	For inputs
((d)) : (0)	((d)) : (0.1)	((d)) : (0.2)
((e)) : (1)	((e)) : (0.9)	((e)) : (0.9)
Fril gives	assumed to be independent	assumed to be independent
((a)) : (0.0973)	Fril gives	Fril gives
	((a)) : (0.1297)	((a)) : (0.1629)

For inputs	For inputs	For inputs
((d)) : (0 0.1)	((d)) : (0.1)	((d)) : (0 0.1)
((e)) : (0.9 1)	((e)) : (0.9)	((e)) : (0.9 1)
assumed to be independent	assumed to be dependent	assumed to be dependent
Fril gives	Fril gives	Fril gives
((a)) : (0.0964 0.1337)	((a)) : (0.0965 0.1625)	((a)) : (0.0964 0.1625)

4.4.3 Rules with Fuzzy Labels

Both the head and the body of a Fril rule can contain fuzzy sets. For example,

((interest rates should be made larger) (((inflation is rising fast))

((inflation is steady))

((inflation is falling)))) : ((0.7 1)(0 0.2)(0 0))

In this example larger, rising fast, steady and falling are all fuzzy sets. It is assumed that the latter three are the only allowed labels for describing the changing inflation. The conditional probabilities are assumed to be subjective judgments from a group of experts who decided whether interest rates should rise for each of the labels.

A specific input will be specified by a fuzzy set on the set of inflation rate labels, for example

inflation is rising fast / 0.4 + steady / 1 + falling / 0.1

or on the same space that the labels are defined on, for example

inflation is rising slowly.

In the latter case, we can express the specific value as

inflation is rising fast / Π(rising fast | rising slowly) + steady / Π(steady | rising slowly)

+ falling / Π(falling / rising slowly)

where Π is the possibility measure.

Suppose

inflation is rising fast / 0.4 + steady / 1 + falling / 0.1

We can express this as a mass assignment

inflation is : steady : 0.6, {steady, rising fast} : 0.3, {steady, rising fast, falling} : 0.1

from which we can give support pairs for each of the labels, i.e.

steady : (0.6 1), rising fast : (0 0.4), falling : (0 0.1)

with constraint

P'r(steady) + P'r(rising fast) + P'r(falling) = 1

More generally, for the rule

(h ((b1) (b2) ... (bn))) : ((u1 v1)(u2 v2) ... (un vn))

where b_i is a goal containing a fuzzy label, for example (inflation is rising slowly). The specific information can be expressed as

$(b_i) : (\alpha_i \; \beta_i)$; (all i) such that

$$\sum_i P'r(b_i) = 1$$

and the inference rule given above holds.

4.5 FUZZY CONTROL

4.5.1 The Fuzzy Control Problem

In fuzzy control applications and more generally for approximate reasoning IF ... THEN rules of the form

IF $X1 = \mathbf{f1}$ & ... & $Xn = \mathbf{fn}$ THEN $Y = \mathbf{g}$

where fuzzy sets $\mathbf{fi} \subseteq_f Fi$ and $\mathbf{g} \subseteq_f G$

are given.

In addition we are also given the facts

$X1 = \mathbf{f'1}, ..., Xn = \mathbf{f'n}$

where fuzzy sets $\mathbf{f'i} \subseteq_f Fi$

The given facts and rule can be used to conclude

$Y = \mathbf{g'}$

where $\mathbf{g'} \subseteq_f G$

The fundamental question is how do we perform this inference. Various approaches can be used to generalise from the classical logic case in which the $\mathbf{fi}$ are subsets of F and $\mathbf{g}$, $\mathbf{g'}$ are subsets of G.

One approach is to interpret the rule as representing a fuzzy implication and to derive a fuzzy relation to represent this implication. There are various choices for this derivation and there should be good reasons for using a particular one. Given this fuzzy relation the inference $\mathbf{g'}$ is then obtained using max-min composition. We will call this the **fuzzy implication method**. Various interpretations for the fuzzy implication relation are given in the next Section.

A second approach is to interpret the IF ... THEN rule as a logic rule with the understanding that $Pr(\text{head} \mid \text{body}) = 1$ and $0 \le Pr(\text{head} \mid \neg \text{body}) \le 1$. If, as will in general be the case, $Pr(\text{body})$ takes some value in the interval $[0, 1]$ then

$Pr(\text{body}) \le Pr(\text{head}) \le 1$

This inference can be written as

$Y = \mathbf{g'} : [Pr(\text{body}), 1]$

The $Pr(\text{body})$ is determined from comparison of the $\mathbf{fi}$ and $\mathbf{f'i}$. This will be done using the concept of **semantic unification** which we have used many times in this book. This provides an interval containing $Pr(\mathbf{fi} \mid \mathbf{f'i})$, i.e.

$\alpha i \le Pr(\mathbf{fi} \mid \mathbf{f'i}) \le \beta i$ for all i

This approach allows for the extension of the above formulation to one in which the rule is probabilistic in nature in addition to containing fuzzy sets. The extended rule is of the form

IF $X1 = \mathbf{f1}$ & ... & $Xn = \mathbf{fn}$ THEN $Y = \mathbf{g} : ((x1\ x2)(y1\ y2))$

where this rule is interpreted as

$x1 \leq \Pr(\text{head} \mid \text{body}) \leq x2$ and $y1 \leq \Pr(\text{head} \mid \neg \text{body}) \leq y2$

The inference in this case will be a probability interval, $[z1, z2]$ say, for the head of the rule which can be represented as

$$Y = \mathbf{g'} : [z1, z2]$$

and this interval will depend on the interval for $\Pr(\text{body})$ and the intervals $[x1, x2]$ and $[y1, y2]$. The inference rule for this case is, as we have seen, an interval valued Jeffrey's rule. This we justified using a relative entropy minimisation criterion for updating a prior distribution based on the IF ... THEN rule with a distribution representing the specific information of the given facts. We called this the **Fril inference method**.

A third approach is to interpret the IF ... THEN rule as a simple observation, namely that of the conjunction

$$X1 = \mathbf{f1} \ \& \ X = \mathbf{fn} \ \& \ Y = \mathbf{g}$$

and to determine a relation for this fuzzy logic statement. Max-min composition is then used to obtain the conclusion. This can be thought of as the application of Hebb's rule for unsupervised learning in a fuzzy associative memory. We will call this the **Mamdani method of inference**.

In practice multiple rules of the following form are given:

$$\text{IF } X1 = \mathbf{f1_r} \ \& \ ... \ \& \ Xn = \mathbf{fn_r} \text{ THEN } Y = \mathbf{g_r}$$

for $r = 1, ..., N$ where $\mathbf{fi_r}$ are fuzzy sets on F and $\mathbf{g_r}$ a fuzzy set on G

and these will be used with the given facts $Xi = \mathbf{f'i}$ to determine the conclusion $Y = \mathbf{g'}$.

Two approaches which we will call the **direct and indirect methods** are applicable in this case of multiple rules. In the direct method the rules are first combined and then the inference is made. In the indirect method inference is made using each rule separately and then the inferences are combined. In the classical logic case both these approaches would give the same solution but this is not true in the fuzzy case or in the combined fuzzy and probabilistic cases.

The fuzzy implication method of inference above in which a fuzzy relation is determined for a rule can be generalised to form a fuzzy relation for all the rules. If Ri is the fuzzy relation for rule i then the relation for all rules is given by

$$R = \bigcap_i Ri$$

and max-min composition is then applied. This corresponds to the direct method. In the indirect method a conclusion $\mathbf{g'i}$ is determined using max-min composition with the fuzzy relation for the ith rule, and the final conclusion is given by

$$\mathbf{g'} = \bigcap_i \mathbf{g'i}$$

For the second approach above the direct method corresponds to using the theory of mass assignments to determine a mass assignment for each rule and combining these mass assignments by finding their meet. This mass assignment represents a family of probability distributions. This family of distributions is updated using the mass assignment for the combined given facts using the minimum relative entropy criteria. This will not be further discussed in this book since it has been described elsewhere (see notes at end of Chapter).

For the indirect method the Fril method of inference is used with each rule to obtain a conclusion of the form

$$\mathbf{g_i}' : (z1 \; z2)$$

These conclusions are combined by a possibilistic averaging process or a mass assignment method given below. For the case of discrete fuzzy sets either method is applicable and in certain special cases, both will give the same solution. For continuous fuzzy sets the averaging process is easier to implement. We will call this indirect approach the **Fril method for multiple rules** since this is used by Fril to derive inferences.

We can extend this without modification to the probabilistic fuzzy rules

$$\text{IF } X1 = \mathbf{fl_r} \; \& \; ... \; \& \; Xn = \mathbf{fn_r} \text{ THEN } Y = \mathbf{g_r} : ((x1 \; x2)(y1 \; y2))$$

for r = 1, ..., N

For the third approach the direct method would form the multiple rule relation using

$$R = \bigcup_i Ri$$

where Ri is the fuzzy relation for a given rule using the Mamdani method. Max-min composition is used for deriving the conclusion.

In the indirect approach the inferences could be combined using

$$\mathbf{g} = \sum_i w_i \mathbf{g_i}$$

where $\mathbf{g_i}$ is the inference from using max-min composition with the Mamdani relation for the ith rule and {wi} is a set of weights. It should be noted that if union is used to combine solutions then the Mamdani direct and indirect approaches are equivalent.

4.5.2 Fuzzy Relation for If ... Then Rules

Let A and B be two variables taking values in the frames of discernment X and Y respectively.

We will consider the fuzzy rule

IF B is **g** THEN A is **f**

where $\mathbf{g} \subseteq Y$ and $\mathbf{f} \subseteq X$ are fuzzy sets defined on Y and X with membership functions

χ_g and χ_f respectively .

This has been discussed and interpreted by several researchers (see notes at end of Chapter).

The statements B is **g** and A is **f** can be interpreted as inducing possibility distributions

$$\Pi_B(u) = \chi_g(u), \text{ for all } u \ \varepsilon \ Y \quad \text{and} \quad \Pi_A(v) = \chi_f(v), \text{ for all } v \ \varepsilon \ X$$

for B and A respectively.

The conditional possibility distribution for A | B can be expressed as

$$\Pi_{A \mid B}(u, v) = \chi_{g \supset f}(u, v) = I(\chi_g(u), \chi_f(v)) \text{ for all } u \ \varepsilon \ Y \text{ and } v \ \varepsilon \ X.$$

where I is a multiple valued logic implication.

We review briefly various interpretations for the fuzzy implication I as discussed in the fuzzy set literature (see notes at end of Chapter).

Three approaches have been considered to interpret the implication I.

(1) This is based on the classical view of implication, i.e. $g \supset f$ is equivalent to $\neg g \vee f$

$$I(u, v) = S(n(u), v) \qquad ; \qquad \text{S implication}$$

where S is a t co-norm standing for a multi-valued disjunction

n is a strong negation

(2) This is based on the idea that implication reflects a partial ordering on propositions such that $I(u, v) = 1$ iff $u \leq v$ and a residuation concept in lattice structures equipped with a semi-group operation T that may stand for conjunction.

$$I(u, v) = \sup(c \ \varepsilon \ [0. \ 1] \mid T(u, c) \leq v) \text{ for all } u \ \varepsilon \ Y \text{ and } v \ \varepsilon \ X. \qquad ; \qquad \text{R implication}$$

where T is a triangular norm.

(3) This is based on viewing the above fuzzy rule as an IF ... THEN ... ELSE statement which leads to a form of implication used in quantum logic.

$$I(u, v) = S(n(u), T(u, v)) \qquad ; \qquad \text{QL implication}$$

where S is a t co-norm, n a strong negation and T is the n-dual of S i.e.

$$T(u, v) = n(S(n(u), n(v)))$$

This arises naturally for the rule of the form

A is **f** IF B is **g** ELSE A is X

which we can express as

$$\Pi_{(A \mid B)}(u, v) = \chi_{(g \times f) \cup (\bar{g} \times X)}(u, v)$$

so that

$$I(u, v) = S(T(\chi_g(u), \chi_f(v)), \ T(n(\chi_g(u)), \chi_X(v))) = S(T(\chi_g(u), \chi_f(v)), \ 1 - \chi_g(u))$$

since $\chi_X(v) = 1$ all $v \varepsilon X$.

We next give some examples of these various forms of implication.

FORM	NAME	TYPE
max(1 - u, v)	Kleene-Dienes	S imp with S = max
		QL imp with S = min(1, u+v)
1 - u + uv	Rechenbach	S imp with S = u+v-uv
min(1, 1 - u + v)	Lukasiewicz	S imp with S = min(1, u+v)
		R imp with T = max(0, u+v-1)
1 if u ≤ v else v	Godel	R imp with T = min
1 if u=0 else max(1, v/a)	Goguen	R imp with T = product
max(1 - u, min(u, v))	Zadeh	QL imp with S = max

4.5.3 Fuzzy Sets with Support Pairs

Suppose that we have an inference of the form

((variable Av is a)) : (x y)

where a is a fuzzy set on Sa

Thus Av is 'a' with probability x, $\bar{a}$ with probability (1 -y) and Sa with probability (y - x)

We can therefore determine

((variable Av is a'))

where a' is the expected fuzzy set and

$\chi_{a'}(t) = x \chi_a(t) + (1 - y) \chi_{\bar{a}}(t) + (y - x)$ where $\bar{a}$ is the complement of a.

Example

If variable Av takes value $\alpha / 1 + \beta / 0.6 + \gamma / 0.2$ defined on F = $\{\alpha, \beta, \gamma, \delta\}$, represented by

((variable Av is [α : 1, β : 0.6, γ : 0.2])) : (0.7 0.9)

then the expected value for Av is $\alpha / 0.9 + \beta / 0.66 + \gamma / 0.42 + \delta / 0.3$ represented by

((variable Av is [α : 0.9, β : 0.66, γ : 0.42, δ : 0.3]))

4.5.4 Fuzzy Control in Fril

The control rules will take the form

$$((\text{control is } g_i)$$

$$(\text{variable } x1 \text{ is } f_{1i}) \dots (\text{variable } xn \text{ is } f_{ni}) \;) : ((a_{1i} \; a_{2i})(b_{1i} \; b_{2i}))$$

for $i = 1, \dots, m$; where g_i is a fuzzy set on G and f_{ij} is a fuzzy set on F.

Specific data will take the form

$$((\text{variable } x1 \text{ is } g_1)) : (c_1 \; d_1)$$

$$. \qquad . \qquad .$$

$$((\text{variable } xn \text{ is } g_n)) : (c_n \; d_n)$$

where $f_{ki} \subset_f F_k$, $g_k \subset_f F_k$, are fuzzy sets.

Often in control problems

$$(a_{1i} \; a_{2i}) = (1 \; 1) \text{ all i}, \qquad (b_{1i} \; b_{2i}) = (0 \; 1) \text{ all i}, \qquad (c_k \; d_k) = (1 \; 1) \text{ all k}.$$

The control value for specific data will be determined by the Fril inference mechanism in conjunction with a method of combining the results from the various rules given below. This method converts the heads with support pairs to heads containing the expected fuzzy sets as given in 4.5.3 and combines the expected fuzzy sets using intersection or an extension of the Dempster method for fuzzy sets.

Fril inference

$$\text{qs}((\text{control is } X))$$

using semantic unification to determine the support pair for $f_{ki} \mid g_k$ will give the results

$$((\text{control is } g_i)) : (x_i \; y_i)$$

for $i = 1, \dots, m$.

We convert these statements to statements with expected fuzzy sets only, i.e.

$$((\text{control is } g'_i))$$

for $i = 1, \dots, m$ and where g'_i is determined as in 4.4.3.

These inferences are combined using the intersection rule or the extended Dempster rule given in Section 4.5.6. Using the intersection rule the final solution is

$$((\text{control is } g))$$

where $g = g_1 \cap \dots \cap g_m$

Another method of combining the inferences is to use a weighted sum of the solutions. Suppose the weighted fuzzy combination is the fuzzy set g; then

$$\chi_g(x) = \sum_i w_i \chi_{g_i}(x) \ ; \ \sum_i w_i = 1$$

The choice of combination rule is left to the user. Fril provides these various possibilities corresponding to different semantics. A small Fril program could be written to allow some other rule of combination. In addition the MIN intersection rule used above can easily be replaced by some other definition of intersection given in Chapter 3.

4.5.5 Example

We will discuss a very simple example involving discrete fuzzy sets so that the calculations are simple. The module for fuzzy control to be described later will illustrate fuzzy control using more realistic examples involving continuous fuzzy sets. This example illustrates the method which can be used for both discrete and continuous fuzzy sets.

This is a variant of an earlier example discussed when dealing with Fril inference from multiple rules.

IF X is **f1** THEN Y is **g1**
IF X is **f2** THEN Y is **g2**
X is **fd**

―――――――――――――

Therefore Y is **g'**

where **f1** = a / 1 + b / 0.7 + c / 0.3 ; F = {a, b, c, d} ; **fd** = a / 0.7 + b / 1 + c / 0.2
    f2 = a / 0.5 + b / 1 + c / 0.1

    g1 = α / 1 + β / 0.5 + γ / 0.1 ; G = {α, β, γ} ; **g2** = α / 0.3 + β / 1
We will determine the inference using both the interval semantic unification and point semantic unification.
The Fril program for this problem is:

```
set(univ1 (a b c d))
set(univ2 (α, β, γ))

(f1{a : 1, b : 0.7, c : 0.3}univ1)
(f2 {a : 0.5, b : 1, c : 0.1} univ1)
(fd {a : 0.7, b : 1, c : 0.2}univ1)

(g1 {α : 1, β : 0.5, γ : 0.1}univ2)
(g2 {α : 0.3, β : 1} univ2)
```

        ((value of y is g1) (value of x is f1))
        ((value of y is g2) (value of x is f2))
        ((value of x is fd)

The query

        qs((value of y is X))

provides solutions

        ((value of y is g1)) : (0.62 1)
        ((value of y is g2)) : (0.57 1)

We can convert these to expected fuzzy sets to give

        ((value of y is {α : 1, β : 0.69, γ : 0.442})
        ((value of y is {α : 0.601, β : 1, γ : 0.43})

so that

        Y is α / 1 + β / 0.69 + γ / 0.442 from the first rule
        Y is α / 0.601 + β / 1 + γ / 0.43 from the second rule

We can combine these two solutions using the intersection rule to give

        Y is α / 0.601 + β / 0.69 + γ / 0.43

using the fuzzy logic MIN rule for intersection.

If the multiplication rule for intersection is used instead then we would obtain

        Y is α / 0.601 + β / 0.69 + γ / 0.19006

We can use other rules of combination such as the extended Dempster rule of combination discussed in the next section or a weighted sum of the individual solutions. For an equal weighting combination, which corresponds to taking the average, the result would be

        Y is α / 0.8005 + β / 0.845 + γ / 0.436

4.5.6 Combining Inferences from Various Rules using the Extended Dempster Rule

        The method of combining inferences using the Dempster rule must be extended when the similar heads contain fuzzy sets. A head in a Fril rule can contain only one fuzzy set. Heads which are the same apart from this fuzzy set can be combined. Suppose we have the inferences

        ((predicate f arguments)) : (x1 x2)
        ((predicate g arguments)) : (y1 y2)

where **f** and **g** are fuzzy sets defined on S.

Let **S** be the fuzzy set with membership function $\chi_S(x) = 1$ for x ϵ S.

The multiplication meet is given by

	$\dfrac{y1}{g}$	$\dfrac{1-y2}{g}$	$\dfrac{y2-y1}{S}$
$\mathbf{f}:x1$	$\mathbf{f}\cap\mathbf{g}$ $x1y1$	$\mathbf{f}\cap\overline{\mathbf{g}}$ $x1(1-y2)$	$\mathbf{f}$ $x1(y2-y1)$
$\overline{\mathbf{f}}:1-x2$	$\overline{\mathbf{f}}\cap\mathbf{g}$ $(1-x2)y1$	$\overline{\mathbf{f}}\cap\overline{\mathbf{g}}$ $(1-x2)(1-y2)$	$\overline{\mathbf{f}}$ $(1-x2)(y2-y1)$
$\mathbf{S}:x2-x1$	$\mathbf{g}$ $(x2-x1)y1$	$\overline{\mathbf{g}}$ $(x2-x1)(1-y2)$	$\mathbf{S}$ $(x2-x1)(y2-y1)$

Cell entries correspond to intersection of corresponding row and column fuzzy sets.

Multiplication Meet

Fig 4.28

In general, $\mathbf{f}\cap\overline{\mathbf{g}}$ and $\overline{\mathbf{f}}\cap\mathbf{g}$ will be non-normalised fuzzy sets, corresponding to some degree of inconsistency. The degree of inconsistency for $\mathbf{f1}\cap\mathbf{f2}$ will be

$$1 - \underset{h}{\mathrm{MAX}}\ \{\chi_{\mathbf{f1}\cap\mathbf{f2}}(h)\}$$

Any cell mass corresponding to a non-normalised fuzzy set is multiplied by the degree of inconsistency for that fuzzy set, i.e.

The mass for any cell with a non-normalised fuzzy set, $\mathbf{f1}\cap\mathbf{f2}$ say, and a mass x becomes

$$x \times \underset{h}{\mathrm{MAX}}\ \{\chi_{\mathbf{f1}\cap\mathbf{f2}}(h)\}$$

The other mass cell entries, x say, are then modified to

$$x\left(1 - \dfrac{\underset{\text{cells with non-normalised fuzzy sets}}{\sum}\ \text{modified masses})}{\underset{\text{cells with normalised fuzzy sets}}{\sum}\ \text{meet masses}}\right)$$

This is a renormalisation process so that the resultant masses add to 1.

Suppose this gives the modified meet

	$\dfrac{y1}{g}$	$\dfrac{1-y2}{g}$	$\dfrac{y2-y1}{S}$
$\mathbf{f}:x1$	$\mathbf{f}\cap\mathbf{g}$ m_{11}	$\mathbf{f}\cap\overline{\mathbf{g}}$ m_{12}	$\mathbf{f}$ m_{13}
$\overline{\mathbf{f}}:1-x2$	$\overline{\mathbf{f}}\cap\mathbf{g}$ m_{21}	$\overline{\mathbf{f}}\cap\overline{\mathbf{g}}$ m_{22}	$\overline{\mathbf{f}}$ m_{23}
$\mathbf{S}:x2-x1$	$\mathbf{g}$ m_{31}	$\overline{\mathbf{g}}$ m_{32}	$\mathbf{S}$ m_{33}

Fig 4.29

The final inference is

((predicate **f*** arguments))

where **f*** is the expected fuzzy set determined from the modified meet cell matrix, i.e.

$$\chi_{f^*}(x) = \sum_{i,j} m_{ij}\, \chi_{f_{ij}}(x) \;;\; x\, \varepsilon\, S$$

where **f$_{ij}$** is the fuzzy set in the ij th cell of the modified meet matrix.

4.5.7 Example using the Extended Dempster Rule of Combination

We use the example of 4.5.5. The two rules give

Y is α / 1 + β / 0.5 + γ / 0.1 : [0.62, 1]

Y is α / 0.3 + β / 1 : [0.57, 1]

Combining using the modified Dempster rule gives the mass assignment

m = α / 0.3 + β / 0.5 : 0.1767, α / 0.3 + β / 1 : 0.2758,

α / 1 + β / 0.5 + γ / 0.1 : 0.3395, {α, β, γ} : 0.2081 since

Fig 4.30

Top numbers in cells are products of the cell row and column masses.

The top left cell entry is multiplied by max membership value of the fuzzy set a / 0.3 + b / 0.5, i.e. 0.5.

The other cell top numbers x are modified using

$$\frac{x(1 - 0.1767)}{(0.2166+0.1634+0.2666)}$$

The expected fuzzy set for the deduction is therefore

Y is α / 0.6833 + β / 0.742 + γ / 0.242

4.5.8 Comparison with Fuzzy Logic Methods

For comparison purposes we will solve the problem given in Section 4.5.5 using various fuzzy logic approaches. Further results and comparisons can be found in the control module. We refer to 4.5.1 and 4.5.2 for the various definitions of approaches used here.

140

IF X is **f1** THEN Y is **g1**

IF X is **f2** THEN Y is **g2**

X is **fd**

_____

Therefore Y is **g'**

where **f1** = a / 1 + b / 0.7 + c / 0.3 ; F = {a, b, c, d} ; **fd** = a / 0.7 + b / 1 + c / 0.2

f2 = a / 0.5 + b / 1 + c / 0.1

g1 = α / 1 + β / 0.5 + γ / 0.1 ; G = {α, β, γ} ; **g2** = α / 0.3 + β / 1

Lukasiewicz Direct Method

We will use the Lukasiewicz rule for fuzzy implication. The implication matrix is found for each rule and combined using intersection. Inference is then made by max-min composition.

The implication fuzzy logic relations for the two rules are

	α / 1	β / 0.5	γ / 0.1
a / 1	1	0.5	0.1
b / 0.7	1	0.8	0.4
c / 0.3	1	1	0.8

First Rule

Fig 4.31

	α / 0.3	β / 1	γ / 0
a / 0.5	0.8	1	0.5
b / 1	0.3	1	0
c / 0.1	1	1	0.9

Second Rule

Fig 4.32

Intersecting these relations gives the intersection relation below. This is used to perform the max-min composition as shown using the data fuzzy set **fd**.

max-min composition

0.8	0.5	0.1
0.3	0.8	0
1	1	0.8

Intersection Relation

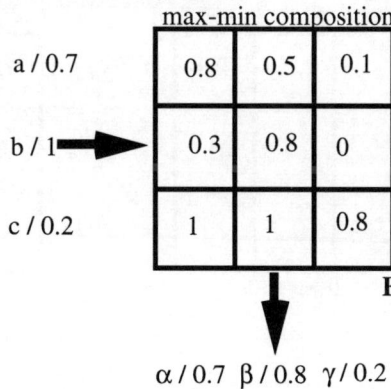

Fig 4.33

a / 0.7

b / 1 ➡

c / 0.2

0.8	0.5	0.1
0.3	0.8	0
1	1	0.8

Fig 4.34

⬇

α / 0.7 β / 0.8 γ / 0.2

The final solution is therefore

Y is α / 0.7 + β / 0.8 + γ / 0.2

Lukasiewicz Indirect Method

The relations of the two rules above are used separately for the max-min composition and the results intersected to give the final solution. The compositions are

max-min composition

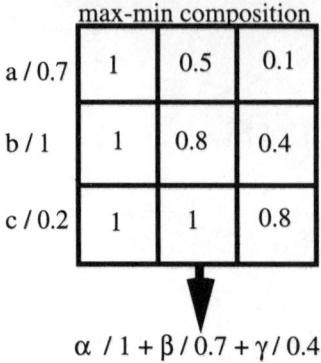

$$\alpha \,/\, 1 + \beta \,/\, 0.7 + \gamma \,/\, 0.4$$

Fig 4.35

max-min composition

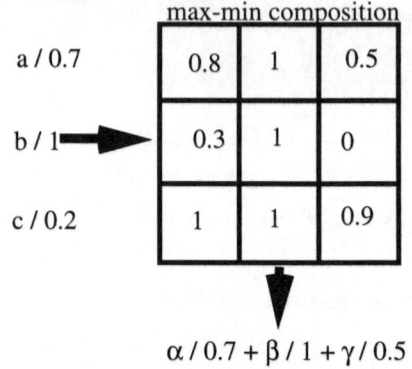

$$\alpha \,/\, 0.7 + \beta \,/\, 1 + \gamma \,/\, 0.5$$

Fig 4.36

Thus we obtain from the two rules the inferences

$$Y \text{ is } \alpha \,/\, 1 + \beta \,/\, 0.8 + \gamma \,/\, 0.4 \quad \text{and} \quad Y \text{ is } \alpha \,/\, 0.7 + \beta \,/\, 1 + \gamma \,/\, 0.5$$

Intersecting these inferences gives the final inference

$$Y \text{ is } \alpha \,/\, 0.7 + \beta \,/\, 0.8 + \gamma \,/\, 0.4$$

Mamdani Direct Method

The implication fuzzy logic relations for the two rules are given below. The min rule is used to define these relations. These are combined using a union operation corresponding to the MAX rule of fuzzy logic. Max-min composition is then performed on the resulting relation to obtain the final inference. The final result is

Y is $\alpha \,/\, 0.7 + \beta \,/\, 1 + \gamma \,/\, 0.1$ since

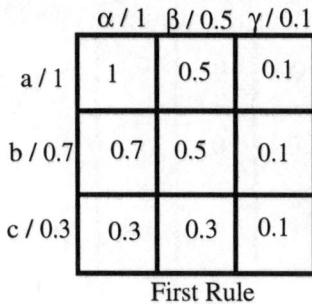

First Rule

Fig 4.37

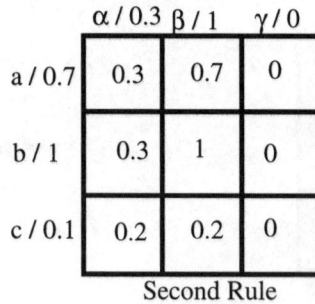

Second Rule

Fig 4.38

Unioning these relations gives the union relation below. This is used to perform the max-min composition as shown using the data fuzzy set **fd**.

142

1	0.7	0.1
0.7	1	0.1
0.3	0.3	0.1

Union Relation
Fig 4.39

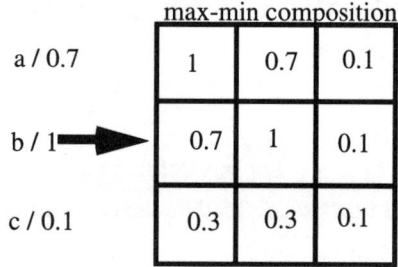

max-min composition

a / 0.7

b / 1 →

c / 0.1

1	0.7	0.1
0.7	1	0.1
0.3	0.3	0.1

↓

α / 0.7 β / 1 γ / 0.1
Fig 4.40

Mamdani Indirect Method

Max-min composition is performed separately on the two relations for the two rules. The results are either averaged or combined as a weighted sum.

The max-min compositions are

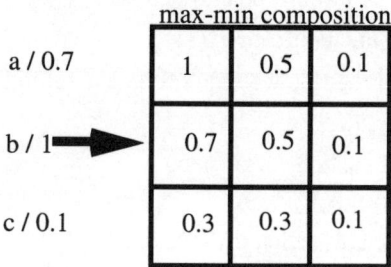

max-min composition

a / 0.7

b / 1 →

c / 0.1

1	0.5	0.1
0.7	0.5	0.1
0.3	0.3	0.1

↓

α / 0.7 β / 0.5 γ / 0.1
Fig 4.41

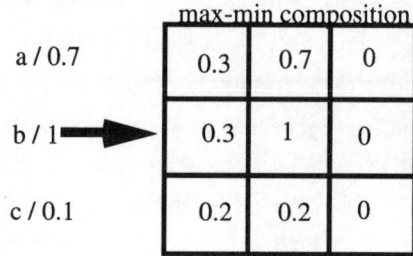

max-min composition

a / 0.7

b / 1 →

c / 0.1

0.3	0.7	0
0.3	1	0
0.2	0.2	0

↓

α / 0.3 β / 1 γ / 0
Fig 4.42

If these results are unioned the final result is

Y is α / 0.7 + β / 1 + γ / 0.1

which is the same as that given above. This will always be the case as discussed in the fuzzy control module (Section 6.5).

If an equal weighting combination is used then the final result is

Y is α / 0.5 + β / 0.75 + γ / 0.05

4.5.9 Precise Values for Fuzzy Control using Mass Assignment Theory

The fuzzy logic rule

IF X_1 is $\mathbf{f_1}$ AND ... AND X_n is $\mathbf{f_n}$ THEN Y is $\mathbf{g}$

where

$\mathbf{f_1}$ ... $\mathbf{f_n}$ are fuzzy sets defined on universes F1, ..., Fn respectively and

$\mathbf{g}$ is a fuzzy set defined on the universe G

is written in Fril as

((value of Y is $\mathbf{g}$)

(value of X_1 is $\mathbf{f_1}$) ... (value of X_n is $\mathbf{f_n}$))

Suppose we know that

(value of X_1 is $\mathbf{f_1'}$)

.   .   .

(value of X_n is $\mathbf{f_n'}$)

then Fril can use this with the rule above to make an inference concerning the value of Y.

We can determine support pairs for the conditional probabilities $\Pr(X$ is $\mathbf{f_i} \mid X$ is $\mathbf{f_i'})$ using interval value semantic unification, or point values for these conditional probabilities using point value semantic unification.

$\Pr(X$ is $\mathbf{f_i} \mid X$ is $\mathbf{f_i'}) \in [\theta_{li}, \theta_{ui}]$ if we use interval semantic unification.

$\Pr(X$ is $\mathbf{f_i} \mid X$ is $\mathbf{f_i'}) = \theta_i$ if we use point semantic unification.

In order to determine the probability for the body of the rule we require some assumption about the dependency of the terms in the body of the rule.

With the independence assumption the probability of the body is given by

$\Pr((\text{value of } X_1 \text{ is } \mathbf{f_1}) ... (\text{value of } X_n \text{ is } \mathbf{f_n})) = \theta_1\theta_2 ... \theta_n$

where θ_i is $\Pr(X$ is $\mathbf{f_i} \mid X$ is $\mathbf{f_i'})$ when point semantic unification is used, and

$\Pr((\text{value of } X_1 \text{ is } \mathbf{f_1}) ... (\text{value of } X_n \text{ is } \mathbf{f_n})) = [\theta_1, \theta_u]$

where

$\theta_1 = \text{MIN}[\theta_1\theta_2 ... \theta_n]$ subject to $\theta_{li} \le \theta_i \le \theta_{ui}$; all i

$\theta_u = \text{MAX}[\theta_1\theta_2 ... \theta_n]$ subject to $\theta_{li} \le \theta_i \le \theta_{ui}$; all i

when interval semantic unification is used.

Using the Fril inference rule

$\Pr((\text{value of } Y \text{ is } \mathbf{g})) \; \varepsilon \; \theta + [0, 1](1-\theta) = [\theta, 1]$

where θ is given by

$\theta = \theta_1\theta_2 ... \theta_n$ for the point semantic unification case

$\theta = \theta_1$ for the interval semantic unification case.

Thus we can conclude the Fril fact

((value of Y is $\mathbf{g}$)) : (θ 1)

where (θ 1) is a support pair representing a probability interval containing the probability of

((value of Y is $\mathbf{g}$)).

This corresponds to a mass assignment

$m = \{(\text{value of Y is } \mathbf{g})\} : \theta, \ \{(\text{value of Y is } G)\} : 1\text{-}\theta$

From this mass assignment we can calculate an expected fuzzy set $\tilde{g}'$ where

$$\mu_{\tilde{g}'}(x) = \theta\mu_{\tilde{g}}(x) + (1 - \theta) \quad \text{for any } x \varepsilon G$$

to give the inference

$$((\text{value of Y is } \mathbf{g}'))$$

The inference is expressed in terms of a fuzzy set $\mathbf{g}'$. For control purposes we require to choose a value from G consistent with this fuzzy set $\mathbf{g}'$. There are various defuzzification algorithms used to perform this task but they are not within the spirit of Fril and we require an approach which is in keeping with the Fril semantics of fuzzy sets.

We interpret the statement

$$((\text{value of Y is } \mathbf{g}'))$$

as defining a possibility distribution over G for the value of Y. This possibility distribution is equivalent to a family of probability distributions given by the mass assignment $m\mathbf{g}'$. From this family of distributions we choose the least prejudiced probability distribution by redistributing the mass associated with a group of elements equally among those elements. For example, suppose we have the fuzzy set

$$\mathbf{f} = a / 1 + b / 0.7 + c / 0.3$$

defined on $F = \{a, b, c, d\}$. The mass assignment associated with this fuzzy set is

$$m\mathbf{f} = \{a\} : 0.3, \ \{a, b\} : 0.4, \ \{a, b, c\} : 0.3$$

This defines a family of probability distributions. A valid distribution can be obtained by redistributing the masses associated with a group of more than one element in some way. For example, we could derive the distribution

$$p_f = a : 0.3, b : 0.4, c : 0.3$$

by allocating 0.4 associated with $\{a, b\}$ to b and 0.3 associated with $\{a, b, c\}$ to c.

The least prejudiced distribution is

$$p_f^{lp} = a : 0.6, b : 0.3, c : 0.1$$

found by allocating 0.4 associated with $\{a, b\}$ equally among a and b and allocating 0.3 associated with $\{a, b, c\}$ equally among a and b and c.

We can generalise this process from the discrete to the continuous case to provide a least prejudiced probability distribution $p_{\tilde{g}'}^{lp}$ associated with the fuzzy set $\mathbf{g}'$. We then calculate the mean of this distribution to give our inferred value, i.e.

$$(\text{value of Y is } \bar{y})$$

where

$$\bar{y} = \int y p_{\tilde{g}'}^{lp}(y) dy$$

An Example using Discrete Fuzzy Sets
IF X is a / 1 + b / 0.7 THEN Y is A / 1 + B / 0.8

X is a / 0.7 + b / 1

where X takes values from {a, b, c} and Y from {A, B, C}

Pr(a / 1 + b / 0.7 | a / 0.7 + b / 1) = 0.805 using point semantic unification

Therefore Y is A / 1 + B / 0.8 : [0.805, 1]

Therefore Mass Assignment m_Y = A : 0.161, {A, B} : 0.644, {A, B, C} : 0.195 giving

Probability distribution over {A, B, C} for Y = A : 0.548, B : 0.387, C : 0.065

A dice example
A dice is thrown and a high score is shown where high is a fuzzy set on {1, 2, ..., 6} defined by

high = 3 / 0.2 + 4 / 0.5 + 5 / 0.9 + 6 / 1

The associated mass assignment is

m_{high} = 6 : 0.1, {5, 6} : 0.4, {4, 5, 6} : 0.3, {3, 4, 5, 6} : 0.2

The least prejudiced probability distribution is therefore

p^{lp}_{high} = 6 : 0.45, 5 : 0.35, 4 : 0.15, 3 : 0.05

The mean value of this distribution is 5.2

We can use the voting model to justify this approach. A representative set of voters when told the dice shows a high score would accept the following as possible scores

voters	1	2	3	4	5	6	7	8	9	10
	6	6	6	6	6	6	6	6	6	6
	5	5	5	5	5	5	5	5	5	
	4	4	4	4	4					
	3	3								

A voter is selected at random and a score chosen from the voter's set of possible scores with equal probability. For example, if voter 4 is chosen then he will randomly select from the set {6, 5, 4}. He will therefore choose 4 with probability 1/3. Thus 4 will be selected with probability

$$Pr(4) = \sum_{i=1}^{10} Pr(4 | \text{voter } i) \, Pr(\text{voter } i) = 1/10\{1/4 + 1/4 + 1/3 + 1/3 + 1/3\} = 0.15$$

Similarly Pr(3) = 0.05, Pr(5) = 0.35 and Pr(6) = 0.45 giving the same probability distribution as above.

If a person is told that the score of a dice throw was high then the probability that the person will select 4 given that he / she must select one value is 0.15 assuming the above fuzzy set for high was derived from a fair representative voting procedure.

4.5.10 Justification for Expected Fuzzy Set

We will now show by a simple example that taking the expected fuzzy set using the support pair associated with the head is consistent with the general mass assignment treatment of fuzzy sets. Generalising from the simple example to the general case is straightforward but messy so we will not present the general case in detail.

Consider the inference

$$f:[\theta,1] \quad \text{where } f = a/1 + b/0.8 + c/0.3 \text{ defined on } \{a,b,c,d\}$$

then

inference is $f:0.7, \{a/1 + b/1 + c/1 + d/1\}:0.3$

corresponding to mass assignment inference

$$0.7(a : 0.2, \{a, b\} : 0.5, \{a, b, c\} : 0.3), 0.3(\{a, b, c, d\} : 1)$$

The expected mass assignment

$$a : 0.14, \{a, b\} : 0.35, \{a, b, c\} : 0.21, \{a, b, c, d\} : 0.3$$

corresponds to the mass assignment from the expected fuzzy set

$$a/1 + b/0.86 + c/0.51 + d/0.3$$

But we can also show that the least prejudiced probability distribution formed from the expected fuzzy sets is the same as the expected least prejudiced probability distribution formed from the least prejudiced distributions from the mass assignment

$$a : 0.2, \{a, b\} : 0.5, \{a, b, c\} : 0.3 \text{ with probability } 0.7$$

and the mass assignment $\{a, b, c, d\} : 1$ with probability 0.3

Least prejudiced distribution for $a : 0.2, \{a, b\} : 0.5, \{a, b, c\} : 0.3$ is

$$a : 0.55, b : 0.35, c : 0.1$$

Least prejudiced distribution for $\{a, b, c, d\} : 1$ is

$$a : 0.25, b : 0.25, c : 0.25, d : 0.25$$

The expected least prejudiced distribution is therefore

$$0.7(a : 0.55, b : 0.35, c : 0.1) + 0.3(a : 0.25, b : 0.25, c : 0.25, d : 0.25)$$
$$= a : 0.46, b : 0.32, c : 0.145, d : 0.075$$

The mass assignment for the expected fuzzy set is

$$a : 0.14, \{a, b\} : 0.35, \{a, b, c\} : 0.21, \{a, b, c, d\} : 0.3$$

which has the following least prejudiced probability distribution

$$a : 0.46, b : 0.32, c : 0.145, d : 0.075$$

4.5.11 An Example using Continuous Fuzzy Sets

Consider the rules

IF X is f_1 THEN Y is g_1

IF X is f_2 THEN Y is g_2

IF X is f_3 THEN Y is g_3

where f_i are defined on the domain [0, 10] and g_i defined on domain [0, 100] and

$$f_1 = [0 : 0, 1 : 1, 4 : 1, 5 : 0]$$

$f_2 = [2:0, 3:1, 6:1, 7:0]$

$f_3 = [4:0, 5:1, 8:1, 9:0]$

and

$g_1 = [0:0, 1:1, 16:1, 25:0]$

$g_2 = [4 \cdot 0, 9:1, 36:1, 49:0]$

$g_3 = [16:0, 25:1, 64:1, 81:0]$

The Fril notation is used for representing fuzzy sets. This is in the form of a list of pairs of the form 'value : membership level'. For the fuzzy set **f** defined on F the value represents the position in F of a vertex of the fuzzy set **f**, and the membership level represents the membership level corresponding to that value. Linear interpolation is used between vertices to calculate membership values.

These fuzzy sets are shown in Fig. 4.43.

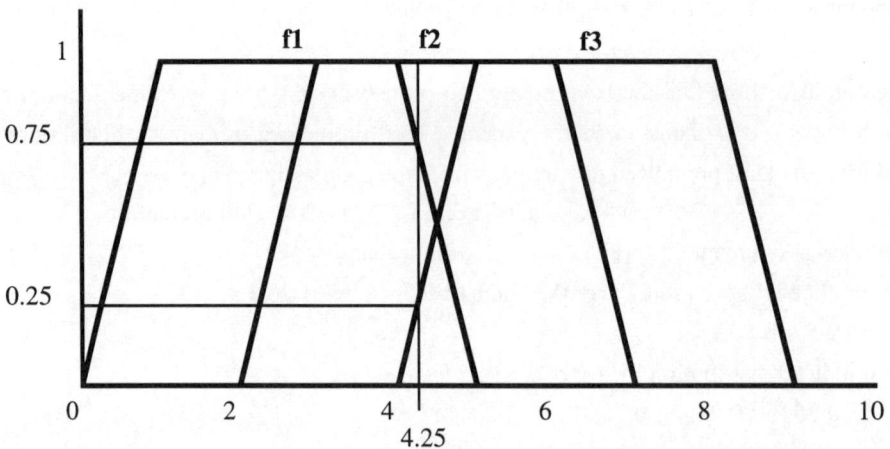

Fig 4.43

If we now have an input

X is 4.25

then using semantic unification we obtain

$Pr(X \text{ is } f_1 \mid X \text{ is } 4.25) = 0.75$

$Pr(X \text{ is } f_2 \mid X \text{ is } 4.25) = 1$

$Pr(X \text{ is } f_3 \mid X \text{ is } 4.25) = 0.25$

These are shown in Fig. 4.43.

Therefore

Y is g_1 : [0.75, 1]

Y is g_2 : [1, 1]

Y is g_3 : [0.25, 1]

The expected fuzzy sets are therefore

Y is $g'_1 = [0.25:0, 1:1, 16:1, 25:0.25, 100:0.25]$

Y is $g'_2 = [4 : 0, 9 : 1, 36 : 1, 49 : 0] = g_2$

Y is $g'_3 = [0 : 0.75, 16 : 0.75, 25 : 1, 64 : 1, 81 : 0]$

These fuzzy sets, with the intersection

$$g' = g'_1 \cap g'_2 \cap g'_3$$

$= [4 : 0, 7.75 : 0.75, 16 : 0.75, 18.25 : 0.8125, 25 : 0.25, 45.75 : 0.25, 49 : 0]$

are shown in Fig 4.44.

The mean value from the least prejudiced probability distribution is 18.15 giving

Y is 18.15

These fuzzy rules came from patches to represent the function $Y = x^2$. The solution can therefore be compared with the exact value of $(4.25)^2 = 18.0625$. This gives surprisingly good results considering the rules we used to model this function. Results will not be as good as this for many points, e.g. for $x = 4.75$ these fuzzy rules gives $y = 28.6865$ while the true solution is $y = 22.5625$. We can also use fuzzy sets as the input. For example $x = $ approx$4.25 = [4.0 : 0, 4.25 : 1, 4.5 : 0]$ gives the solution $y = 19.1567$. We could more carefully choose the fuzzy sets and rules to give accurate answers over a wider range of x values. Below we show this using triangular fuzzy sets and 6 rules (Fig 4.45).

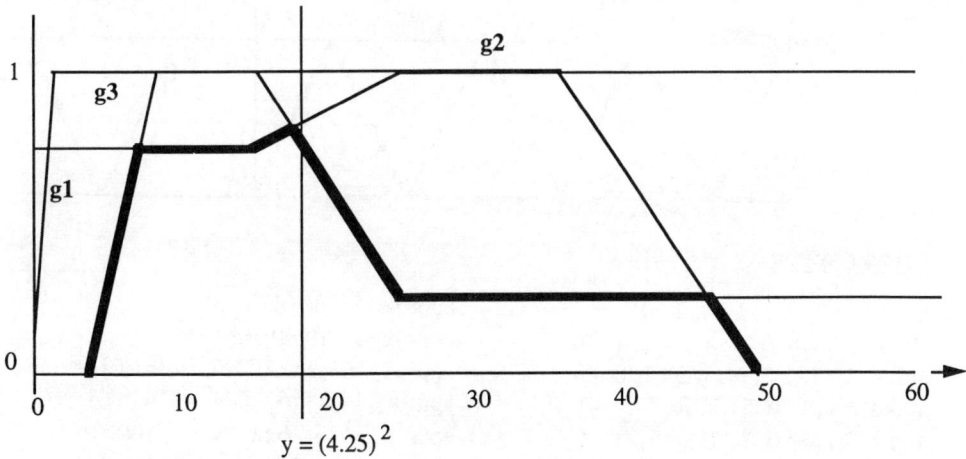

$y = (4.25)^2$

Fig 4.44

149

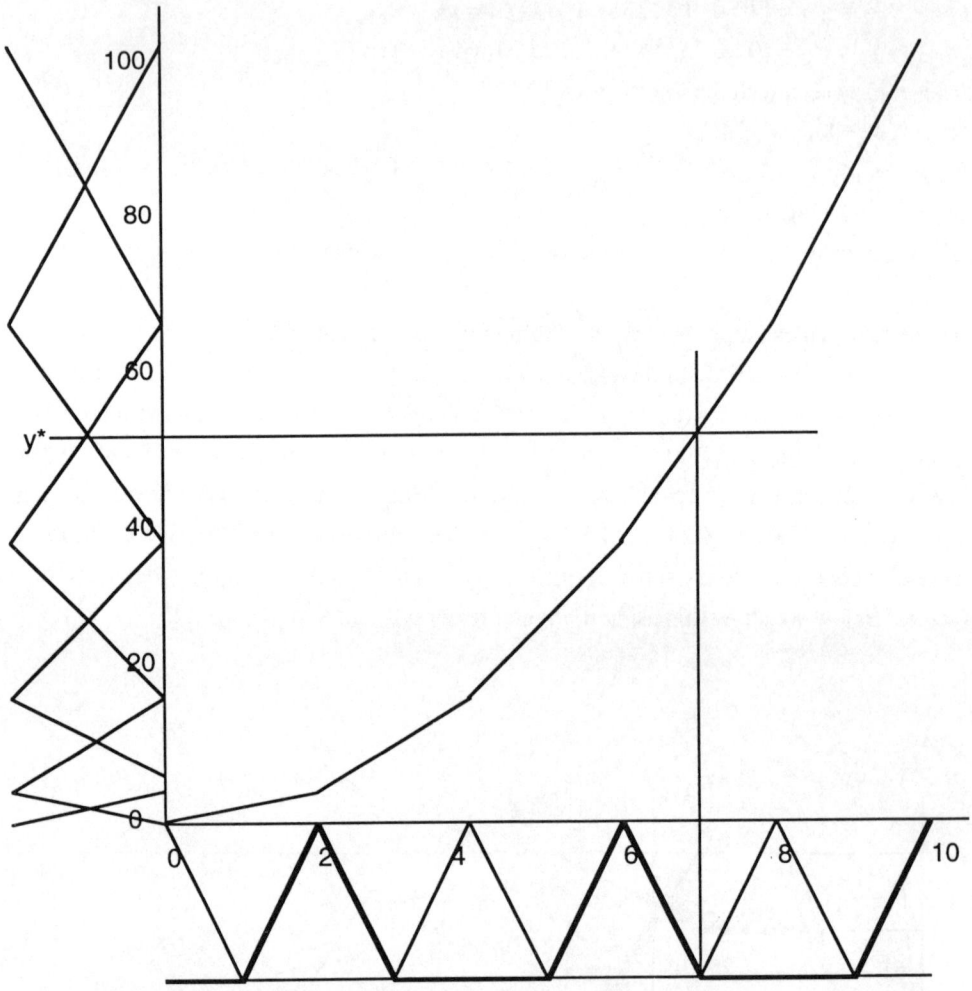

FUZZY SETS

about_0 = [0 : 1, 1 : 1, 2 : 0]
about_2 = [0 : 0, 1 : 1, 3 : 1, 4 : 0]
about_4 = [2 : 0, 3 : 1, 5 : 1, 6 : 0]
about_6= [4 : 0, 5 : 1, 7 : 1, 8 : 0]
about_8= [6 : 0, 7 : 1, 9 : 1, 10 : 0]
about_10 = [8 : 0, 9 : 1, 10 : 1]

x*

approx_0 = [0 : 1, 4 : 0]
approx_4 = [0 : 0, 4 : 1, 16 : 0]
approx_16 = [4 : 0, 16 : 1, 36 : 0]
approx_36 = [16 : 0, 36 : 1, 64 : 0]
approx_64 = [36 : 0, 64 : 1, 100 : 0]
approx_100 = [64 : 0, 100 : 1]

RULES

IF X is about_0 THEN Y is approx_0
IF X is about_2 THEN Y is approx_4
IF X is about_4 THEN Y is approx_16

IF X is about_6 THEN Y is approx_36
IF X is about_8 THEN Y is approx_64
IF X is about_10 THEN Y is approx_100

FIG.4.45

An alternative set of rules and mixed trapezoidal / triangular fuzzy sets is shown in Fig 4.46.

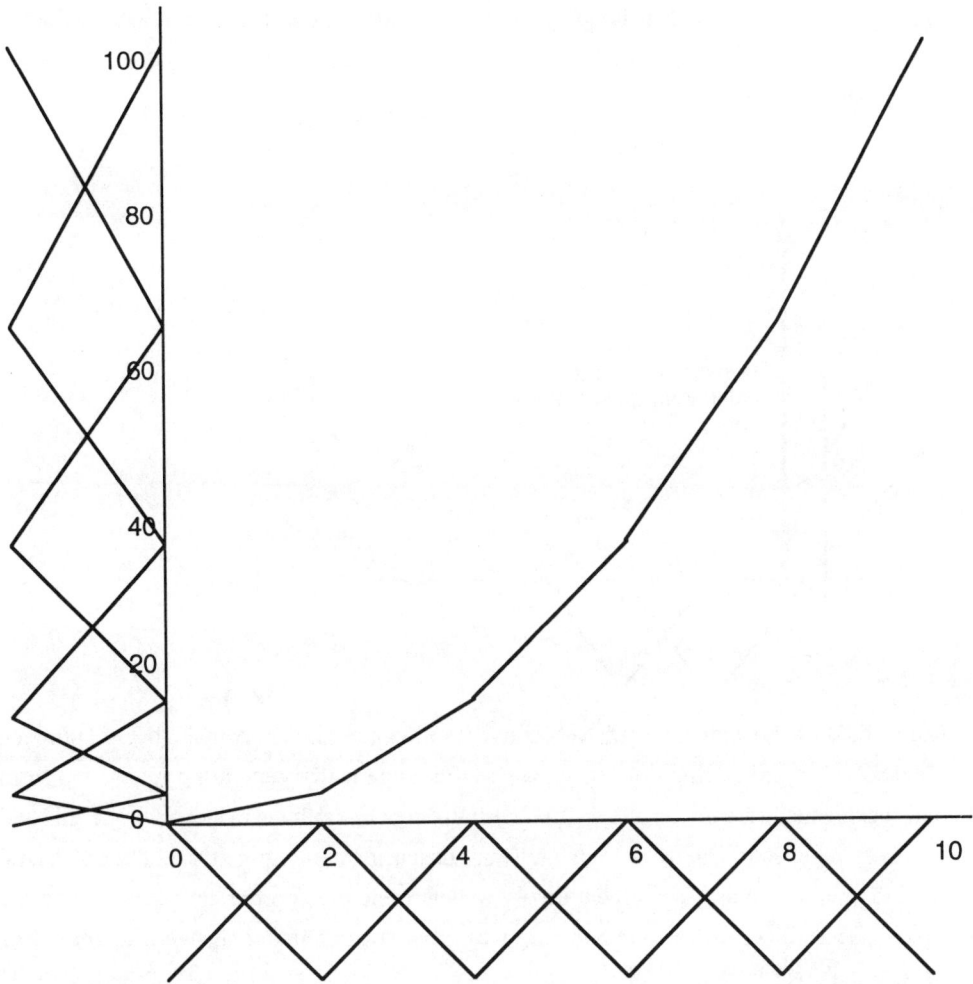

Fig 4.46

FUZZY SETS

about_0 = [0 : 1, 2 : 0]
about_2 = [0 : 0, 2 : 1, 4 : 0]
about_4 = [2 : 0, 4 : 1, 6 : 0]
about_6= [4 : 0, 6 : 1, 8 : 0]
about_8= [6 : 0, 8 : 1, 10 : 0]
about_10 = [8 : 0, 10 : 1]

approx_0 = [0 : 1, 4 : 0]
approx_4 = [0 : 0, 4 : 1, 16 : 0]
approx_16 = [4 : 0, 16 : 1, 36 : 0]
approx_36 = [16 : 0, 36 : 1, 64 : 0]
approx_64 = [36 : 0, 64 : 1, 100 : 0]
approx_100 = [64 : 0, 100 : 1]

RULES

IF X is about_0 THEN Y is approx_0   IF X is about_6 THEN Y is approx_36
IF X is about_2 THEN Y is approx_4   IF X is about_8 THEN Y is approx_64
IF X is about_4 THEN Y is approx_16   IF X is about_10 THEN Y is approx_100

Greater accuracy can be achieved if, having obtained the final expected fuzzy set, we then determine the mean value of the least prejudiced probability distribution using a domain

151

equal to the range of Y values lying in the support of the union of the two fuzzy sets on the Y axis used for the fuzzy interpolation. For example, for the point x = 4.25 we use the domain shown in Fig 4.47.

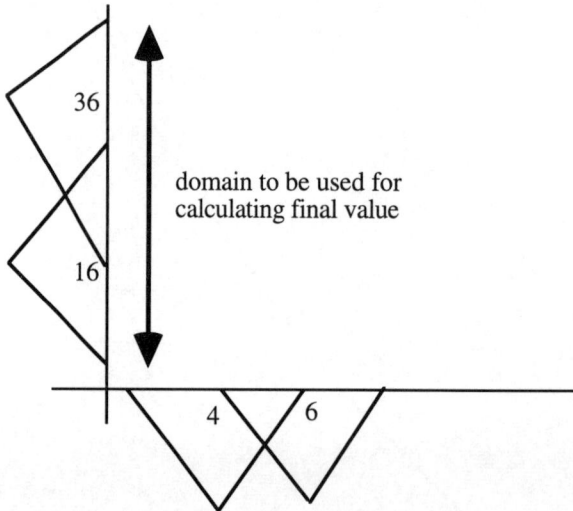

Fig 4.47

The method of choosing the fuzzy sets above is only approximate. A much better approach is described in 4.6.9 which discusses ways of automatically generating fuzzy sets from data. The methods are applicable for finding fuzzy sets for both the evidential logic rule and the fuzzy logic rule. The fuzzy sets are first chosen for the output space. The automatic method then uses mass assignment theory to determine the appropriate fuzzy sets on the input spaces. Fuzzy sets found in this way give overall better answers to the cases discussed above.

Example

We illustrate the Fril method for fuzzy control with the well-known truck example discussed in detail by [Kosko 92]. A truck with the centre of the rear at (x, y) is to be backed up into a loading dock at (x_f, y_f). For a serious study of this problem we would use methods described later for the automatic generation of fuzzy sets from data to obtain the fuzzy sets for the rules. The fuzzy rules used here are from [Kosko 92] in a simplified version of the problem.

The Fril program is

```
set (dom1 0 100)
set (dom2 -100 280)                            ; define domains
set (dom3 -30 30)

(le [0:0 0.0001:1 10:1 35:0] dom1)
(lc [30:0 40:1 50:0] dom1)
```

152

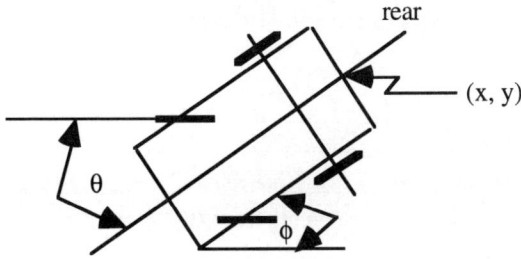

Fig 4.48

```
(ce [45:0 50:1 55:0] dom1)                    ; define fuzzy sets on X
(rc [50:0 60:1 70:0] dom1)
(ri [65:0 90:1 99.9999:1 100:0] dom1)

(rb [-100:0 -45:1 10:0] dom2)
(ru [-10:0 35:1 60:0] dom2)
(rv [45:0 67.5:1 90:0] dom2)
(ve [80:0 90:1 100:0] dom2)                   ; define fuzzy sets on PHI
(lv [90:0 112.5:1 135:0] dom2)
(lu [120:0 155:1 190:0] dom2)
(lb [170:0 225:1 280:0] dom2)

(nb [-30:0 -29.9999:1 -15:0] dom3)
(nm [-25:0 -15:1 -5:0] dom3)
(ns [-12:0 -6:1 0:0] dom3)
(ze [-5:0 0:1 5:0] dom3)                       ; define fuzzy sets on THETA
(ps [0:0 6:1 12:0] dom3)
(pm [5:0 15:1 25:0] dom3)
(pb [18:0 29.9999:1 30:0] dom3)

((theta is ps)(phi is rb)(x is le))
((theta is pm)(phi is rb)(x is lc))
((theta is pm)(phi is rb)(x is ce))
((theta is pb)(phi is rb)(x is rc))
((theta is pb)(phi is rb)(x is ri))

((theta is ns)(phi is ru)(x is le))
((theta is ps)(phi is ru)(x is lc))
((theta is pm)(phi is ru)(x is ce))
((theta is pb)(phi is ru)(x is rc))
((theta is pb)(phi is ru)(x is ri))
```

((theta is nm)(phi is rv)(x is le))
((theta is ns)(phi is rv)(x is lc))
((theta is ps)(phi is rv)(x is ce))
((theta is pm)(phi is rv)(x is rc))
((theta is pb)(phi is rv)(x is ri))   ; define rules

((theta is nm)(phi is ve)(x is le))
((theta is nm)(phi is ve)(x is lc))
((theta is ze)(phi is ve)(x is ce))
((theta is pm)(phi is ve)(x is rc))
((theta is pm)(phi is ve)(x is ri))

((theta is nb)(phi is lv)(x is le))
((theta is nm)(phi is lv)(x is lc))
((theta is ns)(phi is lv)(x is ce))
((theta is ps)(phi is lv)(x is rc))
((theta is pm)(phi is lv)(x is ri))

((theta is nb)(phi is lu)(x is le))
((theta is nb)(phi is lu)(x is lc))
((theta is nm)(phi is lu)(x is ce))
((theta is ns)(phi is lu)(x is rc))
((theta is ps)(phi is lu)(x is ri))

((theta is nb)(phi is lb)(x is le))
((theta is nb)(phi is lb)(x is lc))
((theta is nm)(phi is lb)(x is ce))
((theta is nm)(phi is lb)(x is rc))
((theta is ns)(phi is lb)(x is ri))

((phi is 50.0))
((x is 50.0))

For the inputs given in the program, Fril gives the answer
Fuzzy set [-30:0.6 5:0.6 10.6731:0.826923 12:0.777778 20.5556:0.777778
                                25:0.6 30.0024:0.6 30.006:0]
which, using mass assignment theory to obtain the least prejudiced probability distribution,
defuzzifies to 12.9646 over sub-domain (0 25).
We illustrate the Fril calculation diagrammatically:

154

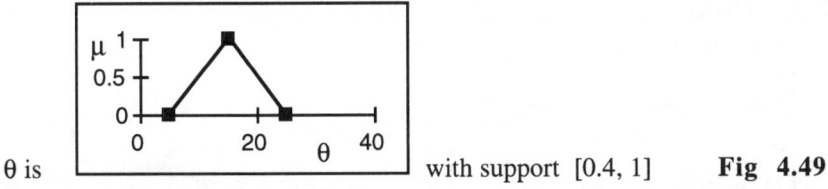

θ is ... with support [0.4, 1]   **Fig 4.49**

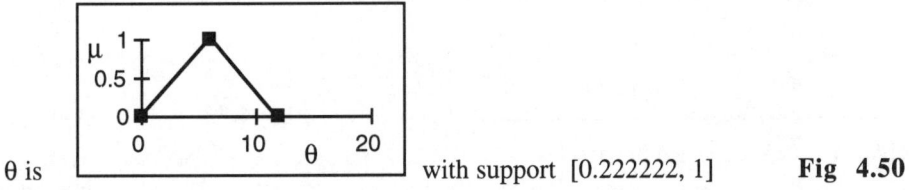

θ is ... with support [0.222222, 1]   **Fig 4.50**

giving expected fuzzy sets

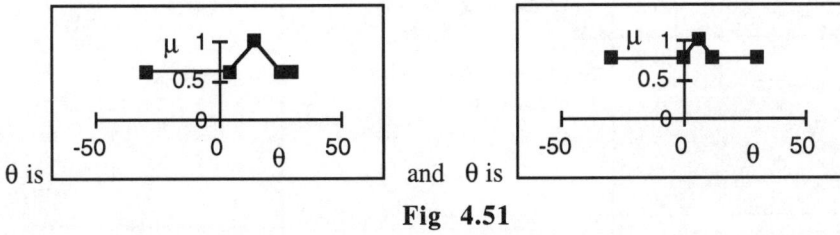

θ is ... and θ is ...

Fig 4.51

Intersecting and defuzzifying using mass assignment theory gives the result in Fig 4.52. In general, four expected fuzzy sets will be produced by Fril.

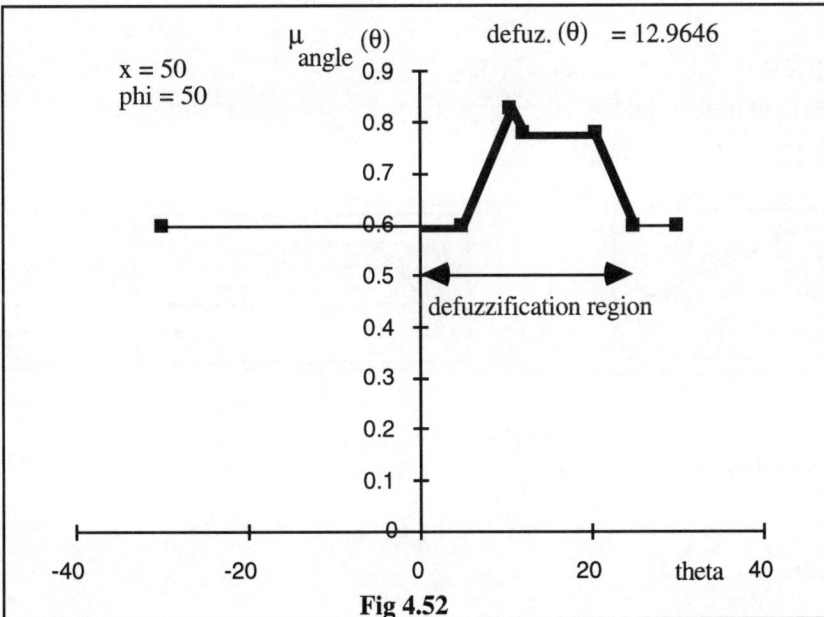

Fig 4.52

155

We can also use fuzzy set inputs. For example, with inputs

((phi is [49:0 50:1 55:0]))

((x is 50.0))

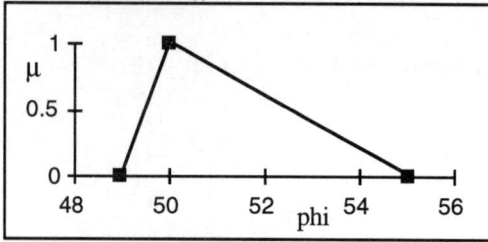

Fig 4.53

we obtain the final expected fuzzy set

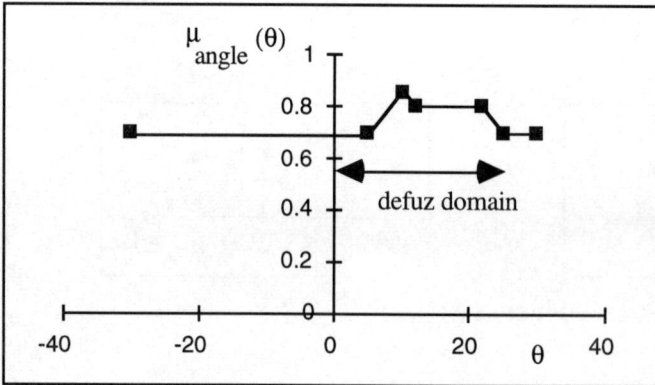

Fig 4.54

and from the least prejudiced distribution we obtain a mean of

12.3441

We can fuzzify both inputs. If we use the inputs

((phi is [49:0 50:1 55:0]))

((x is [45:0 47:1 50:1 52:0))

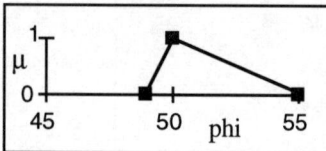 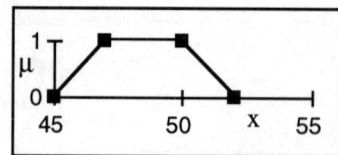

Fig 4.55

we obtain the final expected fuzzy set

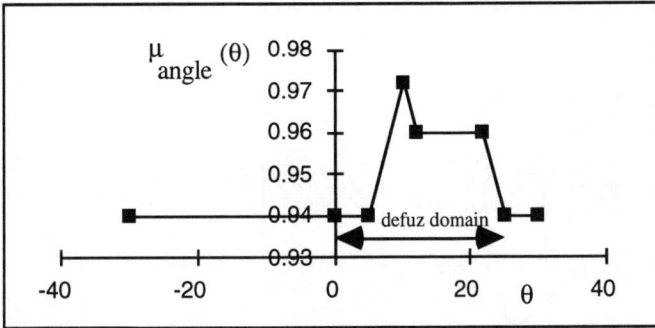

Fig 4.56

giving the final value

$$\theta = 12.1745$$

4.5.12   Case-based Reasoning Fuzzy Interpolation-type Problems

Suppose we have a database of values of a particular function for various argument values. For the function $Y = F(X1, ..., Xn)$ we have a database of the form

F	X1	X2	X3		Xn

Suppose we wish to find the value of F for a point $(x_1, ..., x_n)$ which is not in the database. We determine those points $\mathbf{x_i} = (x_{1i}, ..., x_{ni})$ in the database which are near to the point $\mathbf{x}$. A point $\mathbf{x_i}$ is near if it satisfies $\|\mathbf{x_i} - \mathbf{x}\| \, \xi \, \varepsilon$ where $\| \ \|$ is some distance metric. We form a rule for each of the points $\mathbf{x_i}$ of the form

Y is approx_F($\mathbf{x_i}$) IF X1 is approx_x_{1i} & ... & Xn is approx_x_{ni}

The fuzzy sets approx_F($\mathbf{x_i}$), approx_x_{1i}, ..., approx_x_{ni} are defined as triangular fuzzy sets with membership 1 at F($\mathbf{x_i}$), x_{1i}, ... , x_{ni} respectively. For example

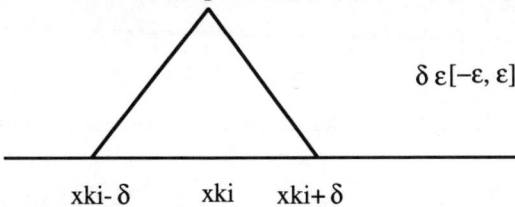

$$\delta \, \varepsilon [-\varepsilon, \varepsilon]$$

xki- δ xki   xki+ δ

Fig 4.57

We illustrate this with a function of two variables example.

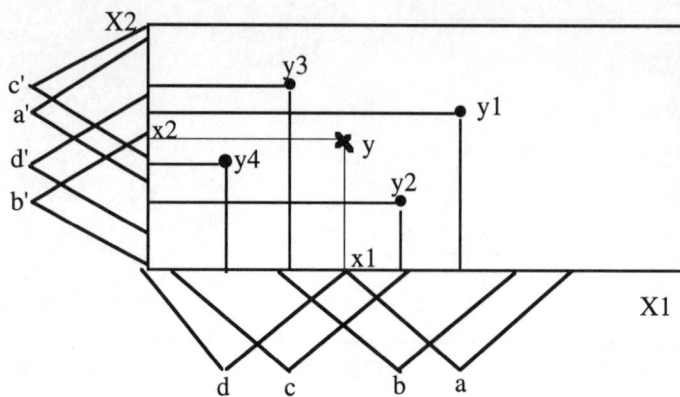

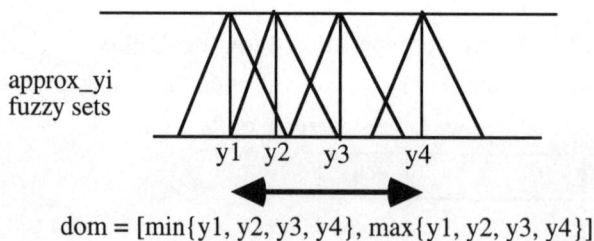

$$\text{dom} = [\min\{y1, y2, y3, y4\}, \max\{y1, y2, y3, y4\}]$$

Fig 4.58

The rules are

        Y is **y1** IF X1 is **a** & X2 is **a'**

        Y is **y2** IF X1 is **b** & X2 is **b'**

        Y is **y3** IF X1 is **c** & X2 is **c'**

        Y is **y4** IF X1 is **d** & X2 is **d'**

The facts are

        X1 is x1

        X2 is x2

The Fril inference from each rule will be the following expected fuzzy sets

        Y is **y1**

        Y is **y2**

        Y is **y3**

        Y is **y4**

Intersecting these fuzzy sets gives

        Y is **y1** ∩ **y2** ∩ **y3** ∩ **y4** = **y**

The mean of the least prejudiced distribution for **y** is determined using the domain dom shown in Fig. 4.58. This gives the final solution Y is $\bar{y}$.

158

This method will provide reasonable accuracy and will be suitable for many applications. If the database contains sufficient data then optimal fuzzy rules can be derived using methods discussed in 4.6.9.

This forms part of the fuzzy data browser discussed in 4.6.7. The approach has many applications and combined with other parts of Fril modules can be used for AI case-based reasoning problems.

Example

We will apply the fuzzy data browser approach to determine the value of F(x) for x = 5.25 given the database

x	F(x)
0	0
2	4
4	16
6	36
8	64
10	100

Fig 4.59

Nearest points for (x=5.25, F(x)) are (x, F(x)) = (4, 16) and (x, F(x)) = (6, 36)

We therefore use the fuzzy sets and rules

Domains are:

        set (domx 0 10)

        set (domy 0 100)

Fuzzy sets are

        (about_4 [2:0 4:1 6:0] domx)

        (about_6 [4:0 6:1 8:0] domx)

        (approx_16 [0:0 16:1 36:0] domy)

        (approx_36 [16:0 36:1 56:0] domy)

Rules are

        Y is approx_16 IF X is about_4

        Y is approx_36 IF X is about_6

If we use the fact

        X is 5.25

Fril provides the solution Y is 27.249. This solution is accurate to about 1%.

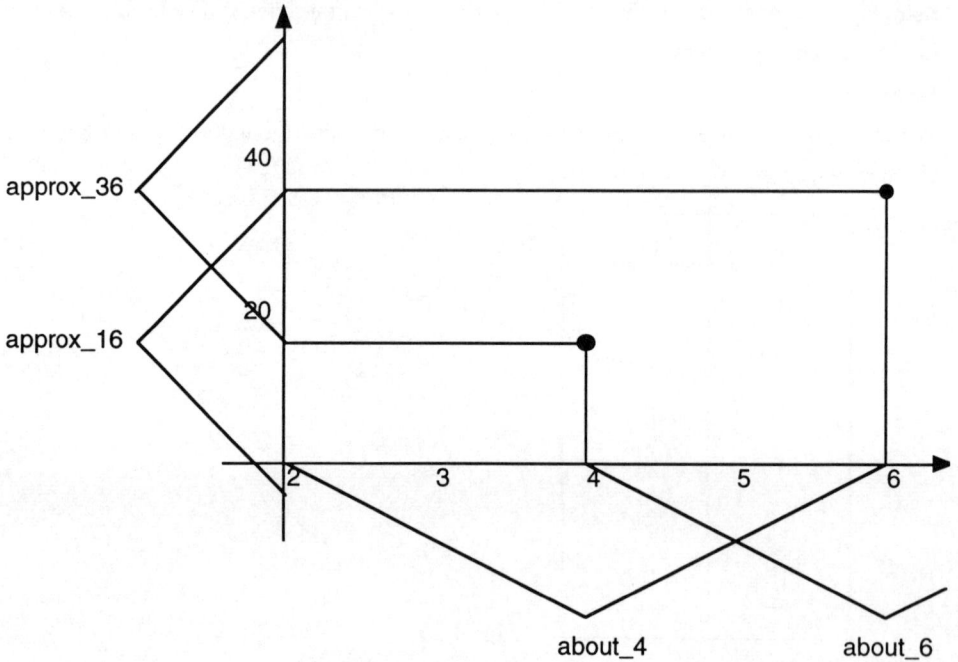

Fig 4.60

If we add an additional point to the database, namely x = 5, F(x) = 25, then we have rules and fuzzy sets given by

about_4 = [2:0, 4:1, 6:0]   approx_16 = [0:0, 16:1, 32:0]
about_5 = [3:0, 5:1, 7:0]   approx_25 = [9:0, 25:1, 41:0]
about_6 = [4:0, 6:1, 8:0]   approx_36 = [20:0, 36:1, 52:0]

Y is approx_16 IF X is about_4
Y is approx_25 IF X is about_5
Y is approx_36 IF X is about_6
sol_dom = [16, 36]

shown in Fig 4.61.

160

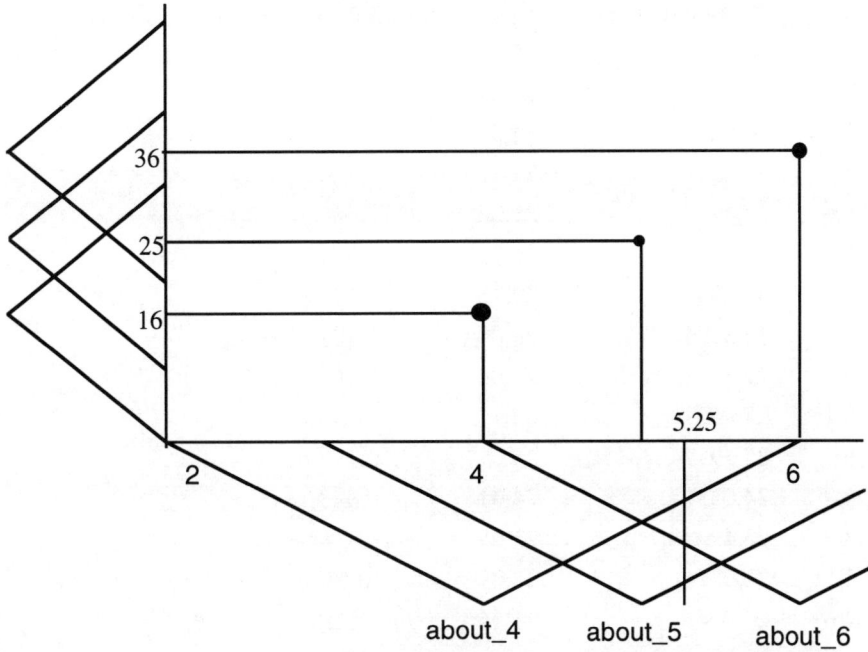

Fig 4.61

and these give the solution

F(5.25) = 27.287

which is slightly more accurate than for the case above.

    We will obtain better accuracy by using narrower fuzzy sets on the x domain. Below we use a Fril program to determine an interpolated value of F(x) for any x in range [4, 6] using the points (4 16) and (6 36) from the database.

       set (domx 0 10)

       set(domy 0 100)

       (about_4 [2:0 4:1 6:0] domx)

       (about_6 [4:0 6:1 8:0] domx)

       (approx_16 [10:0 16:1 22:0] domy)

       (approx_36 [30:0 36:1 42:0] domy)

       ((y is approx_16)(x is about_4))

       ((y is approx_36)(x is about_6))

to obtain the results given in the table below and in Figs 4.62 - 4.65.

x	Predicted F(x	F(x)	Error
6	36	36	0
5.9	35.3895	34.81	0.5795
5.8	34.9244	33.64	0.7495
5.7	34.2541	32.49	1.7641
5.6	33.42	31.36	2.06
5.5	32.6133	30.25	2.3633
5.4	31.8057	29.16	2.6457
5.3	30.3774	28.09	2.2874
5.2	29.6	27.04	2.56
5.1	27.9669	6.01	1.9569
5	25.1999	25	0.1999
4.9	24.0331	24.01	0.0231
4.8	22.4	23.04	-0.64
4.7	21.5774	22.09	-0.5126
4.6	20.0343	21.16	-1.1257
4.5	19.28	20.25	-0.97
4.4	18.62	19.36	-0.74
4.3	17.6424	18.49	-0.8476
4.2	17.0578	17.64	-0.5822
4.1	16.4842	16.81	-0.3258
4	16	16	0

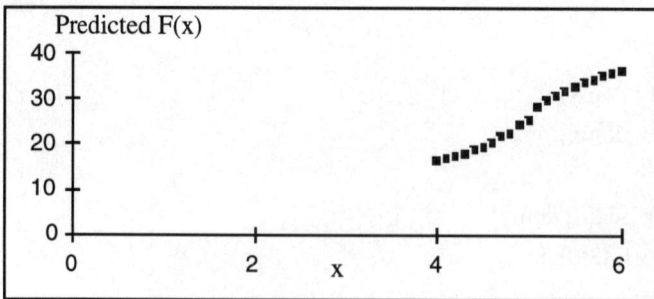

Fig 4.62

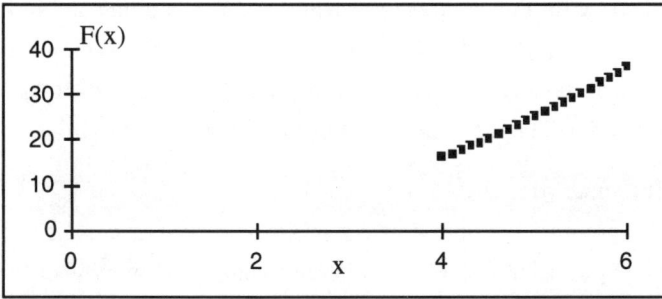

Fig 4.63

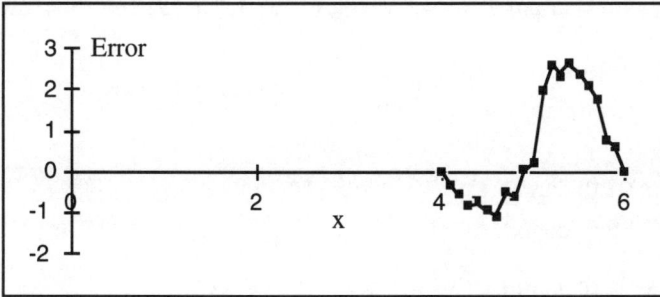

Fig 4.64

We can compare this with the error from using linear interpolation between points (4, 16) and (6, 36)

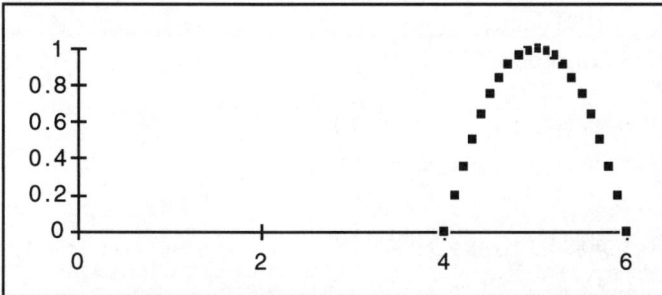

Fig 4.65

An improvement in the fuzzy logic performance can be achieved using the following Fril program

```
set (domx 0 10)
set(domy 0 100)

(about_4 [1:0 3:1 5:1 7:0] domx)
(about_6 [3:0 5:1 7:1 9:0] domx)

(approx_16 [0:0 16:1 32:0] domy)
(approx_36 [20:0  36:1 52:0] domy)

((y is approx_16)(x is about_4))
((y is approx_36)(x is about_6))
```

163

The fuzzy sets used on the X space for this program are such that for all x points in [4, 6] the head of one of the rules will have a support of [1, 1] and the defuzzification region will be the support of this fuzzy set. The error will not be 0 at x=5 but at approx 4.8. It will also be 0 at x=4 and x=5. The error at 5 will be the same as that given by linear interpolation.

Function of two variables example

We can use the following Fril program to approximate $z = F(x, y) = x^2 + y^2$ for $4 \xi x \xi 6$ and $4 \xi y \xi 6$. This is equivalent to using fuzzy interpolation to answer a query about the value of z, given a database with near points (4, 4, 32), (6, 6, 72), (4, 6, 52) and (6, 4, 52).

```
set (domx 0 10)
set(domy 0 10)                              ; domain definitions
set (domz 0 150)

(x_about_4 [1:0 3:1 5:1 7:0] domx)
(x_about_6 [3:0 5:1 7:1 9:0] domx)

(y_about_4 [1:0 3:1 5:1 7:0] domy)          ; Fuzzy Sets
(y_about_6 [3:0 5:1 7:1 9:0] domy)

(approx_32 [0:0 32:1 64:0] domz)
(approx_72 [40:0 72:1 104:0] domz)
(approx_52 [20:0 52:1 84:0] domz)

((z is approx_32) (x is x_about_4)(y is y_about_4))
((z is approx_72) (x is x_about_6)(y is y_about_6))
((z is approx_52) (x is x_about_4)(y is y_about_6))          ; Rules
((z is approx_52) (x is x_about_6)(y is y_about_4))
```

A table showing values with errors computed using this program is shown below.

x	y	z	Value from Program	Error
4	4	32	32	0
4	4.5	36.25	36.5297	-0.2797
4	5	41	42.3849	-1.3849
4	5.5	46.25	48.384	-2.134
4	6	52	52	0
4.5	4.5	40.5	37.0182	3.4818
4.5	5	45.25	45.0443	0.2057
4.5	5.5	50.5	52	-1.5
4.5	6	56.25	55.616	0.634
5	5	50	52	-2
5	5.5	55.25	58.9557	-3.7057
5	6	61	61.6151	-0.6151
5.5	5.5	60.5	66.9818	-6.9818
6	6	72	72	0

Support pairs can be associated with the fuzzy logic rules to tune the rules to give greater accuracy. For example, the following rules provide better accuracy than those above.

((z is approx_32) (x is x_about_4) (y is y_about_4)) : ((1 1)(0 0))

((z is approx_72) (x is x_about_6) (y is y_about_6)) : ((0.94 1)(0 0))

((z is approx_52) (x is x_about_4) (y is y_about_6))

((z is approx_52) (x is x_about_6) (y is y_about_4))

Using these rules we obtain 61.9269 for F(x, y) for x = y = 0.55, an error of 1.4269. With the Fril program

set (domx 0 10)

set(domy 0 10)

set (domz 0 88)

(x_about_4 [2:0 4:1 6:0] domx)

(x_about_6 [4:0 6:1 8:0] domx)

(y_about_4 [2:0 4:1 6:0] domy)

(y_about_6 [4:0 6:1 8:0] domy)

(approx_32 [16:0 32:1 48:0] domz)

(approx_72 [56:0 72:1 88:0] domz)

(approx_52 [36:0 52:1 68:0] domz)

((z is approx_32) (x is x_about_4)(y is y_about_4))

((z is approx_72) (x is x_about_6)(y is y_about_6))

((z is approx_52) (x is x_about_4)(y is y_about_6))

((z is approx_52) (x is x_about_6)(y is y_about_4))

we obtain the results

x	y	z	Fuzzy(x, y)	Error
4	4	32	32	0
4	4.5	35.36	35.0102	0.3498
4	5	41	42	-1
4	5.5	46.25	48.9898	-2.7398
4	6	52	52	0
4.5	4.5	40.5	43.3162	-2.8162
4.5	5	45.25	49.3469	-4.0969
4.5	5.5	50.5	52.0355	-1.5355
4.5	6	56.25	55.0102	1.2398
5	5	50	51.9991	-1.9991
5	5.5	55.25	54.653	0.597
5	6	61	62	-2
5.5	5.5	60.5	60.6837	-0.1837
5.5	6	66.25	68.9897	-2.7397
6	6	72	72	0

4.5.13   A Note on Multiple Rules

Multiple rules are treated separately to form the expected fuzzy set inferences in each case. These expected fuzzy sets are then intersected to obtain a final expected fuzzy set. The least prejudiced probability distribution and the mean value are then found as described above.

When the sets of values that variables can take in the factual information contain the corresponding sets in the rules, treating rules separately will give only a very approximate solution.

Example

Universe for Y = {a, b, c, d, e}   ;   Universe for X = {c1, c2, c3}

$\qquad$ Y = {a, b} IF X = c1

$\qquad$ Y = {c, d} IF X = c2

$\qquad$ X = {c1, c2}

First rule gives Y = {a, b, c, d, e}

Second rule gives Y = {a, b, c, d, e}

Intersecting gives Y = {a, b, c, d, e}

The rules are written slightly differently but are IF THEN rules.

Logically it follows that we can use other rules from which the correct solution can be inferred.

Example

From the above example, the following rule is valid

$\qquad$ Y = {a, b, c, d} IF X = {c1, c2}

so that we can infer

$\qquad$ Y = {a, b, c, d}

In general from the rules

$\qquad$ Y is S1 IF X is T1

$\qquad$ Y is S2 IF X is T2

where S1, S2 are subsets of the universe for Y and T1, T2 are subsets of the universe for X, we can logically deduce the rule

$\qquad$ Y is (S1 $\cup$ S2) IF X is (T1 $\cup$ T2)

The compositional approach to inference does not suffer from this difficulty.

Example

From above the relation for the first rule is

	a	b	c	d	e
c1	1	1	0	0	0
c2	1	1	1	1	1
c3	1	1	1	1	1

$R1 =$ (table above)

Fig 4.66

	a	b	c	d	e
c1	1	1	1	1	1
c2	0	0	1	1	0
c3	1	1	1	1	1

$R2 =$ (table above)

Fig 4.67

Intersecting gives

	a	b	c	d	e
c1	1	1	0	0	0
c2	0	0	1	1	0
c3	1	1	1	1	1

$R1 \cap R2 =$ (table above)

Fig 4.68

from which we can make the inference

$$Y = \{a, b, c, d\}$$

This is equivalent to forming the new rule above.

This idea can be generalised to apply to fuzzy rules with supports.

It is necessary to find new rules as we did in the pure logic case above. For this purpose we use the theorem:

From the rules

Y is s_1 IF X is t_1

Y is s_2 IF X is t_2

where s_1, s_2 are fuzzy subsets of the universe for Y and t_1, t_2 are fuzzy subsets of the universes for X

we can deduce the rule

Y is $(s_1 \cup s_2)$ IF X is $(t_1 \cup t_2)$ where $\cup$ is a fuzzy union.

Example

Universe for Y is $\{a, b, c, d, e\}$;   Universe for X is $\{c1, c2, c3\}$

$Y = a / 1 + b / 0.5$ IF $X = c1 / 1 + c2 / 0.2$

$Y = c / 1 + d / 0.8$ IF $X = c2 / 1 + c3 / 0.3$

$X = c1 / 1 + c2 / 0.7 + c3 / 0.1$

A combined rule is

$Y = a / 1 + b / 0.5 + c / 1 + d / 0.8$ IF $X = c1 / 1 + c2 / 1 + c3 / 0.3$

We now have the equivalent problem

$Y = a / 1 + b / 0.5$ IF $X = c1 / 1 + c2 / 0.2$

$Y = c / 1 + d / 0.8$ IF $X = c2 / 1 + c3 / 0.3$

$Y = a / 1 + b / 0.5 + c / 1 + d / 0.8$ IF $X = c1 / 1 + c2 / 1 + c3 / 0.3$

$X = c1 / 1 + c2 / 0.7 + c3 / 0.1$

Using the first rule with the data given for X and the semantic unification method gives

$Y = a / 1 + b / 0.5 : [0.42, 1]$

giving

$Y = a / 1 + b / 0.79 + c / 0.58 + d / 0.56 + e / 0.56$

Using the second rule with the data given for X and the semantic unification method gives

$Y = c / 1 + d / 0.8 : [0, 1]$

giving

$Y = a / 1 + b / 1 + c / 1 + d / 1 + e / 1$

Using the third rule with the data given for X and the semantic unification method gives

$Y = a / 1 + b / 0.5 + c / 1 + d / 0.8 : [0.93, 1]$

giving

$Y = a / 1 + b / 0.535 + c / 1 + d / 0.814 + e / 0.07$

Intersecting these three results gives the final inference

$Y = a / 1 + b / 0.535 + c / 0.58 + d / 0.58 + e / 0.07$

The compositional method using Lukasiewicz implication gives

R1 =

	a	b	c	d	e
c1	1	0.5	0	0	0
c2	1	1	0.8	0.8	0.8
c3	1	1	1	1	1

Fig 4.69

R2 =

	a	b	c	d	e
c1	1	1	1	1	1
c2	0	0	1	0.8	0
c3	0.7	0.7	1	1	0.7

Fig 4.70

Intersecting gives

R1 ∩ R2 =

	a	b	c	d	e
c1	1	0.5	0	0	0
c2	0	0	0.8	0.8	0
c3	0.7	0.7	1	1	0.7

Fig 4.71

From this relation and the data for X we obtain the following inference for Y,

$Y = a / 1 + b / 0.5 + c / 0.7 + d / 0.7 + e / 0.1$

Theoretically one uses all given rules with all possible combination rules which will include rules obtained by combining rules to date including newly formed rules. In practice one can write a Fril program to choose only those combinations which will give a restricted inference. If the necessary support in the semantic unification of the body given the data is 0, then the resulting inference will be unrestricted. An efficient Fril program can detect when this will occur without having to carry out numerous numeric computations. If the body is defined over a multidimensional space, only one of the terms in the body is required to have a necessary support of 0 to provide an unrestricted inference.

If the body of the rule contains more than one term the method of combining is as given below.

Generalisation

Consider the more general statements

Y is s_1 IF X_1 is $t_1 \wedge X_2$ is u_1

Y is s_2 IF X_1 is $t_2 \wedge X_2$ is u_2

where s_1, s_2 are fuzzy subsets of the universe for Y and t_1, t_2 are fuzzy subsets of the universe for X_1 and u_1, u_2 are fuzzy sets on the universe for X_2.

We can combine these statements to form an additional rule:

Y is $s_1 \cup s_2$ IF $(X_1$ is $t_1 \wedge X_2$ is $u_1) \vee (X_1$ is $t_2 \wedge X_2$ is $u_2)$

which can be re-written as

Y is $s_1 \cup s_2$ IF (X_1, X_2) is $t_1 \times u_1 \vee (X_1, X_2)$ is $t_2 \times u_2$

which can be re-written as

Y is $s_1 \cup s_2$ IF (X_1, X_2) is $(t_1 \times u_1 \cup t_2 \times u_2)$

Example

Let $s_1 = y_a / 1 + y_b / 0.3$; $s_2 = y_a / 0.2 + y_b / 1$;   Universe for Y is $\{y_a, y_b, y_c\}$

Let $t_1 = x_{1a} / 1 + x_{1b} / 0.1$; $t_2 = x_{1a} / 0.2 + x_{1b} / 1$;   Universe for X_1 is $\{x_{1a}, x_{1b}, x_{1c}\}$

Let $u_1 = x_{2a} / 1 + x_{2b} / 0.6$; $u_2 = x_{2a} / 0.4 + x_{2b} / 1$;   Universe for X_2 is $\{x_{2a}, x_{2b}, x_{2c}\}$

From the rules:

1. Y is $y_a / 1 + y_b / 0.3$ IF X_1 is $x_{1a} / 1 + x_{1b} / 0.1 \wedge X_2$ is $x_{2a} / 1 + x_{2b} / 0.6$

2. Y is $y_a / 1 + y_b / 0.7$ IF X_1 is $x_{1a} / 0.2 + x_{1b} / 1 \wedge X_2$ is $x_{2a} / 0.4 + x_{2b} / 1$

we can form the rule

3. Y is $y_a / 1 + y_b / 0.7$

       IF (X_1, X_2) is $(x_{1a}, x_{2a}) / 1 + (x_{1a}, x_{2b}) / 0.6 + (x_{1b}, x_{2a}) / 0.4 + (x_{1b}, x_{2b}) / 1$

These three rules can be used with data

       $(X1, X2) = (x_{1a}, x_{2a}) / 1 + (x_{1b}, x_{2b}) / 1$

Rules 1 and 2 give $Y = y_a / 1 + y_b / 1 + y_c / 1$

Rule 3 gives Y is $Y = y_a / 1 + y_b / 0.7$

Intersecting gives $Y = y_a / 1 + y_b / 0.7$

The compositional method using Lukasiewicz implication gives the same solution.

The requirement of finding the cross product of all fuzzy sets in the body of the rule prior to taking the union of the bodies to be combined presents certain computational inefficiencies. Rules should be constructed so that combining in this way is avoided as far as possible. The compositional method suffers from similar computational inefficiencies. This is avoided if the data given to the rules are more precise than the fuzzy sets occurring in the body of the rules.

The example nevertheless shows how using a fuzzy extension of the logic programming format does not restrict one in any way from obtaining the correct inferences.

Example

We will use the method for combining rules in the following problem

IF X is **f1** THEN Y is **g1**
IF X is **f2** THEN Y is **g2**
X is **fd**

Therefore Y is **g'**

where
f1 = a / 1 + b / 0.7 + c / 0.3 ; **f2** = a / 0.5 + b / 1 + c / 0.1 ; **fd** = a / 0.7 + b / 1 + c / 0.2
all defined on F = {a, b, c, d}, and
g1 = α / 1 + β / 0.5 + γ / 0.1 ; **g2** = α / 0.3 + β / 1
all defined on G = {α, β, γ}.
We use the additional rule
    IF X is (**f1** $\cup$ **f2**) THEN Y is (**g1** $\cup$ **g2**)
i.e. we use the additional rule
    IF X is (a / 1 + b / 1 + c / 0.3) THEN Y is (α / 1 + β / 1 + γ / 0.1)
Fril uses this additional rule to obtain the solution
    Y is α / 1 + β / 1 + γ / 0.1 : [0.86, 1]
which is equivalent to
    Y is α / 1 + β / 1 + γ / 0.226
When this is intersected using the MIN rule with the results obtained from the first two rules, we obtain
    Y is (α / 0.601 + β / 0.69 + γ / 0.226)
This can be compared with the result
    Y is α / 0.601 + β / 0.69 + γ / 0.43)
obtained if we do not use the additional rule.

4.6 EVIDENTIAL LOGIC

4.6.1 Evidential Logic Rule

We introduce evidential support logic as an alternative to deductive logics for artificial intelligence applications which require a means of inductive and abductive reasoning. It is therefore suitable for such applications as case-based reasoning in which concepts are defined in terms of examples illustrating the concept rather than by means of necessary and sufficient conditions. The logic allows generalisation from examples to new situations. The body of a rule does not have to be fully supported in order that the conclusion of the rule be supported. If most of the terms in the body are supported then the head of the rule will have a high support. The terms in the body of the rule can be given different degrees of importance and these weights are taken into account when determining the support for the body. The support of the body is a function of the linear weighted sum of the individual term supports. This function can be chosen to give various interpretations for the body which can vary between the extremes of a conjunction of terms to a disjunction of terms. Intermediate interpretations can be thought of as softer forms of conjunction and softer forms of disjunction. Applications to handwritten character recognition have been shown to be successful.

The logic is derived for support pairs rather than single supports. One reason for deriving an evidential logic in terms of support pairs is to allow for partial matchings of terms. If we ask if a given object satisfies a certain concept which is defined in terms of a set of features then we can ask how many of these features are satisfied by the object. The answer might be that some are satisfied, some are not and no decision can be made concerning the others. This gives rise to a support for the match and a support against the match but these supports will not add up to 1. Thus a support pair is needed to represent the support for the match.

The form of representation allows the inclusion of fuzzy sets. Fuzzy sets are also important for generalisation in inductive reasoning. The fuzzification of precise values of features for a given example of a concept allows a new set of examples to represent the concept. This will be a fuzzy set, so there will be an ordering for this set of similar cases.

Partial matching in terms of fuzzy sets is achieved using the notion of semantic unification.

4.6.2 An Example to Illustrate Syntax

The syntax for an evidential logic rule has been discussed in 4.1.2 and takes the form

$$(h \ (evlog \ f \ (c1 \ n1 \ \ c2 \ n2 \ ... \ cn \ nn) \ ) \ ) : ((x1 \ x2)(y1 \ y2))$$

The following is an evidential reasoning program

(f [0 : 0, 1 : 1])
(good {a : 1, b : 0.7, c : 0.4})
(recent [1970 : 0, 1982 : 1, 1992 : 1])
((book X is worth reading)
      (evlog f ((famous writer is author of X) 0.2
               (key words of text of X relevant) 0.25
               (gives impression from scan through of X ok) 0.3
               (review of X good) 0.1
               (lngth of X suitable) 0.05
               (publication date of X recent) 0.1))   ) : (0.9 1)
(not_too_big [150 : 0, 200 : 1, 250 : 1, 300 : 0])
(approx_250 [240 : 0, 250 : 1, 260 : 0])
(fairly_good {a : 0.3, b : 1, c : 0.5})
((lngth of X suitable)
  (conj   (last page number of X is not_too_big) (page size of X normal))
) : ((1 1)(0 0))
((famous writer is author of mind)) : (0.8 1)
((key words of text of mind relevant)) : (0.6 0.8)
((gives impression from scan through of mind ok)) : (0.7 0.9)
((review of mind fairly_good))
((publication date of mind 1980))
((last page number of mind is approx_250))
((page size of mind normal)) : 0.7

We could ask the query
    qs ((book mind is worth reading))

The evidential support logic system would return a support pair for the fact that the book "mind" is worth reading. To determine this support pair the system determines a support for each of the terms of the body of the main rule and combines these in some way. The rule for this combination is part of the evidential support theory and takes account of the weights given in each term of the body and the function given as the first entry of the body. If this entry is missing then a default function is used. The support pairs for each of the terms are either found as facts or determined using other rules. These other rules may be evidential support rules involving ordinary support rules. An example of an ordinary support rule is the one defining suitable length, (lngth).

4.6.3 Inference from a Single Evidential Logic Rule

For the evidential logic rule

(h (evlog f (c1 w1 c2 w2 ... cn wn)) : ((x1 x2)(y1 y2))

Fril evaluates a support pair $(\alpha_i \beta_i)$ for each term (ci) of the body of the rule. These support pairs are either obtained directly from the program data or evaluated using semantic unification if (ci) contains a fuzzy set. If (ci) is of the form (... fi ...) where fi is a fuzzy set on Fi, and a program data clause (c'i) exists of the same form as (ci) except that fi is replaced by f'i where f'i is a fuzzy set on Fi, then the semantic unification fi | f'i determines $(\alpha_i \beta_i)$.

The evidential logic rule is then replaced by

(h body) : ((x1 x2)(y1 y2))

where

(body) : $(\alpha \ \beta)$

and $(\alpha \ \beta)$ is determined from $\{(\alpha_i \beta_i)\}$, $\{w_i\}$ and f.

The basic Fril inference rule is then used to determine the support for the head, i.e. the inference

(h) : $(\gamma_1 \ \gamma_2)$

In what follows we determine

(1) how to compute $(\alpha \ \beta)$ from the list of support pairs $\{(\alpha_i \beta_i)\}$, the function f, and the weights $\{w_i\}$

(2) how to determine $(\gamma_1 \ \gamma_2)$ from $(\alpha \ \beta)$ and ((x1 x2)(y1 y2)).

Let f = S(x) where

$$S(x) : [0, 1] \rightarrow [0, 1]$$

This will be further discussed below.

The evidential support logic determines $(\alpha \ \beta)$ using

$$(\alpha \ \beta) = (\ S(\sum_i^n w_i\alpha_i) \quad S(\sum_i^n w_i\beta_i) \ )$$

The choice of S(x) determines the nature of this combining operation.

The inference $(\gamma_1 \ \gamma_2)$ is computed using the Fril rule of inference, namely

$$\gamma_1 = \begin{pmatrix} x1.\beta + y1.(1 - \beta) \text{ if } x1 \leq y1 \\ x1.\alpha + y1.(1 - \alpha) \text{ if } x1 > y1 \end{pmatrix} \qquad \gamma_2 = \begin{pmatrix} x2.\alpha + y2.(1 - \alpha) \text{ if } x2 \leq y2 \\ x2.\beta + y2.(1 - \beta) \text{ if } x2 > y2 \end{pmatrix}$$

173

A **special case** of this inference rule occurs when

$$((x1\ x2)(y1\ y2)) = ((\theta 1\ \ \theta 2)\ (0\ 1))$$

The inference then gives the support pair $(\gamma_1\ \gamma 2)$ for the head where

$$\gamma_1 = \alpha\theta 1 \ \ ; \ \ \gamma 2 = \alpha\theta 2 + (1 - \alpha)$$

This special case can be used for case-based reasoning. A more detailed treatment of case-based reasoning has been given by Baldwin.

The combining function S determines the interpretation of the body and hence the interpretation of the overall inference.

For example, if $w_i = 1/n$, (all i), and S(x) is defined as

$$S(x) = \begin{pmatrix} 1 \text{ if } x = 1 \\ 0 \text{ otherwise} \end{pmatrix}$$

then the body is equivalent to a logic conjunction of terms.

In this case $(\alpha\ \beta) = (1\ 1)$ or $(\alpha\ \beta) = (0\ 0)$ or $(\alpha\ \beta) = (0\ 1)$ depending on whether the support pairs $(\alpha_i\ \beta_i) = (1\ 1)$, (all i), or $(\alpha_i\ \beta_i) = (0\ 0)$ for some i, or $\alpha_i = 0$ for some i and

$$\beta_i = 1, \text{ (all i), respectively.}$$

If $w_i = 1/n$, (all i), and S(x) is defined as

$$S(x) = \begin{pmatrix} 1 \text{ if } x \geq 1/n \\ 0 \text{ if } x = 0 \end{pmatrix}$$

then the body, when the support pairs are $(0\ 0)$ or $(1\ 1)$, is equivalent to a logic disjunction of terms. If the support pairs are not restricted in this way, then the body is supported with support pair $(1\ 1)$ if the lower supports of the terms of the body sum to at least 1. This is a generalisation of the disjunction interpretation.

To understand more clearly the various interpretations of S(x) we first consider the body to consist of two terms of equal weighting, each having a single support x1, x2 or equivalently support pairs (x1 x1) and (x2 x2). Thus x = (x1 + x2) / 2. Since x1 and x2 are probabilities of the terms being true, then the probability that both terms are true, i.e. that the conjunction is true lies in the interval [x1 + x2 - 1 $\vee$ 0, x1 $\wedge$ x2].

Now, for a given x, the probability of the conjunction of body terms, where x1 + x2 = 2x, lies in the interval [2x - 1 $\vee$ 0, x].

More generally for x = (x1 + ... + xn) / n, then the probability of the conjunction of the body lies in the interval [(nx - (n - 1)) $\vee$ 0, x] which we can represent graphically in Fig. 4.72.

Similarly the probability of the disjunction of the body terms lies in the interval [x, nx $\wedge$ 1], shown graphically in Fig. 4.73.

Combining these interpretations gives the graphical representation in Fig. 4.74.

174

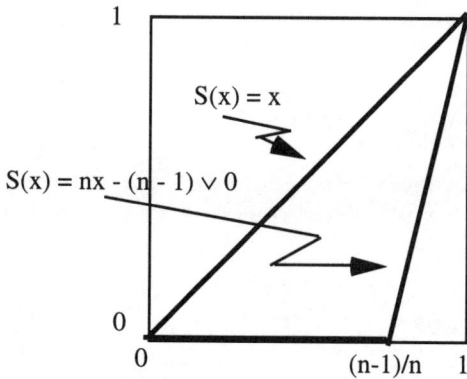

Fig 4.72

We can call this a conjunction region. Lower parts of the region correspond to more pessimistic interpretations of conjunction and the upper parts to more optimistic interpretations of conjunction.

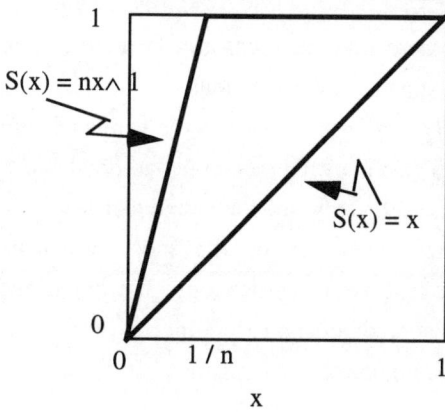

Fig 4.73

We can call this a disjunction region. Lower parts of the region correspond to more pessimistic interpretations of disjunction and the upper parts to a more optimistic interpretations of disjunction.

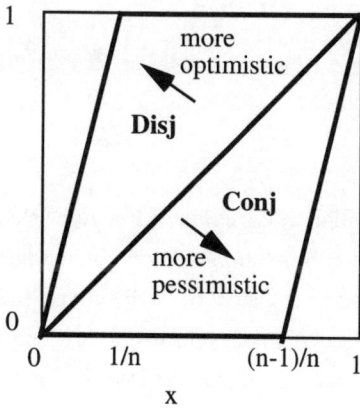

Fig 4.74

The independent conjunction and disjunction, namely

$$S(x) = x^2 \text{ and}$$
$$S(x) = 2x - x^2$$

lie in the conjunction and disjunction regions respectively.

In the limit, as n tends to ∞, we obtain the hard logic conjunction interpretation for the lower curve and the hard logic interpretation for disjunction for the upper curve.

175

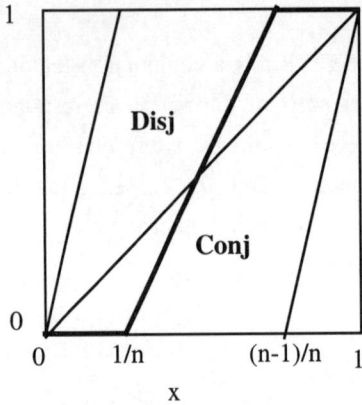

Fig 4.75

An S function such as that given in Fig. 4.75 behaves as a disjunction for $x > 0.5$ and as a conjunction for $x < 0.5$.

When the weights are not equal, then these interpretations can be modified to represent weighted conjunction and weighted disjunction interpretations.

We can also interpret S(x) as follows. The argument value x is the weighted sum of the necessary or possible degrees of match given by the semantic unifications. S depends only on this one argument and has no knowledge of the individual semantic unifications. To obtain the most pessimistic disjunction or the most optimistic conjunction we allocate x equally among all the semantic unifications. To obtain the most optimistic disjunction or the most pessimistic conjunction we allocate x to as few semantic unifications as possible, maximising the number of total mismatches.

More generally one can choose S as

$$S(x) = \begin{cases} 0 \text{ if } x \leq a \\ \dfrac{x-a}{b-a} \text{ if } a < x < b \\ 1 \text{ if } x \geq b \end{cases} \quad ; \quad 0 \leq a \leq b \leq 1$$

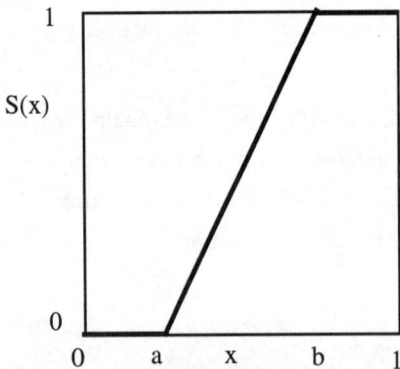

Fig 4.76

which is similar to the logistic function used in neural net computations. A suitable choice of parameters a and b will give the appropriate degree of optimism for high values of x and pessimism for low values of x.

4.6.4 Example

We will consider the book example given by the program in Section 4.6.2 concerning estimating whether to read a given book.

Body support pair calculation :

	Support	Weight
famous_writer is author of mind	[0.8 1]	0.2
key_words of text of mind relevant	[0.6 0.8]	0.25
scan_through of mind gives good impression	[0.7 0.9]	0.3
review of mind good	[0.55 0.79]	0.1
length of mind suitable	[0.6 0.7]	0.05
publication date of mind recent	[0.8333 0.8333]	0.1

using

Semantic Unification	Support
good I fairly good	[0.55 0.79]
recent I 1980	[0.8333 0.8333]

where the support pair for length of mind suitable is calculated as

Semantic Unification	Support
not_too_big I approx_250	[0.9 1]
normal	[0.7 0.7]
giving (conj ...)	[0.6 0.7]

Therefore the support pair for the body is given by

$$(\alpha \ \beta) = (S(0.6833) \ \ S(0.8673)) = (0.6744 \ \ 0.9497)$$

Thus the head of the rule has support pair

$$(\gamma 1 \ \gamma 2) = ((0.9)(0.6744 \ \ 1) = (0.6069 \ \ 1)$$

4.6.5 Combining Inferences from Several Rules

Several rules may be relevant to answering a given query. Each rule is used separately to obtain a support pair for the head of the rule. Let this be denoted by

X is **fi** : $(\gamma i1 \ \gamma i2)$ where **fi** is a fuzzy set on F ;   i = 1, .., n ;

These are combined as given in Sections 4.3, 4.5.4 and 4.5.6. The method of combining depends on the type of query and the form of the heads of the rules. The predicate in the head of an evidential logic set of rules can be defined as a dempster predicate in which case the dempster rule or extended rule will be used to combine the inferences.

The inference rule for a given rule of the form

$$((h) \ (evlog \ f \ (\ (c1) \ n1 \ (c2) \ n2 \ ... \ (cn) \ nn) \ ) \ ) : (\theta1 \ \theta2)$$

where the body support pair is found to be $(\alpha \ \beta)$

can be represented by the neural net type partition

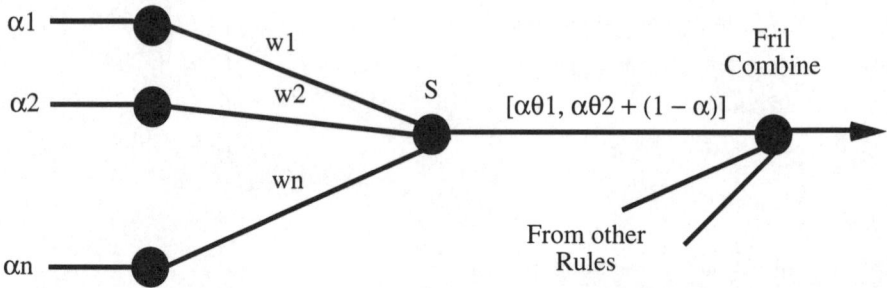

Fig 4.77

The input neurons pass the necessary supports of the partial feature matchings to the combining neuron. The combining neuron combines the necessary feature matchings support as a weighted sum of inputs passed through the S filter to give a support pair as output. This is passed to the inference combining neuron which combines the inferences from different rules according to the Fril method of combining inferences.

We could use neural net technology for this problem by choosing the weights {wi} by a learning algorithm. The strength support pair $(\theta1, \theta2)$ could also be chosen in this way.

We should note that other forms of knowledge representation can be used to describe the prototypical examples. For example, conceptual graphs as given by Sowa in which referent fields can take fuzzy sets as values are also suitable. A similar theory of evidential support logic to that given here is derivable, and a neural net-like architecture given. What value is gained in the understanding of neural net architecture in such mappings is an open question. We could also use causal nets. Relating symbolic representations and inference methods to those of neural net theory may give new concepts and understanding for the development of intelligent computer systems.

4.6.6 Example of Case-based Reasoning

This is a simple example of a practical type of problem. More sophisticated versions can be applied to such tasks as character recognition and scene analysis. The features in the body of the main rule are defined in terms of other rules using the evidential support logic inference rule.

A line drawing representation for the definition of a half moon is given in Fig. 4.78. The pixels are grouped into regions. For each region the number of pixels that the upper line goes through, the number of pixels the lower line goes through and the number of pixels contained in the regions part of the figure are calculated. The number of corners the figure contains is also a feature. The importances of these different features is 0.2 for the line features and 0.3 for the area and corners features.

These weights have simply been chosen subjectively but a more detailed study could provide a statistical method for evaluating the feature importances. For real practical problems some form of evaluating the weightings other than simple subjective judgment would be expected.

For each of the features, upper line, lower line and area, the feature is that of a half moon if the feature vector of region values for the figure is that of fuzzified values for this figure. The fuzzy sets used to provide this generalisation are given below. It is assumed that the region values have equal importance in determining the support for one of these features.

Other figures, namely (a), (b) and (c) are given below. These are to be tested against the definition of a half moon given by the first figure below to determine the support for classifying them as a half moon.

The final classification support will depend on the weights used for the main rule and those used for the feature rules. It also depends on the definition of the fuzzy sets used to generalise the given example of a half moon.

Only one example of a half moon is given but we could add more definition examples, repeat the calculations done here for these examples and combine the results using the theory discussed above.

Example of partial moon

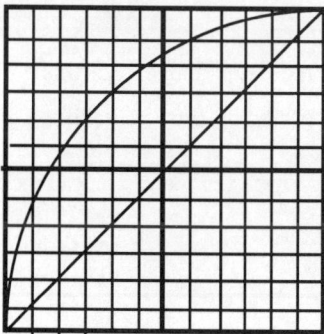

Upper Line (5 6 6 0)
Lower Line (0 6 6 0)
Area   (15 20 20 0)
corners   (2)

Fig 4.78

Upper line feature value given by vector (n1, n2, n3, n4) where ni is number of small squares the upper curve goes through in region i. There are four regions (1, 2, 3, 4) delimited by the bold lines in the diagram and numbered from left to right.

Lower line feature value given by vector as for upper line.

Area feature value given by the number of small squares enclosed in each of the regions.

Corner feature value given by the number of corners in diagram.

Below are given objects we wish to compare with the half moon object above to assess the degree to which each one is a half moon. The first three features in the half moon above and in each case below have vector values. Each element of the vector is a region feature and we will assume these features have equal weighting. Therefore each feature in a vector has weight 0.25.

Given object A

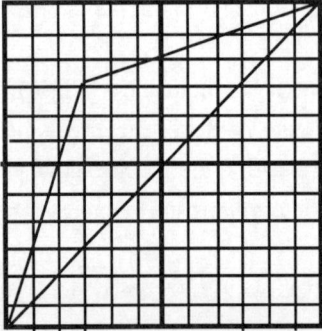

Upper Line   (6 6 6 0)
Lower Line   (0 6 6 0)
Area   (15 19 18 0)
corners   (3)

Fig 4.79

The support for this object to be a half moon is to be determined by comparing its feature values with those of the half moon defined above. For this comparison, importance weights for the features are given by
upper line -- weight 0.2
lower line -- weight 0.2
area -- weight 0.3
corners -- weight 0.3

Given Object B

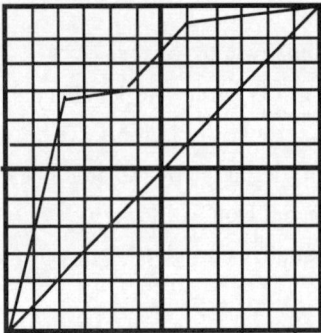

Upper Line   (8 7 6 0)
Lower Line   (0 6 6 0)
Area   (17 21 19 0)
corners   (5)

Fig 4.80

The support for this object to be a half moon is to be determined by comparing its feature values with those of the half moon defined above. For this comparison, importance weights for the features are given by
upper line -- weight 0.2
lower line -- weight 0.2
area -- weight 0.3
corners -- weight 0.3

Given object C

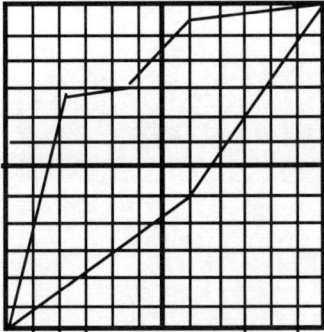

Upper Line   (8 7 6 0)
Lower Line   (0 8 6 2)
Area   (16 25 24 3)
corners   (6)

Fig 4.81

The support for this object to be a half moon is to be determined by comparing its feature values with those of the half moon defined above. For this comparison, importance weights for the features are given by

upper line -- weight 0.2

lower line -- weight 0.2

area -- weight 0.3

corners -- weight 0.3

In the half_moon definition example given above we generalise the vector feature values to those given below.

upper line vector

$$(\quad 4/0.4 + 5/1 + 6/0.4,$$
$$5/0.4 + 6/1 + 7/0.4,$$
$$5/0.4 + 6/1 + 7/0.4,$$
$$0/1 + 1/0.4) = (g11, g12, g13, g14)$$

lower line vector

$$(\quad 0/1 + 1/0.4,$$
$$5/0.4 + 6/1 + 7/0.4,$$
$$5/0.4 + 6/1 + 7/0.4,$$
$$0/1 + 1/0.4) = (g21, g22, g23, g24)$$

area vector

$$(\quad 13/0.3 + 14/0.7 + 15/1 + 16/0.7 + 17/0.3$$
$$18/0.3 + 19/0.7 + 20/1 + 21/0.7 + 22/0.3$$
$$18/0.3 + 19/0.7 + 20/1 + 21/0.7 + 22/0.3$$
$$0/1 + 1/0.7 + 2/0.3) = (g31, g32, g33, g34)$$

The corner feature value is also generalised to:

corners

$$2/1 + 3/0.4 + 4/0.2 = g41$$

The notation for the rules is that most appropriate for this problem and Fril. The rules are

((half_moon support for X)
     (evlog ((upper_line satisfactory for X) 0.2
           (lower_line satisfactory for X) 0.2
           (area satisfactory for X) 0.3
           (corners satisfactory for X) 0.3   ))) : (1 1)

((upper_line satisfactory for X)
     (evlog ((region 1 has **g11** black squares for upper line for X) 0.25
            (region 2 has **g12** black squares for upper line for X) 0.25
            (region 3 has **g13** black squares for upper line for X) 0.25
            (region 4 has **g14** black squares for upper line for X) 0.25
                ))) : ((1 1)(0 0))

((lower_line satisfactory for X)
     (evlog ((region 1 has **g21** black squares for lower line for X) 0.25
            (region 2 has **g22** black squares for lower line for X) 0.25
            (region 3 has **g23** black squares for lower line for X) 0.25
            (region 4 has **g24** black squares for lower line for X) 0.25
                )) : ((1 1)(0 0))

((area satisfactory for X)
     (evlog ((region 1 has **g31** black squares inside figure for X) 0.25
            (region 2 has **g32** black squares inside figure for X) 0.25
            (region 3 has **g33** black squares inside figure for X) 0.25
            (region 4 has **g34** black squares inside figure for X) 0.25
              ))) : ((1 1)(0 0))

((corners satisfactory for X)
     (evlog f ((figure has **g41** corners for X) 1))) : ((1 1)(0 0))

Facts from the given objects (a), (b) and (c) to be classified are given by

((region 1 has 6 black squares for upper line for a))
((region 2 has 6 black squares for upper line for a))
((region 3 has 6 black squares for upper line for a))
((region 4 has 0 black squares for upper line for a))
((region 1 has 0 black squares for lower line for a))
((region 2 has 6 black squares for lower line for a))

((region 3 has 6 black squares for lower line for a))
((region 4 has 0 black squares for lower line for a))

((region 1 has 15 black squares inside figure for a))
((region 2 has 19 black squares inside figure for a))
((region 3 has 18 black squares inside figure for a))
((region 4 has 0   black squares inside figure for a))

((figure has 3 corners for a))

((region 1 has 8 black squares for upper line for b))
((region 2 has 7 black squares for upper line for b))
((region 3 has 6 black squares for upper line for b))
((region 4 has 0 black squares for upper line for b))

((region 1 has 0 black squares for lower line for b))
((region 2 has 6 black squares for lower line for b))
((region 3 has 6 black squares for lower line for b))
((region 4 has 0 black squares for lower line for b))

((region 1 has 17 black squares inside figure for b))
((region 2 has 21 black squares inside figure for b))
((region 3 has 19 black squares inside figure for b))
((region 4 has 0   black squares inside figure for b))

((figure has 5 corners for b))

((region 1 has 8 black squares for upper line for c))
((region 2 has 7 black squares for upper line for c))
((region 3 has 6 black squares for upper line for c))
((region 4 has 0 black squares for upper line for c))

((region 1 has 0 black squares for lower line for c))
((region 2 has 8 black squares for lower line for c))
((region 3 has 6 black squares for lower line for c))
((region 4 has 2 black squares for lower line for c))

((region 1 has 16 black squares inside figure for c))
((region 2 has 25 black squares inside figure for c))
((region 3 has 24 black squares inside figure for c))
((region 4 has 3   black squares inside figure for c))

((figure has 6 corners for c))

We include only the lower supports in the support pairs for the semantic unification since upper supports do not enter the final calculation. The body supports for the main rule are given by

For a	vector supports	vector equal weighted sum	weights	weighted sum
upper line	0.4, 1, 1, 1	0.85	(0.2)	0.17
lower line	1, 1, 1, 1	1	(0.2)	0.2
area	1, 0.7, 0.3, 1	0.75	(0.3)	0.225
corners	0.4	0.4	(0.3)	0.12
				0.715

For b	vector supports	vector equal weighted sum	weights	weighted sum
upper line	0, 0.4, 1, 1	0.6	(0.2)	0.12
lower line	1, 1, 1, 1	1	(0.2)	0.2
area	0.3, 0.7, 0.7, 1	0.675	(0.3)	0.2025
corners	0	0	(0.3)	0
				0.5225

For c	vector supports	vector equal weighted sum	weights	weighted sum
upper line	0, 0.4, 1, 1	0.6	(0.2)	0.12
lower line	1, 0, 1, 0	0.5	(0.2)	0.1
area	0.7, 0, 0, 0	0.175	(0.3)	0.0525
corners	0	0.0	(0.3)	0
				0.2725

so that the supports, assuming $S(x) = x$, for the three cases are
support for a being half moon shape is [0.715, 1]
support for b being half moon shape is [0.5225, 1]
support for c being half moon shape is [0.2725, 1]

The upper support of 1 means there is no support against objects being half moons. The lower supports give support for objects being half moons.

4.6.7 Learning Evidential Logic Rules from Examples

Scientists, engineers, managers, business decision makers from many disciplines collect large amounts of data in the form of databases. A database represents a collection of records to be used to answer important queries. Sometimes the answer to a query can be obtained from the database. More often than not the answer is not directly available. Answers to similar queries are available and these must be used to interpolate or extrapolate to the conditions of the actual query. This is a form of case-based reasoning and requires the ability to generalise from a set of similar cases to the case in hand. The Fril evidential logic rule can be used for this purpose, and this section is concerned with automatically deriving these rules from data supplied in the form of a database of factual information. The rules can be used not only for the required case-based reasoning but also for providing the user with a full explanation for the prediction and the ability to converse with the computer to improve its performance. The computer knowledge base is not restricted to evidential logic rules but can use other types of Fril rules.

Knowledge acquisition in this case uses frequency analysis, mass assignments and semantic unification to automatically generate the fuzzy sets and weights occurring in the evidential logic rules. It can also use genetic programming to allow the knowledge to evolve from a state of high performance to even better performance sets of rules. This is achieved by allowing algebraic combinations of database features and not simply a selection of the features themselves.

The user can use this knowledge to gain an understanding of the domain of application, criticise the form of knowledge with reference to the original data, determine where further data should be acquired, use his / her creativity to try out the validity of various relationships satisfied by the data, have a summary of the data in the form of fuzzy rules and generally use the computer as a tool in the aid to discovery within an environment of the original database.

A Fril case-based reasoning program provides an easy-to-use computing environment with a window menu driven front end that can be used by persons of varying computer literacy.

The user prepares a database with one column corresponding to a classification and all other columns corresponding to features which can be measured or subjectively assessed. Each row of the database corresponds to an example. More generally, suppose that the variable Y is dependent on the vector $\mathbf{x} = (X_1, ..., X_n)$ where

$$Y = F(\mathbf{x}) + n$$

n represents a noise term. It is often the case that F is not known and it is only required to give a value for Y belonging to the set of classifications $\{g_1, ..., g_n\}$ where g_i is a label. A database of examples of the form

Class for Y	Value of X1	Value of X2		Value of Xn

Fig 4.82

where values in the class column can be fuzzy sets on $\{g1, ..., gn\}$ and values in X_i columns are values of the variable X_i which can be point values or fuzzy sets on the value space associated with X_i. The value space of X_i can be a discrete set or an interval.

Fril uses this database to construct an evidential logic rule. The user can add further examples to the database, add more simple features and suggest complex features involving algebraic combinations of existing features.

For example, the classification could be the suitability of a house for a given customer and the features would be the various qualities of the house such as size of garden, number of bedrooms, size of lounge etc. A representative number of examples of suitable houses would be chosen by the customer. A new house on the market could then be tested to see for which customers it would be suitable.

The database could be the classification of credit worthiness of persons. The classification of credit worthiness could be {very_good, good, average, poor, very_poor}. The database would consist of past customers with their details and subjective credit worthiness as features.

Another example might be a classification of change in interest rate with features representing measurable economic conditions.

Classes of {very_good, good, average, poor, very_poor} for the potential for oil at a given place with geological measurement and other features is another obvious example.

The form of the head of the classification evidential logic rule for such a program is of the form

classification is CLASS

or

feature FEATURE has value contained in FUZZY_SET

where words in capitals represent variables which can be instantiated to the chosen classification, feature or chosen fuzzy set.

The body of the rule consists of a weighted list of features, where each feature is simple or complex and has an associated weight representing the importance of that feature. Each feature has the form

feature FEATURE has value contained in FUZZY_SET

where FEATURE is a variable instantiated to some particular feature, either simple or complex, and FUZZY_SET is a variable instantiated to a fuzzy set representing the collection of allowed values for the feature FEATURE.

The body of the rule also contains a filter, FILTER, represented by a fuzzy set defined on the truth space [0, 1].

The evidential logic rule can be written in the form

classification is CLASS

IF

[feature FEATURE_1 has value contained in FUZZY_SET_1 with weight w_1
  feature FEATURE_2 has value contained in FUZZY_SET_2 with weight w_2

  feature FEATURE_N has value contained in FUZZY_SET_N with weight w_N]
with filter FILTER : [X1, X2], [Y1, Y2]

or in the form

feature FEATURE has value contained in FUZZY_SET

IF

[feature FEATURE_1 has value contained in FUZZY_SET_1 with weight w_1
  feature FEATURE_2 has value contained in FUZZY_SET_2 with weight w_2

  feature FEATURE_N has value contained in FUZZY_SET_N with weight w_N]
with filter FILTER : [X1, X2], [Y1, Y2]

This is not the actual notation for an evidential logic rule in Fril. This was discussed previously and the reader can easily translate this pseudo code into actual Fril code.

A feature defined by a rule is called a complex feature. A complex feature can be defined using any type of Fril rule and not just the evidential logic rule. A simple feature represents a measured data variable or a subjective input.

The fuzzy sets used for the features are determined using frequency methods on data supplied from a learning set of examples as shown below.

The weights used in an evidential logic rule are obtained from the rules of classification and a semantic unification algorithm which is also discussed below.

It should be emphasised that the features in the rules can be simple or complex. An example of a complex feature would be

musicianship of X

This would appear in a rule as

feature musicianship of X has value contained in **f** with weight w

where **f** is a fuzzy set on {negligible, v poor, poor, average, good, v good, excellent}.

This complex feature could be defined using another evidential logic Fril rule.
Another example is the feature

$$X - Y$$

which would appear in a rule as

feature X - Y has value contained in **f** with weight w

where **f** is a fuzzy set defined on the space for differences in measurements of X and Y.
For example in one rule, **f** may be the fuzzy set **large** and in another rule it may be the
fuzzy set **small**.

Another example of a complex feature is

$$X \text{ AND } Y$$

This would appear in a rule as

feature X AND Y has value contained in **h** with weight w

where **h** is a fuzzy set on the cross product space of the spaces for X and Y. The actual
fuzzy set would be determined from the learning set. It could be decomposed as

$$\mathbf{h} = \mathbf{f} \times \mathbf{g}$$

where **f** is the fuzzy set on the space of measurements for X and **g** is the fuzzy set on the
space of measurements for Y. In this case this would appear in the rule as

feature X is contained in **f** AND feature Y is contained in **g** with weight w

More generally, features can occur in the body of evidential logic rules as S_Exp's where
Fril uses a clause of the form

S_Exp is **f**

where **f** is a fuzzy set and S_Exp is an expression formed from the generating set

$$G = \{+, -, *, /, \text{Variables}\}$$

where Variables are simply variables which can act as terminals, and the operators +, -, *, /
can take elements in G as values of their two arguments. For example

$$X^2 + Y$$

is an S_Exp and the corresponding feature would be

$$(X^2 + Y) \text{ is } \mathbf{f}$$

Features can be combined using logical operators AND, OR and we can also use NOT. For
example

$$(X^2 + Y) \text{ is } \mathbf{f} \text{ AND } Z \text{ is } \mathbf{g}$$

$$\text{NOT}\{(X^2 + Y) \text{ is } \mathbf{f}\}$$

4.6.8 Choosing the Weights using a Semantic Unification Algorithm

Suppose the rules for classification of objects with features f_1, ..., f_n and classifications c_1, ..., c_m have the form

classification is c_i

IF

[feature f_1 has value contained in $\mathbf{f_{i1}}$ with weight w_{i1}

feature f_2 has value contained in $\mathbf{f_{i2}}$ with weight w_{i2}

feature f_n has value contained in $\mathbf{f_{in}}$ with weight w_{in}]

with filter FILTER : [1, 1], [0, 0]

for $i = 1$, ..., m

We will consider the choice of weights in rule k. The importance of a given feature, say fr in this rule depends on how well the fuzzy set $\mathbf{f_{kr}}$ discriminates from the corresponding feature values in the other rules, i.e. the greater overlap the fuzzy set $\mathbf{f_{kr}}$ has with the corresponding fuzzy set in each of the other rules the less important this feature is in this rule. We can use point semantic unification to determine the degree of match of $\mathbf{f_{kr}}$ with $\mathbf{f_{ir}}$ for all i, $i \neq k$. Let this result in the unifications

$$\mathbf{f_{kr}} \mid \mathbf{f_{ir}} : \theta_{kir} \; ; \; \text{all i, } i \neq k$$

The degree of importance of fr in rule k with respect to the ith rule is $1 - \theta_{kir}$. The degree of importance of fr depends on $\sum_{\substack{i=1 \\ i \neq k}}^{m} 1 - \theta_{kir}$ so that we define the relative weights of rule k as

$$w'_{kr} = 1 - \frac{\sum_{\substack{i=1 \\ i \neq k}}^{m} \theta_{kir}}{m - 1} \qquad \text{for } r = 1, ..., n$$

The relative set of weights for rule k, namely $\{w'_{k1}, ..., w'_{kn}\}$ are then normalised to give the importance weights for rule k

$$w_{ki} = \frac{w'_{ki}}{\sum_{j=1}^{n} w'_{kj}} \qquad \text{for } i = 1, ..., n$$

The features in the body of the evidential logic rules can be complex rather than simple as assumed above. The above method is easily modified for these more general cases. We need only consider the form of the feature and the point semantic unification for that feature with respect to the corresponding feature in the other classification rules. For example, consider a complex feature

189

X - Y

appearing in the kth rule as

feature X - Y is contained in $\mathbf{f_k}$

The corresponding semantic unifications for determining w_k would be

$\mathbf{f_k} \mid \mathbf{f_i} : \theta_{ik}$ for all i, i ≠ k

As another example we can consider the Fril clause

X is $\mathbf{f_k}$ AND Y is $\mathbf{g_k}$

appearing in the kth rule. The corresponding semantic unifications for determining w_k would be

$\mathbf{f_k} \mid \mathbf{f_i} : \alpha_{ik}$ for all i, i ≠ k

$\mathbf{g_k} \mid \mathbf{g_i} : \beta_{ik}$ for all i, i ≠ k

giving

X is $\mathbf{f_k}$ AND Y is $\mathbf{g_k} \mid$ X is $\mathbf{f_k}$ AND Y is $\mathbf{g_k} : \theta_{ik}$ where $\theta_{ik} = \alpha_{ik} \wedge \beta_{ik}$ for all i, i ≠ k

The MIN operator ∧ is used since we have a conjunction of conditions and this conforms with the fuzzy logic algebra. For a disjunction we would use the MAX operator ∨.

If we use NOT in an S_Expression such as (NOT X) in the rule form

NOT(X is $\mathbf{f_k}$)

then we use

$\mathbf{f_k} \mid \mathbf{f_i} : \theta_{ik}$ for all i, i ≠ k

giving NOT(X is $\mathbf{f_k}$) | NOT(X is $\mathbf{f_k}$) : 1 - θ_{ik} for all i, i ≠ k

A similar method of obtaining the required semantic unifications for any feature expressed as a general S_Expression can be used.

4.6.9 Choosing the Feature Fuzzy Sets using Frequency Methods

The features in the body of an evidential logic rule are S_Expressions with fuzzy sets. The fuzzy sets in cases like this are to be determined by reference to a set of learning examples. An example is an object with measured values for the simple features and also the classification found from the database. A portion of this database is used to learn the fuzzy sets and the remainder used to test the overall performance of the fuzzy classification rules. The performance is the percentage of successful classifications given by the rules for the test portion of the database.

Suppose we wish to estimate the fuzzy set $\mathbf{f}$ for a given feature F in rule k with head 'class k'. This fuzzy set must be such that the statement

value of feature F is contained in $\mathbf{f}$

provides a reasonable statement for the body of the rule. In one sense the fuzzy set represents an aggregate of values allowed for F when the object has classification 'class k'. We can display the data given for the values of a given feature for a given classification by means of a frequency plot. When the value of the feature F can take a continuum of values we plot the number of objects with classification 'class k' which have a value in the interval

$[f_i, f_{i-1}]$. The interval for values of F can be divided into many such intervals : $[f_1, f_2]$, $[f_2, f_3]$, ..., $[f_{N-1}, f_N]$. We must estimate the fuzzy set **f** from this frequency distribution. In the case when F can take only distinct values then a frequency plot for these values is obtained.

Two methods have been used to determine initial estimates for the fuzzy sets. These can then be tuned for optimal performance. Optimal performance is concerned not only with the collection of values for the example set but also the ability of the resultant fuzzy set to give good generalisation for the test set.

We will first illustrate the two methods with a simple discrete fuzzy set example. The semantics of the methods will then be discussed. The general algorithm is easily constructed from this illustrative case and the details will not be given here.

Suppose that feature F can take values from the set {a, b, c, d, e} and that in the learning portion of the example set for which the head of the rule is true the following frequency distribution of values is recorded

frequency distribution $Pr(a) = 0.2$, $Pr(b) = 0.3$, $Pr(c) = 0.4$, $Pr(d) = 0.1$

METHOD 1:

We normalise the frequency distribution so that the largest frequency is 1 to give the fuzzy set   **f** = a / 0.5 + b / 0.75 + c / 1 + d / 0.25

This is obtained by dividing each frequency by 0.4.

METHOD 2:

We choose a fuzzy set for **f** such that the least prejudiced probability distribution obtained from the mass assignment associated with **f** is the given frequency distribution. By the least prejudiced probability distribution we mean that distribution formed from the mass assignment associated with the fuzzy set obtained by distributing a mass associated with a set of elements equally among the set of elements. This was discussed in 4.5.9.

Let   **f** = a / μ_a + b / μ_b + c / 1 + d / μ_d

where $\mu_b \geq \mu_a \geq \mu_d$ so that

$m_f = c : 1 - \mu_b$, {b, c} : $\mu_b - \mu_a$, {a, b, c} : $\mu_a - \mu_d$, {a, b, c, d} : μ_d

so that least prejudiced probability distribution is

$Pr(c) = (1 - \mu_b) + 1/2(\mu_b - \mu_a) + 1/3(\mu_a - \mu_d) + 1/4\mu_d = 0.4$

$Pr(b) = 1/2(\mu_b - \mu_a) + 1/3(\mu_a - \mu_d) + 1/4\mu_d = 0.3$

$Pr(a) = 1/3(\mu_a - \mu_d) + 1/4\mu_d = 0.2$

$Pr(d) = 1/4\mu_d = 0.1$ so that

$\mu_d = 0.4$, $\mu_b = 0.9$, $\mu_a = 0.7$ giving the fuzzy set

f = a / 0.7 + b / 0.9 + c / 1 + d / 0.4

This provides an easy algorithm described below.

These two methods are easily generalised to the case of continuous fuzzy sets.

We can show the method 2 diagrammatically in Fig 4.83. The method is easily generalised for the case in which the examples have classifications which are fuzzy sets over the universe of classifications. This will be discussed in detail.

191

Examples Set

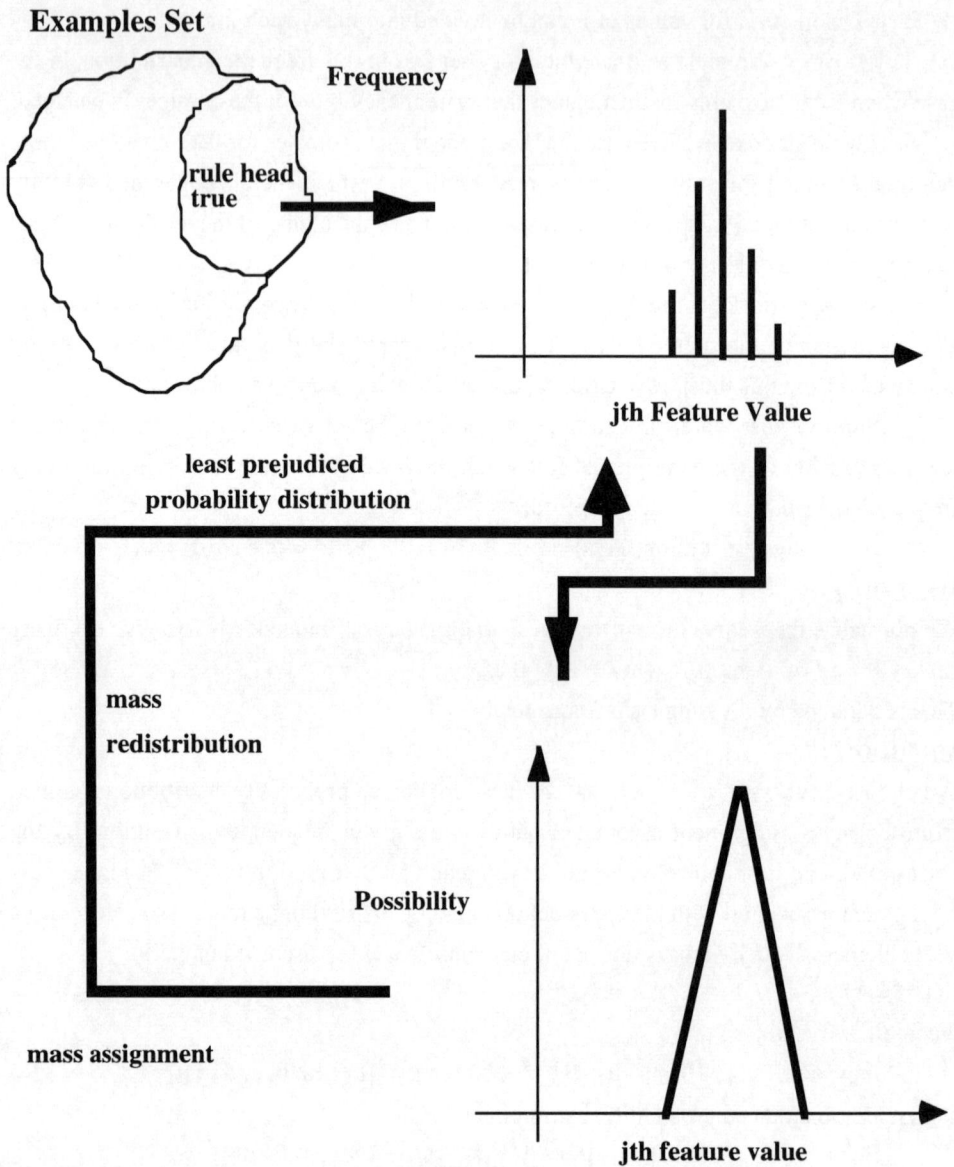

Fig 4.83

Algorithm for deriving fuzzy set from frequency distribution

sum = 0

order elements in increasing values of their probabilities

(1) membership value of first entry = sum + num_of_elements*probability of first entry

sum =: sum + membership value just derived

new probability of element = old value - value of first entry

delete first entry

IF one entry remaining give it membership value of 1 ELSE repeat (1)

Example

      sum = 0

      num of elements = 4

d : 0.1

a : 0.2

b : 0.3

c : 0.4

        $\mu(d) = \text{sum} + 4*0.1 = 0.4$

      sum = $\mu(d)$ = 0.4

      num of elements = 3

a : 0.1

b : 0.2

c : 0.3

        $\mu(a) = \text{sum} + 3*0.1 = 0.7$

      sum = $\mu(a)$ = 0.7

      num of elements = 2

b : 0.1

c : 0.2

        $\mu(b) = \text{sum} + 2*0.1 = 0.9$

      sum = $\mu(b)$ = 0.7

      num of elements = 1

c : 0.1

        $\mu(c) = 1$

If there are elements with equal probabilities, they are treated as a group in the same way as a single element.

What justification can we give for the two methods? The optimal fuzzy sets approximate closely to the fuzzy sets found using these methods.We will not attempt to justify method 1. It is easy to use and gives fuzzy sets which can be useful but we cannot justify treating a frequency distribution as if it were a fuzzy set. Of course, such a fuzzy set could perform very well as a means of generalising from the example learning set to the test set of data and it is only used as a first approximation to the final fuzzy set for this feature.

The following justification can be given for method 2. Suppose you are told that for all objects with a certain classification 'class k' the value of feature F is **f**, where **f** is a fuzzy set. You are asked to provide a representative set of objects for the example set with classification 'class k'. The correct method for you to use would be to form the mass assignment m_f, determine the least prejudiced probability distribution from this mass assignment and select a representative set of objects using this distribution. This justifies method 2 provided the data given are in fact a truly representative selection of examples. To further amplify this explanation consider the non-fuzzy case. Suppose you are told that all persons with a certain quality have heights in the range [5ft 10", 6ft 2"] and you must provide a representative set of examples of heights of persons with this quality. You would use the uniform distribution over the interval [5ft 10", 6ft 2"] to select your examples. The uniform distribution in this case corresponds to the least prejudiced distribution from the mass assignment with a mass of 1 on the interval [5ft 10", 6ft 2"] which is associated with the possibility distribution in which all values in interval [5ft 10", 6ft 2"] have membership 1 and all other values have membership 0.

We can illustrate this further with a simple example. Consider a representative group of persons. Each person must first choose a set of die values corresponding to high values. They are forced to make a binary decision with regard to whether a particular die value is high or not. Each person is then asked to randomly select n die values from his or her set of high die values. These are all pooled to provide a sequence of high die values. Using this sequence we are asked to give a membership function for the fuzzy concept **high**. We give a frequency distribution of the various scores in the set of high scores. Let this be

frequency distribution = 3 : 0.05, 4 : 0.1833, 5 : 0.3833, 6 : 0.3833

Let the fuzzy set for high be

high = 3 / x + 4 / y + 5 / 1 + 6 / 1

then the mass assignment for this fuzzy set is

m_{high} = {5, 6} : 1 - y, {4, 5, 6} : y - x, {3, 4, 5, 6} : x

and the least prejudiced probability distribution is

$$3 : \; 1/4(x)$$
$$4 : \; 1/3(y - x) + 1/4(x)$$
$$5 : \; 1/2(1 - y) + 1/3(y - x) + 1/4(x)$$
$$6 : \; 1/2(1 - y) + 1/3(y - x) + 1/4(x)$$

We equate this with the given frequency distribution above, so that

$1/4(x) = 0.05$

$1/3(y - x) + 1/4(x) = 0.1833$

$1/2(1 - y) + 1/3(y - x) + 1/4(x) = 0.3833$

$1/2(1 - y) + 1/3(y - x) + 1/4(x) = 0.3833$

giving

$x = 0.2, \; y = 0.6$

so that the fuzzy set for high is

high = 3 / 0.2 + 4 / 0.6 + 5 / 1 + 6 / 1

The approach used here to determining the fuzzy set **high** is consistent with the voting model interpretation of a fuzzy set given earlier.

If we reverse the argument and are asked to give a set of high die scores where high is a fuzzy set defined as above, then we would use the probability distribution

3 : 0.05

4 : 0.1333 + 0.05 = 0.1833

5 : 0.2 + 0.1333 + 0.05 = 0.3833

6 : 0.3833

obtained as the least prejudiced probability distribution from the mass assignment m_{high} .

This distribution can thought of as a local maximum entropy distribution. The maximum entropy distribution is 3 : 0.2, 4 : 0.2667, 5 : 0.2667, 6 : 0.2667 which intuitively would not be the correct distribution to use. When dealing with a given set of feature values we can do exactly what we have described above, namely find a frequency distribution and form a fuzzy set by equating the frequency distribution with the least prejudiced, i.e. local maximum entropy, distribution for this fuzzy set. We can then say that the features values satisfy the fuzzy set found.

Finally we modify the method of obtaining the frequency distribution of values of a given feature corresponding to a given object classification when the classification is a fuzzy set on the set of classifications. Suppose the set of classifications is $C = \{C_1, ..., C_r\}$ and an object is given the classification

object classification = $C_1 / \mu_1 + ... + C_r / \mu_r$

What frequency count do we give for a given feature value of this object in class i? We use the value p_i, the probability of C_i in the least prejudiced probability distribution obtained from the mass assignment corresponding to this fuzzy set.

Example   Consider C = {strong, average, weak} and an object with the fuzzy classification

object = strong / 1 + average / 0.7 + weak / 0.3

Let one feature for this object have the value x lying in the feature value interval I. What counts do we give to the frequency distributions for the fuzzy sets for this feature in the case of each of the rules for the three heads?

Form the mass assignment m_{object} = strong : 0.3, {strong, average} ; 0.4, {strong, average, weak} : 0.3 and the least prejudiced probability distribution

p = strong : 0.6, average : 0.3, weak : 0.1

We therefore give a count of 0.6 for feature value I in rule with head strong, 0.3 in rule with head average and 0.1 in rule with head weak.

Automation of feature fuzzy sets for fuzzy rules

We will show the general method with a simple example already considered in Section 4.5.11, namely $Y = X^2$. We will use the following fuzzy sets (Fig. 4.84) on the Y axis

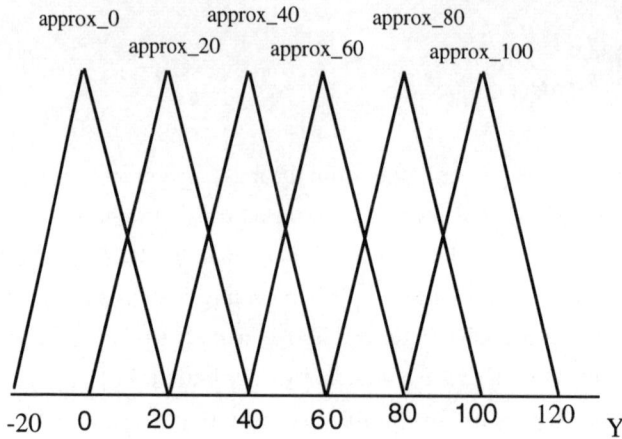

Fig 4.84

and show how to produce the fuzzy set on X for the rule with head 'Y is approx_20. We need only consider values of x in the range R, which give Y values in the range [0, 40], for this case. A value of X, say x, will have a corresponding value of y which will have membership in approx_0 and approx_20 if x is in a certain range and in approx_20 and approx_40 if in the complement of this range. We consider each x to be an object to be split among the different heads as described above in the simple example. Thus we count a proportion of x, p say, for the fuzzy set , **f2** say, in the rule with approx_20 in the head. The value of p is determined using the method above. It is easy to show that for **f2** p is

given by
$$p(x) = \begin{cases} \dfrac{3\mu_{approx\_20}(y)-1}{2\mu_{approx\_20}(y)} & \text{for } 10 \le y \le 30 \\[2ex] \dfrac{\mu_{approx\_20}(y)}{2(1-\mu_{approx\_20}(y))} & \text{for } 0 \le y \le 10 \ \text{ or } \ 30 \le y \le 40 \end{cases}$$

where $y = x^2$.

From p(x) we can determine a frequency distribution corresponding to the least prejudiced distribution for **f2**, i.e.

$$f(x) = \frac{p(x)}{\int\limits_0^{\sqrt{40}} p(x)dx}$$

which simply corresponds to normalising p(x).

From this least prejudiced probability distribution we can determine the fuzzy set f2 using the mass assignment algorithm described above. In this case the calculation is particularly simple. If we are given the distribution

$\{x_i : f_i\}$ for $i = 1, ..., n$ in decreasing order of f_i, i.e. $f_{i+1} < f_i$ (all i)

then $\mu_i = i(f_i - f_{i+1}) + \mu_{i+1}$

with $f_{n+1} = 0$, $\mu_{n+1} = 0$; for $i = n, n-1, ..., 1$

This gives $\mu_1 = 1$.

We can display this fuzzy set f2 graphically

196

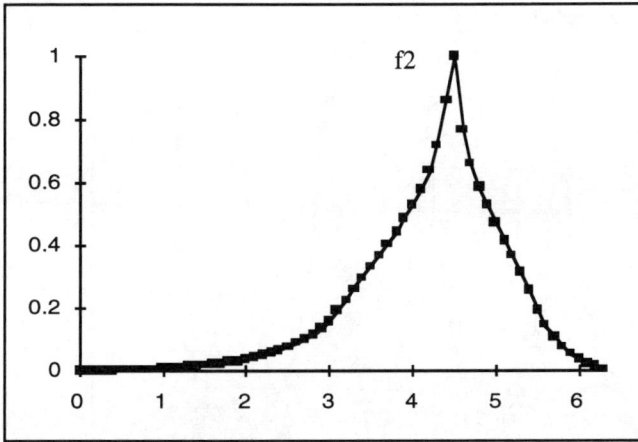

Fig 4.85

We can then form the rule

Y is	**approx_20**	IF	X is	**f2**

If we have the rules

Y is	**approx_0**	IF	X is	**f1**
Y is	**approx_20**	IF	X is	**f2**
Y is	**approx_40**	IF	Y is	**f3**
Y is	**approx_60**	IF	Y is	**f4**
Y is	**approx_80**	IF	Y is	**f5**
Y is	**approx_100**	IF	Y is	**f6**

then the fuzzy sets **f1**, **f3**, **f4**, **f5**, and **f6** can be determined using the same method which we used to find **f2**. These fuzzy sets are shown in Fig 4.86. If we use these rules in Fril to determine the value F( ) we obtain the results

x	Fuzzy F(x)	F(x)	|Error|
10	100	100	0
9.75	96.9422	95.0625	1.8797
9.5	89.2292	90.25	1.0208
9.25	84.5486	85.5625	1.0139
9.00	80.4516	81	0.5484
8.75	77.8794	76.5625	1.3169
8.5	74.2526	72.25	2.0026
8.25	66.5687	68.0625	1.4938
8.00	62.7125	64	1.2875
7.75	59.8411	60.0625	0.2214
7.5	57.6343	56.25	1.3843
7.25	53.5232	52.5625	0.9607
7.00	48.5208	49	0.4792
6.75	44.882	45.5625	0.6805
6.5	41.5456	42.25	0.7044
6.25	39.5464	39.0625	0.4839

197

Fuzzy Sets on X axis

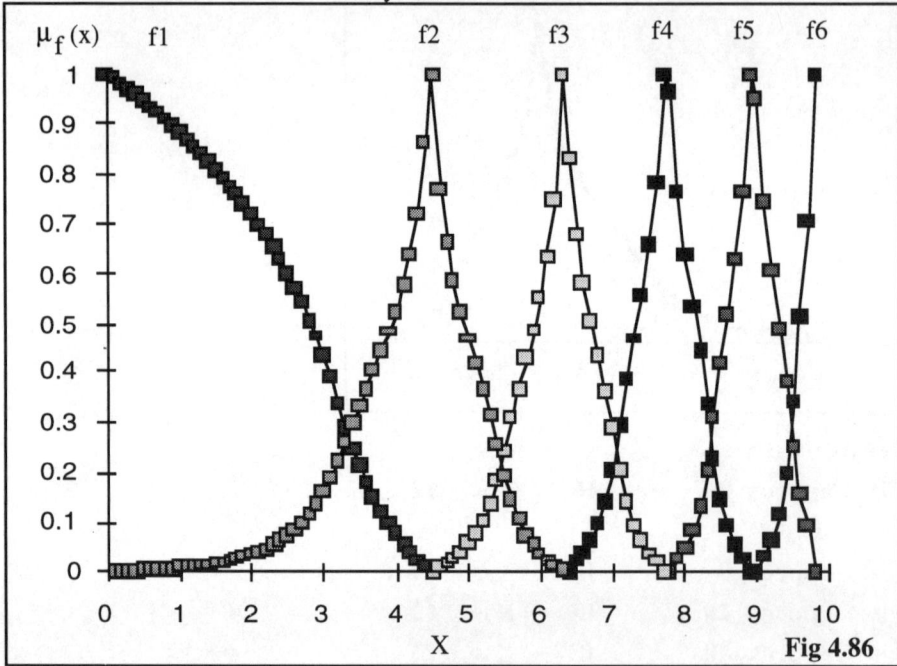

Fig 4.86

6.00	37.6578	36	1.6578
5.75	35.2637	33.0625	2.2012
5.5	31.7729	30.25	1.5229
5.25	26.9474	27.5625	0.6151
5.00	24.4288	25	0.5712
4.75	22.1132	22.5625	0.4493
4.5	20.1874	20.25	0.0626
4.25	19.3487	18.0625	1.2862
4.00	17.8714	16	1.8714
3.75	16.7683	14.0625	2.7058
3.5	14.4018	12.25	2.1518
3.25	12.9763	10.5625	2.4138
3.00	9.06507	9	0.06507
2.75	7.18732	7.5625	0.37518
2.5	4.2248	6.25	2.0252
2.25	3.58012	5.0625	1.48238
2.00	3.19092	4	0.80908
1.75	2.806	3.0625	0.2565
1.5	2.78459	2.25	0.53459
1.25	2.41719	1.5625	0.85469
1.00	2.05709	1	1.05709
0.75	1.12303	0.5625	0.56053
0.5	0.706412	0.25	0.456412
0.25	0.237834	0.0625	0.175334
0	0	0	0

198

The error will be 0 for those x values corresponding to peak membership values of the fuzzy sets f_i and also for those x values for which two membership functions, f_i and f_{i+1} say, cross. It is important that the fuzzy sets on the Y space are symmetrical for the error to be zero at the values of x corresponding to peak membership values. This is why we chose extensions of the fuzzy sets **approx_0** and **approx_100**. We show the results in Fig 4.87.

This approach for automatically finding fuzzy sets from data can be used, in general, for fuzzy control. The fuzzy sets are first chosen for the output space and the above method used to determine the fuzzy sets on each of the input spaces. The error oscillates as shown in Fig 4.88.

4.6.10 Optimising Feature Fuzzy Sets

The fuzzy sets found using the method in the last section for the feature values may not be the optimal ones for generalisation purposes although one would expect the optimal ones to be approximately the same. The overall performance of the classifier can therefore be optimised by allowing small variations in these feature fuzzy sets in the bodies of the evidential logic rules.

Consider the problem with 10 possible classifications and 20 features. Each classification will have a rule with the body containing at most 20 fuzzy sets. We have therefore a set of rules with at most 200 fuzzy sets. These fuzzy sets are known approximately but require variation to optimise the performance of the classifier. This optimisation can be performed incrementally. The system is used with each example in the test example set. After each test it is known whether a correct classification was performed. If the classification was correct we pass to the next test case. If the classification was incorrect we consider the rule associated with the classification which the system gave and that corresponding to the correct classification. These two rules are compared and the fuzzy sets modified so that the correct solution is obtained. This modification takes the form of widening the fuzzy sets associated with large contributions in the rule corresponding to the correct classification and reducing the width of those fuzzy sets associated with large contributions in the body of the rule giving the incorrect classification. This will cause the support for the correct classification to be increased and that for the incorrect classification to be decreased. This is performed for each test example. The performance of the overall system is then tested, and if there is an improvement the new fuzzy sets are accepted and the whole process is repeated. If no improvement results then the old fuzzy sets are kept and the incremental optimisation is stopped. This process is under development and many questions concerning convergence etc. are being investigated. The overall method has been shown to be very effective for some practical problems but more experience is required before any general statements can be made.

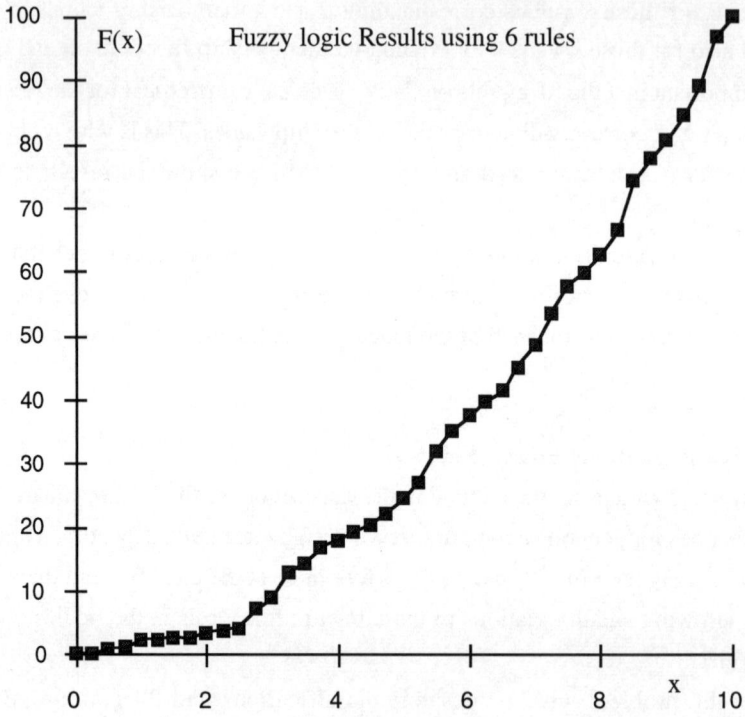

Fig 4.87

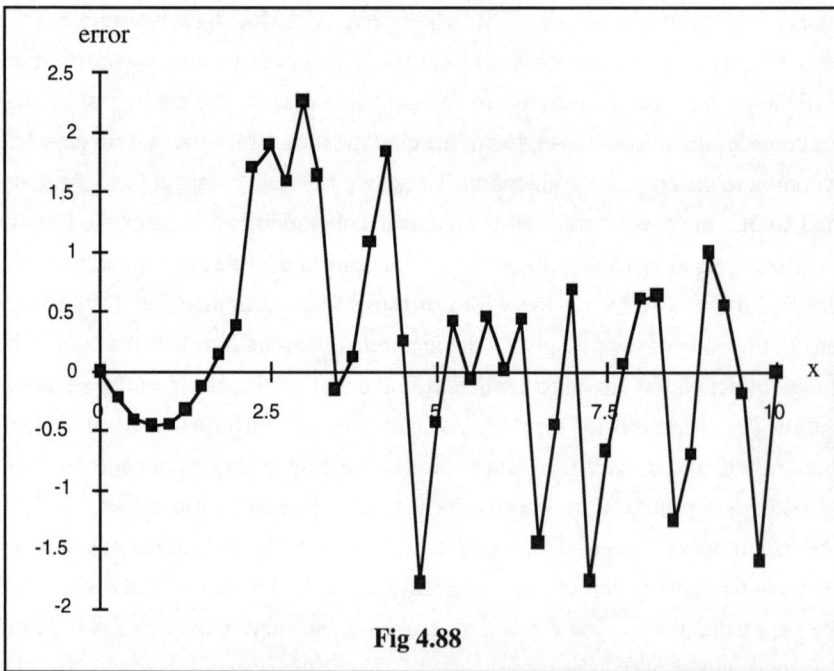

Fig 4.88

4.6.11 Optimising what Features to Use

Feature selection is important to the success of this process. The database contains all features which the user can usefully supply. These will correspond to measurements the user can make on the objects in the example set. The user may be advised by the system that the features supplied are not adequate to provide a good classification. He or she would then be asked for some more features. These features supplied by the user are all treated as simple features. Complex features can be formed from these simple features by combining two or more in some algebraic form. The user can be asked to suggest possible complex features and these will be tried by the system. The system will determine a set of values for a complex feature using the database of simple feature values and the algebraic form. A fuzzy set can then be formed in the normal way and the process completed.

As an alternative to the user supplying the complex features we can use a genetic algorithm for this purpose. A set of programs is chosen at random. Each program consists of a set of rules, one for each classification. All the rules in a given program have the same form of body, i.e. the same features. The features selected for a given program are selected at random from the generating set

$$G = \{+, -, *, /, X1, ..., Xn\}$$ using a probability distribution over the set G.

The Xi correspond to the simple features in the database. Thus we could generate the feature $$X1 + (X2 - X3)^2$$

by generating the string

$$+(X1, (* (-(X2, X3)) (-(X2, X3))))$$

The probability distribution over G is such that simple features have a higher probability of being chosen than the other elements, so that the probability of producing the more complex features is reduced. Even though all the rules of a given program have the same features the rules will have different fuzzy sets for the features and different weights found using methods given above. The optimised program produced using the methods given above is included in the set of programs. The performance of each program is evaluated and a probability distribution over the set of programs given with probability being proportional to the performance.

New programs can be generated by mutation and cross-fertilisation. A new program can replace any program in the original set for which it has a higher performance. Mutation chooses a program using the probability distribution from the set of programs and changes one of the features drawn at random to a new feature selected at random from G. Cross-fertilisation chooses two programs from the set of programs using the fitness probability distribution and separates the bodies of the rules of these programs into two parts. The division point is chosen at random. New programs are then selected by swapping the parts between programs.

The use of genetic programming is under investigation and it is too early to draw any conclusions.

4.6.12 Fuzzy Data Browser and Soft Computing

The methods described in Sections 4.6.7 to 4.6.11 can be used to produce a fuzzy data browser. This is a Fril module which can answer queries with reference to a database. It also contains fuzzy control methods described in 4.5.9 to 4.5.12. This forms the basis of a more general Fril module concerned with soft computing.

The term soft computing was introduced by Lotfi Zadeh. He has stated that the emergence of effective ways of dealing with complex, large scale systems through the use of fuzzy logic (FL), neural networks (NN), probabilistic reasoning (PR) and other techniques can be referred to collectively as soft computing (SC). Viewed as branches of soft computing, FL is concerned mainly with imprecision, NN with learning and PR with uncertainty. Zadeh has also pointed out that there is considerable overlap between FL, NN and PR and often they can be used to advantage in combination. Fril is an ideal computer language for soft computing since it contains all the basic elements of FL and PR, and 'C' programs for NN algorithms can easily be linked to Fril, producing a powerful combined system with a friendly user interface.

Fril has been linked to the Mathematica system, which provides a powerful extension to a soft computing environment. Fril has been used for unsupervised and supervised neural net type learning to form rules for classification. This work has provided good results.

A database attribute value can be given as a specified precise value, a set of possible values or a range of values, a discrete or continuous fuzzy set or as unknown.

A query will be answered either directly by reference to the database or by automatically generating fuzzy logic or evidential logic rules from the database. The methods are general so that any relevant question can be given an answer. If the answer is too vague the user can be asked for further information and the module will determine what is the most valuable information to be asked for. The user can ask for an assessment of the accuracy of the solution and general 'what if' questions. Rules generated are stored in the knowledge base for further use. Fuzzy interpolation methods and case-based reasoning can also be used to answer queries. Explanations of how the solution was obtained can be given to the user in a layered format. The user can ask for further details about certain aspects but is not presented with a complete trace of the solution. The user can ask for relationships between variables to be tested. The relationships may be fuzzy. Suggestions for improvement in rules formed and new rules can be made by the user and the system will test such ideas and report back any relevant conclusions.

This type of module has numerous applications in many areas of engineering, medicine, economics and business, social sciences and domestic affairs.

4.7 BIBLIOGRAPHY

Further reading on Fril, support logic programming and mass assignment theoretical issues relevant to Fril, is as follows:

Baldwin J.F, Guild N.C.F, (1979), "FUZLOG: A computer program for Fuzzy Reasoning", Proc. 9th Symp. on Multi-Valued Logic, Bath, pp 38-45.

Baldwin J.F, Guild N.C.F, (1980), "Modelling Controllers using fuzzy relations", Kybernetes, Vol 9, pp 223-229.

Baldwin J.F, Guild N.C.F, (1981), "Fuzzy Reasoning applied to Control Models", Third IMA Conf. on Control Theory, Academic Press, pp 647-660.

Baldwin J.F, (1981), "Fuzzy Logic and Fuzzy Reasoning", in Fuzzy Reasoning and its applications (Eds Mamdani E.H, Gaines B.R.), pp 133-148, Academic Press.

Baldwin J.F, Zhou S.Q, (1984), "An Introduction to FRIL - A Fuzzy Relational Inference Language", Fuzzy Sets and Systems **14**, pp 155-174.

Baldwin J.F, (1985), "A Knowledge Engineering Fuzzy Inference Language", In Management Decision Support Systems using Fuzzy Sets and Possibility Theory, (Eds Kacprzyk J, Yager R.R.), Verlag Press, pp 253-269.

Baldwin J.F, (1985), "Automated Fuzzy and Probabilistic Inference", Fuzzy Sets and Systems **18**, pp 219-235.

Baldwin J.F, (1986), "An Uncertainty Calculus for Expert Systems", Artificial Intelligence: Applications of Quantitative Reasoning, (Eds Sanchez E, Zadeh L.A.), Pergamon Press, pp 33-54.

Baldwin J.F, (1986), "Support Logic Programming", Int J. of Intelligent Systems, Vol 1, pp 73-104.

Baldwin J.F, (1986), "Support Logic Programming", in Fuzzy Sets Theory and Applications, Proc. of NATO Advanced Study Institute (1985), (Eds Jones A.I. et al), Reidel Pub. Co, pp 133-171.

Baldwin J.F, Crabtree B, (1986), "CRIL - A Concept Relational Inference Language for Knowledge Engineering", in Fuzzy Logics in Knowledge Engineering, (Eds Negoita C.V, Prade H.), Verlag TUV (1986), pp 209-234.

Baldwin J.F, (1987), "Evidential Support Logic Programming", Fuzzy Sets & Systems **14**, pp 1-26.

Baldwin J.F, (1989), "Computational Models of Uncertainty Reasoning in Expert Systems in Artifical Intelligence", J. Computers Math. Applic, pp 1-15.

Baldwin J.F, (1991), "Combining Evidences for Evidential Reasoning", Int J. of Intelligent Systems **6**, pp 1-40.

Baldwin J.F, (1991), "Inference under Uncertainty for Expert Systems", Proceedings of AI and Computer Power: The Impact on Statiistics., Unicom Seminars, pp 48-60.

Baldwin J.F, Martin T.P, Pilsworth B.W, (1991), "FRIL: A support logic programming system", Proceedings of AI and Computer Power: The Impact of Statistics., Unicom Seminars, pp 159-172.

Baldwin J.F, Martin T.P, (1991), "Fast Operations on Fuzzy Sets in the abstract FRIL Machine", Proc. FUZZ-IEEE 92.

Baldwin J.F, (1991), "A Calculus for Mass Assignments in Evidential Reasoning", in "Advances in the Dempster-Shafer Theory of Evidence", pp 513-533, (Eds Fedrizzi M, Kacprzyk J, Yager R.R.), 1992, John Wiley.

Baldwin J.F, (1991), "Approximate Reasoning, Fuzzy & Probabilistic Control using a theory of Mass Assignments", Proc. of IFES, Japan, 1991, pp 611-622.

Baldwin J.F, (1991), "A Theory of Mass Assignments for Artificial Intelligence", Proc. IEEE AI Conference (Australia 1991), To be published in Lecture notes of Computer Science, Springer Verlag 1994.

Baldwin J.F, (1993), "Evidential Support Logic, Fril and Case based Reasoning", Int J. of Intelligent Systems, pp 939-960.

Baldwin J.F, (1992), "A mass assignment theory for uncertainty reasoning", Proc. FUZZ-IEEE 92.

Baldwin J.F, (1992), "Fuzzy and Probabilistic Uncertainties", in Encyclopedia of AI, 2nd edition, (Ed Shapiro), pp 528-537, Wiley.

Baldwin J.F, (1992), "Evidential Reasoning under Probabilistic and Fuzzy Uncertainties", in An Introduction to Fuzzy Logic Applications in Intelligent Systems (Eds Yager R.R, Zadeh L.A.), Dordrecht: Kluwer, pp 297-333.

Baldwin J.F, (1993), "A Mass Assignment Theory and Memory Based Reasoning", in Intelligent Systems with Uncertainty, (Eds Bouchon-Meunier B, Valverde L, Yager R.R.), Elsevier, pp 97-107.

Baldwin J.F, Ribeiro R, (1994), "Fuzzy Reasoning by Case for Decision Support Systems", Int J. Uncertainty, Fuzziness and Knowledge Based Systems, **2**.1, pp 11-25.

Baldwin J.F, (1993), "Fuzzy, Probabilistic and Evidential Reasoning in Fril", Proc. FUZZ-IEEE 93, San Francisco, pp 459-465.

Baldwin J.F, Coyne M.R, Martin T.P, (1993), "Connectionist vs Symbolic Feature Representation in Evidential Support Logic", Proc FUZZ-IEEE 93, San Francisco, pp 827-833.

Baldwin J.F, Martin T.P, Zhou Y, (1993), "A Fril Knowledge Base for the Management of Uncertainty in Performance Assessment of Hazardous Waste Repositories", Proc. FUZZ-IEEE 93, San Francisco, pp 739-745.

Baldwin J.F, (1993), "Fuzzy Reasoning in Fril for Fuzzy Control and Knowledge-based Applications", Asia-Pacific Engineering Journal, (Part A) **3** (Parts 1, 2), pp 59-81.

Baldwin J.F, (1993), "Fuzzy Sets, Fuzzy Clustering and Fuzzy rules in AI", Fuzzy Logic in AI Workshop, 13th Int Joint Conf. on AI, Chambery, France, pp 1-11.

Baldwin J.F, Martin T.P, (1993), "From Fuzzy Databases to an Intelligent Manual using Fril." Journal of Intelligent Information Systems **2**, pp 365-395.

Baldwin J.F, Martin T.P, Zhou Y, (1993), "Fuzzy Cellular Automata - a practical approach to fuzzy differential equations", in Uncertainty in Intelligent Systems, (Eds Bouchon-Meunier B, Valverde L, Yager R.R.), North-Holland, Elsevier Science Pub, pp 235-247.

Dubois D, Prade H, (1986), "On the Unicity of the Dempster Rule of Combination", Int J. of Intelligent Systems **1**, No 2, pp 133-142.

Dubois D, Prade H, (1990c), "Consonant Approximations of Belief Functions", Int J. of Approx. Reasoning, Vol 4, No 5/6, pp 419-445.

Dubois D, Prade H, (1990d), "Resolution Principles in Possibilistic Logic", Int J. of Approx. Reasoning, Vol 4, 1, pp 1-21.

Filev D.P, Yager R.R, (1991), "A generalized defuzzification method via bad distributions", Int J. Intelligent Systems, Vol 6, pp 687-697.

Jeffrey R, (1965), The Logic of Decision, McGraw-Hill, New York.

Kosko B, (1992), Neural Networks and Fuzzy Systems - A Dynamical Systems Approach to Machine Intelligence, Prentice-Hall Int.

Lopez de Mantaras R, (1990), Approximate Reasoning Models, Ellis Horwood.

Nilsson N, (1986), "Probabilistic Logic", Artificial Intelligence **28**, pp 71-87.

Pearl J, (1988), Probabilistic Reasoning in Intelligent Systems, Morgan Kaufmann.

Pearl J, (1990), "Reasoning with Belief Functions; An analysis of compatibility", Int J. of Approx Reasoning, Vol 4, No 5/6, pp 363-389.

Ralescu A, Baldwin J.F, (1988), "Concept Classification from Examples and counter examples", Int J. Man-Machine Studies **30**, pp 1 -26 (Also published in Machine Learning and Uncertain Reasoning (Eds Gaines B.R, Boose, 1990).

Sugeno M. et al, (1989), "Fuzzy algorithm control of a model car by oral instructions", Fuzzy Sets and Systems **32**, No 2, pp 207-221.

Trillas E, Valverde L, (1985), "On mode and implication in approximate reasoning", in Approximate Reasoning in Expert Systems, (Eds Gupta et al), pp 157-166, North Holland.

Yager R.R, (1988), "On ordered weighted averaging aggregation operators in multi-criteria decision making", IEEE Trans. Syst, Man & Cybernetics, Vol 18, **1**, pp 183-190.

Yager R.R, (1990), "A general approach to rule aggregation in fuzzy logic control", Tech Report MII-1208, Iona College, New Rochelle, New York.

Yager R.R, (1992), "Families of OWA Operators", Tech. Report M11-1301, Iona College, New Rochelle, New York.

Zadeh L.A, (1978), "PRUF - a meaning representation language for natural languages", Int J. of Man-Machine Studies **10,** pp 395-460.

Zadeh L.A, (1983), "The role of fuzzy logic in the management of uncertainty in expert systems", Fuzzy Sets and Systems **11,** pp 198-228.

CHAPTER 5

Systems Programming in Fril

5.1 INTRODUCTION

The fundamental ideas of logic programming were introduced in Chapter 2. In this chapter we show how the list processing and search facilities of the language may be harnessed to develop powerful programs using Fril. A particular feature of Fril is the similarity between data (lists) and programs, since clauses are list-structured. Fragments of Fril programs can be manipulated using list processing techniques, and we discuss various aspects of meta-programming including different uses of meta-variables, a simple Fril interpreter, and an elementary inference engine. Finally, the chapter covers practical aspects of logic programming in Fril, focussing on aspects of efficiency in the language and ways of measuring and improving the time and space requirements of programs. In all cases we try to illustrate the points under discussion by means of example programs.

5.2 MORE ADVANCED LIST PROCESSING

In Chapter 2 we outlined a simple search program *(travel X Y)* that would check for the existence of a path in a directed acyclic graph (defined by the *flight* clauses). In this Section, we progressively refine a similar program to search an arbitrary graph. This illustrates a number of points about Fril programming and list processing techniques.

5.2.1 A Simple Search Program

We start with a simple program which will find whether a path exists between two nodes in a directed acyclic graph such as that shown in Fig. 5 - 1. The program is

```
((path START END)              /* Can we get there in one step ? */
   (edge START END))

((path CURRENT END)
   (edge CURRENT NEXT)         /* otherwise, move one step */
   (path NEXT END))            /* and continue recursively */

((edge a b))                   /* definition of graph */
((edge b c))
((edge b g))
((edge c d))
```

```
((edge c i))
((edge d j))
((edge d e))
((edge e j))
((edge e f))
((edge f i))
((edge i h))
((edge g h))
((edge k h))
((edge k l))
((edge k m))
((edge m n))
```

Apart from a few name changes, this program is virtually identical to the *travel* and *flight* knowledge base described in Chapter 2. It can easily be used to check whether a path exists between two nodes, or to generate pairs of nodes connected by a path, e.g.

```
?((path a h))
    yes

?((path h a))
    no

?((path X h)(pp X)(fail))
    i
    g
    k    ... etc
    no
```

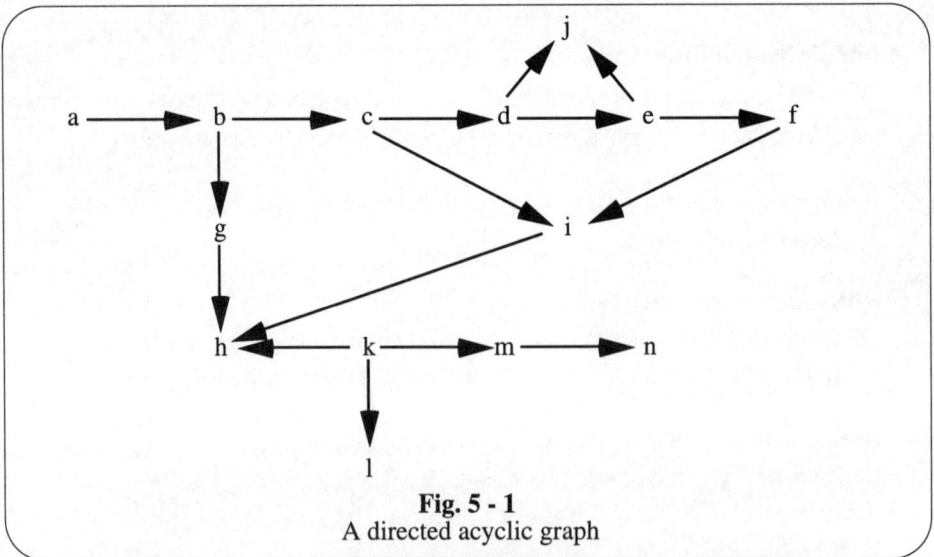

Fig. 5 - 1
A directed acyclic graph

This program implements a simple depth-first backtracking search, i.e. whenever there are alternatives, it always chooses the next edge in the same way, by selecting the first available. If a path is found to lead to a dead end, the most recent choice is undone and the next possibility is tried, until the destination is found or there are no more choices. We will improve this program first to report on the path found, and then to handle more complicated cases such as undirected graphs and cyclic graphs.

The first improvement requires an extra parameter to store the nodes visited on the path. This enables the path between two nodes to be reported, rather than the query just succeeding or failing according to whether or not a path exists. The revised program is

```
((path1 START END  (START  END))        /* Can we go in one step */
    (edge START  END))

((path1 CURRENT END  (CURRENT|REST))
    (edge CURRENT  NEXT)                  /* otherwise, move one step */
    (path1 NEXT END  REST))              /* and continue */
```

Each call to *path1* using the second clause adds an extra node onto the route and makes a recursive call to *path1* to fill in the rest of the route. The route is thus built up one node at a time, until the recursion terminates and the final pair of nodes is added to the route. The query

```
?((path1 a h X)(pp X))
```

produces

```
(a b c d e f i h)
yes
```

Notice that this is not the easiest path from *a* to *h*. Using the query

```
qh((path1 a h P))
```

produces all solutions:

```
((path1 a h (a b c d e f i h)))
((path1 a h (a b c i h)))
((path1 a h (a b g h)))
no (more) solutions
yes
```

The shortest path in this case is produced last. The paths are produced in this sequence because of the ordering of clauses within the knowledge base. We could try to reorder the *edge* clauses, so that the paths were produced in a different order; however, it would not be possible to reorder the facts so that the shortest path was produced for every pair of nodes.

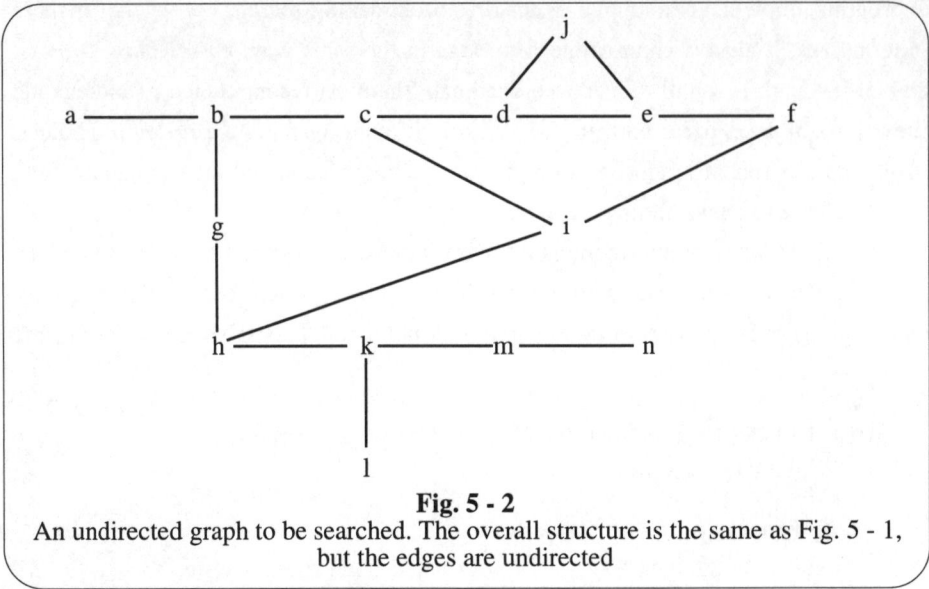

Fig. 5 - 2
An undirected graph to be searched. The overall structure is the same as Fig. 5 - 1,
but the edges are undirected

5.2.2 Searching Undirected Graphs

The next improvement allows undirected graphs to be searched. We will use an undirected version of the graph in Fig. 5 - 1, as shown in Fig. 5 - 2. In this graph it is possible to travel from node *a* to node *b*, or from *b* to *a*. A naive way of reflecting this in the Fril program would be to duplicate the set of *edge* clauses, but reverse the arguments in each duplicate, i.e. add the clauses

```
((edge b a))
((edge c b))
  .
  .
  .
((edge m k))
((edge n m))
```

to the program. This is adequate but rather inelegant, as for every clause of the form *(edge node1 node2)* we have its inverse *(edge node2 node1)*. It is tempting to stick with the original set of clauses and supplement them with a rule to cover the inverse cases:

```
((edge a b))                    /* definition of graph */
((edge b c))
((edge b g))
  .
  .
  .
((edge k m))
((edge m n))
((edge X Y) (edge Y X))
```

The rule states that the inverse of every edge in the graph is also an edge. This rule must appear after the facts, so that if an edge between a pair of nodes is not recorded as an *edge* fact, the system will look for the inverse *edge* fact, since if none of the facts match then the rule will be tried. On the surface, this seems like an elegant solution. However, it is fundamentally flawed, as consideration of the goal

> *(edge a h)*

will show. No fact will match this goal, but the rule will match, giving the bindings (X=a, Y=h), and yielding the new goal

> *(edge h a)*

Again, this is not matched by any facts but will match the rule with (X'=h, Y'=a) yielding the goal

> *(edge a h)*

This is identical to the original goal; thus the system will cycle repeatedly between these two unsatisfiable goals. The solution to this problem is to separate the rule and facts. We define a rule such as

> ((joined X Y) (edge X Y))
>
> ((joined X Y) (edge Y X))

with the original set of *edge* clauses. This covers all possibilities and fails correctly when two nodes are not linked by an undirected edge, e.g. *(joined a h)* will fail. We must modify the definition of *path1* to work with this:

```
((path2 START END (START END))    /* Can we go in one step */
   (joined start END))            /*look for undirected edge*/

((path2 CURRENT END (CURRENT|REST))
   (joined CURRENT NEXT)          /*move one (undirected) step*/
   (path2 NEXT END REST))         /* and continue */
```

This is identical to the definition *path1*, except it calls *joined* rather than *edge* to reflect the fact that we are working with an undirected graph whose edges are defined by the *joined* clauses. The program works adequately in some cases but suffers from a serious problem in others. Consider the goal *(path2 d h L)*. Nodes *d* and *h* are not joined directly, so the first clause for *path* fails. The goal list develops as follows:

(path2 d h L)	uses clause 2, CURRENT=d END=h L=(d|REST)
(joined d NEXT) (path2 NEXT h REST)	matches clause 1, X=d Y=NEXT
(edge d NEXT) (path2 NEXT h REST)	matches clause 6, NEXT=j
(path2 j h REST)	uses clause 2, CURRENT'=d END'=h ,REST=(j|REST')
(joined j NEXT') (path2 NEXT' h REST')	usesmatches clause 2, X'=j Y'=NEXT'
(edge NEXT' j) (path2 NEXT' h REST')	matches clause 6, NEXT'=d
(path2 d h REST')	

The last goal is identical to the initial goal (except for the different variable used). Clearly the program will loop, building an infinite path of the form *d-j-d-j....* To alleviate this problem we need to keep a record of nodes already visited, and prevent further visits to those nodes. It is not immediately clear how to achieve this, as a call to *path2* builds up the route one node at a time, with the recursive call filling in the remainder of the path. The information on nodes already visited is not available to pass down to the recursive call. We must add another argument, this time to allow calls which are later in the recursion to access the nodes that have already been visited. The general form of the head is

    (path3 *node1 node2 route visited*)

where the *route* argument is used as above to build up the path between nodes and the *visited* argument is used to pass down a list of nodes that should not be revisited. The definition is:

```
((path3 START END  (START  END) VISITED)
     (joined START  END)
     (negg member END  VISITED))

((path3 CURRENT END  (CURRENT |REST) VISITED)
     (joined CURRENT  NEXT)
     (negg member NEXT VISITED)
     (path3 NEXT END  REST  (NEXT|VISITED)))

((member E (E|T)))
((member E (H|T)) (member E T))
```

where the definition of *member* was discussed in Section 2.6.3. The program can be run via the query

    ?((path3 a h P (a))(pp P))

    (a b c d j e f i h)
    yes

The final argument to *path3* is a list, VISITED, which at each stage in the recursion contains the nodes already included on the path. We can check that no loops are created by ensuring that the NEXT node chosen has not already been visited. If it has, it will be a member of the list VISITED and the call *(negg member NEXT VISITED)* will fail, forcing the system to backtrack and choose another candidate NEXT node by resatisfying the goal *(joined CURRENT NEXT)*.

For completeness, we also check in the first clause that the END node has not already been visited. This is only relevant in certain circumstances when the program backtracks.

212

```
           goal                                    bindings
1  (path3  a  h  P  (a))                    P     = (a|REST1)
2  (path3  b  h  REST1  (b  a))             REST1 = (b|REST2)
3  (path3  c  h  REST2  (c  b  a))          REST2 = (c|REST3)
4  (path3  d  h  REST3  (d  c  b  a))       REST3 = (d|REST4)
5  (path3  j  h  REST4  (j  d  c  b  a))    REST4 = (j|REST5)
6  (path3  e  h  REST5  (e  j  d  c  b  a)) REST5 = (e|REST6)
7  (path3  f  h  REST6  (f  e  j  d  c  b  a)) REST6 = (f|REST7)
8  (path3  i  h  REST7  (i  f  e  j  d  c  b  a)) REST7 = (i  h)
```

Fig. 5 - 3

Evolution of the goal using the definition *path3* to find a path from node *a* to node *h* in the undirected graph shown in Fig. 5 - 2. The final binding for P is *(a b c d j e f i h)*.

The goal list develops as shown in Fig. 5 - 3. For clarity, we only show the calls to *path*, and omit the intermediate calls to other goals; instances of variables in the recursive calls are subscripted 1,2,etc.

At step 6, *d* is initially chosen as the *NEXT* node, but is then rejected as it has already been visited. At step 7, *j* is tried and rejected in the same way. The final binding for *P* is *(a b c d j e f i h)*. This is built up step by step, and the answer is available at the top level - each lower level passes back to its caller the answer from the next level down, augmented by one more node. In contrast, the list of nodes visited (fourth argument) is augmented and passed down to the next level. This different usage of arguments is an important point and must be appreciated in order to design programs correctly.

Because of the need to avoid revisiting the first node, we call *path3* with the initial node already in the list of visited nodes. This could be avoided by changing the definition of the second clause:

```
((path4 START  END  (START  END) VISITED)
    (joined START  END)
    (negg member START  VISITED)
    (negg member END  VISITED))

((path4 CURRENT  END  (CURRENT |REST) VISITED)
    (joined CURRENT  NEXT)
    (negg member CURRENT  VISITED)
    (path4 NEXT END  REST  (CURRENT|VISITED)))
```

i.e. we add the *current* node to the list of those visited, rather than the *next* node. This definition would require the query

?((path4 a h P ())(pp P))

However, this has the disadvantage of moving the test for the acceptability of a node down to the next stage of the recursion. Thus if *CURRENT* is a member of *VISITED*, it is

213

possible that several solutions to the goal *(joined CURRENT NEXT)* may be produced unnecessarily - the goal *(negg member CURRENT VISITED)* will fail no matter what binding is found for *NEXT*.

We note that in Fig. 5 - 3 when the recursion terminates at step 8, the list of nodes visited is the reverse of the path found. An obvious question is whether we can make use of this list to answer the query, instead of having to build up a separate list for the route. The subject of returning the correct value to the top level where the program was called is frequently confusing to programmers who are used to thinking in the constructs of procedural languages, and expect to be able to return a value from any point in a program. Because Fril is a relational language rather than a functional language, all passing of values must be done via arguments - both inputs to a procedure and outputs from a procedure. This makes the language more flexible since more than one "return value" may be passed back, and it is frequently not necessary to define in advance which arguments are input and which are output. In order to make a value accessible to the caller as a return value, it must be passed back via one of the head arguments. Thus we could replace the definition of *path3* by

```
((path5 START  END  ROUTE VISITED)
    (joined START  END)
    (negg member END  VISITED)
    (reverse VISITED ROUTE))

((path5 CURRENT  END  ROUTE  VISITED)
    (joined CURRENT  NEXT)
    (negg member NEXT VISITED)
    (path5 NEXT END  ROUTE  (NEXT|VISITED)))
```

with a suitable definition of *reverse*, such as that given in Section 2.6.6. Instead of building up the path as we go down the recursion, we wait until the recursion terminates (first clause) and then create the path in one go by reversing the list of nodes visited. In the definition of *path5*, the third parameter is simply present as a 'place-holder', to enable the answer to be passed back from the lowest level of the recursion up to the top level where the answer is required. There is one drawback to this program, related to flexibility in the use of the list of nodes to be visited. For instance, if we want to find a route from *a* to *h* avoiding node *d*, we could use the query

```
qh((path3 a h P (a d)))

((path3 a h (a b c i h) (a d)))
((path3 a h (a b g h) (a d)))
no (more) solutions
yes
```

214

However, with the definition *path5*, this would not be possible as the list of nodes visited is also used to form the route. Instead, we would have to use a query such as

?((path5 a h P (a)) (negg member d P) (pp P))

Whilst this would produce the same answers, it is less efficient, as an entire path is produced before being checked for passing through node *d*. Backtracking to find another path does not necessarily produce a path without node *d* - in this case, the first two paths produced by the call to *path5* are

(a b c d j e f i h)

(a b c d e f i h)

both of which contain *d* and thus fail the call *(negg member d P)*. Backtracking in this case does not go far enough to undo the inclusion of *d* in the path, although the next solution found by *path5 would* be acceptable. As a general rule, it is best to place a test (such as checking that node *d* is not on the path) as close as possible to the part of the program which generates the value being tested. This is the case in the definition *path3*, as nodes are only added to the path when it is known that they are not on the forbidden list; however in the definition of *path4* and the query using *path5*, the tests are performed considerably later. In a simple benchmark using the programs and queries shown, *path3* was found to be well over an order of magnitude faster than the query using *path5*.

5.2.3 Searching Other Graphs

A depth-first backtracking search is simple to write in Fril, as every program executes using exactly this strategy. The program above can be used to search any graph, by replacing the definition of *joined* with one appropriate to the new problem. Many problems can be represented as a search through a state-space graph - for example, a classic AI problem is the "jugs puzzle". In this problem, two containers (jugs) of capacity 5 and 7 litres are provided, together with a source of water and a sink. The only actions allowed are to fill either container from the tap, empty either container completely into the sink, or transfer water from one container to the other until one is either full or empty. The object of the exercise is to find a way of getting a specified quantity of water in one of the containers, say 4 litres in the small container.

The problem can be represented easily by a graph in which each node is labelled with a pair of numbers representing the quantity of water in the small and large container respectively. Thus (0 0) represents the state in which both are empty, (5 7) represents the state in which both are full. A portion of the graph is shown in Fig. 5 - 4. It is straightforward to write a set of Fril clauses which define the edges of the graph as allowed transitions between states, e.g.

((joined (S L) (S 7)))

would represent the action of filling the large jug from the tap as (S L) represents the initial (unknown) state, and (S 7) represents the state in which the large jug is filled and the small jug is unchanged from the initial state. Similarly

((joined (S L) (S 0)))

would represent the action of emptying the large container. The above search program can then be used to find a path from the state (0 0) to the state (4 0). As in the maze example, the path found may not be the simplest path, but with further refinement the program could find it. Similarly it is easy to extend this program to deal with weighted arcs so that different costs or distances may be ascribed to different paths within the graph. It is also straightforward to program more sophisticated search

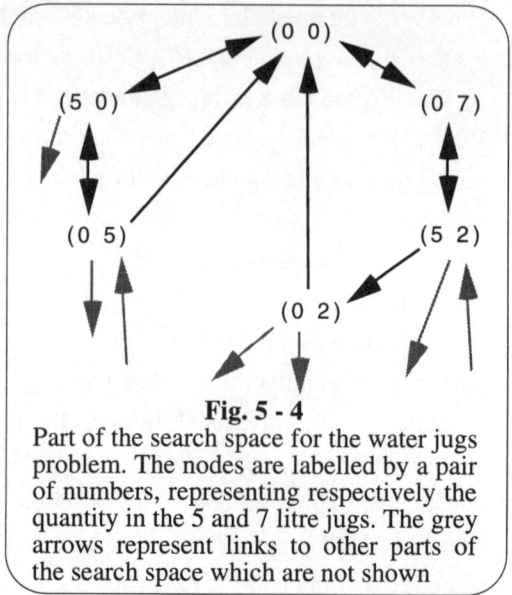

Fig. 5 - 4
Part of the search space for the water jugs problem. The nodes are labelled by a pair of numbers, representing respectively the quantity in the 5 and 7 litre jugs. The grey arrows represent links to other parts of the search space which are not shown

strategies such as breadth-search, heuristic search etc., using Fril. These topics are covered in the Fril tutorial manual, and in more general terms in most fundamental texts on AI. The interested reader is referred to one of these sources for further details.

5.2.4 An Elementary Interface for the Search Program

Finally, we embed the search program *path3* in an elementary user interface that prompts for start and end nodes, checks that these are valid, and then prints out the route between them. This illustrates the use of various Fril built-in predicates and shows how we could start to build up a usable system. It is included as motivation for the various issues - a true user-friendly system would probably use more advanced features of the Fril system to build up a complete 'point-and-click' mouse-driven interface. The tasks that the system must perform are:

1. prompt for the nodes and read the values typed in
2. ensure that nodes are valid
3. find the route and display the message

Thus our top-level program looks like this:

```
((find_path)
    (get_valid_node start START)
    (get_valid_node end END)
    (path3 START END ROUTE (START))
    (output START END ROUTE))
```

where we have used the same procedure to read in the start and end nodes, distinguishing them by the first argument which will be used in the prompt. Getting a valid node should

216

print a prompt, read the input, and then check it is valid:

```
((get_valid_node NTYPE NODE)
    (p What is your NTYPE node)
    (r NODE)
    (valid_node NODE) (!))

((get_valid_node NTYPE NODE)
    (get_valid_node NTYPE NODE))

((valid_node N) (con N) (joined N _) (!))
((valid_node N) (p Sorry N is not a valid node)(pp)(fail))
```

We define a node to be valid if it is a constant, and it is joined to another node. This definition would be inadequate (for example) in the case where a node was not connected to any other nodes; however, in our example this is a convenient test for ensuring nodes are valid. The second clause for *valid_node* covers the failure case, when the node is not valid. Logically we want this case to fail and from this point of view we should only include the first clause. However, from the practical point of view we would like to indicate that the node is not valid; thus we print a message and cause the *valid_node* goal to fail. This is logically equivalent to omitting the clause, but has the useful side-effect of printing information.

The goal *(r NODE)* in the first clause for *get_valid_node* calls the built-in predicate *r*, which reads the next term type on the input stream and binds it to the argument *NODE*. The second clause for *get_valid_node covers* the case where *valid_node* fails, and simply repeats the call. Once two valid nodes have been read, *find_path* is called to search for a route between the two nodes, and *output* prints the path:

```
((output START END ROUTE)
    (p One possible path between START and END is ROUTE )
    (pp))
```

If there is no route between the selected nodes, *find_path* will fail. It would be simple to add a clause warning the user of this situation.

The program runs as shown below:

```
?((find_path))
        What is your start node      s
        Sorry s is not a valid node
        What is your start node      a
        What is your end node        h
        One possible path between a and h is (a b c d j e f i h)
        yes
```

Clearly this is a very rudimentary system, but it forms the basis for a more sophisticated approach. Search is a fundamental aspect of many programs, and is straightforward to program using the logic programming features of Fril.

5.3 SYSTEMS PROGRAMMING IN FRIL

One of the aspects of Fril which distinguishes it from many other languages is the fact that program source and data have a very similar form, namely lists. This enables standard list processing techniques to be applied to fragments of Fril code (either clauses or queries). Meta-programming is an extremely useful technique in the Fril programmer's repertoire which exploits this feature. Essentially it allows us to use a *variable* in place of the predicate in a goal, provided that the variable is instantiated to a constant by the time the goal is called. More generally, we can use a variable in place of any code fragment, as long as the variable is instantiated to a valid structure when the code is executed.

5.3.1 Use of a Variable in place of a Predicate

Consider the following program which checks that the elements of a non-empty list are in strictly ascending order:

    ((ordered (E)))
    ((ordered (E1 E2|T)) (less E1 E2) (ordered (E2|T)))
where *less* is a built-in predicate that succeeds if E1< E2.

?((ordered (1 2 3 4 10)))
    yes

?((ordered (1 2 3 3 10)))
    no

We could write a less strict version of *ordered* which simply checked that the elements were in non-descending order, allowing for the second case above where adjacent elements are equal:

    ((ordered2 (E)))
    ((ordered2 (E1 E2|T)) (less_eq E1 E2) (ordered2 (E2|T)))

where*(less_eq E1 E2)* succeeds if E1 ≤ E2.

    ?((ordered2 (1 2 3 3 10)))
    yes

    ?((ordered2 (1 2 3 2 10)))
    no

218

There is a large degree of similarity between these two definitions - so much so that we could write a common definition and pass the ordering predicate, *less* or *less_eq*, as an argument:

        ((ordered_by ANY (E)))
        ((ordered_by ORDER (E1 E2|T)) (ORDER E1 E2)(ordered (E2|T))

which would be called by

        ?((ordered_by less (1 2 3 4 10)))
        yes

        ?((ordered_by less (1 2 3 3 10)))
        no

        ?((ordered_by less_eq (1 2 3 3 10)))
        yes

From the theoretical point of view this is a departure from first order logic, because the clause corresponds to a logic statement quantified over the *predicate*. As a practical technique, it allows great flexibility in programming, as the example above illustrates.

The use of a variable predicate symbol is a very powerful mechanism, but the technique is restricted to cases where the predicate is instantiated at the time of the call. It is tempting, given a goal of the form *(X a b)*, to expect it to generate values for *X*, i.e. to succeed with different predicates naming relations satisfied by the pair *a* and *b*. For example, given a simple "blocks world" knowledge base:

            ((is–block block–1))
            ((is–block block–2))
            ((is–red block–1))
            ((is–red block–2))
            ((is–cube block–1))
            ((is–cylinder block–2))
            ((on–table block–1))   … etc

we might hope to find a common property of two blocks by means of a program such as

        ((common PROP B1 B2) (PROP B1) (PROP B2))

This will work if it is used to check that a property holds for two named blocks, e.g.

        ?((common is–red block–1 block–2))
        yes

or to generate pairs of blocks for which the property holds, e.g.

        qh((common is–red X Y))
        ((common is–red block–1 block–1))
        ((common is–red block–1 block–2))
        ((common is–red block–2 block–1))   … etc.
        yes

Unfortunately it cannot be used to generate properties which are common to two blocks, so that the query

   ?((common PR block–1 block–2) (p PR))

would cause an error as Fril would try to execute the goal *(PR block–1)* without instantiating the predicate *PR*. There are a number of ways around this. The first is simply to adopt the convention that this use of the program will not be allowed, and stipulate that it must only ever be used to check that a property is common, or to generate one or both blocks for which a given property holds. Clearly this may require additional code to enforce the constraint. Alternatively, we can modify the rule to ensure that the predicate is always instantiated before it is called. One way to do this would be to replace the rule by:

   ((common PROP B1 B2) (dict PROP) (PROP B1) (PROP B2))

where *dict* is a built-in predicate that checks or generates the names of predicates currently defined. A safer and more elegant way of achieving this would be to define a predicate *property* which lists all possible properties that a block might satisfy, and use this to generate or check the predicate names:

   ((property is–block))
   ((property is–red))
   ...etc
   ((common PROP B1 B2) (property PROP) (PROP B1) (PROP B2))

Then the query

   ?((common PR block–1 block–2) (p PR))
   is–block
   yes

generates a property which is common to both blocks.

Given this one limitation, the use of a variable in place of a predicate symbol leads to a powerful programming tool which enables techniques such as data abstraction to be implemented easily. The method can be extended quite straightforwardly to allow an object-oriented style of programming in Fril.

5.3.2 Use of Head and Tail Notation when Calling a Clause

We can use a similar technique to map a predicate over a list of arguments. Suppose that we have a list of numbers and we wish to check that a certain property is true of them all. We can use the definition

   ((map PRED ()))
   ((map PRED (H|T)) (PRED H) (map PRED T))

Then a query such as

   ?((map int (1 2 3)))

succeeds by executing the goals *(int 1)*, *(int 2)*, and *(int 3)* at successive levels of the recursion (*int* is a built-in predicate which is true if its argument is an integer), and

> ?((map int (1.2 2 3 a)))

fails as the first element of the list leads to the goal *(int 1.2),* which fails.

The idea can be extended to predicates which generate a value, e.g. the built-in predicate *square* is true if its second argument is the square of its first, and can be used to generate squares or square roots as well as checking values. We define the predicate *(apply pred list1 list2)* which is true if each element of *list2* is the result of applying the predicate *pred* to the corresponding argument of *list1*.

> ((apply PRED () ()))
> ((apply PRED (H|T) (RESULT|REST))
>   (PRED H RESULT)
>   (apply PRED T REST))

This behaves as shown by the following queries:

> ?((apply square (2 4 6) R) (p R))
> (4 16 36)
> yes

> ?((apply square L (2 4 6)) (p L))
> (1.41421 2 2.44949)
> yes

Notice that the second example returns only the positive square roots, as the negative root is not given by the Fril built-in predicate. We could define a more general clause that gave both positive and negative square roots of a positive number:

> ((sqroot X P N) (less 0 X)(square P X)(times -1 P N))

Now, we could try to apply this to a list of numbers, using a query of the form

> ?((apply sqroot (2 4 6 7) L)(pp L))

The definition of *apply* given above is inadequate, since it relies on the predicate having arity 2, i.e. it would call the goal *(sqroot 2 RESULT).* Clearly this will not match the head of the clause for *sqroot*, and so the goal will fail. We could add a new definition of *apply*,

> ((apply2 PRED () ()))
> ((apply2 PRED (H|T) ((RES1 RES2)|REST))
>   (PRED H RES1 RES2)
>   (apply2 PRED T REST))

which caters for the fact that the definition of *sqroot* uses two arguments to return the values. However, this is contrary to the spirit of logic programming propounded in this book, as it requires a specialised version of *apply* for each different arity. We therefore change the definition to

```
((applyn PRED () ()))
((applyn PRED (H|T) (RESULTS|REST))
    (PRED H | RESULTS)
    (applyn PRED T REST))
```

This copes with *any* number of arguments, and only requires that the "input" argument is the first, i.e. that the predicate to be mapped over the list has the general form

(pred input output1 output2 ... outputn)

In the goal *(PRED H | RESULTS)*, the Fril system unifies the argument *RESULTS* with any additional arguments there are present in the clause head. This is easy to understand if we consider the calling process as a simple unification between a goal and the head of a clause. There is no problem in unifying the two terms

(sqroot X P N)   and *(sqroot 2|RESULTS)* with X=2, RESULTS=(P N)

        or

(square X XSQ)   and *(square 2|RESULTS)* with X=2, RESULTS=(XSQ)

One can use this mechanism in a variety of ways, for example to write a predicate with a variable number of arguments. We have already seen the *append* program in Section 2.6.5, which can be used to concatenate two lists. Let us assume that we need to extend this to an arbitrary number of lists, so that the predicate *concat* is true if its first argument is the result of concatenating the remaining lists, i.e. it has the following behaviour:

```
?((concat X (a b c) (d e f))(p X))
(a b c d e f)
yes

?((concat X (a b c) (d e f) (g h i) (j) (k l))(p X))
(a b c d e f g h i j k l)
yes
```

The program can be written as:

```
((concat () ()))
((concat RESULT L1|REST)
    (concat R REST) (append L1 R RESULT))
```

with the definition of *append* given in Chapter 2.

We note in passing that whilst a definition such as *concat* could be convenient from the programming point of view, it is not desirable from the logical point of view as it is difficult to define the meaning of the clauses. In addition, there is a practical limitation on the use of the program arising from Fril's restriction of the arity of a goal

(31 on most hardware platforms). A more elegant definition would have two arguments, the second being a list of the lists to be concatenated and the first being the result of the concatenation process:

```
((clean_concat () ()))
((clean_concat RESULT (L|REST))
    (clean_concat R REST)
    (append L R RESULT))
```

This works correctly with any number of lists to be concatenated.

5.3.3 Using Variables to Represent Larger Fragments of Program

Finally we examine a more general use of meta-variables to represent larger fragments of code. Let us suppose that we wish to write an *if...then...else* construct for Fril. This will have the general form

```
(if (test)
    ((list of goals to be executed if test succeeds))
    ((list of goals to be executed if test fails)) )
```

e.g.

```
?((if (less 2 1) ((p something wrong)(pp))
            ((p all ok)(pp)) ))
all ok
yes
```

In this case, the test fails, so the *then* branch is ignored and the goals in the *else* branch are executed. We will assume that the test is deterministic, i.e. once it has succeeded it should not be resatisfied. This can be programmed quite simply as

```
((if TEST THEN ELSE)  TEST (!) | THEN)
((if TEST THEN ELSE)   | ELSE)
```

The variables *THEN* and *ELSE* are used to form either part or all of the bodies of the two clauses. Thus with the goal above, the two clauses become

```
((if (less 2 1)((p something wrong)(pp))((p all ok)(pp)))
    (less 2 1)
    (!)
    (p something wrong)(pp))
```

```
((if (less 2 1) ((p something wrong)(pp))((p all ok)(pp)))
    (p all ok)(pp))
```

The bodies of the two clauses are replaced at run-time by structures which are valid lists of goals. This is an extremely powerful tool in systems programming, and enables very general programs to be written compactly. The *if-then-else* construct above is actually one of the Fril built-in predicates, and is implemented in Fril as shown. Its use can clarify programs in some instances but in others can lead to very confused and poorly structured code, particularly if the programmer is still wedded to the procedural constructs of conventional languages.

5.3.4 Use of *cl* to Decompile Clauses

The discussion above may give the impression that Fril is an interpreted system, with clauses being examined and executed at run-time. In fact much of the work of an interpreted system can be performed at the time when the clauses are first read into the system, and Fril clauses are actually compiled on loading into a series of instructions for an abstract machine. These instructions are either compiled further into machine code or are executed by means of an emulator. The use of variables to represent parts of Fril code which can be instantiated at run-time requires special treatment within this architecture. Since clauses are input as lists of lists, we may ask whether the list processing facilities can be used to pattern-match against larger sections of code, rather than just within the execution of a single goal. The built-in predicate *cl* can be used to decompile clauses back to their source list structure. Effectively this gives us a means of matching the entire list structure of a clause against another list. Thus we can find a clause which matches a particular list pattern without having to execute the clause.

In its simplest form, *cl* takes a list which could represent a clause, i.e. one in which the first element is a list whose first element is a constant:

$(cl\ ((<const>\ |X)\ |Y)\ )$

where *<const>* is an arbitrary constant. Other forms of *cl* allow the support associated with a clause to be determined, and more sophisticated searching and indexing of the knowledge base. The interested reader is referred to the Fril manual for details. *cl* is one of the few built-in predicates that are resatisfiable, and it successively returns different clauses which match the given pattern, in the order in which they appear in the knowledge base. This means that we can simulate the execution of a Fril program - in order to execute a list of goals, we take the first goal and find the first clause whose head matches this goal. If necessary, we execute the body of the clause, and then continue with the second goal in the original list. The body of the matching clause is, of course, just another list of goals which can be treated in exactly the same way. If at any stage there is no clause whose head matches a goal then that goal fails and we return to the most recent point at which alternative clauses existed. This account, of course, does not cater for built-in predicates. We will return to this point later.

The simulation program is:

```
((exec () ))                          /* no goals - success */
((exec ((PRED|ARGS)|GOALS))
    (cl ((PRED|ARGS)|BODY))           /* is there a matching clause*/
    (exec BODY)                       /* execute the body */
    (exec GOALS))                     /* continue with other goals */
```

We can easily extend this to handle most built-in predicates. These will not return any matching clauses for the *cl* built-in predicate; however, we can use the built-in predicate *sys* to filter out these cases:

```
((exec2 () ))                         /* no goals - success */
((exec2 ((PRED|ARGS)|GOALS))
    (sys PRED)                        /* is it a built-in pred */
    (PRED|ARGS)                       /* execute it */
    (exec2 GOALS))                    /* continue with other goals */
((exec2 ((PRED|ARGS)|GOALS))
    (cl ((PRED|ARGS)|BODY))           /* is there a matching clause*/
    (exec2 BODY)                      /* execute the body */
    (exec2 GOALS))                    /* continue with other goals */
```

This program could form the basis of a crude debugging package to trace the execution of programs, for example by printing a message each time the execution of a goal is simulated. This approach would work adequately in many cases - there are, however, a number of disadvantages in the handling of built-in predicates. For example, if a goal such as *(negg pred1 a (b c a))* is encountered, it would be trapped by the second clause as *(sys negg)* succeeds. The goal *(negg pred1 a (b c a))* would then be executed by the second goal in the body of clause 2. We might prefer to examine the workings of the call to *pred1*, and this could be arranged by suitable further processing of certain built-in predicates such as *negg*. More seriously, the simulation does not handle the cut correctly. To illustrate this, consider the program for finding the maximum of two numbers given in Section 2.7.1.

```
((max X Y X) (less Y X) (!))
((max X Y Y))
```

As discussed at the time, this program is efficient and works correctly on backtracking, but it is not a "logical" definition of the relation because it relies on the use of the cut to control execution rather than being a logical specification of the relation. The query

?((max 4 2 M)(pp M)(fail))

leads to the execution tree shown in Fig. 5 - 5. The first clause for *max* matches the first goal in the list, *(max 4 2 M)*, and its body succeeds. The value 4 is printed, and the *(fail)* goal causes backtracking to take place. Although the head of the second *max* clause

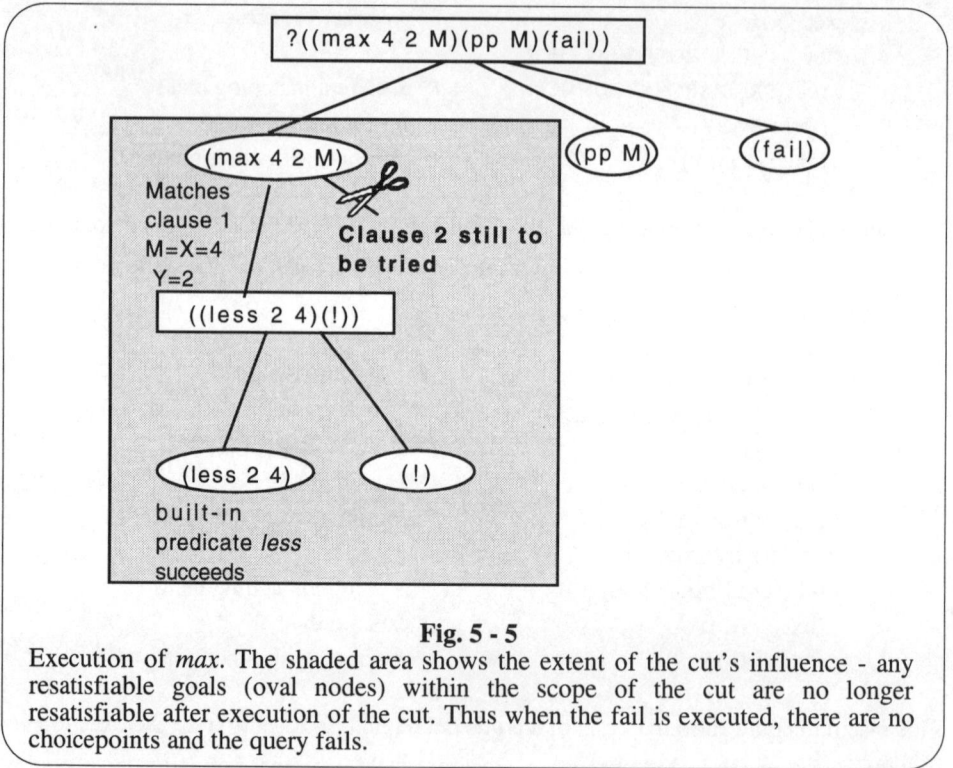

Fig. 5 - 5

Execution of *max*. The shaded area shows the extent of the cut's influence - any resatisfiable goals (oval nodes) within the scope of the cut are no longer resatisfiable after execution of the cut. Thus when the fail is executed, there are no choicepoints and the query fails.

would also match the first goal, it is not considered because the cut in the body of the first clause removes this choicepoint from consideration.

Thus no further solutions are produced. However, in the simulation of execution produced by *exec2*, a different situation is found (see Fig. 5 - 6). Because the cut is absorbed into the body of the second clause for *exec2*, its scope does not extend as far as the goal *(cl ((max 4 2 M)|BODY)* which generates the clauses whose bodies are "executed". On backtracking, the second possible matching clause is produced by *cl* and an alternative (but incorrect) solution is printed.

The problem arises from the cut being executed at the wrong level. It is impossible to interfere with the Fril execution mechanism to extend the scope of the cut; however, with a little ingenuity it is possible to use the meta-variable facilities of the language to pass a cut back to the correct place and execute it there. In Fig. 5 - 6, we wish the cut to affect all goals to the left of and below the goal

(exec2 ((less 2 4) (!)))

If we separate the treatment of the first goal in any list from the treatment of the remaining goals in the list, we can devise a mechanism. Let each goal pass back a goal to be executed. In the case of a cut, this goal will also be a cut; in all other cases it will be some neutral goal which simply succeeds (*no_cut* below). Then following the (simulated) execution of the goal body, we can execute the additional goals and achieve the desired effect.

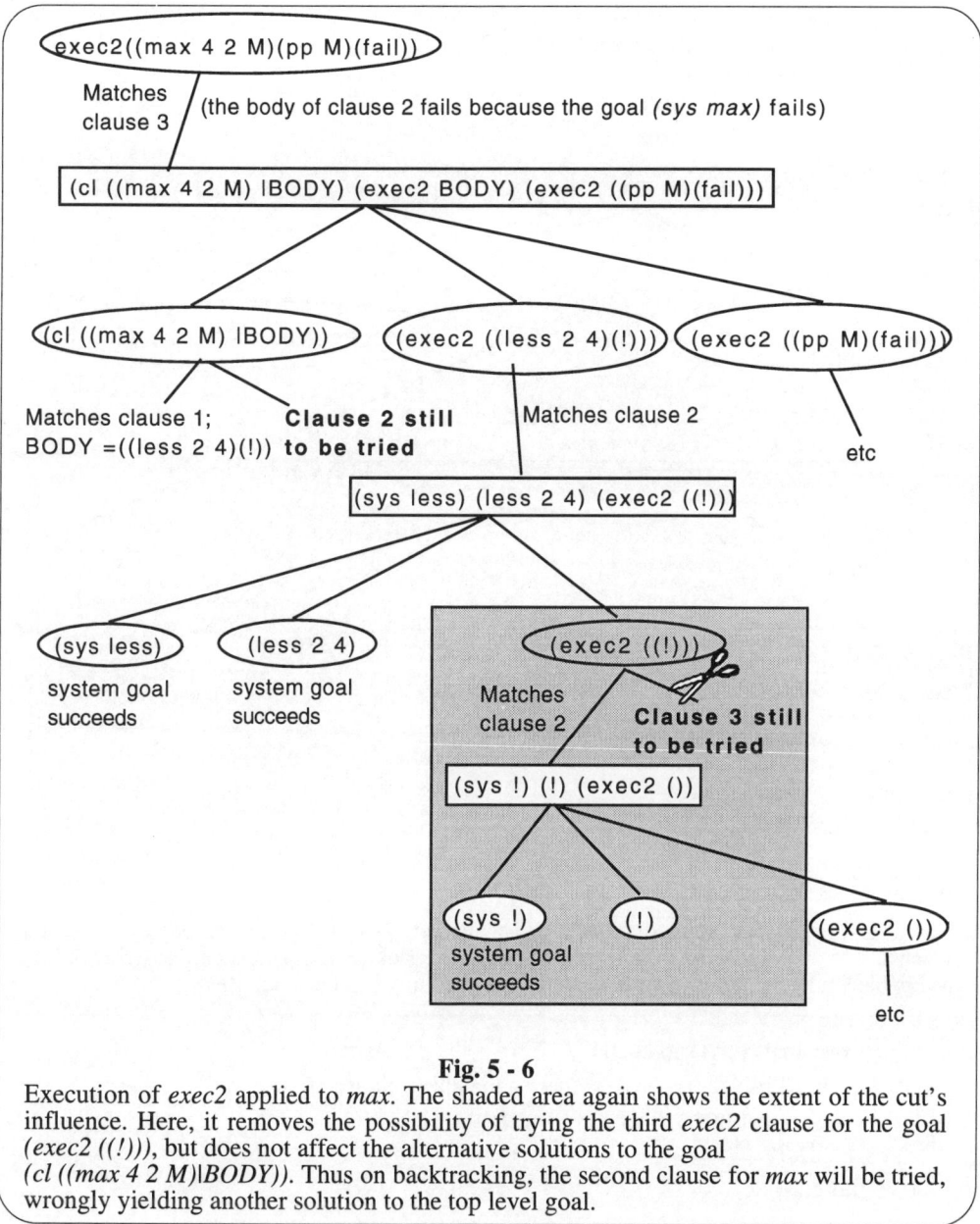

exec2((max 4 2 M)(pp M)(fail))

Matches clause 3 / (the body of clause 2 fails because the goal *(sys max)* fails)

(cl ((max 4 2 M) IBODY) (exec2 BODY) (exec2 ((pp M)(fail))))

(cl ((max 4 2 M) IBODY))　　(exec2 ((less 2 4)(!)))　　(exec2 ((pp M)(fail)))

Matches clause 1;　　**Clause 2 still**　　Matches clause 2
BODY =((less 2 4)(!))　**to be tried**
　　　　　　　　　　　　　　　　　　　　　　　　　etc

(sys less) (less 2 4) (exec2 ((!)))

(sys less)　　(less 2 4)　　(exec2 ((!)))
system goal　　system goal　　Matches　　**Clause 3 still**
succeeds　　succeeds　　clause 2　　**to be tried**

(sys !) (!) (exec2 ())

(sys !)　　(!)　　(exec2 ())
system goal
succeeds　　　　　　　　etc

Fig. 5 - 6
Execution of *exec2* applied to *max*. The shaded area again shows the extent of the cut's influence. Here, it removes the possibility of trying the third *exec2* clause for the goal *(exec2 ((!)))*, but does not affect the alternative solutions to the goal *(cl ((max 4 2 M)|BODY))*. Thus on backtracking, the second clause for *max* will be tried, wrongly yielding another solution to the top level goal.

```
((exec-list () ()))
((exec-list ((P|A)|G)(EXT|EXTRAS))
    (exec-goal (P|A) EXT)
    (exec-list G EXTRAS))

((exec-goal (!) (!)) )
((exec-goal (P|A)
    (no-cut)) (sys P)(P|A))
```

227

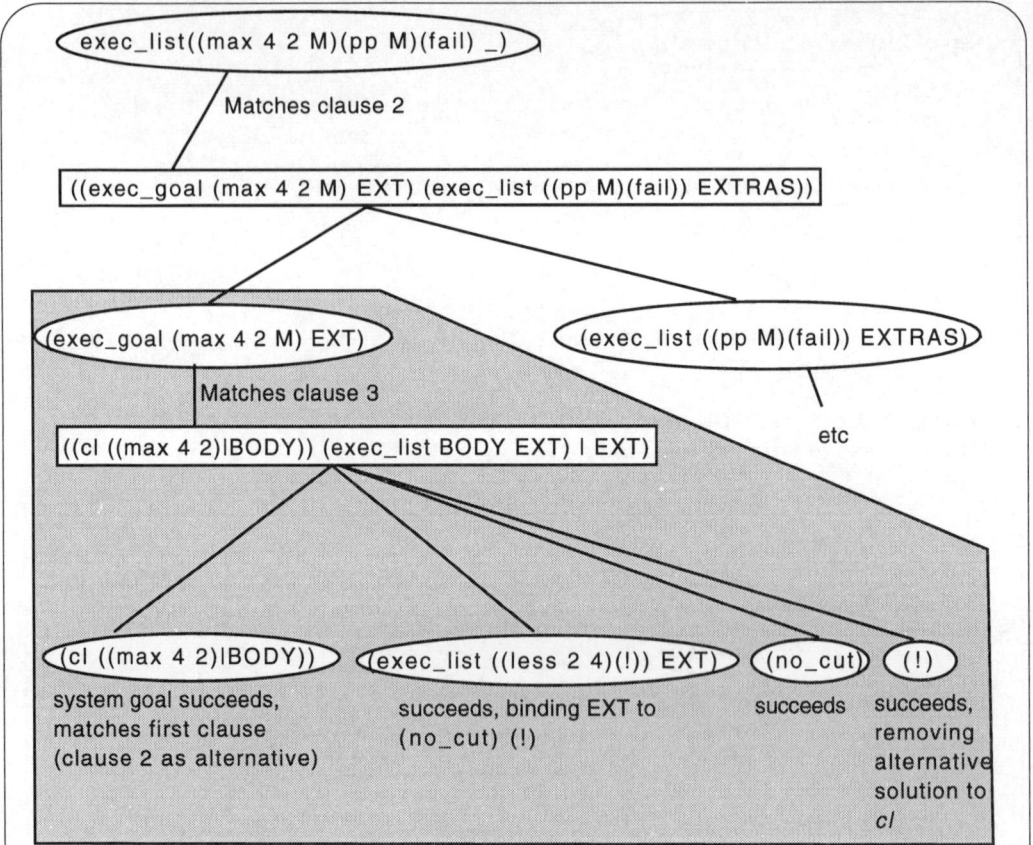

Fig. 5 - 7

Execution of *exec_list* applied to *max*. The shaded area shows the extent of the cut's influence which would lead to correct behaviour on backtracking. This can be achieved by passing back a list of goals to be executed once the body has been satisfied.

```
((exec-goal (P|A) (no-cut))
    (cl ((P|A)|BODY)) )   /* is there a matching clause */
    (exec-list BODY EXT)  /* execute the body */
    |EXT)
((no-cut))
```

The operation of this program is shown in Fig. 5 - 7. We note that there is a minor flaw in this program, if a goal of the form *(X)* is encountered, where *X* is an uninstantiated variable, then the definition will bind *X* to *!* and proceed as though a cut had been encountered. Also, the cut will be simulated incorrectly if a goal to the right of the cut in the body has alternative solutions. These matters have been ignored, as the aim is to illustrate the principles involved rather than actually implementing a completely robust system - it would be straightforward to add another test to detect the case of a variable predicate or goal and abort execution or take other suitable action. In a similar vein, a full

228

tracing system would require special treatment for a number of other system goals; however, apart from the cut, all of these cases can be treated straightforwardly. The interested reader is referred to the Fril manual for further discussion of the implementation of a trace package and treatment of the cut within it.

5.3.5 A Simple Inference Engine

We will explore another refinement, namely how to augment the system so that it can request information when none is present in the knowledge base. This is the situation in many knowledge-based systems, where the program is expected to work with the information available but to consult a human expert in certain cases where no information is recorded. Let us consider a simple knowledge base representing the rule:

the reliability of any system is acceptable if the design of the system is well-structured and the development of the system is high quality

together with the following information on two systems:

the design of system-a is well-structured

the design of system-b is well-structured

the development of system-a is high quality

This can be represented by the Fril clauses

```
((reliability-of SYSTEM is acceptable)
    (design–of SYSTEM is well–structured)
    (development–of SYSTEM is high–quality))
((design–of system–a is well–structured))
((design–of system–b is well–structured))
((development–of system–a is high–quality))
```

Clearly there is a great deal of uncertainty involved in these rules and terms, which would need to be included in a real system; for the purposes of illustrating the simple inference engine, we will ignore the uncertainty. Our inference engine is based on the simulator of Fril execution discussed in the previous section:

```
((show () ))                     /* no goals left - success */
((show ((PRED|ARGS)|GOALS))
    (cl ((PRED|ARGS)|BODY))      /* is there a matching clause*/
    (show BODY)                  /* execute the body */
    (show GOALS))                /* continue with other goals */
```

This allows goals of the form

```
show((reliability-of system-a is acceptable))
show((reliability-of system-b is acceptable))
```

to be executed - the first would succeed, the second would fail, because the fact

```
((development–of system–b is high–quality))
```

is not present. It would be helpful to recognise this, and be able to update the knowledge base if the information has been omitted accidentally. It would also be useful to explain the reasoning behind a conclusion. We extend the definition of *show* to cater for the missing information first:

```
((show2 () ))
((show2 ((PRED|ARGS)|GOALS) )
    (cl ((PRED|ARGS)|BODY) )
    (show2 BODY)
    (show2 GOALS))
((show2 ((PRED|ARGS)|GOALS) )
    (negg cl ((PRED|ARGS)|BODY))        /* no clause present */
    (missing-info (PRED|ARGS))           /* check on missing  information */
    (show2 GOALS))
((missing-info GOAL)
    (added-info GOAL RESPONSE)          /*has it already been added*/
    (!)                                  /* don't ask again */
    (eq RESPONSE yes))                   /* may be true or false */
((missing-info GOAL)
    (ask-about GOAL RESPONSE)           /* otherwise, ask */
    (addcl ((added-info GOAL RESPONSE)))) /* and record it*/
((ask-about GOAL RESPONSE)
    (p is it true that |GOAL)
    (pp)
    (p please answer yes or no)
    (r RESPONSE))
```

The built-in predicate *addcl* regards its argument as a clause, and adds this clause to the knowledge base. Running the second query illustrates the way information is elicited and stored in the knowledge base:

```
show2((reliability-of system-b is acceptable))
    is it true that development-of system-b is high-quality
    please answer yes or no   yes
    yes

show2((reliability–of system–b is acceptable))
    yes
```

The second time that the query is run, it is not necessary to prompt for the missing information since it has been entered into the knowledge base:

```
list added-info

    ((added-info (development-of system-b is high-quality) yes))
    yes
```

Clearly we would need to be more sophisticated about validating the response in the definition of *ask_about*, and we would also need to incorporate facilities for managing the information added under the clause *added_info*; however, this shows how a simple inference shell can be developed very rapidly with just a few lines of Fril code. Further enhancements could display the facts and rules used to derive a solution by adding print statements to the definition of *show2*, or include another argument to store all of the information in a tree structured list. This could then be interrogated to whatever depth is desirable from the top level.

5.3.6 Other Applications of Meta-Programming

Many of the built-in predicates of Fril are implemented in the Fril language using meta-programming techniques. For example, the predicates below fall into this category:

snips	makes a goal succeed only once
neg	negation as failure
negg	negation as failure
orr	standard Prolog disjunction
if	simulates if ... then ... else
forall	checks that a condition holds for all solutions to a goal
qh	finds and prints all solutions to a query
wh	finds all solutions to a query and prints an answer pattern for each
oh	finds and prints one solution to a query, backtracking to find another on request
isall	returns all solutions to a query, in a list
findall	similar to "isall" above, but with different syntax

5.4 IMPROVING THE EFFICIENCY OF FRIL PROGRAMS

In an ideal logic programming language, we could write a program as a declarative description of the problem under consideration, and then execute the program to produce a solution. Fril is a step towards such a language, but is only an approximation to the goal of logic programming. Consequently, a Fril program cannot always be written simply as a set of logical statements about the problem - it may be necessary to take the Fril execution strategy into account when writing the program. At the simple level, this means considering the order in which Fril solves goals and searches the knowledge base, as we have seen above in the development of a search program. As more complex programs are written, it becomes necessary to consider other aspects of program execution such as the amount of space required and the computations performed.

231

5.4.1 Measuring the Efficiency of Fril Programs

Fril programs are compiled into code for a virtual machine, which is then compiled further or executed by means of a byte-code emulator depending on the hardware platform. Many optimisations are performed automatically by the Fril compiler, and significant increases in efficiency can be obtained by knowledge of some of the optimisation strategies.

The main space requirements of Fril execution arise from
• the need to keep track of variable bindings so they can be undone on backtracking
• the need to remember goals which can be resatisfied on backtracking
• the need to remember goals which have not yet been executed.

The main factor influencing the time required by a Fril program is the number of goals which are executed. This can be estimated quite precisely by considering an execution tree similar to those illustrated in Chapter 2 and Fig. 5 - 5 to Fig. 5 - 7.

The Fril built-in predicate *statistics* can give a good guide to the amount of space required by a program. As a general guide, the amount of space is governed by
• the number of goals still to be executed (*control* and *environment* stacks)
• the number of goals that have been executed but are resatisfiable (*control* and *environment* stacks and *trail*)
• the number of lists created during execution (*copystack*).
The support stack is used during the evaluation of the support for a query, and is not considered here. The space used by the knowledge base and symbol table is related to the memory needed to store the compiled Fril program.

5.4.2 Recursion, Tail Recursion, and Accumulating Parameter Techniques

One of the most important factors influencing the space required by a program is the amount of recursion in the code. Recursion is invariably the natural programming style in Fril. It provides a compact and elegant method of breaking a problem down into one or more similar but less complex sub-problems. As an example, consider the program to find the length of a list.

```
((length () 0))
((length (H|T) L) (length T LT) (sum LT 1 L))
```

Here, the problem of finding the length of a list is reduced to the simpler problem of finding the length of the tail, T. This is simpler in the sense that the new problem is closer to the terminating condition given by the first clause. Once the length of the list T is known, the length of (H|T) is found by adding 1. We can write a general recursive clause:

```
((pred a1...an) (g1 b1...bm) ... (pred a1'...an') ... (gk c1...cj))
```

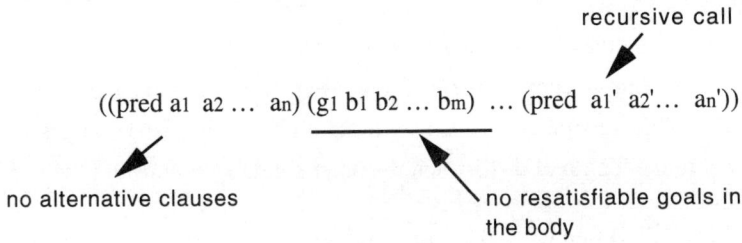

Fig. 5 - 8
General form of a tail recursive clause

where $a_1 \dots a_n$ are the arguments to the head, and the terms *(gi ...)* represent an arbitrary collection of goals in the body. A special case of recursion is known as *tail recursion* which occurs when the recursive call is the last goal in the body, there are no alternative clauses that match the head, and none of the goals in the body are resatisfiable (see Fig. 5 - 8). This may arise when the clause is the last in the definition of a predicate, or when other alternatives have been removed by means of a cut. In some circumstances, the Fril compiler can detect the fact that a clause is the last possible match because other clauses have incompatible arguments. Tail recursive definitions are subject to special optimisations which drastically reduce the amount of memory necessary for execution. In fact, tail recursion is formally equivalent to iteration, and the Fril system takes advantage of this by converting tail recursive calls to iterative calls which do not increase the control stack at all. This is known as *tail recursion optimisation..* A more general form, implemented in Fril is known as *last-call optimisation*. This is not restricted to recursive definitions and allows similar improvements to be made (say) in a pair of mutually recursive calls. Writing tail recursive programs is good practice and can lead to substantial savings in execution time and space as shown in the examples below. On the other hand, tail recursive Fril programs can be less easy to understand than the equivalent non-tail-recursive 'natural' definitions and it is often helpful to write the 'obvious' program first, and transform it to the more efficient tail-recursive form later, if efficiency considerations demand this.

To illustrate the process, consider the execution of *length*. This is a recursive program, but is not tail recursive as the recursive call to length is not the last call in the body. To find the length of the list *(a b c)*, the list of goals develops as follows :

```
(length (a b c) N)
(length (b c) LT) (sum LT 1 N)
(length (c) LT1) (sum LT1 1 LT) (sum LT 1 N)
(length () LT2) (sum LT2 1 LT1) (sum LT1 1 LT) (sum LT 1 N)
(sum 0 1 LT1) (sum LT1 1 LT) (sum LT 1 N)
(sum 1 1 LT) (sum LT 1 N)
(sum 2 1 N)
```

giving the solution N=3.

We can see that by the time the recursion terminates and the first goal matches the terminating condition (line 4 above), there is one *(sum ...)* goal outstanding for each element of the list. This version of the *length* program requires space (on the control stack) proportional to the length of the list. On the other hand, if we consider the program

```
((length LIST LEN) (len LIST 0 LEN))
((len () N N))
((len (H|T) C N) (sum C 1 C1) (len T C1 N))
```

the second clause for *len* is tail recursive. For the query
        ?((length (a b c) N)
the list of goals develops as follows

```
(length (a b c) N)
(len (a b c) 0 N)
(sum 0 1 C1) (len (b c) C1 N)
(len (b c) 1 N)
(sum 1 1 C1') (len (c) C1' N)
(len (c) 2 N)
(sum 2 1 C1") (len () C1" N)
(len () 3 N)
```

which matches the first clause for *len*, giving the solution N=3.

In this case, there are never more than two goals in the list, and the program executes in constant space irrespective of the length of the list. The number of goals executed is almost the same in the two cases, but the space requirement of the second definition is constant, as opposed to the order-N requirement of the first definition.

An equivalent program in a conventional language could be to take an array of unknown length and count the number of elements before a particular value is found. This would be simple to program iteratively, and would execute in constant space. The Fril program *len* is equivalent to such an iterative program.

5.4.3 Transforming Recursive Definitions into Tail Recursive Definitions

To investigate this process further, consider the factorial program
        ((fact 0 1) (!))
        ((fact N FN) (sum M 1 N) (fact M FM) (times N FM FN))
In a similar manner to *length* above, this requires space proportional to N, the number whose factorial is to be calculated. To find the factorial of 3, the list of goals develops as follows:

```
(fact 3 X)
(sum M 1 3) (fact M FM) (times 3 FM FN)
(fact 2 FM) (times 3 FM FN)
(sum M' 1 2)(fact M' FM') (times 2 FM' FM) (times 3 FM FN)
(fact 1 FM') (times 2 FM' FM) (times 3 FM FN)
(sum M"1 1) (fact M" FM") (times 1 FM" FM') (times 2 FM' FM) (times 3 FM FN)
(fact 0 FM") (times 1 FM" FM) (times 2 FM' FM) (times 3 FM FN)
(times 1 1 FM') (times 2 FM' FM) (times 3 FM FN)
(times 2 1 FM) (times 3 FM FN)
(times 3 2 FN)
```

ending with X bound to 6.

Execution gradually moves towards finding the factorial of 0, the terminating condition. When this matches the first goal in the list, there is one *(times …)* goal outstanding for each call to factorial. This version of the factorial program requires space proportional to N.

In a conventional language, factorial would probably be written iteratively :

```
fact(num)
{
        count = 0 ;
        ans = 1 ;
        while(count < num)
                count = count+1;
                ans = ans*count;
        endwhile
        return(ans)
}
```

where *count*, *ans*, and *num* are integer variables and the language is intended to be self-explanatory "pseudo-code". This program is iterative, and executes in constant space. Let us consider the Fril program as

```
((fact 0 1) (!))
((fact M_i F_i) (sum M_{i-1} 1 M_i)(fact M_{i-1} F_{i-1})(times M_i F_{i-1} F_i))
```

where the subscript i is used to index different occurrences of similar variables. We will consider the general query

```
?((factorial N X)(pp X))
```

where N is an arbitrary positive integer value. The program is essentially identical to the one discussed above and in Section 2.5.2, but we have renamed and subscripted the

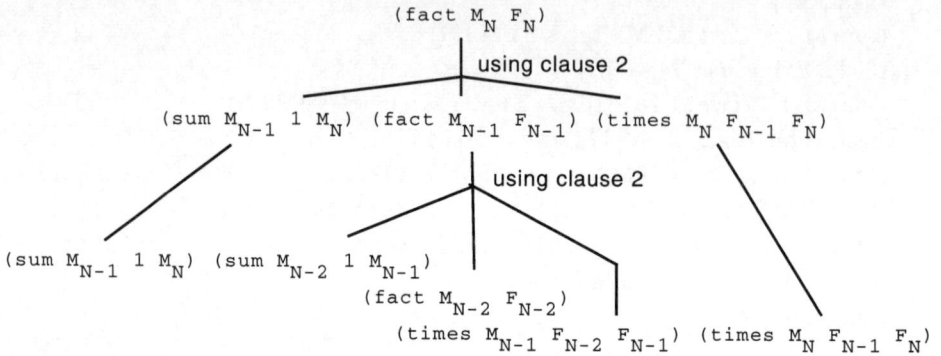

$$(\text{fact } M_N \; F_N)$$

using clause 2

$$(\text{sum } M_{N-1} \; 1 \; M_N) \quad (\text{fact } M_{N-1} \; F_{N-1}) \quad (\text{times } M_N \; F_{N-1} \; F_N)$$

using clause 2

$$(\text{sum } M_{N-1} \; 1 \; M_N) \quad (\text{sum } M_{N-2} \; 1 \; M_{N-1})$$
$$(\text{fact } M_{N-2} \; F_{N-2})$$
$$(\text{times } M_{N-1} \; F_{N-2} \; F_{N-1}) \quad (\text{times } M_N \; F_{N-1} \; F_N)$$

Fig. 5 - 9

The first two stages in the unfolding process for *(fact N X)*. NB this is not an execution tree - it is an expansion of the original query. The goals in the expansion are the leaf nodes of the execution tree if the expansion is continued as far as possible.

variables. We can unfold the Fril factorial definition. The unfolding process replaces a goal by the body of a clause whose head matches the goal. The first two stages of unfolding are shown in Fig. 5 - 9.

Eventually the unfolding process will terminate, as the goal (fact M_i F_i) will be replaced by the first clause rather than the second; e.g. for N=3, we obtain the conjunction of goals:

$$(\text{sum } M_2 \; 1 \; M_3) \; (\text{sum } M_1 \; 1 \; M_2) \; (\text{sum } M_0 \; 1 \; M_1)$$
$$(\text{fact } M_0 \; F_0)$$
$$(\text{times } M_1 \; F_0 \; F_1) \; (\text{times } M_2 \; F_1 \; F_2) \; (\text{times } M_3 \; F_2 \; F_3)$$

In general we will then have a list of goals of the form:

$$\left(\bigwedge_{i=1}^{N} (\text{sum } M_{N-i} \; 1 \; M_{N-i+1}) \right) (\text{factorial } M_0 \; F_0) \left(\bigwedge_{i=1}^{N} (\text{times } M_i \; F_{i-1} \; F_i) \right)$$

Since we know $M_0 = 0$ and $F_0 = 0$ from the terminating clause, we can rearrange this sequence of goals as:

$$\left(\bigwedge_{i=1}^{N} (\text{sum } M_{i-1} \; 1 \; M_i) (\text{times } M_i \; F_{i-1} \; F_i) \right)$$

as, from a logical point of view, the order of elements in a conjunction is immaterial. To illustrate this, for N=3 we rearrange the goals as follows:

$$(\text{sum } M_0 \; 1 \; M_1) \; (\text{times } M_1 \; F_0 \; F_1)$$
$$(\text{sum } M_1 \; 1 \; M_2) \; (\text{times } M_2 \; F_1 \; F_2)$$
$$(\text{sum } M_2 \; 1 \; M_3) \; (\text{times } M_3 \; F_2 \; F_3)$$

Let us define a new predicate, say *f2* to represent

$$\left(\bigwedge_{k=i}^{N} (\text{sum } M_{k-1} \ 1 \ M_k)(\text{times } M_k \ F_{k-1} \ F_k) \right)$$

To convert this to Fril, we must include N as an argument since the recursion will not stop otherwise. Also, the result is calculated at the bottom level of the recursion and is not available at the top, so we must include an argument in which to pass the answer back to the top level. We therefore make the following definition:

((fact M_N F_N) (f2 0 1 M_N F_N))

((f2 M_N F_N M_N F_N) (!))

((f2 M_{i-1} F_{i-1} M_N F_N) (sum M_{i-1} 1 M_i) (times M_i F_{i-1} F_i) (f2 M_i F_i M_N F_N))

which executes the goal (fact 3 X) as follows:

(fact 3 X)
(f2 0 1 3 X)
(sum 0 1 M) (times M 1 F) (f2 M F 3 X)
(times 1 1 F) (f2 1 F 3 X)
(f2 1 1 3 X)
(sum 1 1 M') (times M' 1 F') (f2 M' F' 3 X)
(times 2 1 F') (f2 2 F' 3 X)
(f2 2 2 3 X)
(sum 1 1 M') (times M' 1 F') (f2 M' F' 3 X)
(times 2 1 F') (f2 2 F' 3 X)
(f2 2 2 3 X)
(sum 2 1 M") (times M" 2 F") (f2 M" F" 3 X)
(times 3 2 F") (f2 3 F" 3 X)
(f2 3 6 3 X)

This matches the first clause for f2, and binds X to 6.

We can improve further on this definition, since the multiplications can be done in any order. In the definition

((fact MN FN) (f3 MN 1 FN))

((f3 0 FN FN) (!))
((f3 M F FN) (sum M 1 MNEW)(times M F FNEW)(f3 MNEW FNEW FN))

the first argument is a counting parameter which decreases to zero in steps of 1, the second argument is the accumulating parameter in which the answer is built up, and the third argument is a slot in which the answer is passed back. This definition is perhaps marginally better than f2 as it uses three arguments rather than four, although the difference is barely detectable in practice. Both definitions can be interpreted declaratively. In the first case (f2), the head states

factorial of argument 1 is argument 2 and factorial of argument 3 is argument 4, and in the second case (f3)

factorial of argument 1 is argument 2 divided by argument 3

We can think of these clauses as solving a more general problem than the one we are interested in. We can then use the generalised predicate as a special case to solve the problem of interest. In a similar fashion the definition for *length* can be interpreted as finding the difference between the length of a list and a specified number. In the special case of this number being zero, the definition can be read as :

1. the length of list X is N if the length of X is N-0
2. the length of the empty list is N-N (= 0)
3. the length of the list (H|T) is L-D if the length of the tail, T, is L - (D+1).

An alternative way to develop the definition is to think completely procedurally in order to convert a non-tail recursive definition to a tail-recursive version. As a rule of thumb, the computation after the recursive call should be an associative operation so that we can reverse the order of the computation and start with the finishing value, working down to produce the answer when the terminating clause is reached. As the answer is required at the top of the tree rather than at the bottom, we also have to add an argument so that the answer can be passed back up to the top level.

It is good practice to insulate the modified definition from being called at the top level, as we have done in the examples above, e.g. we would call *length* or *fact* rather than the tail recursive versions *len* or *f2*. This mechanism also provides a useful opportunity to perform any type-checking of arguments, e.g. we could ensure that only factorials of positive integers were evaluated by defining

```
((fact N FN) (int N) (less 0 N) (!) (f2 0 1 N FN))
((fact N FN) (p positive integer needed instead of N))
```

This is preferable to including the check in the definition of *f2*, as we can be certain that if a valid argument is supplied at top level then all recursive calls will also have valid arguments. The cut is used in the first clause to guard against unwanted backtracking once it is known that the argument *N* is of the required form. It would be slightly more elegant to include two alternative clauses, one to handle each possible error condition.

5.4.4 A Tail Recursive Version of Reverse

As another example of improved efficiency, consider the simple list reversal program covered in Section 2.6.7:

```
((reverse () ()))
((reverse (H|T) R) (reverse T RT) (append RT (H) R))
((append () L L))
((append (H|L1) L2 (H|L3)) (append L1 L2 L3))
```

Consideration of execution shows that for a list of N elements this program requires space proportional to N^2, whereas an equivalent iterative program can run in space proportional to N.

The tail recursive definition of *reverse* has some similarities to the definition of *len* above. However, instead of using the difference between two numbers to represent the length of the list, we use the difference between two *lists* to represent the result of reversing a list. Instead of considering the problem of reversing a list, consider the problem of appending an arbitrary list to the reverse of a list, e.g.

(d e f) appended to the reverse of *(a b c)* would give *(c b a d e f)*

An alternative way of expressing this idea is to say that the list *(a b c)* reversed is the *difference* between the lists *(c b a d e f)* and *(d e f)*

Then the generalised predicate has the head *(reva L R A)* where R is the result of appending A to the reverse of L. It can be written:

```
((reva () A A))
((reva (H|T) R A) (reva T R (H|A)))
```

The first clause states that if list A is appended to the reverse of an empty list, then the result is simply A. The second clause states that R is the result of appending list A to the reverse of *(H|T)* if R is the result of appending *(H|A)* to T. Alternatively, we can interpret the clauses as:

1. the reverse of the empty list is the difference between a list and itself, i.e. ()
2. the reverse of (H|T) is the difference between R and A
   if the reverse of T is the difference between R and (H|A).

We solve the problem of reversing a list by simply taking the special case in which A is the empty list, i.e. define

```
((reverse L R) (reva L R ()))
```

Another way of understanding this definition is to interpret the clauses procedurally with the second argument being a slot for the answer and the third argument a slot in which the answer is built up. Execution of a simple query proceeds as follows :

```
((reverse (a b c) X))
((reva (a b c) X ()))
((reva (b c) X (a)))
((reva (c) X (b a)))
((reva () X (c b a)))
Solved X = (c b a)
```

The answer gradually "accumulates" in the third argument, until the terminating condition is reached, at which time the complete answer has been built up. For this reason, the technique is also known as the accumulating parameter method. We note that one unfortunate consequence of these more sophisticated definitions is that programs are also more specialised, and only work in one direction, e.g. the definition of *reverse* given above requires the first argument to be an input.

5.4.5 Removing Redundant Computations

In some logic programs, execution may repeat computations that have already been performed. A commonly used example arises in the calculation of the Fibonacci function, which is discussed below. Another occurrence would be in a search program such as that discussed in Section 5.2, where we might use the program several times to find the best routes between different pairs of nodes. For example, using the graph shown in Fig. 5 - 2, suppose we initially find the shortest route between nodes i and m, and later wish to find the shortest route between nodes f and n. Examination of the graph reveals the first problem is a sub-problem of the second, so if we have already solved the first problem (i-m) we should be able to utilise this information in the second problem (f-n).

In the Fibonacci case, calculating the value of *(fib n)* requires separate calculation of *(fib n-1)* and *(fib n-2)*; however, in the course of computing the value of *(fib n-1)*, we must again calculate *(fib n-2)*; e.g., to calculate *(fib 4)*, *(fib 3)* and *(fib 2)* are found; in the process of calculating *(fib 3)*, *(fib 2)* is found again, along with *(fib 1)*. There is a large amount of repeated work here, which could be avoided in one of two ways. The elegant approach, which works for the Fibonacci case, is to reformulate the problem to remove the doubly recursive definition and replace it with a singly recursive definition. Thus we would calculate both *(fib n-1)* and *(fib n-2)* in one recursive step; the next level of the recursion would calculate *(fib n)* and *(fib n-1)*. This is illustrated by the definition

```
((fib 0 1) (!))
((fib 1 1) (!))
((fib F FN) (fib2 F FN 1 1))
((fib2 1 FN FN1 FN) (!))
((fib2 N F FM2 FM1)
     (sum N1 1 N)
     (sum FM1 FM2 FM)
     (fib2 N1 F FM1 FM))
```

The first argument of *fib2* is a counter that decreases to zero in steps of 1; the second argument is a place-holder for the answer which is calculated when the recursion finishes, and the third and fourth arguments are used to store successive pairs of values *(fib m-1)* and *(fib m)*. Execution of *(fib 6 X)* proceeds as follows:

```
((fib 6 X))
((fib2 6 X 1 1))
((fib2 5 X 1 2))
((fib2 4 X 2 3))
((fib2 3 X 3 5))
((fib2 2 X 5 8))
((fib2 1 X 8 13))
```

which matches the first clause for *fib2* with X=13.

Whilst this removes the double recursion, it does not solve the problem of recalculating results unnecessarily if the program is called more than once. We can consider some way of storing intermediate results so that they do not need to be recalculated. Clearly this requires an equivalent of "global storage" in a conventional programming language. It is achieved by adding information to the knowledge base during program execution. Fril provides a number of built-in predicates which change the knowledge base, such as *addcl* which adds a new clause, *delcl* which deletes an existing clause, and *kill* which removes the entire set of clauses defining a particular predicate. Full details are given in the Fril manual.

From the logical point of view, changing the knowledge base may be a dangerous thing to do, since execution of a logic program can be viewed as proving a theorem (the query) from a set of axioms (the knowledge base). Because predicates such as *addcl* and *delcl* change the knowledge base, it is possible for a program using these predicates to derive a solution which is not logically implied by the initial set of clauses. Although this can be useful at times, it is also very dangerous if we attempt to relate a program to its logical "meaning".

One way of using *addcl* in a manner which avoids this problem is to add only clauses which are derived from the original knowledge base as intermediate results. In this way, no solutions can be found which were not implied by the original program. This is often known as lemma generation. To illustrate this, consider the standard definition of the Fibonacci function, in which many calculations are repeated, with the effect becoming more serious as larger numbers are used. The repetition can be avoided by asserting facts as they are derived:

```
((fib 0 0) (!))
((fib 1 1) (!))
```

```
((fib N FN) (known fib N FN) (!))
((fib N FN)
        (sum P 1 N)
        (sum Q 2 N)
        (fib P FP)
        (fib Q FQ)
        (sum FP FQ FN)
        (addcl ((known fib N FN))))
```

Thus *(fib X)* is calculated once only for each required value of *X*, with later calls to recalculate this value caught by the third clause. This results in a substantial saving of execution time, without altering the meaning of the initial program. Note however that the run time behaviour of the program may vary according to how many times the code has been run before. In this case there will be no difference in the answer provided, only in the time taken to run the program. It is not difficult to imagine programs which are so dependent on the use of the knowledge base as global storage that they can produce completely different results at different times using the same set of input data. The best policy on such programs is not to write them in the first place; if they are written, it is essential that the use of the knowledge base as global storage is well documented and supported by functions to initialise the global storage predicates and "insulate" the remainder of the program as far as possible from any unwanted side-effects.

In any program such as this there is a tradeoff between the speed gained by not repeating computations and the overhead of compiling clauses and adding them to the knowledge base and then having to search through the facts which have been derived. The best treatment in a particular case is dependent on many factors such as the number of intermediate results to be stored, the number of times the intermediate results will be required, etc. Careful analysis is necessary to obtain the optimum approach.

If large numbers of facts are to be stored, it may be worth using a Fril relation rather than a table of facts. Relations are similar to tables of facts, but tuples may be stored in a system-defined order. This allows optimised access if one or more arguments are specified, and enables Fril to search a reduced set of possible candidates. In the case where all arguments are specified, the Fril search may only examine a small percentage of the total entries in the relation, with a consequent increase in the speed of execution.

5.5 PRACTICAL FRIL PROGRAMMING

5.5.1 Program Development in Fril

Fril provides either a built-in editor or an interface to a system editor which can be called from within Fril. This enables programs to be developed quickly through an edit - reload - test cycle. As with most logic programming systems, there are facilities to trace and debug programs, including code which uses the uncertainty-handling aspects of the language. Normally, Fril uses an incremental compiler when code is loaded, and all clauses are globally accessible. From a software engineering viewpoint, it is often convenient to have a modular structure of code broken down into self-contained units communicating by well-defined interfaces. Fril allows sections of code to be compiled into modules. A module is loaded as a compiled entity, and consists of "public" clauses which enable the module code to be called from elsewhere, and "private" clauses which are not accessible to the outside world. Because a module is compiled as a unit, more optimisations than normal are possible, as code can be considered in larger units than single clauses.

Fril provides a facility for trapping and dealing with program errors and other interrupts, and for programming control keys so that Fril commands may be run with a single keystroke. Most Fril systems incorporate a sophisticated set of window-management facilities incorporating the capability to build a custom user-interface with menus and mouse-driven dialogs.

5.5.2 Comparison to Prolog

Readers who are familiar with Prolog should have little difficulty in understanding or writing standard logic programs in Fril. The main differences at this level are syntactic - Fril lists are delimited by parentheses ( ) rather than brackets [ ] and Fril clauses are in Cambridge Polish form, i.e. the predicate is the first element of the list, rather than the standard Prolog which uses a functional form *pred(a,b,c)*. One advantage of this is to make meta-programming much simpler - a goal of the form *(X a b c)* can be called directly, provided *X* is instantiated at the time of calling. In contrast, an Edinburgh Prolog system has to use built-in predicates such as *univ, =.., functor, arg*, etc. to facilitate meta-programming.

The built-in predicates are comprehensive, and little difficulty should be encountered in converting between Prolog and Fril. The arithmetic capabilities are adequate although it is sometimes slightly tedious to split a calculation into the component steps.

The major difference between Fril and Prolog systems is that Fril has many uncertainty-handling features which make it particularly useful for writing systems which have to deal with real-world knowledge. By its very nature, this is often clouded in uncertainty to a greater or lesser degree and Fril is ideally suited to modelling these uncertainties, as discussed in other chapters of this book.

5.5.3 Extending the Fril System

As we have seen, Fril is a very powerful programming system which can be used to write flexible knowledge-based systems for a wide variety of purposes. Increasingly, there is a trend towards the integration of knowledge-based systems into a wider context -

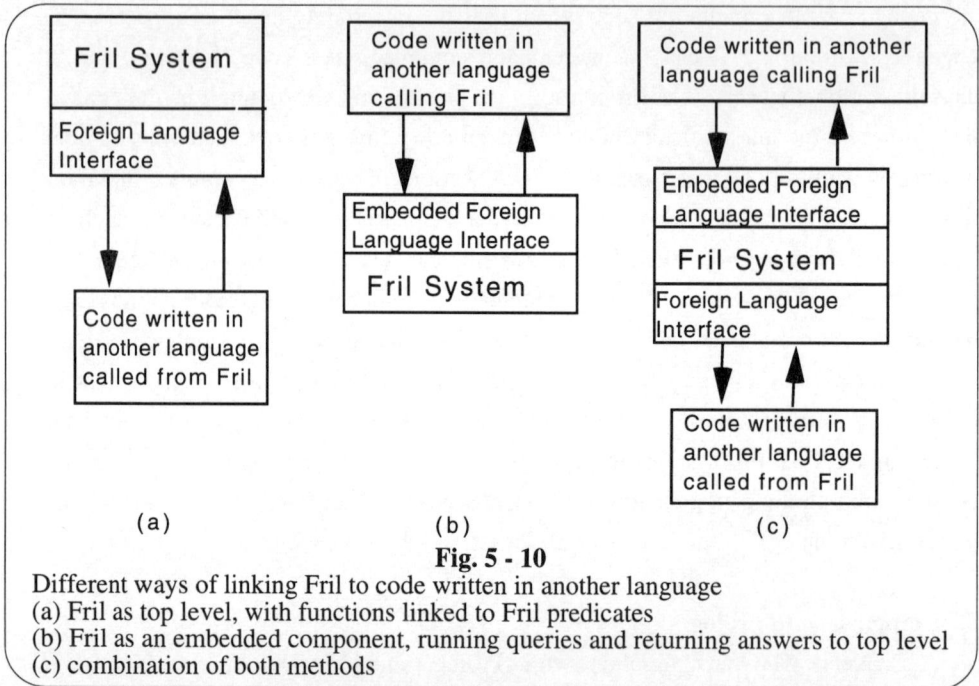

Fig. 5 - 10
Different ways of linking Fril to code written in another language
(a) Fril as top level, with functions linked to Fril predicates
(b) Fril as an embedded component, running queries and returning answers to top level
(c) combination of both methods

for example, a real-time system may control an industrial process and handle routine data collection with a knowledge-based system to deal with alerts, plan maintenance, tune the performance of the control system, etc. Fril can be linked with other systems, either at the top level or as an embedded component in a larger system, as shown in Fig. 5 - 10. The Fril Foreign Language Interface enables code written in a language other than Fril to be linked into the Fril system and executed by calling a Fril procedure in the normal way. Fril provides the "top level" of the resultant system, i.e. control is normally with the Fril core, and only passes to the external code when the appropriate procedures are called during Fril execution. This is represented pictorially in Fig. 5 - 10 (a), and can be used (for example) where some intensive numerical processing or handling of graphics must be performed. In some circumstances, it is more convenient for the user code to be in control of processing, with information and control passed to Fril when appropriate (see Fig. 5 - 10(b)). It is possible to combine the two mechanisms (Fig. 5 - 10(c)) so that Fril is called by the top-level user code and in turn can pass control to user-defined functions during program execution.

A complete knowledge-based system can be written in Fril (possibly with exten- sions in another language as described above), and used by people with little or no expe- rience of Fril. The Fril Application Generator incorporates additional code into the top level of Fril, creating a stand-alone system which may be run without knowledge of, or access to, the underlying Fril language. The executable application does not go through the usual Fril cycle of prompting for input, reading input, and executing a query or compiling a clause into the knowledge base. Instead, it executes a top level predicate specified by the application, which performs all of the run time processing. The top level predicate has an arity of one, and is called with the one of the arguments *initialise, run, reset,* or *exit.*

5.5.4 Procedural Control of Execution

Most problems can be expressed tail-recursively in Fril, and, as we have seen, tail-recursive programs execute efficiently by compilation into iterative code. In some circumstances, a tail-recursive program may still use significant amounts of copystack space by creating list structure. Fril has a garbage collector which attempts to minimise the amount of copystack space used; however, there are situations where it may not be possible to recover all of the space. If the program in question does not pass any data from one level of recursion to the next, it may be possible to replace the recursive definition by a procedural construct, the *repeat-fail* loop. This should be used as a last resort, but enables code to run in constant space (including copystack) as all stack space is recovered when the system backtracks. For example, consider a program that repeatedly reads in a single piece of information, performs some processing on the data, and prints a result. The program terminates when some keyword (e.g. stop) is read. It could be programmed recursively:

```
((test) (r INPUT) (recurse INPUT))
((recurse stop) (!))
((recurse INPUT)
       (process INPUT RESULT)
       (pp RESULT)
       (r NEXT-INPUT)
       (recurse NEXT-INPUT))
```

The input is read before being passed to the recursive call, so that the terminating condition (input of *stop*) may be detected. We could code this in the alternative fashion, using the built-in predicate *repeat* which is always resatisfied on backtracking:

```
((test2)
       (repeat)
       (r INPUT)
       (process INPUT RESULT)
       (pp RESULT)
       (eq INPUT stop))
```

In this case, the final goal *(eq INPUT stop)* will fail in all cases except when the computation should terminate. On failure, the system backtracks to the *repeat* goal which is resatisfied and the code is re-executed. Note that the call to *process* should not be resatisfiable, and should behave appropriately when given the input *stop*. This program is less elegant than the recursive formulation, but may be necessary on grounds of efficiency.

5.5.5 Comparison to Procedural Languages

The following correspondences may be useful to those having difficulty adjusting from the procedural style of programming:

iterative loop . . . . recursive rule

test for termination . . . . fact (or non-recursive rule) giving terminating condition

temporary variable . . . . argument to a goal in the body

global variable . . . . argument in head and to at least one goal in the body (in certain circumstances the knowledge base may be used to store "global" values as discussed in Section 5.4.5)

destructive assignment . . . . . new temporary variable

disjunction. . . . . different clauses

variable type . . . . unification mechanism or explicit check using *con,int...*

arguments . . . . terms in clause head (input or output according to call)

return value . . . . terms in clause head (input or output according to call)

Note that variables are not 'typed' - a variable will match any term. However, type checking is carried out implicitly as part of the unification process since two terms which are not variables will only match if they are identical. Type checking of arguments can be further enforced by built-in predicates such as *con*, *int*, *num*, etc.

5.6 BIBLIOGRAPHY

The Fril manual contains a detailed description of a tracing predicate and discusses how to treat the cut within the package. There is also a section on how to write simple systems predicates such as those listed in Section 5.3.6, and a number of more advanced search routines. Search is covered in most general AI texts, such as Nilsson, and in many books on Prolog such as Bratko, Sterling and Shapiro. The latter also contains interesting material regarding efficiency and programming "tricks" in Prolog.

Baldwin J.F, Martin T.P, Pilsworth B.W, (1988), "Fril Manual, version 4.0", Fril Systems Ltd, Bristol Business Centre, Bristol BS8 1QX, UK.

Baldwin J.F, Martin T.P, Pilsworth B.W, (1993), "Fril Manual, version 5.0", Fril Systems Ltd, Bristol Business Centre, Bristol BS8 1QX, UK.

Bratko I, (1986), Prolog Programming for Artificial Intelligence, Addison Wesley.

Nilsson N, (1982), Artificial Intelligence, Springer-Verlag.

O'Keefe R, (1988), The Craft of Prolog, MIT Press.

Sterling L, Shapiro E, (1986), The Art of Prolog, MIT Press.

CHAPTER 6

Modules for Uncertain Inference in Fril

6.1 INTRODUCTION

This Chapter builds upon the foundations of uncertain inference in Fril which were laid in Chapter 4. The Chapter describes the content and use of Fril programs which can be found on the accompanying diskettes. The principal focus will be on describing tools and applications associated with recent developments and extensions of the Fril language. These include Evidential Logic reasoning and examples, the extended inference rule for Fril and its application to Causal Nets, and Fuzzy Control tools and applications. Many of the developments and extensions are built into the Fril language, for example the predicate 'evlog' for evidential logic reasoning, the extended Fril rule with multiple conditional support pairs, and methods of combination of fuzzy sets and inferences from multiple Fril rules. For the purposes of demonstration of the inference processes of Fril in this Chapter, many of these built-in utilities are simulated in Fril as well. These run much less efficiently than the built-in utilities, but they nevertheless can help to animate the inference processes and provide more extensive visualisations of the theoretical results and examples developed in Chapter 4.

The Chapter is concluded (Section 6.7) by giving some examples of how Fril can be used to model a wide variety of other uncertain inference processes, by focussing on PRUF - a meaning representation language for natural languages developed by Lotfi Zadeh between 1978 and 1986. The examples include an implementation of Zadeh's Test-Score semantics.

We begin, however, by presenting examples of straightforward support logic inference in Fril with which existing users of Fril will already be very well familiar. Two examples will be considered, both of which appear in Chapter 4. The first is the design example (Section 4.3.2) and the second is the non-monotonic reasoning example (Section 4.3.6). The examples can be explored in the Fril Demonstration System, provided on the enclosed floppy disks, under the Basic Inference section of the Fuzzy Control module (see Section 6.5). However, if you wish to explore the examples directly, try the following:

- Click on the Fuzzy Control radio button (this is the default) in the top level "Demonstrations" Dialog Box, & click Run to invoke the Fuzzy Control module;
- Click on the Basic Inference radio button in the Problem cluster, and select any one of the bottom three selections in the Queries popup menu - then click on Evaluate to run the example. Try any of the bottom three selections of the Queries

menu and repeat. The Dialog Interface to the Fril Demonstration system is described in more detail in Section 6.2.1. It is very simple to use and the reader should have no problem in using the above guideline instructions to run the examples presented immediately below:

```
/* Combining inferences from multiple Fril rules with the same head, but no fuzzy sets */
      ((design of X is ok)
            (performance of X is good)
            (looks of X is modern)) : (0.9 1)
      ((design of X is ok)
            (cost of X is expensive)) : (0 0.05)
      ((design of X is ok)
            (not reliability of X is high)) : (0 0.2)
      ((performance of X is good)
            (eng_report  of X is ok)
            (reliability of X is high)) : (0.9 1)
      ((looks of d is modern)) : (0.8 1)
      ((reliability of d is high)) : (0.7 0.8)
      ((eng_report of d is ok)) : (0.7 1)
      ((cost of d is expensive)) : (0.6 1)


/* utility 'clauses' for examining support from separate clauses */
      ((clauses (PRED|ARGS) )
            (forall ( (cl ((PRED|ARGS)|BODY) SUPPPAIR 1 N) (kill temp_clause) )
                  ( (addcl ((temp_clause|ARGS)|BODY) : SUPPPAIR)
                  (ws ( (rule N support for (PRED|ARGS) )
                                          (temp_clause|ARGS) )) ) ))


/* non-monotonic reasoning example */
      dempster fly
      ((fly X) (bird X)) : (0.9 0.95)
      ((fly X) (penguin X)) : (0 0)
      ((bird X) (penguin X))
      ((penguin Penny)) : 0.4
      ((bird Penny)) : (0.9 1)
```

Predicate 'clauses' is a simple utility for displaying the support from separate clauses of a predicate with the same head in each clause. The following example session in Fril reproduces examples described in Chapter 4 and shows the kinds of query that can be tried.

qs((design|X))
((design of d is ok)) : (0.31752 0.43)
no (more) solutions

clauses (design|X)
(rule 1 support for (design of d is ok)) : (0.31752 1)
no (more) solutions
(rule 2 support for (design of d is ok)) : (0 0.43)
no (more) solutions
(rule 3 support for (design of d is ok)) : (0 0.84)
no (more) solutions

qs((fly|X))
((fly Penny)) : (0.718935 0.847633)
no (more) solutions

clauses (fly|X)
(rule 1 support for (fly Penny)) : (0.81 0.955)
no (more) solutions
(rule 2 support for (fly Penny)) : (0 0.6)
no (more) solutions

Note how necessary is the dempster definition of the 'fly' predicate, since the supports from the two inference paths, namely (0.81 0.955) and (0 0.6), do not overlap.

The basic query evaluator for support logic queries is the predicate 'supp_query' which takes two arguments. The first argument is a conjunction of support logic goals and the second is initially a variable which is bound to the support pair derived for the support logic conjunction. The following example illustrates such a query, and its corresponding inference is displayed:

? ((supp_query ((performance of X is good) (looks X is modern)) S) (p X : S))
d : (0.3528 1)

There are several utilities for support logic queries which are built-in predicates of the Fril system. For example, predicate 'qs' used above obtains all solutions to a support logic conjunction of goals and displays the conjunctions with associated supports.

((qs X) (pp) (supp_query X S) (p X : S) (pp) (fail))
((qs _) (pp 'no (more) solutions'))

249

An alternative more compact definition for 'qs' is as follows:

```
((qs X)
        (forall ((supp_query X S)) ((p X : S) (pp)) )
        (pp 'no (more) solutions'))
```

The utility 'ws' which was used in the above definition of 'clauses' is similar to 'qs' but displays an answer pattern instead of the whole conjunction of goals, thus:

```
((ws (X|Y) )
        (forall ((supp_query Y S)) ((p X : S) (pp)) )
        (pp 'no (more) solutions'))
```

These predicates are all Fril Prolog utilities. There are also several support logic meta-programming utilities as follows. Predicate 'and' takes any number of goals as argument and returns the support for their conjunction using the default multiplicative conjunction law. It is defined as an equivalence (using ((1 1) (0 0)) pair of conditional support pairs) so that the goal expressed using 'and' returns the same support as the support evaluated for the conjunction of goals. The predicate 'and' is sometimes useful for converting a conjunction of goals into a single goal.

```
((and|X)|X) : ((1 1)(0 0))
```

Predicate 'conj' is similar to 'and' in both syntax and meaning except that it uses the conjunction law where no assumption regarding independence of goals is made. Notice how the predicate 'conj' uses a variable support in its definition. The support pair S is computed by the Fril Prolog goal (dep_conj X S) and S becomes the conditional support for the rule. Note also how 'dep_conj' is called as a Fril Prolog goal using basic Fril Prolog evaluator '?'. This shows how Fril Prolog can be embedded in Support Logic programs.

```
((conj|X) (? ((dep_conj X S)) )) : S
((dep_conj () (1 1) ))
((dep_conj (X|Y) S) (supp_query (X) S1) (dep_conj Y S2) (conj_calc S1 S2 S))
((conj_calc (N1 P1) (N2 P2) (N P) )
        (sum N1 N2 N3) (sum N4 1 N3) (max N4 0 N) (min P1 P2 P))
```

When '?' is used in a support logic context it returns a support of (1 1) if the goal succeeds and a support of (0 0) if it fails. Another example of a support logic meta predicate is 'match', which returns the support pair for the semantic unification of its first argument given the second. Predicate 'not' is the support logic negation operator. Its syntax is similar to 'negg' for 'negation as failure' with Fril Prolog goals, but its meaning is to apply the complement law for support logic negation. For example:

? ((supp_query ((not and (performance of X is good) (looks of X is modern))) S)
        (p X : S))
d : (0 0.6472)

and this inference is the complement of (0.3528 1) evaluated above.

6.2 EVIDENTIAL LOGIC

6.2.1 Introduction to the Fril Demonstration System

The Evidential Support Logic application is the first of six applications described in this book for which there is a demonstration module on the enclosed diskettes. For this reason we preface our discussion of the application with an introduction to the Demonstration System environment and brief instructions on how to use the application modules. It is assumed henceforth that you have installed the Fril Demonstration system on a hard disk as described in the "Read Me" files on each diskette, and that you have opened the Fril Demo application. The top level Demonstrations Dialog box is shown in Fig. 6.1a overleaf. The illustration corresponds to the Apple Macintosh Demo version.

Each of the six radio buttons in the "Choice of modules" cluster represents a different application. To select an application, click the mouse on one of the six choices and then click on the Run button, when a new Dialog Box will appear. Alternatively, you can click on any of the three remaining buttons. Clicking on the Quit button will enable you to exit from the Demonstration. Clicking on the Help button will provide two levels of on-line help about the Demonstration system as a whole, about the Fril programming language and about Fril Systems Limited who develop, market and sell the product. Finally, clicking on the "Describe module..." button will provide two levels of on-line help about the particular module currently selected.

The two levels of on-line help operate in the following way. Initially a temporary Information box appears giving summary help or information on the relevant topic. If this is sufficient, then you can click on the OK button, when the Information box will disappear, returning you to the main Dialog box. If more information is required then you can click on "More information..." when a more permanent window of help information is displayed which can be inspected at will. Alternatively, click on Quit which gives the option to exit from the Demonstration system altogether.

251

```
╔════════════════════════════════════════════════════╗
║ ▤▢▤▤▤▤▤▤▤▤▤▤▤ Demonstrations ▤▤▤▤▤▤▤▤▤▤▤ ║
╠════════════════════════════════════════════════════╣
   Fril Demonstration System © Fril Systems Ltd
              Interface to Fril Demo Modules

            ┌─ Choice of modules ─────────────┐
            │                                 │
            │  ◉ Fuzzy Control                │
            │                                 │
            │  ○ Causal Nets                  │
            │                                 │
            │  ○ Fuzzy Database               │
            │                                 │
            │  ○ Intelligent Manual           │
            │                                 │
            │  ○ Evidential Support Logic     │
            │                                 │
            │  ○ PRUF                         │
            └─────────────────────────────────┘

    ╔══════╗  ┌──────┐  ┌────────────────┐  ┌──────┐
    ║ Run  ║  │ Help │  │Describe module…│  │ Quit │
    ╚══════╝  └──────┘  └────────────────┘  └──────┘
```

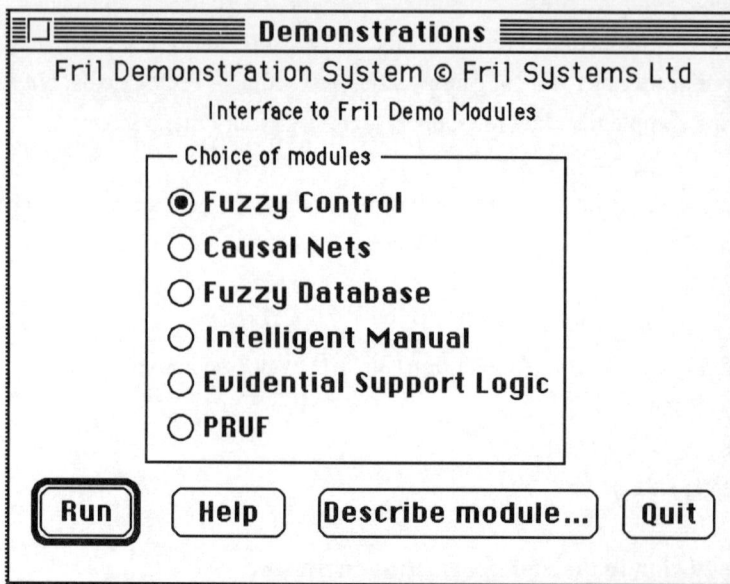

Fig. 6.1a - Introductory Dialog Box for Fril Demonstration System:
for example, click on Evidential Support Logic radio button
and then click on Run to run module.

In this Chapter, four of the modules listed are explored, namely: Fuzzy Control, Causal Nets, Evidential Support Logic and PRUF. The two remaining modules, Fuzzy Database and Intelligent Manual, are discussed in Chapter 7 following.

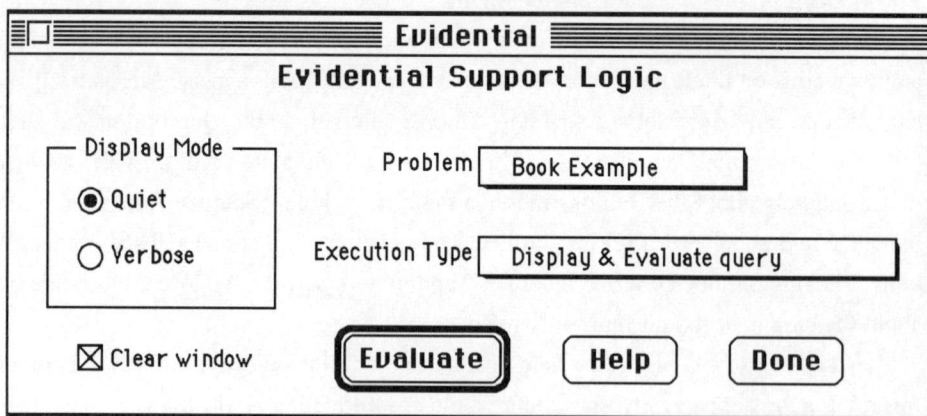

```
╔════════════════════════════════════════════════════╗
║ ▤▢▤▤▤▤▤▤▤▤▤▤▤▤▤ Evidential ▤▤▤▤▤▤▤▤▤▤▤▤▤ ║
╠════════════════════════════════════════════════════╣
              Evidential Support Logic

   ┌─ Display Mode ─┐     Problem ┌──────────────────┐
   │                │             │  Book Example    │
   │  ◉ Quiet       │             └──────────────────┘
   │                │
   │  ○ Verbose     │  Execution Type ┌───────────────────────┐
   │                │                 │ Display & Evaluate query│
   └────────────────┘                 └───────────────────────┘

   ☒ Clear window   ╔══════════╗   ┌──────┐   ┌──────┐
                    ║ Evaluate ║   │ Help │   │ Done │
                    ╚══════════╝   └──────┘   └──────┘
```

Fig. 6.1b - Dialog interface for Evidential Support Logic module

The Evidential Dialog box in Fig. 6.1b above provides the environment for exploring the examples discussed below. The Display mode can be set as Quiet or Verbose. Quiet means that only output directly pertaining to a given query is displayed. Verbose means that additional trace information is displayed to help animate the computation being illustrated. The Problem popup menu includes a choice of two examples: the Book and Moon examples discussed in Section 4.6. There is a choice of four types of execution mode which can be selected from the "Execution Type" popup menu: Display & Evaluate query (this is the default); Evaluate query; Display query; and List relevant knowledge. These are all self-explanatory. Clicking the Evaluate button applies the given Execution Type to the Problem selected in the Display Mode chosen, and the results are displayed in a window immediately below the Dialog Box. If the Clear window box is checked, then the window displaying the results will be cleared prior to the display of the new results. Clicking the Help button provides the two levels of on-line help about the module as described above. Clicking on the button "Done" closes the Dialog Box and returns the user to the top level Demonstrations Dialog Box, where other applications can be selected and explored.

6.2.2 Outline of the Programs

Below is listed the Fril code for the predicate 'evlogic' which simulates the built-in predicate 'evlog', described in Section 4.6. The simulation allows various print options to be incorporated into the code, to help animate the computation process when applied to various examples.

```
((evlogic LIST) (? ((evidential_body [0:0, 1:1] LIST S)) )) : S
((evlogic FUZ LIST) (? ((evidential_body FUZ LIST S)) )) : S

((evidential_body FUZ LIST S)
        (body LIST (0 0) SUPP)
        % intermediate print line: intermediate body support pair SUPP
        (eq SUPP (X Y) )
        (supp_query ((match FUZ X)) S1) (supp_query ((match FUZ Y)) S2)
        (eq S1 (N _)) (eq S2 (P _))
        % final print line: final filtered body support pair (N P)
        (eq S (N P) ))
((body () S S))
((body (G WIL) (N P) SUPP)
        (supp_query (G) S2) (eq S2 (N2 P2))
        (times W N2 WN2) (sum N WN2 NEWN)
        (times W P2 WP2) (sum P WP2 NEWP)
```

253

% body print line: body information: G S2 W (NEWN NEWP)
(body L (NEWN NEWP) SUPP))

There is a one argument and a two argument form for predicate evlogic. The two argument form expects a fuzzy set as its first argument representing the filtering function for the weighted body support - for example, this can represent a soft form of conjunction or disjunction as described in Section 4.6. The one argument form assumes the filtering function is the ramp fuzzy set [0:0, 1:1]. If the Verbose option is selected from the Display Mode cluster of the Evidential module, then the following additional "trace" information is provided about the computation of support in the Evidential Logic rule, as represented by the comments in the above program fragment. Thus, the body print line displays a component goal G of the rule body together with its computed support S2, its weight W and the cumulative support for the rule body; the intermediate print line (predicate evidential_body) displays the body support pair SUPP prior to filtering with the fuzzy set function FUZ; and the final print line displays the filtered body support pair resulting from the match of the components of SUPP with FUZ.

6.2.3 Exploring some Examples

The knowledge base for the Evidential Support Logic module is displayed below, followed by an example session which can be followed in the Fril Demonstration. Discrete or itype fuzzy sets can be used for this problem - itypes have been used here.

```
/* illustrative book example */
    set (probdom (0 1) )
    set (yeardom (1900 1993) )
    set (valdom (a b c) )
    set (extdom (0 1000) )
    (s_curve [0.25:0, 0.9:1] probdom)
    (true_line [0:0, 1:1] probdom)
    (good {a:1, b:0.7, c:0.4} valdom)
    (recent [1970:0, 1982:1] yeardom)

    ((book X is worth reading) (evlogic s_curve (
    (famous writer is author of X) 0.2
    (key words of text of X relevant) 0.25
    (gives impression from scan through of X ok) 0.3
    (review of X good) 0.1
    (extent of X suitable) 0.05
    (publication date of X recent) 0.1) )) : (0.9 1)
```

254

(not_too_big [150:0, 200:1, 250:1, 300:0] extdom)

(approx_250 [240:0, 250:1, 260:0] extdom)

(fairly_good {a:0.3, b:1, c:0.5} valdom)

((extent of X suitable) (conj

       (last page number of X is not_too_big)

       (page size of X normal))) : ((1 1) (0 0))

((famous writer is author of Mind)) : (0.8 1)

((key words of text of Mind relevant)) : (0.6 0.8)

((gives impression from scan through of Mind ok)) : (0.7 0.9)

((review of Mind fairly_good))

((publication date of Mind 1980))

((last page number of Mind is approx_250))

((page size of Mind normal)) : 0.7

The appropriate top level query for this example is as follows:

    qs ((book MIND is worth reading))

and this can be evaluated by clicking on the Evaluate button in the Dialog Box with the appropriate options selected.

/* case based reasoning example */

    set (sqdom (0 144))

    (g11 [3:0, 4:0.4, 5:1, 6:0.4, 7:0] sqdom)

    (g12 [4:0, 5:0.4, 6:1, 7:0.4, 8:0] sqdom)

    (g13 [4:0, 5:0.4, 6:1, 7:0.4, 8:0] sqdom)

    (g14 [0:1, 1:0.4, 2:0] sqdom)

    (g21 [0:1, 1:0.4, 2:0] sqdom)

    (g22 [4:0, 5:0.4, 6:1, 7:0.4, 8:0] sqdom)

    (g23 [4:0, 5:0.4, 6:1, 7:0.4, 8:0] sqdom)

    (g24 [0:1, 1:0.4, 2:0] sqdom)

    (g31 [12:0, 13:0.3, 14:0.7, 15:1, 16:0.7, 17:0.3, 18:0] sqdom)

    (g32 [17:0, 18:0.3, 19:0.7, 20:1, 21:0.7, 22:0.3, 23:0] sqdom)

    (g33 [17:0, 18:0.3, 19:0.7, 20:1, 21:0.7, 22:0.3, 23:0] sqdom)

    (g34 [0:1, 1:0.7, 2:0.3, 3:0] sqdom)

    (g41 [2:1, 3:0.4, 5:0] sqdom)   % pair 4:0.2 included by interpolation

    (true_line [0:0, 1:1] probdom)

((half_moon support for X) (evlogic true_line (

       (upper_line satisfactory for X) 0.2

       (lower_line satisfactory for X) 0.2

(area satisfactory for X) 0.3

(corners satisfactory for X) 0.3))) : (1 1)

((upper_line satisfactory for X) (evlogic true_line (

(region 1 has g11 black squares for upper line for X) 0.25

(region 2 has g12 black squares for upper line for X) 0.25

(region 3 has g13 black squares for upper line for X) 0.25

(region 4 has g14 black squares for upper line for X) 0.25))) : ((1 1) (0 0))

((lower_line satisfactory for X) (evlogic true_line (

(region 1 has g21 black squares for lower line for X) 0.25

(region 2 has g22 black squares for lower line for X) 0.25

(region 3 has g23 black squares for lower line for X) 0.25

(region 4 has g24 black squares for lower line for X) 0.25))) : ((1 1) (0 0))

((area satisfactory for X) (evlogic true_line (

(region 1 has g31 black squares inside figure for X) 0.25

(region 2 has g32 black squares inside figure for X) 0.25

(region 3 has g33 black squares inside figure for X) 0.25

(region 4 has g34 black squares inside figure for X) 0.25))) : ((1 1) (0 0))

((corners satisfactory for X) (evlogic true_line (

(figure has g41 corners for X) 1))) : ((1 1) (0 0))

The definitions of fact predicates 'region' and 'figure' are exactly as appear in Section 4.6.6, and are not repeated here, for example:

((region 1 has 6 black squares for upper line for a))

((region 2 has 6 black squares for upper line for a))

((region 3 has 6 black squares for upper line for a))

((region 4 has 0 black squares for upper line for a))

((figure has 3 corners for a))

... etc.

The appropriate top level query for this example is as follows:

qs ((half_moon support for CASE))

and this can be evaluated by clicking on the Evaluate button in the Dialog Box with the appropriate options selected.

The following is an example of the output from an interactive session using the Fril Demonstration System, when the Verbose option in the Display Mode cluster is selected. Compare the results with those appearing in Section 4.6. There are several pages of output for the case-based reasoning example, and only small portions from the beginning and end of the session are displayed below. Note that discrete fuzzy sets could have been used instead of itypes for the definitions of the gij above.

- Click on "Verbose" in "Display Mode" cluster;
- Select "Book example" from "Problem" popup menu;
- Choose "Display & Evaluate" query option from "Execution Type" popup menu;
- Click on "Evaluate" button.

qs ((book M is worth reading))
(famous writer is author of Mind) (0.8 1) 0.2 (0.16 0.2)
(key words of text of Mind relevant) (0.6 0.8) 0.25 (0.31 0.4)
(gives impression from scan through of Mind ok) (0.7 0.9) 0.3 (0.52 0.67)
(review of Mind {a:1 b:0.7 c:0.4}) (0.55 0.79) 0.1 (0.575 0.749)
(extent of Mind suitable) (0.6 0.7) 0.05 (0.605 0.784)
(publication date of Mind [1970:0 1982:1]) (0.8333 0.8333) 0.1 (0.6833 0.8673)
intermediate body support pair (0.6833 0.8673)
final filtered body support pair (0.6744 0.9497)

((book Mind is worth reading)) : (0.6069 1)

- Click on "Verbose" in "Display Mode" cluster;
- Select "Moon example" from "Problem" popup menu;
- Choose "Display & Evaluate" query option from "Execution Type" popup menu;
- Click on "Evaluate" button.

qs ((half_moon support for X))
(region 1 has [3:0 4:0.4 5:1 6:0.4 7:0] black squares for upper line for a)
(0.4 0.4) 0.25 (0.1 0.1)
(region 2 has [4:0 5:0.4 6:1 7:0.4 8:0] black squares for upper line for a)
(1 1) 0.25 (0.35 0.35)
(region 3 has [4:0 5:0.4 6:1 7:0.4 8:0] black squares for upper line for a)
(1 1) 0.25 (0.6 0.6)
(region 4 has [0:1 1:0.4 2:0] black squares for upper line for a)
(1 1) 0.25 (0.85 0.85)
intermediate body support pair (0.85 0.85)
final filtered body support pair (0.85 0.85)
(region 1 has [3:0 4:0.4 5:1 6:0.4 7:0] black squares for upper line for b)
(0 0) 0.25 (0 0)

......

(region 4 has [0:1 1:0.7 2:0.3 3:0] black squares inside figure for c)

(0 0) 0.25 (0.175 0.175)

intermediate body support pair (0.175 0.175)

final filtered body support pair (0.175 0.175)

(area satisfactory for c) (0.175 0.175) 0.3 (0.2725 0.2725)

(figure has [2:1 3:0.4 5:0] corners for c) (0 0) 1 (0 0)

intermediate body support pair (0 0)

final filtered body support pair (0 0)

(corners satisfactory for c) (0 0) 0.3 (0.2725 0.2725)

intermediate body support pair (0.2725 0.2725)

final filtered body support pair (0.2725 0.2725)

((half_moon support for a)) : (0.715 1)

((half_moon support for b)) : (0.5225 1)

((half_moon support for c)) : (0.2725 1)

These solutions provide a clear ranking of the objects a, b and c in that order as representing the concept half-moon.

6.3 EXTENDED FRIL RULES

The notation for extended Fril rules was defined in Section 4.1.2 and the simple example given in Section 4.2.2 is as follows:

((h) (((b1)) ((b2)) ((b3)) ((b4)))) : ((0.5 0.7) (0.2 0.9) (0.3 0.5) (0.7 0.8))

Given supports for goals (b1) (b2) (b3) and (b4), the allocation algorithm for the optimisation inference problem described in Section 4.2.2 determines the overall support for the goal (h). This rule representation and allocation algorithm are supported by the core Fril system. However, for the purposes of illustration of the inference mechanism, this section and the following (Section 6.4) use a simulation of the extended inference mechanism, with the following equivalent representation:

((h) (general   (((b1)) ((b2)) ((b3)) ((b4)))

                ((0.5 0.7)(0.2 0.9)(0.3 0.5)(0.7 0.8)))) : ((1 1) (0 0))

where predicate 'general' fulfils a role similar to 'evlogic' in Section 6.2 above. Predicate

258

'general' takes two arguments: the first is the body of the extended rule and the second is the support list. The conditional support ((1 1) (0 0)) ensures that the rule is an equivalence so that the support for 'h' is identical to the support derived for the 'general' goal.

In this section we present the Fril program for 'general' as an example of meta-programming in Fril, and as a basis for animating the optimisation algorithm for the extended Fril Rule.

```
((general G S) (? ((minmax_alloc  G  S  SUPP) )) : SUPP

((minmax_alloc G S (N P) )
    (pair_listings G S L R)
    (sortpairs1_ascend L L2) (sortpairs1_descend R R2)
    (p necessary supports in ascending order for minimum - initial ordering) (pp L2)
    (alloc L2 N)
    (p possible supports in descending order for maximum - initial ordering) (pp R2)
    (alloc R2 P2)
    (!)
    (check_supports N P2 P))

((pair_listings () () () () ))
((pair_listings (B|G) ((L U)|S) ((L PAIR)|MIN) ((U PAIR)|MAX) )
    (supp_query B PAIR)
    (!) (pair_listings  G  S  MIN  MAX))
((pair_listings (B|G) ((N)|S) ((N  PAIR)|MIN) ((N  PAIR)|MAX) )
    (num N) (supp_query  B  PAIR)
    (!) (pair_listings  G  S  MIN  MAX))

((alloc L Z)
    (standardise  L  1  LIST) (mult_up  LIST  0  Z)
    (pp) (p dot product list is  LIST  with value  Z) (pp))

((standardise () _ () ))
((standardise ((VAL (N P))|L) IND ((VAL  ALLOC)|R) )
    (pp) (p candidate ranges) (pp) (p ((VAL (N P))|L) )
    (low_sum 0 ((VAL (N P))|L) LOWSUM)
    (pp) (p sum of alpha is  LOWSUM)
    (sum LOWSUM DIFF IND)
    (pp) (p difference from last sum of theta  IND  is  DIFF)
```

```
(sum N DIFF NEW) (pp) (p candidate allocation is NEW)
(constrain_to_interval NEW N P ALLOC)
(pp) (p constrain allocation to lie within range (N P) )
(pp) (p theta allocation is ALLOC)
(sum NEWIND ALLOC IND)
(pp) (p new sum of theta is NEWIND) (pp)
(!)
(standardise L NEWIND R))


((constrain_to_interval CAND _ UPPER UPPER)
   (less UPPER CAND) (!))
((constrain_to_interval CAND LOWER _ LOWER)
   (less CAND LOWER) (!))
((constrain_to_interval CAND _ _ CAND))


((low_sum SUM () SUM))
((low_sum ACC ((VAL (N P))|L) SUM)
   (sum ACC N NEWACC) (!) (low_sum NEW ACC L SUM))


((mult_up () S S))
((mult_up ((VAL COMP)|L) IND RESULT)
   (times VAL COMP PROD) (sum PROD IND INC) (!) (mult_up L INC RESULT))
```

This program uses some utility predicates such as sorting, which are not displayed here. For example, predicate sortpairs1_ascend takes a list of pairs as its first argument and returns this in the second argument as a sorted list of pairs, where the sort is done on the value of the first element of the pairs in ascending order. An efficient quicksort algorithm is employed using difference list techniques. Predicate sortpairs1_descend is similar but sorts the list in descending order of its first element pairs. The print statement annotations of the programs follow very closely the notations used to describe the algorithm in Section 4.2.2.

The elementary examples discussed in Section 4.1.2 and 4.2.2 can be adapted very simply to the notation of predicate 'general' as shown above in the case of example predicate 'h'. The query qs((h)) returns support inference ((h)) : (0.28 0.83) as described in Section 4.2.4. There is no explicit Fril module for demonstrating these particular examples on the diskette, but the extended Fril rule is the basis of the Causal Nets applications for which there is a Demonstration module.

6.4.1 Introducing the Causal Nets Dialog Interface

The Causal Nets application can be invoked from the top level Dialog Box by clicking on the Causal Nets radio button in the Choice of modules cluster, and then clicking the Run button. The Causal Nets modelling dialog box then appears as shown in Fig. 6.2 below.

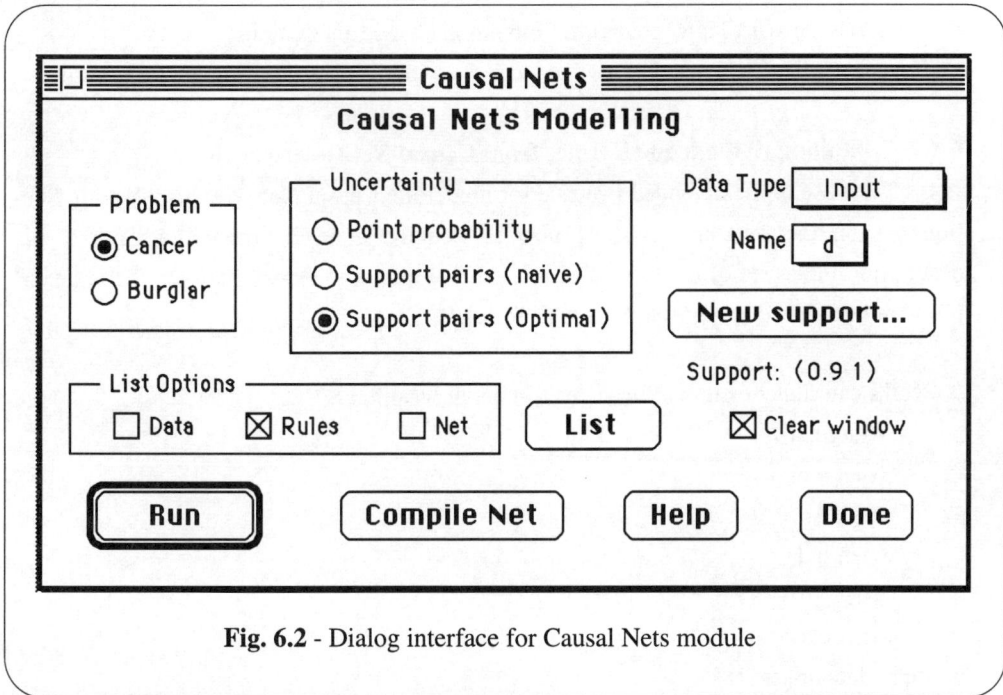

Fig. 6.2 - Dialog interface for Causal Nets module

Two different problems can be explored: the Cancer problem introduced by Pearl and described in Section 4.4.2, and another very simple Belief net example, concerning the detection of a Burglar, described in Section 6.4.3 below.

There is a choice of three different Uncertainty models, of which the Support pairs (Optimal) is the default and subsumes the other two as it is the most general. If the problem has support pairs where the necessary and possible supports are always the same, then the Support Pairs (Optimal) model and the Point Probability model are equivalent and give identical solutions.

The net is defined by a set of Fril clauses, which can be viewed by checking the Net box in the List Options cluster and clicking the List button. Both Apriori and Input Data item uncertainty values can be changed by clicking on the "New support..." or "New probability...' buttons.

•   First choose the "Cancer" or the "Burglar" problem - "Cancer" is the default;

- Next choose the Uncertainty model - "Support Pairs (Optimal)" is the default;
- Next select Apriori values - observe the defaults using the "Name" popup menu;
- Then Click on "Compile Net" to create the extended rules;
- Check "Rules" box in List Options and click on the "List" button to display rules;
- Then select Input data values - observe the defaults from "Name" popup menu;
- Finally Click on "Run" to obtain inference from the rules;
- Try out different Input data values to compare results;
- Note that changing Apriori data will require recompilation of the net;
- Click on "List" after selecting from amongst the List Options;
- Check the Clear window box to clear the window prior to displaying the results.

6.4.2 Compiling Extended Fril Rules from Causal Net Descriptions

The use of the extended Fril rule for modelling Causal Nets was discussed in Section 4.4. In this section we show how to compile a basic probabilistic causal net description into a set of extended Fril rules. The initial knowledge base for the 'Cancer' problem introduced in Section 4.4.2 is as follows:

```
/* Pearl's causal net example - basic causal net description */
        ((target a))
        ((net a b))
        ((net a c))
        ((net b d))
        ((net c d))
        ((net c e))
/* input data nodes */
        ((input d))
        ((input e))
/* apriori and conditional probability data */
        ((apriori a 0.2))
        ((conditional b a 0.8))
        ((conditional b (not a) 0.2))
        ((conditional c a 0.2))
        ((conditional c (not a) 0.05))
        ((conditional d (b c) 0.8))
        ((conditional d ((not b) c) 0.8))
        ((conditional d (b (not c)) 0.8))
        ((conditional d ((not b) (not c)) 0.05))
        ((conditional e c 0.8))
        ((conditional e (not c) 0.6))
```

This knowledge can be displayed by proceeding as follows:

- Click on "Cancer" in the Problem cluster (if not already current);
- Click on "Support pairs (Optimal)" in the "Uncertainty" cluster;
- Click on "Compile Net" to compile the Rules;
- Click on "Data" and "Net" check boxes in the "List Options" cluster;
- Click on the "List" button.

The predicate 'target' identifies the target hypothesis node or nodes (in this case node 'a') which is to be the primary focus of queries, and for which apriori probability data is required. The binary relation 'net' defines the directed arcs between the nodes of the causal net. Predicate 'input' identifies the data nodes of the net. In this implementation, these data nodes can be deduced from predicate 'net' as being the leaf nodes of the net - that is to say those nodes with no directed arcs to any other nodes - in this case nodes 'd' and 'e'. This restriction avoids the difficulties of overspecification and partial conflict in the net. Predicate 'apriori' defines the apriori probability of the target node(s) - in this case $Pr(a) = 0.2$. Predicate 'conditional' defines the conditional probability relations for the net. For example, $Pr(b|a) = 0.8$ is represented by the first clause of conditional above, and $Pr(d|\neg bc) = 0.8$ is represented by the fact clause ((conditional d ((not b) c) 0.8)).

The objective is to derive a set of rules based on the top level node 'a' so that probabilistic support for 'a' can be derived for different choices of specific information (probabilistic data) on the input nodes.

An additional predicate 'projsum' is a utility corresponding to 'general', and is required for projecting supports onto a label from a set of labels. Goal (projsum LAB LABELS) derives support for label LAB by computing support for the labels LABELS and then projecting these appropriately onto LAB. For example, (projsum (b ((b))) ((bc ((b) (c))) ('b~c' ((b) (not c))) ('~bc' ((not b) (c))) ('~b~c' ((not b) (not c)))) computes support for bc and 'b~c' and, if these are singleton probabilities, simply adds them together and this becomes the support which 'projsum' returns. In the case of more general support pairs the sum must be constrained so that probabilities lie in the interval [0, 1]. Note that a label was defined in this context as a pair of the label name and its meaning (e.g. name 'b~c' and its meaning ((b) (not c))).

- Click on "Point probability" in the "Uncertainty" cluster;
- Recompile the net by clicking on the "Compile Net" button;
- Click on the "Rules" check box in the "List Options" cluster;
- Click on the "List" button to display the compiled rules as follows:

((a) (general (((bc)) (('b~c')) (('~bc')) (('~b~c')))
                  ((0.8) (0.457143) (0.2) (0.05)))) : ((1 1) (0 0))

((bc) (general (((d) (e)) ((d) (not e)) ((not d) (e)) ((not d) (not e)))

                          ((0.125) (0.05556) (0.01564) (0.00595)))) : ((1 1) (0 0))

(('b~c') (general (((d) (e)) ((d) (not e)) ((not d) (e)) ((not d) (not e)))

                          ((0.65625) (0.7778) (0.08171) (0.0833)))) : ((1 1) (0 0))

(('~bc') (general (((d) (e)) ((d) (not e)) ((not d) (e)) ((not d) (not e)))

                          ((0.125) (0.05556) (0.01556) (0.00595)))) : ((1 1) (0 0))

(('~b~c') (general (((d) (e)) ((d) (not e)) ((not d) (e)) ((not d) (not e)))

                          ((0.09375) (0.1111) (0.88716) (0.90476)))) : ((1 1) (0 0))

((b) (projsum (b ((b))) ((bc ((b) (c))) ('b~c' ((b) (not c)))

              ('~bc' ((not b) (c))) ('~b~c' ((not b) (not c))))))) : ((1 1) (0 0))

((c) (projsum (c ((c))) ((bc ((b) (c))) ('b~c' ((b) (not c)))

              ('~bc' ((not b) (c))) ('~b~c' ((not b) (not c))))))) : ((1 1) (0 0))

- Now select "Support pairs (Optimal)" from the "Uncertainty" cluster;
- Recompile the net by clicking on "Compile Net";
- Display the compiled rules again, by clicking on the "List" button.

The rules will be equivalent to those observed above except that conditional point proba-bility values will be replaced by support pairs with necessary and possible supports the same as the above point probability values.

    The following results can be displayed by clicking on the Run button, and they can be compared with those appearing in Section 4.4.2. In the first example, both 'd' and 'e' are uncertain (supports (0 1) assumed for each) and this explains the non-singleton support pair inference.

Using apriori (a) : (0.2 0.2)
and inputs
((d)) : (0 1)
and
((e)) : (0 1)
Top level query is:
qs ((a))
((a)) : (0.0888688 0.4603)
no (more) solutions

- Select "Point probability" again from the "Uncertainty" cluster;
- Recompile the net;
- Choose "Input" from the "Data Type" popup menu (this should be the default);
- Select 'd' from the "Name" popup menu (should also be the default);
- Click on "New Probability..." button and enter probability 0 (probability of 'd');
- Select 'e' from the "Name" popup menu;
- Click on "New Probability..." button and enter probability 1 (probability of 'e');
- Finally click on the "Run" button.

    Using apriori (a) : 0.2

    and inputs

    ((d)) : (0 0)

    and

    ((e))

    Top level query is:

    qs ((a))

    ((a)) : (0.0972763 0.0972763)

    no (more) solutions

- Now select probability 0.1 for 'd' and 0.9 for 'e' using similar procedure to above

    ((d)) : 0.1

    ((e)) : 0.9

    qs((a))

    ((a)) : (0.129668 0.129668)

    no (more) solutions

- Now select probability 0.2 for 'd' and 0.9 for 'e'

    ((d)) : 0.2

    ((e)) : 0.9

    yes

    qs((a))

    ((a)) : (0.162859 0.162859)

    no (more) solutions

- Select "Support pairs (Optimal)" from the "Uncertainty" cluster;
- Recompile the net and click on the "New Support..." button;
- Select (0 0.1) support pair for 'd' and (0.9 1) for 'e';
- Click on the "Run" button.

((d)) : (0 0.1)
((e)) : (0.9 1)
qs((a))
((a)) : (0.0964355 0.133745)
no (more) solutions

The application can be explored further by modifying the apriori probability of 'a'. This can be done by selecting Apriori from the Data Type popup menu and clicking the New Probability... or the New support... button. Enter the revised apriori value, recompile the net and Run. Note that each time the apriori value is changed, the net has to be recompiled.

6.4.3 A Second Application

Consider a second application, representing a belief net, in which there are two target nodes (event and thief) and a single input node (phone). A car alarm can be triggered by some relatively harmless event such as vibrations from a passing car, a pedestrian knocking the car as he or she walks by, or a mischievous child rocking the car. Alternatively, the alarm can be triggered by forced entry into the car which in turn may be caused by a thief with malicious intent. In either case, the sounding alarm may provoke a response in some responsible neighbour or passer-by, who may phone the police or inform the owner.

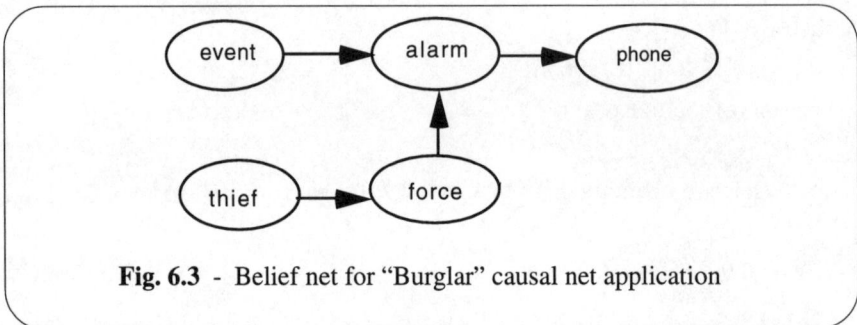

Fig. 6.3 - Belief net for "Burglar" causal net application

((target (event thief)))
((net event alarm))
((net alarm phone))
((net thief force))
((net force alarm))

((input phone))

266

((apriori event 0.2))
((apriori thief 0.05))

((conditional alarm (event force) 0.99))
((conditional alarm (event (not force)) 0.8))
((conditional alarm ((not event) force) 0.99))
((conditional alarm ((not event) (not force)) 0.01))
((conditional force thief 0.9))
((conditional force (not thief) 0.05))
((conditional phone alarm 0.7))
((conditional phone (not alarm) 0.1))

This application can be explored by clicking on the Burglar radio button in the Problem cluster and then compiling the rules by clicking on the Compile Net button. The rules can be displayed by checking Rules box in List Options cluster and clicking on the "List" button as before.

((thief) (general (((force)) ((not force)))
                      ((0.486486) (0.00550964)))) : ((1 1) (0 0))

((eventforce) (general (((alarm)) ((not alarm)))
                      ((0.0750507) (0.00024472)))) : ((1 1) (0 0))

(('event~force') (general (((alarm)) ((not alarm)))
                      ((0.594997) (0.0480181)))) : ((1 1) (0 0))

(('~eventforce') (general (((alarm)) ((not alarm)))
                      ((0.300203) (0.00097888)))) : ((1 1) (0 0))

(('~event~force') (general (((alarm)) ((not alarm)))
                      ((0.0297498) (0.950758)))) : ((1 1) (0 0))

((alarm) (general (((phone)) ((not phone)))
                      ((0.693222) (0.0971504)))) : ((1 1) (0 0))

((event) (projsum (event ((event))) ((eventforce ((event) (force)))
          ('event~force' ((event) (not force))) ('~eventforce' ((not event) (force)))
          ('~event~force' ((not event) (not force)))))) : ((1 1) (0 0))

((force) (projsum (force ((force))) ((eventforce ((event) (force)))

('event~force' ((event) (not force))) ('~eventforce' ((not event) (force)))

('~event~force' ((not event) (not force)))))) : ((1 1) (0 0))

Using apriori (event) : 0.2 and (thief) : 0.05, and appropriate assignments of input data, the following results can be computed:

((phone)) : (0 1)

qs((event))

((event)) : (0.108669 0.479298)

no (more) solutions

qs((thief))

((thief)) : (0.0235755 0.130809)

no (more) solutions

((phone)) : (1 1)   % asserted information

qs((event))

((event)) : (0.479298 0.479298)

no (more) solutions

qs((thief))

((thief)) : (0.130809 0.130809)

no (more) solutions

6.4.4 Deriving the Bayesian Conditional Probabilities

Consider again the problem of Section 6.4.1. The problem is decomposed into two modules ((a) (b c)) corresponding to phase 1 and ((b c) (d e)) corresponding to phase 2. Following the treatment of Section 4.4.2, we use capitals to denote variables - so that for example variable B denotes alternatives b and ¬b. We first compute Pr(A|BC) using Pr(A) as the apriori probabilities for this the first phase. As a consequence of the first phase, the probabilities Pr(BC) will have been computed, and these fulfil the role of apriori probabilities for the second phase so that Pr(BC|DE) can be computed in like manner, to establish the Fril rules. Using Bayes theorem we can compute the following:

Phase 1:

With data:

$Pr(a) = 0.2$; $Pr(b|a) = 0.8$; $Pr(b|\neg a) = 0.2$; $Pr(c|a) = 0.2$; $Pr(c|\neg a) = 0.05$.

Using Bayes:

Pr(A|BC)   = Pr(BC|A).Pr(A)/Pr(BC) where Pr(A) is the apriori on A;

Pr(BC|A)   = Pr(B|A).Pr(C|A) assuming independence of B and C; also

268

Pr(BC)   = Pr(BC|A).Pr(A) + Pr(BC|¬A).Pr(¬A)

               = Pr(B|A).Pr(C|A).Pr(A) + Pr(B|¬A).Pr(C|¬A).(1 - Pr(A))

Therefore, Pr(A|BC) = X/{X + Y} where

X= Pr(B|A).Pr(C|A).Pr(A); and Y = Pr(B|¬A).Pr(C|¬A).(1 - Pr(A))

Whence, X(abc) = 0.8*0.2*0.2 = 0.032; Y(abc) = 0.2*0.05*0.8 = 0.008

Pr(a|bc) = 0.032/0.04 = 0.8

also, X(ab¬c) = 0.8*0.8*0.2 = 0.128; Y(ab¬c) = 0.2*0.95*0.8 = 0.152

Pr(a|b¬c) = 0.128/0.28 = 0.4571

and, X(a¬bc) = 0.2*0.2*0.2 = 0.008; Y(a¬bc) = 0.8*0.05*0.8 = 0.032

Pr(a|¬bc) = 0.008/0.04 = 0.2

and, X(a¬b¬c) = 0.2*0.8*0.2 = 0.032; Y(a¬b¬c) = 0.8*0.95*0.8 = 0.608

Pr(a|¬b¬c) = 0.032/0.64 = 0.05

Phase 2:

With data:

Pr(d|bc) = 0.8; Pr(d|b¬c) = 0.8; Pr(d|¬bc) = 0.8; Pr(d|¬b¬c) = 0.05;

Pr(e|c) = 0.8; Pr(e|¬c) = 0.6;

Pr(a|bc) = 0.8; Pr(a|b¬c) = 0.4571; Pr(a|¬bc) = 0.2; Pr(a|¬b¬c) = 0.05.

Using Bayes:

Pr(BC|DE) = Pr(DE|BC).Pr(BC)/Pr(DE) = Pr(D|BC).Pr(E|C).Pr(BC)/Pr(DE)

with Pr(BC) = {X + Y} from Phase 1 above

Pr(DE) = W1 + W2 + W3 + W4 where

W1 = Pr(D|BC).Pr(E|C).Pr(BC); W2 = Pr(D|B¬C).Pr(E|¬C).P(B¬C);

W3 = Pr(D|¬BC).Pr(E|C).Pr(¬BC); and

W4 = Pr(D|¬B¬C).(Pr(E|¬C).Pr(¬B¬C);

so that Pr(BC|DE) = W1/{W1 + W2 + W3 + W4}

These procedures are easily generalised and depend only on the decomposition of the net into appropriate modules. Clearly, the computations are critically dependent on the apriori probability of the target node (in this case node 'a'), and the net would have to be recompiled for different choices of apriori.

6.4.5 Bayesian Arithmetic with Support Pairs

So far we have considered only probabilistic causal nets where both the apriori and conditional probability values were point valued. In the case that the input data have point valued probabilities and the assumption of independence is made, then the inferences from compiled rules are always point valued probabilities. When the input data are uncertain - for example when they are undefined or characterised by interval support pairs - then we have shown how support pair inferences can be derived from the compiled rules.

269

Of more general interest is the case that the apriori probabilities and/or the conditional probabilities are characterised by non-singleton support pairs. A naive approach to this case is to 'fuzzify' the Bayes computations, illustrated in the previous Section, by performing fuzzy arithmetic on the interval support pairs. For example, to obtain S = S1 + S2, where S1 = (n1 p1), S2 = (n2 p2), we compute n = n1+n2, and p = p1+p2 and derive S = (n p). The product is computed similarly (replacing + by * in the above). For the case of division and subtraction, we must take care to infer the widest possible interval consistent with the support pair constraints. For example, in the case of division, to obtain S = S1/S2 we compute n = n1/p2 and p = p1/n2, truncating p to unity if the ratio p1/n2 > 1. Similarly for subtraction, to obtain S = S1 - S2 we compute n = n1 - p2 and p = p1 - n2, truncating either or both to zero when the differences are less than zero. This approach is adopted when the "Support pairs (naive)" radio button is selected in the Uncertainty cluster.

Consider the Cancer problem again (select Cancer radio button in the Problem cluster), and select the Support pairs (naive) Uncertainty option. Try changing the apriori probability of 'a' by selecting Apriori from the Data Type popup menu and clicking on the New Support... button. Changing the support for 'a' to (0.2 0.3) should derive the following compiled rules:

((a) (general (((bc)) (('b~c')) (('~bc')) (('~b~c')))
                ((0.571429 1) (0.372093 0.735632) (0.181818 0.333333)
                                (0.0487805 0.0851064)))) : ((1 1) (0 0))

((bc) (general (((d) (e)) ((d) (not e)) ((not d) (e)) ((not d) (not e)))
                ((0.10032 0.18843) (0.044827 0.083895) (0.014471 0.024561)
                                (0.00555556 0.00940386)))) : ((1 1) (0 0))

(('b~c') (general (((d) (e)) ((d) (not e)) ((not d) (e)) ((not d) (not e)))
                ((0.503537 0.868139) (0.6 1) (0.0726345 0.113158)
                                (0.074359 0.115533)))) : ((1 1) (0 0))

(('~bc') (general (((d) (e)) ((d) (not e)) ((not d) (e)) ((not d) (not e)))
                ((0.092604 0.14805) (0.041379 0.065917) (0.013358 0.019298)
                                (0.00512821 0.00738875)))) : ((1 1) (0 0))

(('~b~c') (general (((d) (e)) ((d) (not e)) ((not d) (e)) ((not d) (not e)))
                ((0.0680064 0.10347) (0.0810345 0.122846) (0.745547 1)
                                (0.763248 1)))) : ((1 1) (0 0))

((b) (projsum (b ((b))) ((bc ((b) (c))) ('b~c' ((b) (not c)))

('~bc' ((not b) (c))) ('~b~c' ((not b) (not c)))))) : ((1 1) (0 0))

((c) (projsum (c ((c))) ((bc ((b) (c))) ('b~c' ((b) (not c)))

('~bc' ((not b) (c))) ('~b~c' ((not b) (not c)))))) : ((1 1) (0 0))

Now select Input from the Data Type popup menu and change the support pair for 'd' to (0.1 0.1), and the support pair for 'e' to (0.9 0.9). Click the Run button to obtain the following solution.

((d)) : 0.1
((e)) : 0.9
qs((a))
((a)) : (0.100563 0.251604)
no (more) solutions

Compare this result with the result we obtained for apriori Pr(a) = 0.2 which derived inference: ((a)) : (0.129668 0.129668). We could also show that the inference for the case Pr(a) = 0.3 is: ((a)) : (0.195479 0.195479), and we might expect an inference interval close to (0.129668 0.195479) for the above case of apriori in interval [0.2, 0.3]. The reason for this large discrepancy is that the crude fuzzy arithmetic model adopted in the above naive approach does not take into account the probabilistic constraints of the problem. Taking these into account leads to optimisation/allocation problems similar to that described for the extended Fril rule described in Section 4.2.2 and simulated in Section 6.3 above. These optimisations have been incorporated into the Uncertainty option Support pairs (Optimal), which can be used to compile both probabilistic and support pair causal nets (or mixtures of the two - for both apriori and conditional probabilities), and the above example is illustrated below:

- Select: "Support pairs (Optimal)"
- Check that apriori is still (0.2 0.3)
- Recompile the net
- List the Rules and Run

((a) (general (((bc)) (('b~c')) (('~bc')) (('~b~c')))

((0.8 0.872727) (0.457143 0.590769) (0.2 0.3)

(0.05 0.0827586)))) : ((1 1) (0 0))

271

((bc) (general (((d) (e)) ((d) (not e)) ((not d) (e)) ((not d) (not e)))

((0.11375 0.16452) (0.0497281 0.0750213) (0.0155642 0.022869)

(0.00595238 0.00879297)))) : ((1 1) (0 0))

(('b~c') (general (((d) (e)) ((d) (not e)) ((not d) (e)) ((not d) (not e)))

((0.628184 0.693179) (0.763853 0.808081) (0.0817121 0.101351)

(0.0833333 0.103917)))) : ((1 1) (0 0))

(('~bc') (general (((d) (e)) ((d) (not e)) ((not d) (e)) ((not d) (not e)))

((0.109308 0.125) (0.0489297 0.0555556) (0.0155642 0.016632)

(0.00595238 0.00639488)))) : ((1 1) (0 0))

(('~b~c') (general (((d) (e)) ((d) (not e)) ((not d) (e)) ((not d) (not e)))

((0.0742955 0.09375) (0.088685 0.111111) (0.859148 0.88716)

(0.880895 0.904762)))) : ((1 1) (0 0))

((b) (projsum (b ((b))) ((bc ((b) (c))) ('b~c' ((b) (not c)))

('~bc' ((not b) (c))) ('~b~c' ((not b) (not c))))))) : ((1 1) (0 0))

((c) (projsum (c ((c))) ((bc ((b) (c))) ('b~c' ((b) (not c)))

('~bc' ((not b) (c))) ('~b~c' ((not b) (not c))))))) : ((1 1) (0 0))

qs((a))

((a)) : (0.129068 0.196125)

no (more) solutions

This interval is very close to the required interval of (0.129668 0.195479). The reason it differs at all is because the optimisations are only performed locally with respect to each Bayes formula calculation separately, and in theory the whole set of such Bayes computations should be considered. This is far too complex a problem to be treated in general and the local approximation will be sufficiently good in practice.

Consider the following general Bayes computation:

$$\Pr(B_j \ldots C_j | D) = \Pr(D | B_j \ldots C_j).\Pr(B_j \ldots C_j) / \sum_{i=1}^{n} \Pr(D | B_i \ldots C_i).\Pr(B_i \ldots C_i)$$

where $\Pr(B_i \ldots C_i) = \alpha_i \in (n_i \ p_i)$ and $\Pr(D | B_i \ldots C_i) \in (l_i \ u_i)$ for i = 1, ..., n

It can be shown that the solution of:

$$Pr(B_j \ldots C_j | D) \in (x \; y)$$

leads to a pair of optimisations as follows:

$$x = \underset{\alpha_j}{\text{MIN}} \; l_j n_j / (u_1 \alpha_1 + \ldots + l_j n_j + \ldots + u_n \alpha_n) \; \text{with} \sum_{i \neq j} \alpha_i = 1 - \alpha_j = 1 - n_j$$

where α_j is assigned to maximise the denominator expression, and

$$y = \underset{\alpha_j}{\text{MAX}} \; u_j p_j / (l_1 \alpha_1 + \ldots + u_j p_j + \ldots + l_n \alpha_n) \; \text{with} \sum_{i \neq j} \alpha_i = 1 - \alpha_j = 1 - p_j$$

where α_j is assigned to minimise the denominator expression.

These problems can be solved by directly analogous methods to those described in Section 4.2.2.

6.5 FUZZY CONTROL

In this section we describe program utilities for performing fuzzy control inference and apply these to the examples of Section 4.5 of Chapter 4. In Section 6.6 following, we apply these tools to a more realistic application in fuzzy control - the well known Inverted Pendulum problem.

6.5.1 Fuzzy Control Predicates and Notation

The basic query evaluators in the Support Logic model for fuzzy control are the same as for the standard Support Logic inference model, i.e. qs, ws and os. For example, if the following query is evaluated:

qs ((controller of _Plant is _Output))

and there is a Support Logic predicate for controller with rules having heads of the form:

((controller of PLANT is large) . . .) : <support-pair>

where large is a fuzzy set, then the query evaluator 'qs' will operate in the fuzzy control mode of Support Logic programming. The output control inference fuzzy set will be bound to the variable _Output for a given instantiation of plant _Plant, using the expected fuzzy sets model for combining fuzzy sets and inference support pairs described in Sections 4.2.5 to 4.3.5 and 4.5.9 to 4.5.13. In this case the inference support pair will always be (1 1). However, if the "controller" predicate did not have a fuzzy set argument in the heads of rules in the position corresponding to the variable _Output, then the standard Support Logic inference procedure would be applied, obtaining a support pair inference for the goal (controller of _Plant is _Output) for each instantiation of _Plant and _Output derived. These two inference modes have an analogy to data driven (fuzzy control) and goal driven modes of inference in Expert Systems reasoning strategies.

There is an additional family of Support Logic query evaluators: qsd, wsd and osd, which are closely related to qs, ws and os, but which only operate in the fuzzy control mode of inference. In addition to computing the output inference fuzzy set for control, these also display the corresponding defuzzified value using the mass assignment model for defuzzification described in Sections 4.5.9 to 4.5.13.

For the purposes of comparison of various different Fuzzy Control models in the Fuzzy Control module of the Demonstration System, however, there are several additional fuzzy control predicates defined which simulate the built-in Support Logic model for control and implement more traditional Fuzzy Control models based on classical Fuzzy sets reasoning. These incorporate options to display traces of the inference process when the "Verbose" option for output display is selected. The principal predicates for these simulations and illustrations are as follows:

slc   for support logic control with semantic unification
fsc   for fuzzy sets control using max-min composition

These predicates have the following goal forms:

(slc <agg-operator> <pred-name> <list-of-fuzzy-data> <fuz-inf> <de-fuz>)
(fsc <fuzzy-implication-type> <agg-operator> <pred-name> <list-of-fuzzy-data>
            <fuz-inf> <de-fuz>)
where

<agg-operator> is the aggregation operator for combining pairs of fuzzy sets inferred from different rules - for support logic control, this is any of: intersection, multiply, average or dempster;

<pred-name> is the target top-level predicate name;

<list-of-fuzzy-data> is a list of data items - one corresponding to the fuzzy set in each goal in the body of a rule - this notation implies the restriction of every rule having the same format, but this restriction is not necessary and the notation is just a convenience for the purposes of demonstration since the examples considered all follow this restriction;

<fuz-inf> is the final output fuzzy inference;

274

<fuzzy-implication-type> is one of:

Luk   Lukasiewicz implication (union body combination)

                       <agg-operator> is intersection, multiply, or average;

Kleene-D   Kleene-Dienes implication (union body combination)

                       <agg-operator> is intersection, multiply, or average;

Mamdani   Mamdani conjunction (intersection body combination)

                       <agg-operator> is union or average.

<de-fuz> is the defuzzified value of <fuz-inf> - the algorithm used depends on the type of inference process, as follows:

Support Logic Control:

The defuzzified value is the expected output control value based on the modified probability distribution inferred from the output control fuzzy set using mass assignment theory as described in Sections 4.5.9 to 4.5.13.

Lukasiewicz and Kleene-Dienes Fuzzy Control:

The defuzzified value is the average domain value of those with maximum membership if the domain is a continuous interval or a discrete set of numbers, otherwise it is a domain value with maximum membership.

Mamdani Fuzzy Control:

The defuzzified value is the centroid of the output inference possibility distribution, i.e. the domain value of an itype fuzzy set corresponding to the centre of gravity of the area under the membership characteristic function. In the case of a discrete fuzzy set B, with membership function χ_B and real valued domain universe $(y_1, y_2, ..., y_p)$, this is the domain point y, where

$$y = \sum_{j=1}^{p} y_j \chi_B(y_j) / \sum_{j=1}^{p} \chi_B(y_j)$$

The simulations treat two particular cases of fuzzy sets in a special way. Possibility distributions in which the membership value is unity over the whole domain are represented by the constant "unrestricted". This arises frequently with the Support Logic model and the Lukasiewicz and Kleene-Dienes fuzzy sets models of control. In the case of the Mamdani fuzzy set model, fuzzy set inferences with zero membership over the whole domain are frequently encountered, and these are represented by the constant "inconsistent".

The following notations are frequently employed as a shorthand referring to the various different options for exploring fuzzy control:

slc	Support Logic control
fsc	Fuzzy Sets control (including Lukasiewicz, Kleene-Dienes and Mamdani)
fsl	Fuzzy Sets control with Lukasiewicz implication
fsk	Fuzzy Sets control with Kleene-Dienes implication
fsm	Mamdani Fuzzy Sets control
slci	Support Logic control with intersection aggregation of rule inferences
slcd	Support Logic control with modified dempster aggregation
slca	Support Logic control with average aggregation
fsli	Lukasiewicz Fuzzy control with intersection aggregation
fsla	Lukasiewicz Fuzzy control with average aggregation
fski	Kleene-Dienes Fuzzy control with intersection aggregation
fska	Kleene-Dienes Fuzzy control with average aggregation
fsmu	Mamdani Fuzzy control with union aggregation
fsma	Mamdani Fuzzy control with average aggregation

6.5.2 The Dialog Interface for the Fuzzy Control Module

Selecting the Fuzzy Control radio button and clicking on Run in the top level Demonstrations dialog box obtains the Dialog interface for Fuzzy Control Inference Methods shown in Fig. 6.4.

Three different types of problem are represented which can be selected by clicking on one of the radio buttons in the Problem cluster:

- Basic inference corresponds to basic problems of support logic inference with the very simple example of the "value" predicate involving discrete fuzzy sets introduced in Sections 4.2.6, 4.3.3 and 4.3.4 Several examples also explore the Support Logic control mode of inference. In addition, the examples introduced in Section 6.1 at the beginning of the Chapter are included.

- Basic control compares the four different models of Fuzzy control inference in the above "value" example, which was discussed in Sections 4.5.5 to 4.5.8.

- Pendulum control compares the four different models of Fuzzy control inference in a more realistic problem of fuzzy control concerning the balancing of an Inverted Pendulum. This application employs continuous possibility distributions using Fril itype fuzzy set definitions.

There are the familiar Display cluster with "Quiet" and "Verbose" modes for controlling the amount of information displayed, and the Execution Type popup menu with the usual four options for the type of query to be explored, namely: Display & Evaluate query, Display query, Evaluate query, and List relevant knowledge.

The Queries popup menu contains a different selection of options for the Basic Inference problem and the Basic and Pendulum fuzzy control problems. The Basic Inference category will be discussed first.

```
┌─────────────────────────────────────────────────────────────────┐
│ ▤▯ ▤▤▤▤▤▤▤▤▤▤ Fuz Control ▤▤▤▤▤▤▤▤▤▤                              │
│          Fuzzy Control Inference Methods                         │
│                                                                  │
│                                    Data Type: (ang vel) pair     │
│   ┌─ Display ─┐  ┌── Problem ──┐                                 │
│   │           │  │ ○ Basic Inference  Control Input │ User Defined│
│   │ ● Quiet   │  │ ○ Basic Control                  │            │
│   │ ○ Verbose │  │ ● Pendulum Control │ ┌──────────────────────┐ │
│   └───────────┘  └─────────────────┘  │    Enter Data...     │ │
│                                        └──────────────────────┘ │
│                                         User Input: (-90 30)     │
│                                                                  │
│  Execution Type │ Display & Evaluate query              │       │
│                                                                  │
│  Queries │ Support Logic Control with intersection aggregation │ │
│                                                                  │
│   ☒ Clear window   ( Evaluate )    ( Help )    ( Done )          │
└─────────────────────────────────────────────────────────────────┘
```

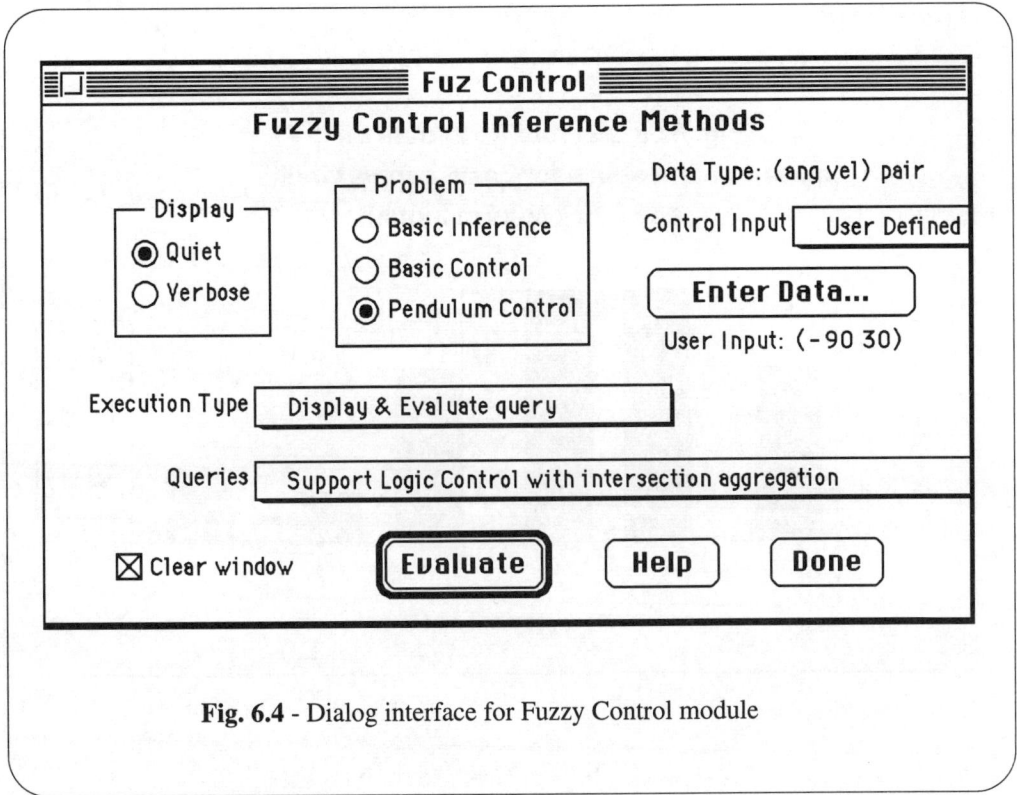

Fig. 6.4 - Dialog interface for Fuzzy Control module

6.5.3 Basic Inference problems

Both the Basic Inference and Basic Control problem queries are based on the following very elementary knowledge base introduced in Sections 4.2 and 4.3. The input space (univ1) and output space (univ2) fuzzy sets are displayed as barcharts in Figs. 6.5a and 6.5b.

```
set (univ1 (a b c d) )
set (univ2 (alpha beta gamma) )
(f1 {a:1, b:0.7, c:0.3} univ1)
(f2 {a:0.5, b:1, c:0.1} univ1)
(fd {a:0.7, b:1, c:0.2} univ1)
(g1 {alpha:1, beta:0.5, gamma:0.1} univ2)
(g2 {alpha:0.3, beta:1} univ2)
(g {alpha:1, beta:0.2} univ2)

((value of y is g1) (val of x is f1))
((value of y is g2) (val of x is f2))
```

277

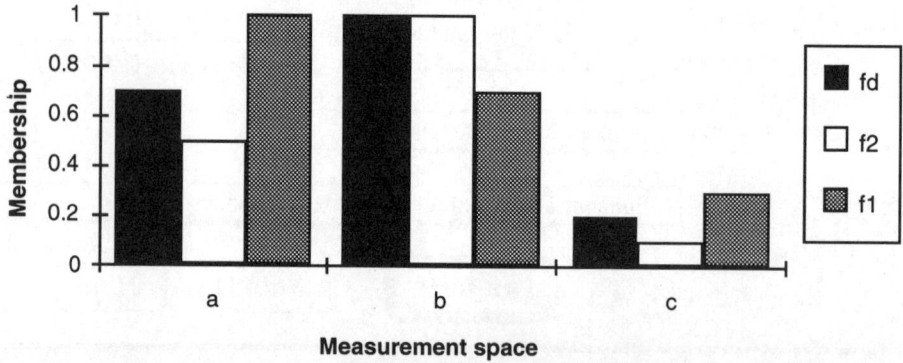

Fig. 6.5a Discrete fuzzy sets on measurement space for basic support logic and fuzzy control model

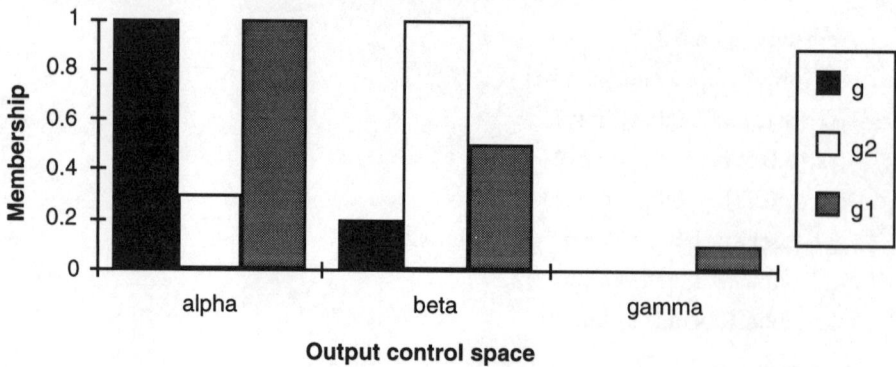

Fig. 6.5b Discrete fuzzy sets on output control space for basic support logic and fuzzy control model

((val of x is fd))

dempster valued
((valued of y is g1) (val of x is f1))
((valued of y is g2) (val of x is f2))

For the Basic Inference problem, the set of Query descriptions is as follows:

1. 'Default Support Logic plus expected value'
2. 'Dempster Support Logic plus expected value'
3. 'Default Support Logic with singleton fset'
4. 'Dempster Support Logic with singleton fset'
5. 'Modified Dempster computation'
6. 'Default Support Logic Control plus defuzzification'
7. 'Dempster Support Logic Control plus defuzzification'
8. 'Support Logic inference with Design example'
9. 'Non-monotonic reasoning with Penguin example'
10. 'Support Logic negation example'

On selecting each of these and clicking the Evaluate button, the following output is displayed:

1. **Support for goal (value of y is g) - case of default rule**
list g
(g {alpha:1 beta:0.2} univ2)
list univ2
set (univ2 (alpha beta gamma))
qs ((value of y is g))
((value of y is {alpha:1 beta:0.2})) : (0.3596 0.5518)
? ((expected2 g univ2 (0.3596 0.5518) _ExpFuz)
    (p Expected Fuzzy Set _ExpFuz) (pp))
Expected Fuzzy Set {alpha:0.5518 beta:0.62268 gamma:0.6404}

In this first example, the support logic goal (value of y is g) is evaluated, which is not support logic control since the fuzzy set 'g' is instantiated in the query. The support pair (0.3596 0.5518) is derived and this is used with the fuzzy set definition of 'g' to obtain the expected Fuzzy Set shown over the given universe 'univ2'.

2. **Support for goal (valued of y is g) - case of dempster rule**

. . . . .

qs ((valued of y is g))

((valued of y is {alpha:1 beta:0.2})) : (0.323586 0.657823)

? ((expected2 g univ2 (0.323586 0.657823) _ExpFuz)

(p Expected Fuzzy Set _ExpFuz) (pp))

Expected Fuzzy Set {alpha:0.657823 beta:0.672696 gamma:0.676414}

This second example is similar to the first with dempster predicate "valued" replacing "value". The dempster combination rule is used to combine the support pair inferences from the two rules for "valued".

3. **Support for goal (value of y is <singleton>) - case of default rule**

? ((forall ((member _Fuz ({alpha:1} {beta:1} {gamma:1})))

((qs ((value of y is _Fuz))))))

((value of y is {alpha:1})) : (0.31 0.472)

((value of y is {beta:1})) : (0.399 0.538)

((value of y is {gamma:1})) : (0 0.43)

In this third example, the fuzzy set 'g' is replaced by the singleton components of the universe of 'g'.

4. **Support for goal (valued of y is g) - case of dempster rule**

? ((forall ((member _Fuz ({alpha:1} {beta:1} {gamma:1})))

((qs ((valued of y is _Fuz))))))

((valued of y is {alpha:1})) : (0.174957 0.564377)

((valued of y is {beta:1})) : (0.263175 0.659587)

((valued of y is {gamma:1})) : (0 0.19006)

The fourth example is the same as the third with dempster "valued" replacing "value".

5. **Modified dempster combination example**

? ((demp_mod g1 (0.62 1) g2 (0.57 1) univ2 X) (pp X))

{alpha:0.683256 beta:0.741922 gamma:0.241999}

The modified (extended) dempster combination rule is discussed in Section 4.5.6.

6. **Evaluation of support logic goal (value of y is X) - default fuzzy control**

qsd ((value of y is X))

((value of y is {alpha:0.601 beta:0.69 gamma:0.43})) : (1 1)

Fuzzy set {alpha:0.601 beta:0.69 gamma:0.43}

                defuzzifies to beta over sub-domain (alpha beta gamma)

This example shows the built-in evaluator 'qsd' for Support Logic control. Note how the variable X in the goal matches with the fuzzy sets in the heads of predicate "value". This is what determines the query as Support Logic control, and contrasts with the first example above.

7. Evaluation of support logic goal (valued of y is X) - dempster fuzzy control

qs ((valued of y is X))

((valued of y is {alpha:0.683256 beta:0.741922 gamma:0.241999})) : (1 1)

Fuzzy set {alpha:0.683256 beta:0.741922 gamma:0.241999}

                defuzzifies to beta over sub-domain (alpha beta gamma)

This example is similar to 6. above with dempster predicate "valued" replacing "value". This means that the modified (extended) dempster combination rule is employed. If the Verbose radio button is selected in the Display cluster and the Evaluate button is clicked again, then you will be able to observe that the above fuzzy set inference derives from the following (fuzzy-set support-pair) pairs:

    ({alpha:1 beta:0.5 gamma:0.1} (0.62 1)) and ({alpha:0.3 beta:1} (0.57 1))

The final three examples (8, 9 and 10) relate to the examples discussed in the introduction to this chapter, Section 6.1, and the reader is invited to try these and refer to that section.

6.5.4 Basic Fuzzy Control

In this section we continue to explore the simple application based on the "value" predicate described above, but focus on comparing the four different inference methods for Fuzzy Control. Selecting the Basic Control option in the Problem cluster sets up the following nine options in the Queries popup menu:

1. 'Support Logic Control with intersection aggregation' (mnemonic: slci)
2. 'Support Logic Control with dempster aggregation' (mnemonic: slcd)
3. 'Support Logic Control with average aggregation' (mnemonic: slca)
4. 'Lukasiewicz Control with intersection aggregation' (mnemonic: fsli)
5. 'Lukasiewicz Control with average aggregation' (mnemonic: fsla)
6. 'Kleene-D Control with intersection aggregation' (mnemonic: fski)
7. 'Kleene-D Control with average aggregation' (mnemonic: fska)
8. 'Mamdani Control with union aggregation' (mnemonic: fsmu)
9. 'Mamdani Control with average aggregation' (mnemonic: fsma)

The Control Input can be selected from the popup menu in the upper right of the Dialog box. This defaults to the discrete fuzzy set 'fd' which is defined as follows:

    set (univ1 (a b c d))

    (fd {a:0.7 b:1 c:0.2} univ1)

Other choices of Control Input provided are: {a:0.7 b:1 c:0.2}, {a:1}, a, b, c, d. Since other applications, such as the Inverted Pendulum example to be described, may involve more than one input, the input data are represented as a list. Assuming that the default Control Input data is selected, clicking the Evaluate button with each of the above nine fuzzy control Query options selected will invoke the following goals:

1. evaluates (slc intersection value (fd) FUZ VAL)
2. evaluates (slc dempster value (fd) FUZ VAL)
3. evaluates (slc average value (fd) FUZ VAL)
4. evaluates (fsc Luk intersection value (fd) FUZ VAL)
5. evaluates (fsc Luk average value (fd) FUZ VAL)
6. evaluates (fsc Kleene-D intersection value (fd) FUZ VAL)
7. evaluates (fsc Kleene-D average value (fd) FUZ VAL)
8. evaluates (fsc Mamdani union value (fd) FUZ VAL)
9. evaluates (fsc Mamdani average value (fd) FUZ VAL)

where, in each case, variable FUZ is bound to the control inference fuzzy set, and variable VAL is bound to the defuzzification value as follows:

Query Type		Fuzzy Output	Defuzz. value
1.	slci	{alpha:0.601 beta:0.69 gamma:0.43}	beta
2.	slcd	{alpha:0.683 beta:0.742 gamma:0.242}	beta
3.	slca	{alpha:0.8005 beta:0.845 gamma:0.436}	beta
4.	fsli	{alpha:0.7 beta:0.8 gamma:0.4}	beta
5.	fsla	{alpha:0.85 beta:0.9 gamma:0.45}	beta
6.	fski	{alpha:0.5 beta:0.5 gamma:0.3}	alpha
7.	fska	{alpha:0.75 beta:0.75 gamma:0.4}	alpha
8.	fsmu	{alpha:0.7 beta:1 gamma:0.1}	beta
9.	fsma	{alpha:0.5 beta:0.75 gamma:0.05}	beta

Strictly, the defuzzified values in examples 6 and 7 ought to be randomised choices between alpha and beta. This randomisation is implemented for the mass defuzzification for support logic control, but in other cases the left-most peak membership value is chosen arbitrarily.

6.6 Fuzzy Control of Inverted Pendulum Examples

6.6.1 Introducing the Application

In this Section we introduce a set of fuzzy control rules for balancing an inverted pendulum in two dimensions. The basic model is based on that discussed by Kosko (1992). There are two fuzzy state variables, namely: the angle that the pendulum shaft makes with the vertical (with zero angle corresponding to the vertical position); and the angular velocity, which is measured as the difference between the angle at the current time step and the previous time step. There is one fuzzy control variable; this is the angular velocity of the motor measured as the motor current. The domains of the variables are taken as (-10 10) for motor current, (-90 90) degrees for angle and (-180 180) degrees for angular velocity. Each of the three spaces is spanned by seven overlapping trapezoid fuzzy sets as shown in Fig. 6.6 below.

There are fifteen linguistic rules which span the control-state space as shown in Fig. 6.7, where the row labels represent angular velocity, the column labels represent angle, and the matrix entries represent motor current. Each of the rules has the following form:

((motor_current <curr-itype>) (angle <ang-itype>) (angular_velocity <vel-itype>))

The Pendulum Control problem is selected from the Problem cluster in the Fuzzy Control Inference Methods dialog module. The same selection of nine queries is available to try from the Queries popup menu as in the Basic Control problem discussed above. There is a wide range of Control Input values to try from the popup menu comprising (angle angular_velocity) pairs, including pairs of numbers and pairs of fuzzy sets; and there is an additional option at the bottom of the menu to select User Defined Data.

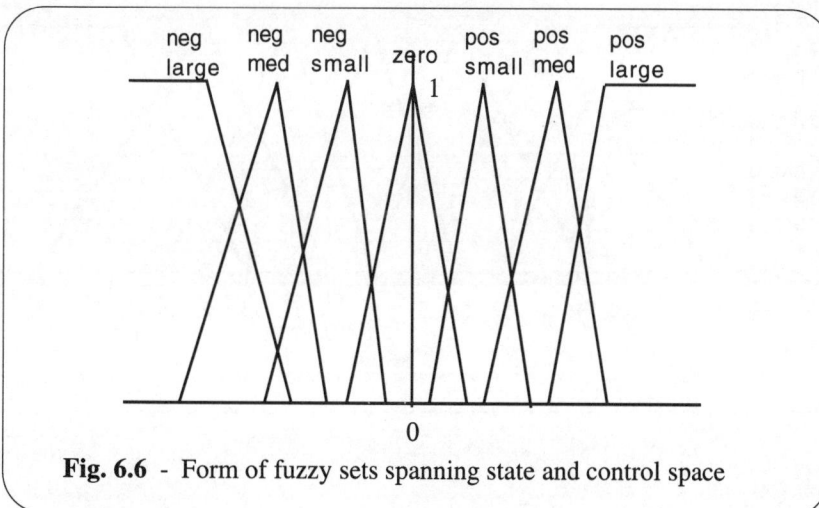

Fig. 6.6 - Form of fuzzy sets spanning state and control space

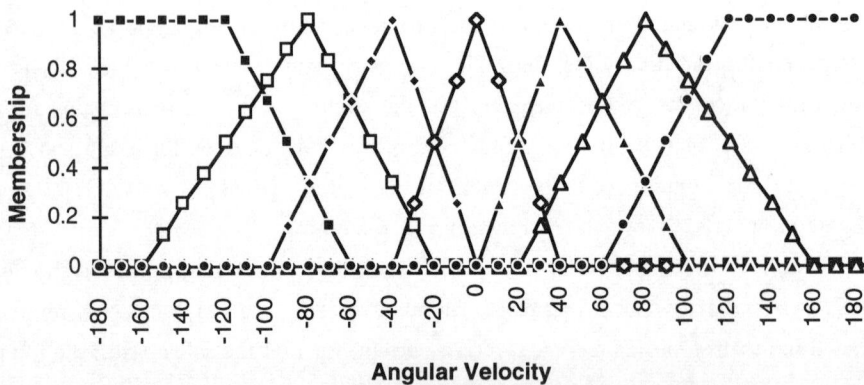

Fig. 6.6a Form of the fuzzy sets spanning the space of Angular Velocity

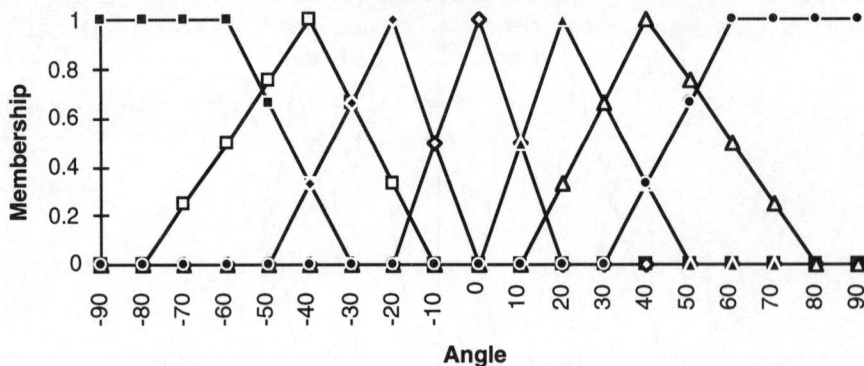

Fig. 6.6b Form of the fuzzy sets spanning the Angle space

Fig. 6.6c Form of the fuzzy sets spanning the Motor Current control space

	nl	nm	ns	ze	ps	pm	pl
nl				pl			
nm				pm			
ns				ps	ns		
ze	pl	pm	ps	ze	ns	nm	nl
ps			ps	ns			
pm				nm			
pl				nl			

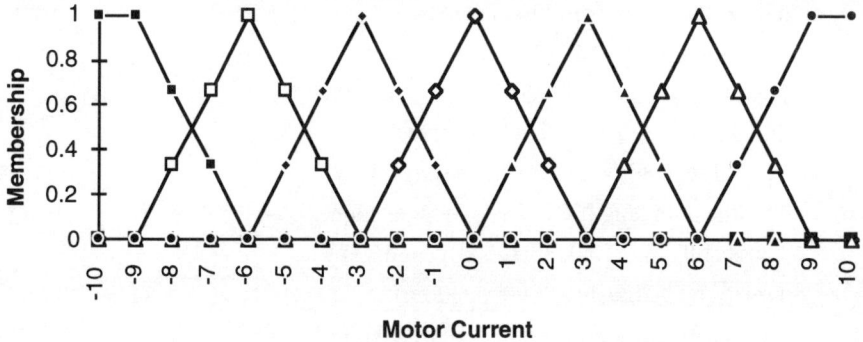

Fig. 6.7 - Matrix of motor current control fuzzy sets, where row labels represent angular velocity; column labels represent angle.

User defined data is entered by clicking on the Enter Data... button, when the user is prompted successively for the value of angle, which must be in the range [-90, 90], and angular_velocity , which must be in the range [-180, 180]. There is no option for the user to enter fuzzy set defined data.

The complete knowledge base of the Inverted Pendulum application is as follows:

set (currdom (-10 10))

```
set (angdom (-90 90) )
set (veldom (-180 180) )
(poslarge_curr [7:0, 9:1] currdom)
(posmedium_curr [4:0, 6:1, 8:0] currdom)
(possmall_curr [1:0, 3:1, 5:0 ] currdom)
(zero_curr [-2:0, 0:1, 2:0] currdom)
(negsmall_curr [-5:0, -3:1, -1:0] currdom)
(negmedium_curr [-8:0, -6:1, -4:0] currdom)
(neglarge_curr [-9:1, -7:0 ] currdom)
(poslarge_ang [60:0, 80:1] angdom)
(posmedium_ang [35:0, 55:1, 75:0] angdom)
(possmall_ang [10:0, 30:1, 50:0] angdom)
(zero_ang [-20:0, 0:1, 20:0] angdom)
(negsmall_ang [-50:0, -30:1, -10:0] angdom)
(negmedium_ang [-75:0, -55:1, -35:0] angdom)
(neglarge_ang [-80:1, -60:0] angdom)
(poslarge_vel [100:0, 150:1] veldom)
(posmedium_vel [50:0, 90:1, 130:0] veldom)
(possmall_vel [0:0, 40:1, 80:0] veldom)
(zero_vel [-30:0, 0:1, 30:0] veldom)
(negsmall_vel [-80:0, -40:1, 0:0] veldom)
(negmedium_vel [-130:0, -90:1, -50:0] veldom)
(neglarge_vel [-150:1, -100:0] veldom)


((motor_current poslarge_curr) (angle zero_ang) (angular_velocity neglarge_vel))
((motor_current poslarge_curr) (angle neglarge_ang) (angular_velocity zero_vel))
((motor_current posmedium_curr) (angle zero_ang) (angular_velocity negmedium_vel))
((motor_current posmedium_curr) (angle negmedium_ang) (angular_velocity zero_vel))
((motor_current possmall_curr) (angle zero_ang) (angular_velocity negsmall_vel))
((motor_current possmall_curr) (angle negsmall_ang) (angular_velocity zero_vel))
((motor_current possmall_curr) (angle negsmall_ang) (angular_velocity possmall_vel))
((motor_current zero_curr) (angle zero_ang) (angular_velocity zero_vel))
((motor_current negsmall_curr) (angle possmall_ang) (angular_velocity negsmall_vel))
((motor_current negsmall_curr) (angle possmall_ang) (angular_velocity zero_vel))
((motor_current negsmall_curr) (angle zero_ang) (angular_velocity possmall_vel))
((motor_current negmedium_curr) (angle posmedium_ang) (angular_velocity zero_vel))
((motor_current negmedium_curr) (angle zero_ang) (angular_velocity posmedium_vel))
((motor_current neglarge_curr) (angle poslarge_ang) (angular_velocity zero_vel))
((motor_current neglarge_curr) (angle zero_ang) (angular_velocity poslarge_vel))
```

6.6.2 Comparison of the Results

The graphs in Figs. 6.8 to 6.13, which follow, illustrate some of the differences between inferences obtained from the knowledge base using a range of data taken from the Control Input popup menu selection. The graphs show compatible inferences for the chosen data sets, but the types and degrees of fuzziness of the outputs vary amongst Support Logic, Lukasiewicz, Kleene-Dienes and Mamdani fuzzy sets control methods.

When input measurements represent wide swings from the nominal so that the output inference is far from the set point (zero) of Motor Current control, the inferences tend to be quite vague, for example in Figs. 6.8, 6.9 and 6.10. This represents the fact that the rules are more concentrated in the region of the nominal measurements of zero Angle and zero Angular Velocity, as shown in Fig. 6.7 above. This vagueness is represented as "almost" unrestricted in the cases of Support Logic, Lukasiewicz and Kleene-Dienes fuzzy controls, and "almost" inconsistent in the Mamdani fuzzy control case.

The first graph in Fig. 6.8 below represents the results for all of the models of aggregation of rule inferences employed. The reason that there is no difference between the various models is that there is minimal interaction between the rules at such an extreme set of measurement data, and the inferences are determined from a single rule in each case.

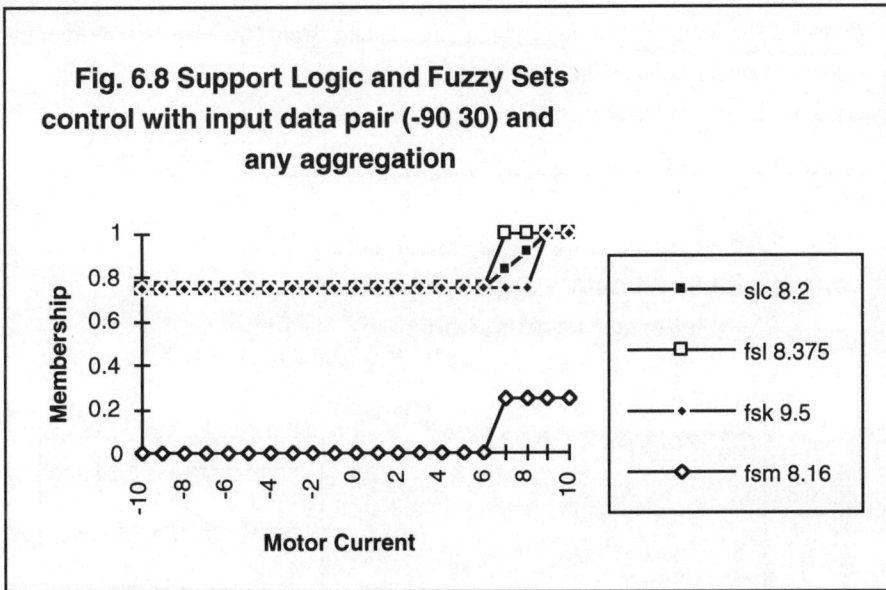

Fig. 6.8 Support Logic and Fuzzy Sets control with input data pair (-90 30) and any aggregation

In the region of maximum membership, the Mamdani method tends to give the smallest peak membership, an in all the examples the output is a non-normal fuzzy set. The Lukasiewicz and Man ani controls tend to have the broadest region of maximum membership, whereas S port Logic and Kleene-Dienes tend to give more triangular shaped outputs in this reg .

287

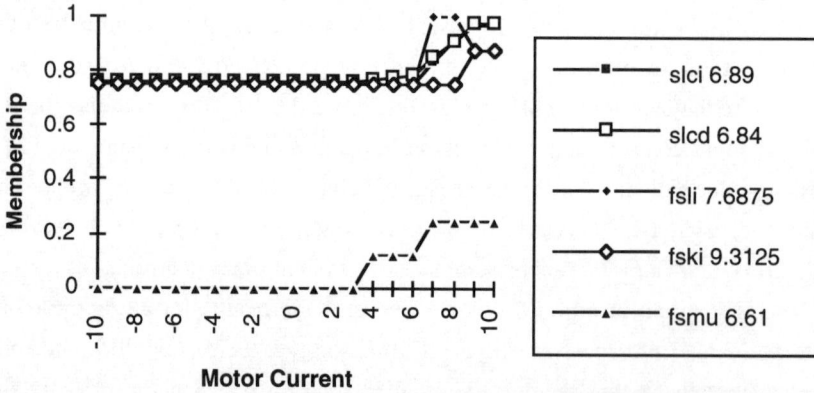

Fig. 6.9a Support Logic and Fuzzy Sets control with input data pair (-75 30) and set theoretic aggregation

slci 6.89
slcd 6.84
fsli 7.6875
fski 9.3125
fsmu 6.61

In regions of the control domain which are distant from the region of maximum membership, Mamdani control gives the smallest membership, whereas Lukasiewicz and Kleene-Dienes have similar degrees of fuzziness with Support Logic slightly more fuzzy.

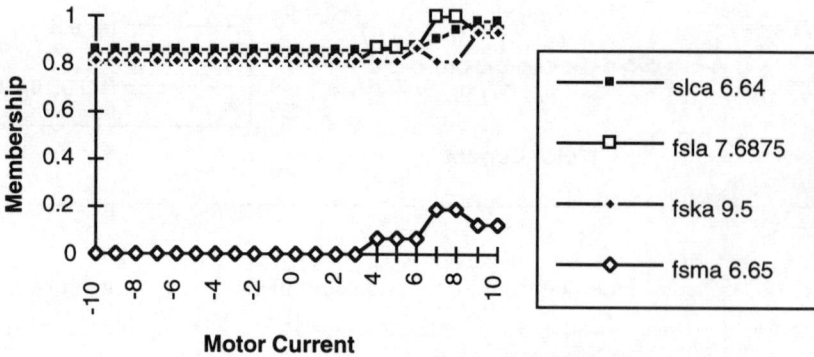

Fig. 6.9b Support Logic and Fuzzy Sets control with input data pair (-75 30) and average aggregation

slca 6.64
fsla 7.6875
fska 9.5
fsma 6.65

The support logic control inference tends to give much the smoothest form of membership function in the region of maximum membership, whereas Kleene-Dienes controls are quite peaky and Mamdani controls have a step like character, in the case of union aggregation operator.

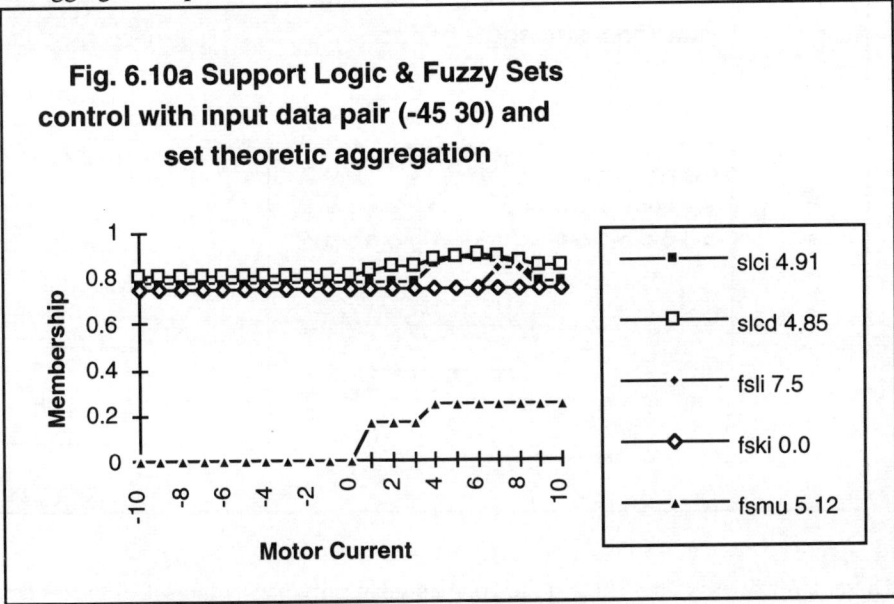

Fig. 6.10a Support Logic & Fuzzy Sets control with input data pair (-45 30) and set theoretic aggregation

Membership vs Motor Current

- slci 4.91
- slcd 4.85
- fsli 7.5
- fski 0.0
- fsmu 5.12

The average aggregation approach tends to give more fuzzy results than the set theoretic approaches of intersection, union (and modified dempster in the Support Logic case).

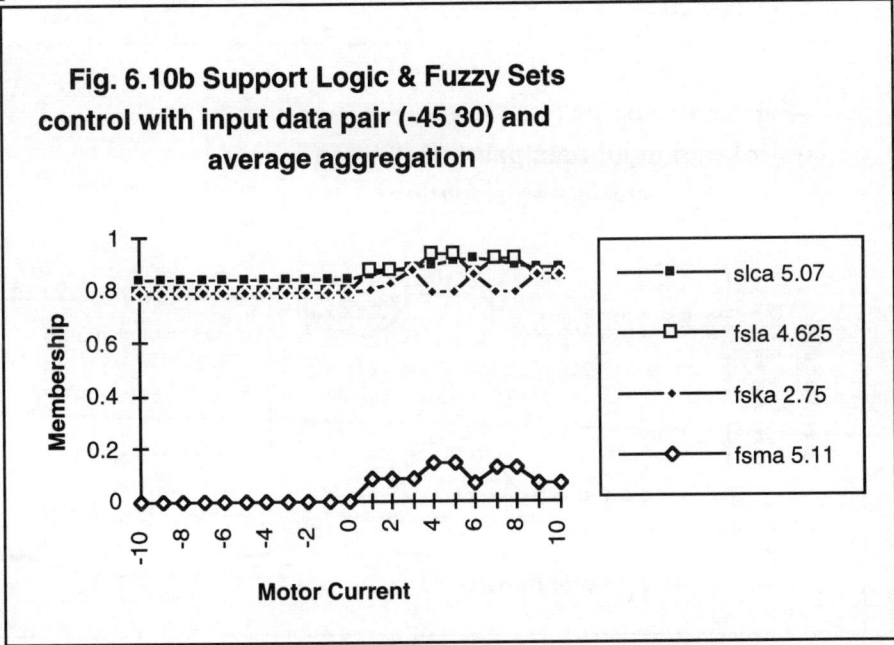

Fig. 6.10b Support Logic & Fuzzy Sets control with input data pair (-45 30) and average aggregation

Membership vs Motor Current

- slca 5.07
- fsla 4.625
- fska 2.75
- fsma 5.11

The graphs show the results of defuzzification of the inferences in the figure legends.

Fig. 6.11a Support Logic & Fuzzy Sets control with input data pair (-35 30) and set theoretic aggregation

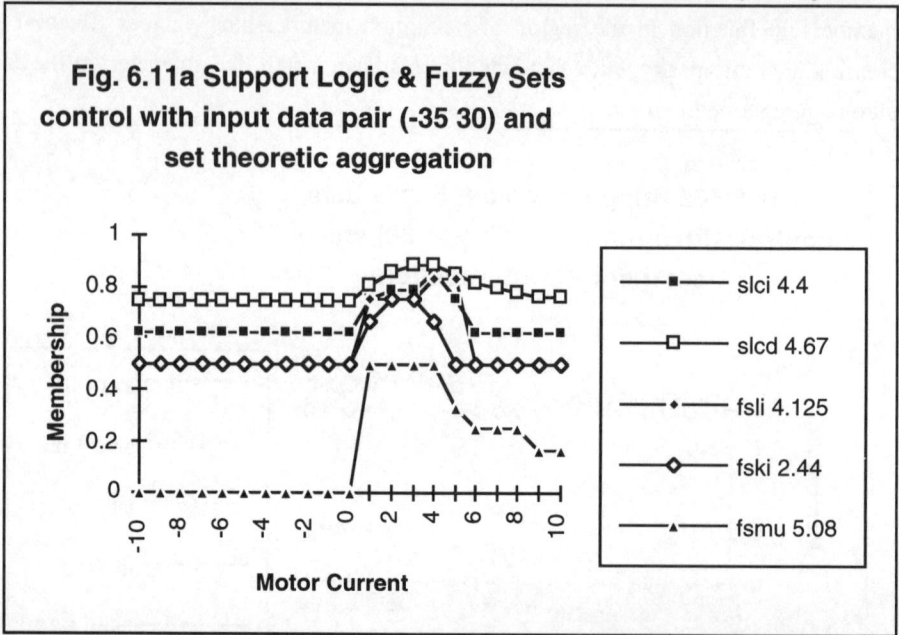

These defuzzified values show quite good compatibility between most of the models, for example between the Support Logic, Lukasiewicz and Mamdani controls. But the Kleene-Dienes is sometimes very different, as in Fig. 6.10a for example, where the inference is almost unrestricted, giving a value of zero for the defuzzification.

Fig. 6.11b Support Logic & Fuzzy Sets control with input data pair (-35 30) and average aggregation

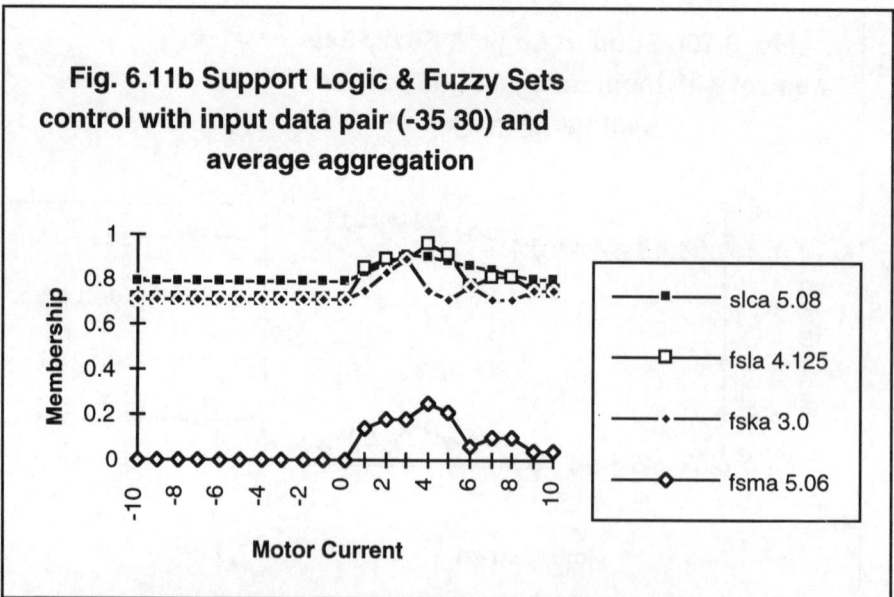

The Support Logic approach gives the smoothest transition of defuzzified value from outlying data through to close to the nominal (measurement values of zero).

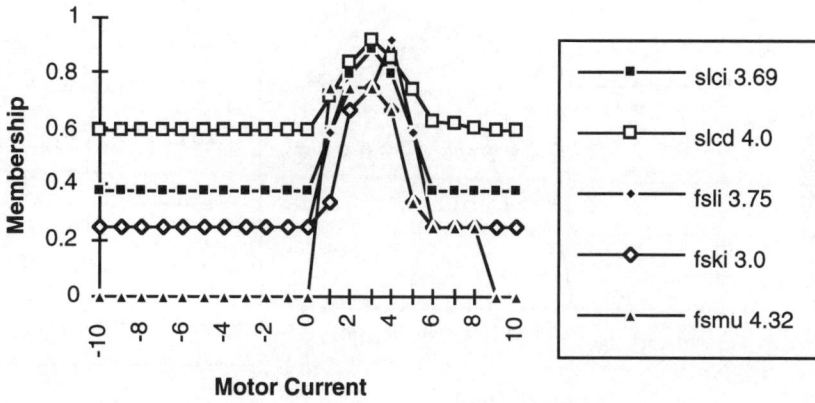

Fig. 6.12a Support Logic & Fuzzy Sets control with input data pair (-25 30) and set theoretic aggregation

For example, the defuzzified value for the set theoretic aggregation method is monotonic decreasing with input measurements over the range of results - Fig. 6.8 to Fig. 6.13a.

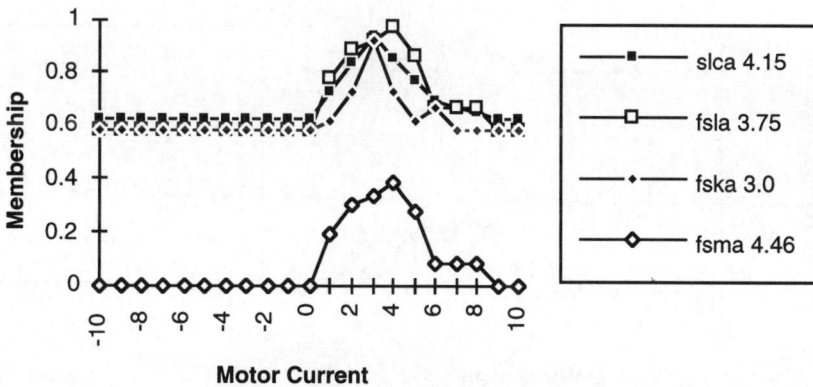

Fig. 6.12b Support Logic & Fuzzy Sets control with input data pair (-25 30) and average aggregation

This monotonicity property is an intuitive and important attribute of the defuzzification method.

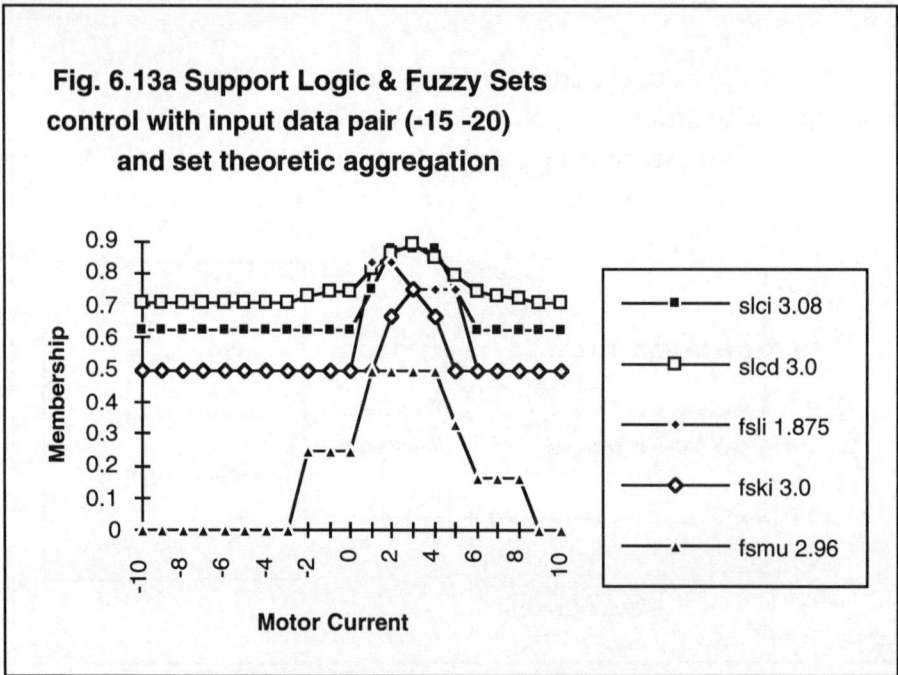

Fig. 6.13a Support Logic & Fuzzy Sets control with input data pair (-15 -20) and set theoretic aggregation

slci 3.08
slcd 3.0
fsli 1.875
fski 3.0
fsmu 2.96

The property is not satisfied for the Support Logic approach in the case of the average aggregation model.

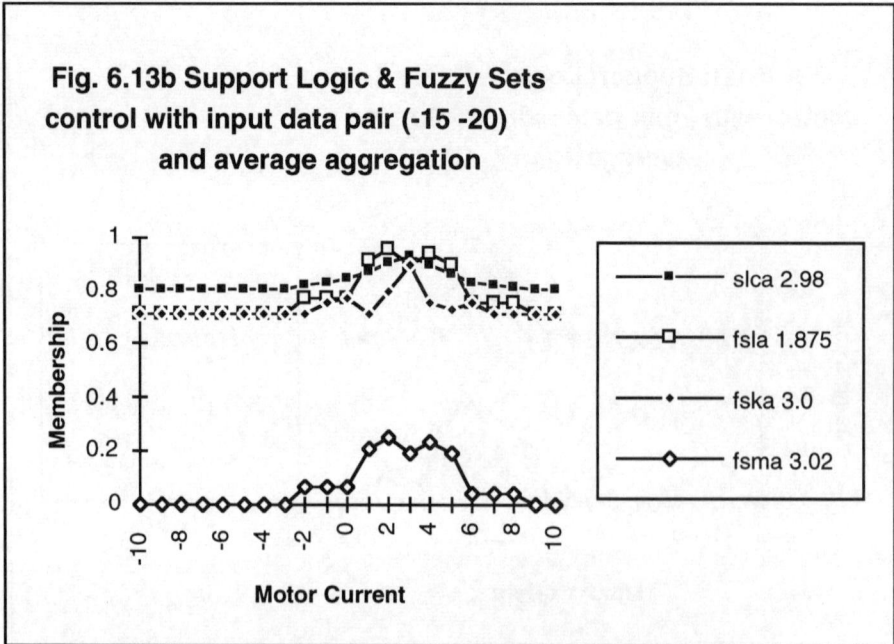

Fig. 6.13b Support Logic & Fuzzy Sets control with input data pair (-15 -20) and average aggregation

slca 2.98
fsla 1.875
fska 3.0
fsma 3.02

This is one amongst several reasons why the average aggregation model is counter-intuitive for the Support Logic case. Another, perhaps more important, reason is that there is no theoretical justification for averaging fuzzy sets when these are interpreted as a conjunction of mass assignments.

The monotonic property appears to be satisfied by the Mamdani control method for both union and average aggregation models. However, both Lukasiewicz and Kleene-Dienes methods fail in this property when using the intersection model of aggregation.

The process of defuzzification is very important to the whole methodology of fuzzy control, and the results of defuzzification can be most effectively illustrated by three dimensional surface plots of defuzzified Motor Current control output inference against Angle and Angular Velocity input measurements. These are shown in Figs. 6.14 to 6.22.

Figs. 6.14a to 6.22 show Control surface overviews for the nine different models discussed, with the given mnemonics: slci, slcd, slca, fsli, fsla, fski, fska, fsmu, and fsma, respectively. The overviews cover the whole domain of measurement spaces - namely interval [-90, 90] for Angle and [-180, 180] for Angular Velocity. For a large part of the outlying regions of the measurement space (i.e. for large values of both Angle and Angular Velocity - positive and negative), the results in all cases show Motor Current inferences of zero. The reason for this is that the inference fuzzy sets obtained were "unrestricted" in the case of Support Logic, Lukasiewicz and Kleene-Dienes fuzzy control models and "inconsistent" in the Mamdani fuzzy control case, so that defuzzifications obtained correspond to the mid point of the domain in every case - i.e. zero Motor Control. This reflects the fact that the problem is not controllable in such extreme cases. For this reason the region close the set point origin is of greater interest, and plots in Figs. 6.14b, 6.17b and 6.21b show control surfaces in greater detail for the more central portions of the measurement space.

The results confirm the observations made in relation to the Fuzzy Set outputs of Figs. 6.8 to 6.13, that the Support Logic models give the smoothest control surface profile, particularly in the case of the intersection aggregation model. Both Mamdani control models give fairly good results in this respect, but have the disadvantage that the surface profile tends to be stepped, giving a multi-level relay effect in the implementation of control.

The Kleene-Dienes control model with intersection aggregation can give rather uneven inferences as, for example, between data sets (-16 90) and (-17 90), and this is somewhat counter intuitive. Note that both Lukasiewicz and Kleene-Dienes algorithms for fuzzy control inference implement approximate reasoning in the case of multiple control rules, and this is the case here. However, it can be shown that the approximate inferences obtained are less restrictive than the theoretically correct inferences [Baldwin & Pilsworth (1979)].

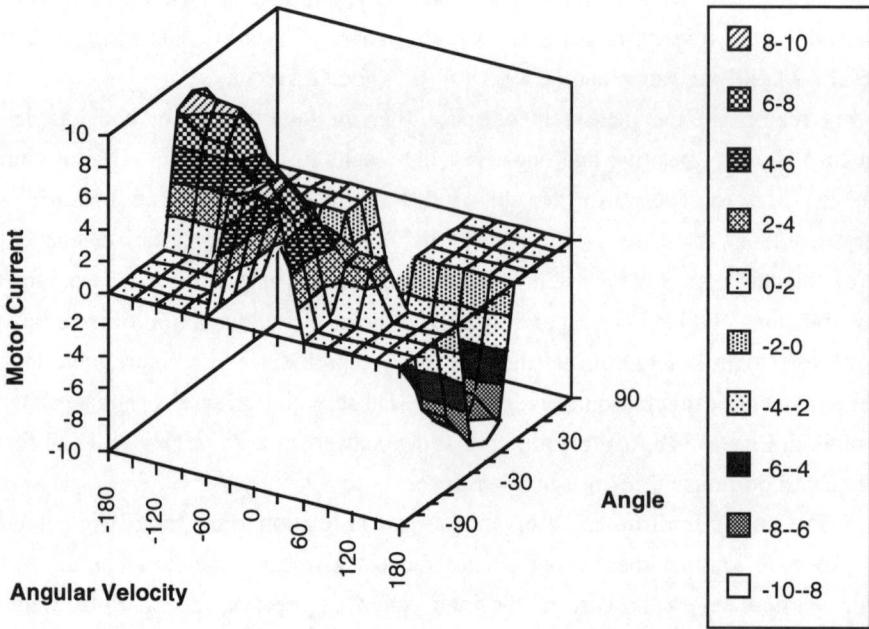

Fig. 6.14a Control surface overview for Support Logic model with intersection aggregation and mass defuzzification

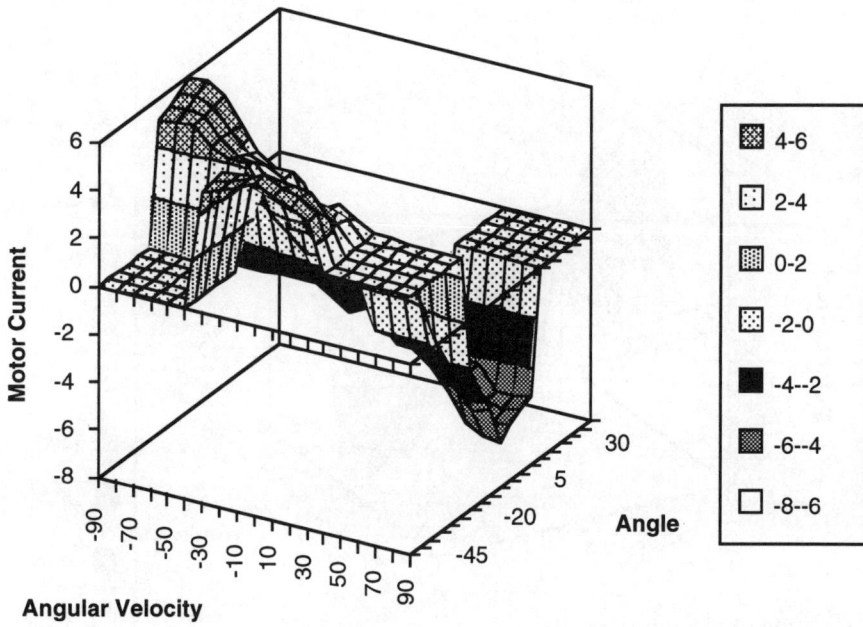

Fig. 6.14b Control surface detail for Support Logic model with intersection aggregation and mass defuzzification

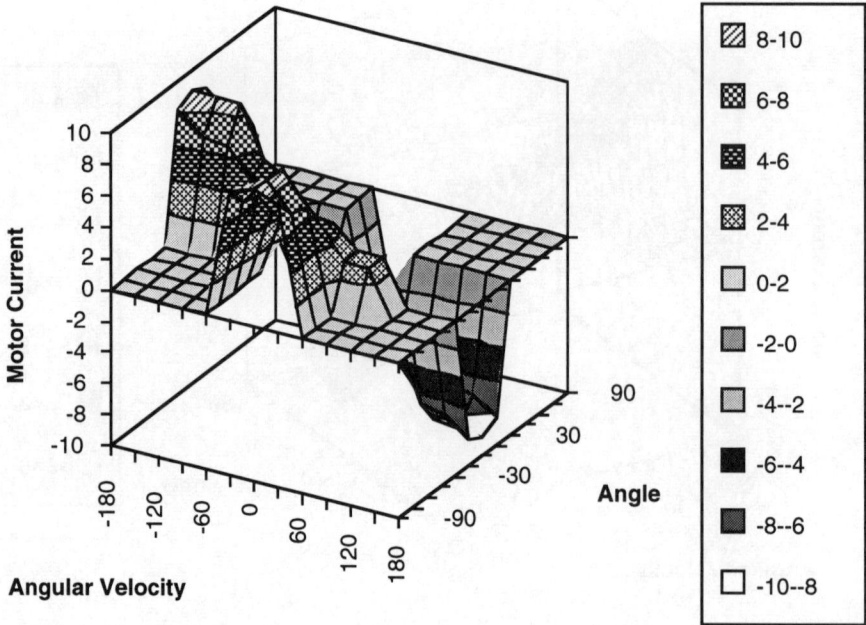

Fig. 6.15 Control surface overview for Support Logic model with modified dempster aggregation and mass defuzzification

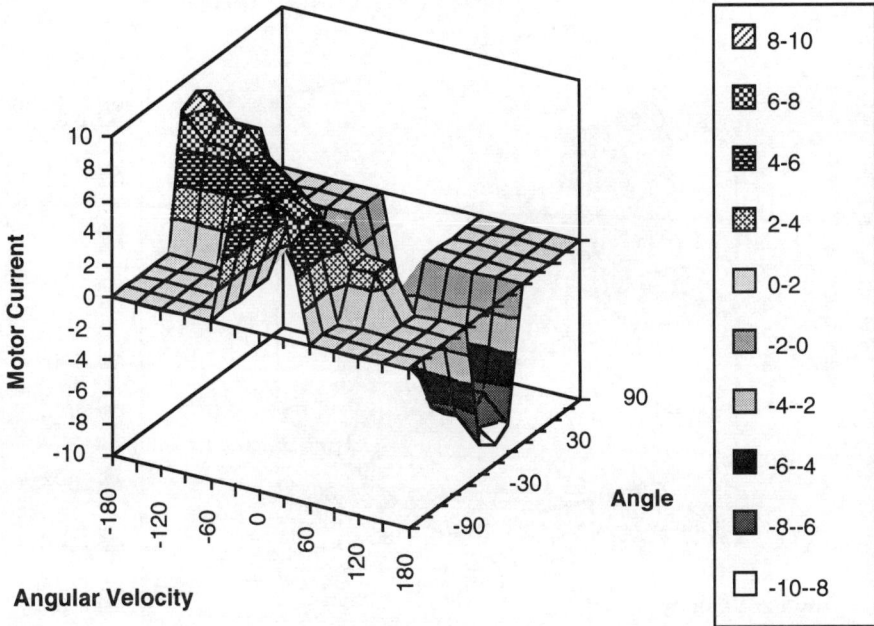

Fig. 6.16 Control surface overview for
Support Logic model with average
aggregation and mass defuzzification

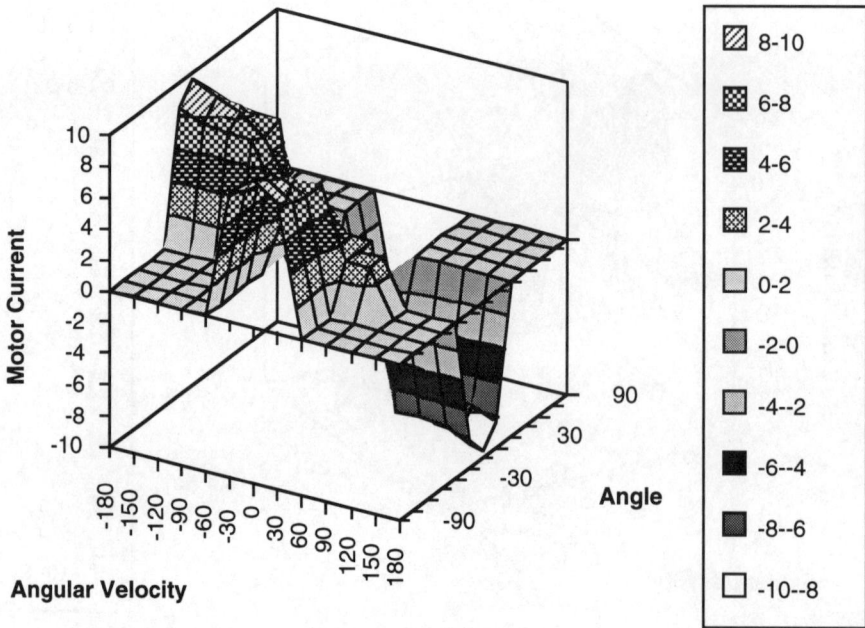

Fig. 6.17a Control surface overview for Lukasiewicz fuzzy control with intersection aggregation and max memb. defuzzification

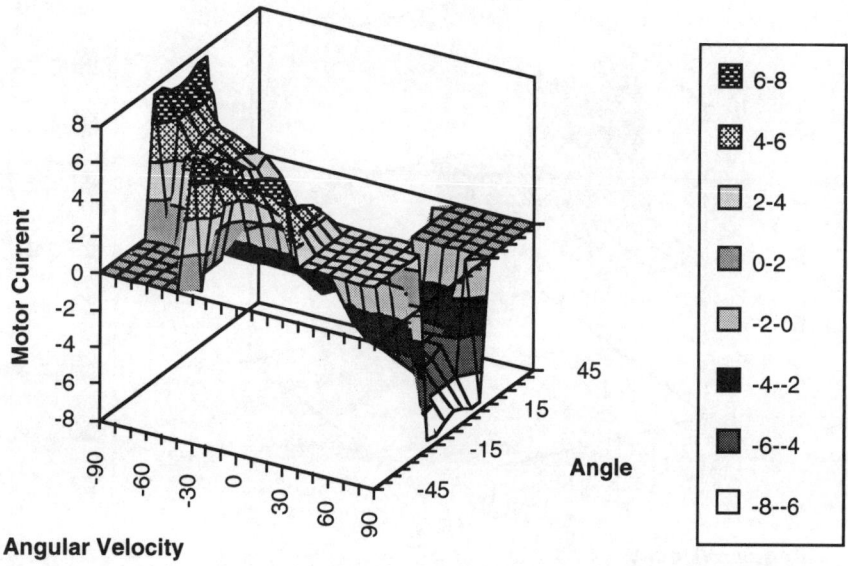

Fig. 6.17b Control surface detail for Lukasiewicz fuzzy control with intersection aggregation and max memb. defuzzification

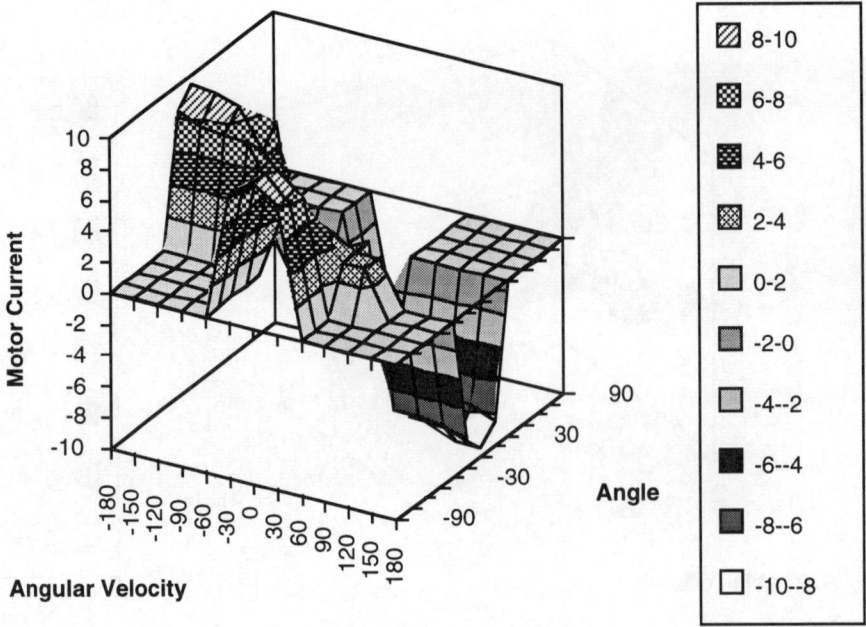

Fig. 6.18 Control surface overview for Lukasiewicz fuzzy control with average aggregation and max memb. defuzzification

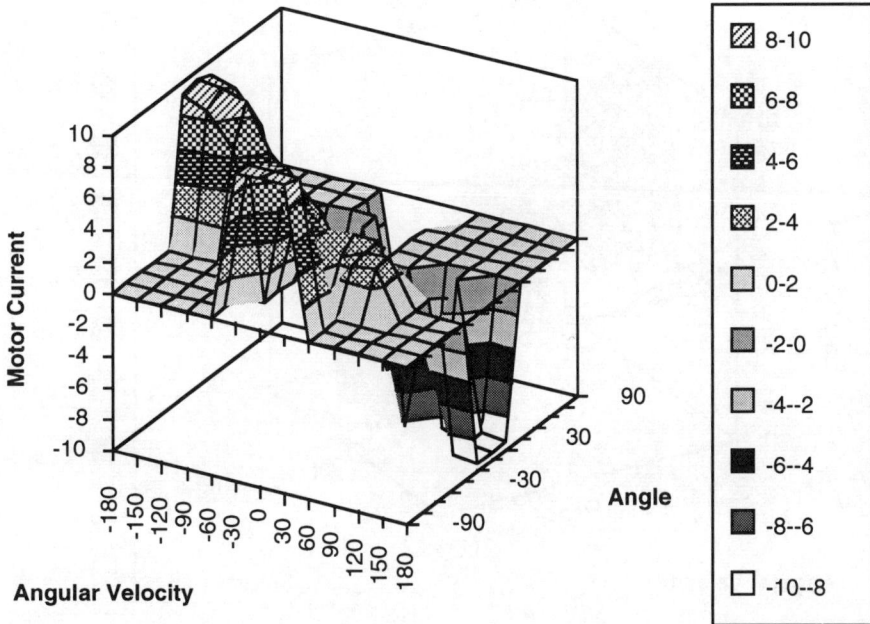

Fig. 6.19 Control surface overview for Kleene-Dienes fuzzy control with intersection aggregation and max memb. defuzzification

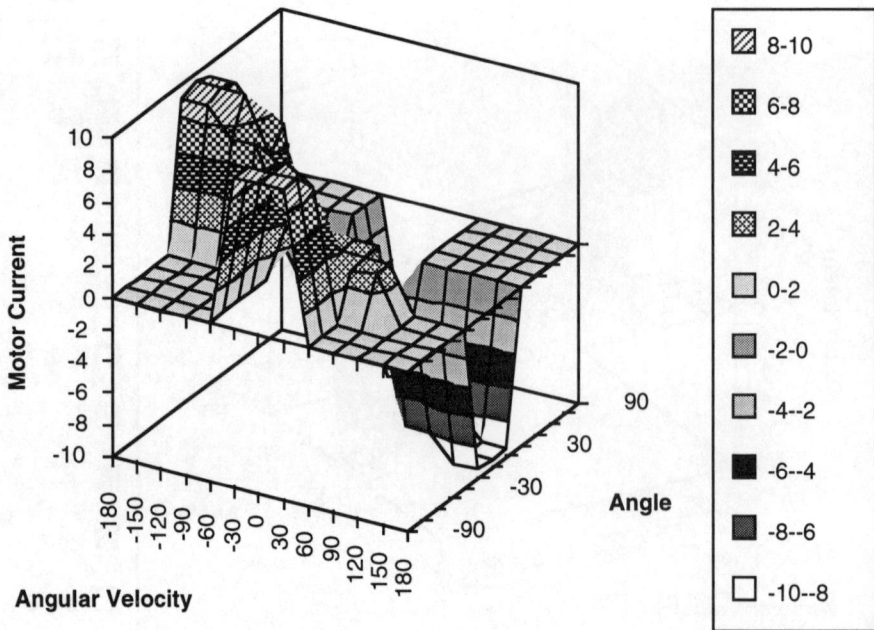

Fig. 6.20 Control surface overview for Kleene-Dienes fuzzy control with average aggregation and max memb. defuzzification

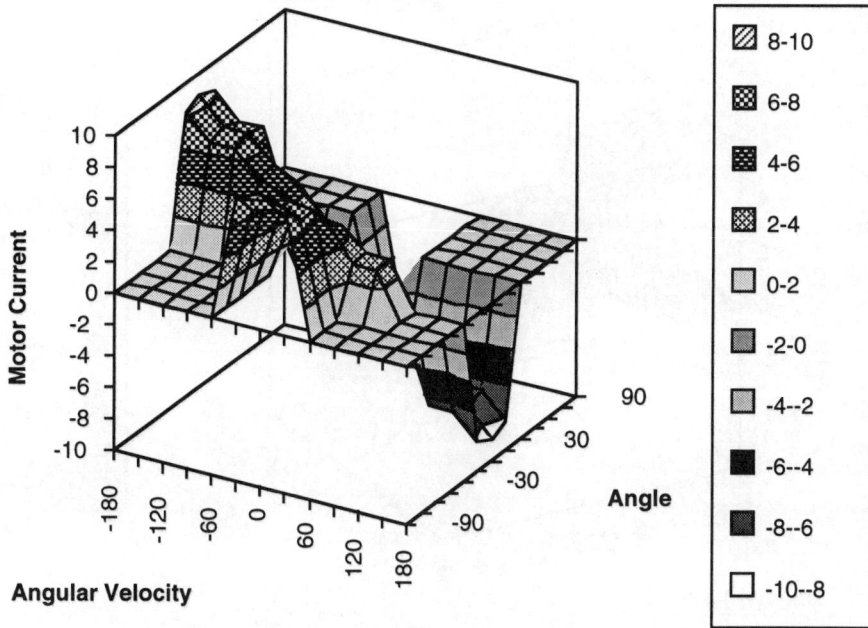

Fig. 6.21a Control surface overview for Mamdani fuzzy control with union aggregation and centroid defuzzification

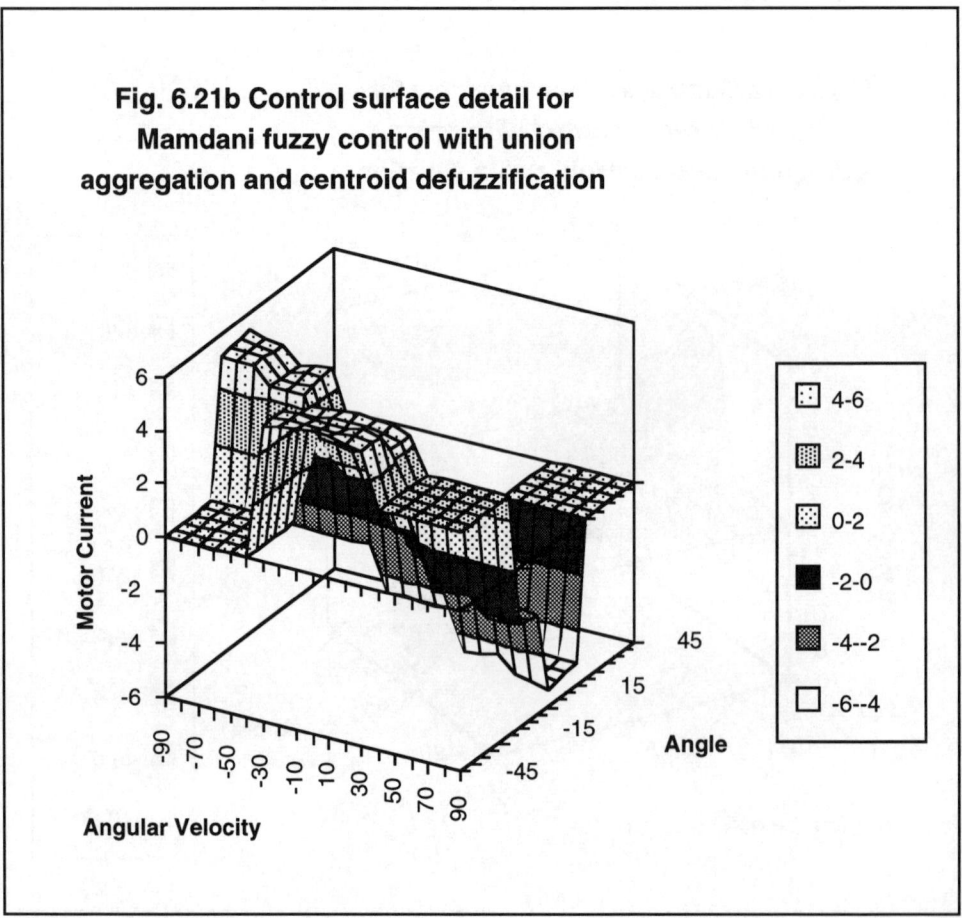

Fig. 6.21b Control surface detail for Mamdani fuzzy control with union aggregation and centroid defuzzification

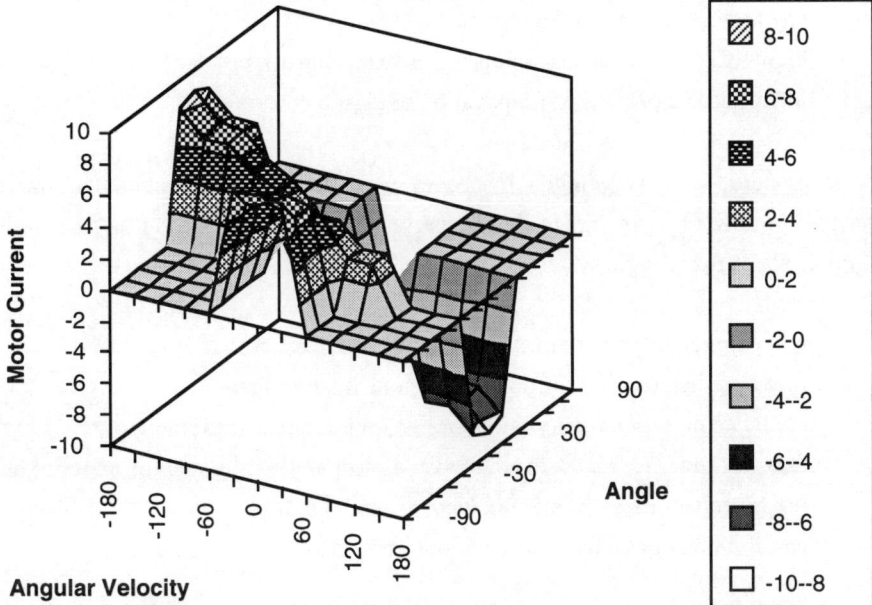

Fig. 6.22 Control surface overview for
Mamdani fuzzy control with average
aggregation and centroid defuzzification

6.7 ZADEH'S FUZZY INFERENCE LANGUAGE - PRUF

6.7.1 Introducing PRUF - Possibilistic, Relational, Universal, Fuzzy

Lotfi Zadeh introduced the theory of Fuzzy Sets in 1965. Zadeh developed PRUF in 1978 as a language for the representation of meaning in natural languages, and he extended this to include Test-Score semantics in 1986 and QSA/FL in 1989 - an approach to Qualitative Systems Analysis based on Fuzzy Logic.

The purpose of this Section is to explore a selection of the inference paradigms modelled in PRUF and its sequels, and show how they can be implemented in Fril. Zadeh identified some of the essential characteristics of fuzzy logic as relating to the following:

exact reasoning is a limiting case of approximate reasoning
in fuzzy logic, everything is a matter of degree
any logical system can be fuzzified
knowledge is a collection of elastic or fuzzy constraints
inference is a process of propagation of elastic constraints

These properties are very much in accord with the spirit and method of modelling uncertain knowledge in Fril. More particularly, Zadeh introduces the following components of fuzzy logic systems:

fuzzy linguistic truth values - true, fairly true, very true
fuzzy predicates - tall, ill, soon, swift, much larger than
predicate modifiers - very, more or less, quite, rather, extremely
fuzzy quantifiers - few, several, most, almost always, frequently, about five
fuzzy probabilities - likely, unlikely, around 0.8, high
possibilities - possibility distributions and elastic restrictions

It will be clear from this and previous chapters how suitable Fril is to model these components. In the following Section we briefly explore some modes of reasoning suggested by Zadeh which use these components, and we then show how to implement some of these in Fril.

6.7.2 Examples of PRUF Inference

(a) Categorical reasoning:

Carol is slim
Carol is very intelligent
Therefore Carol is slim and very intelligent

This kind of inference is straightforward to implement directly in Fril using support logic programming. Another example is as follows:

> Mary is young
>
> John is much older than Mary
>
> Therefore John is "much older than young"

Zadeh solves this via the extension principle as a form of max-min composition with the "much older" relation as follows:

$$\chi_{\text{Age(John)}}(a) = \bigvee_{b} \chi_{\text{"much older"}}(a, b) \wedge \chi_{\text{young}}(b)$$

We implement this as one of our examples using a new predicate 'composing'.

(b) Syllogistic reasoning:

This relates to inference from premises containing fuzzy quantifiers such as:

> most Swedes are blond
>
> most blond Swedes are tall
>
> Therefore most^2 Swedes are blond and tall

Zadeh models most^2 using fuzzy arithmetic as the product of fuzzy quantifier most with itself. This is very simply modelled using the fuzzy arithmetic procedures of FRIL. For example:

> (most [0.5:0, 0.9:1, 1:1, 1.001:0])
>
> ((most2 X) (times most most X))

when query ?((most2 X) (pp X)) displays fuzzy set [0.25:0, 0.81:1, 1:1, 1.002:0] which is a reasonable approximation to the product using piecewise linear segments.

(c) Qualitative reasoning: Fuzzy if ... then rules such as:

> volume is small if pressure is high
>
> volume is large if pressure is low
>
> pressure is medium high
>
> Therefore volume is "more or less average"

Clearly this is just the kind of reasoning we have been discussing under Fuzzy Control.

(d) Test-Score semantics for fuzzy quantification:

Consider the proposition: "most young women are attractive"

Let $P = \{w_1, w_2, ..., w_n\}$ denote the population of women. The concept of a test score involves finding the proportion of young and attractive women counted over the population of young women and testing this against the fuzzy quantifier 'most'. Zadeh counts the number of women satisfying a fuzzy concept by summing the associated membership function over domain P. Thus Zadeh introduces the idea of a relative sigma

307

count ρ as follows:

$$\rho = (\sum_{i=1}^{n} \chi_{young}(w_i) \wedge \chi_{attractive}(w_i))/ \sum_{i=1}^{n} \chi_{young}(w_i)$$

and this value ρ is tested against 'most' by test-score = $\chi_{most}(\rho)$, which represents the compatibility of the proposition "most young women are attractive" with the knowledge base. In our own implementation of test score semantics, we generalise the concept by counting supports instead of membership function values. The support pair characterisation of proportion ρ is then tested against 'most' by semantic unification, so that if ρ is represented by support pair (a b), then the final support pair inference is:

(most|a, most|b)

where 'most|a' denotes the semantic match of 'most' given 'a'.

Zadeh treats the following kind of dispositional knowledge using a similar approach:

"young men like young women" interpreted as

"most young men like mostly young women"

This is treated in two parts as follows:

Let R(x) denote the relation: "x likes mostly young women"

where x is taken from the domain of men. Then we can express the dispositional knowledge as:

"most young men are R"

We can determine a support relation R by computing a test score for each instance x of the population of men, then the relative sigma count of 'young men are R' can be tested against 'most' to give a final support pair. These examples are treated in the following Section.

6.7.3 Using the PRUF module

The PRUF module is selected by clicking on the PRUF radio button in the Choice of modules cluster of the top level Demonstrations Dialog of the Fril Demonstration System. This module can then be run by clicking on the Run button when the Dialog box, shown in Fig. 6.23, is displayed.

The Dialog includes the usual Quiet and Verbose options in the Display Mode cluster and the usual four Execution Types in the popup menu. There are ten choices of Linguistic problem to be selected from the corresponding popup menu and these are described in detail below.

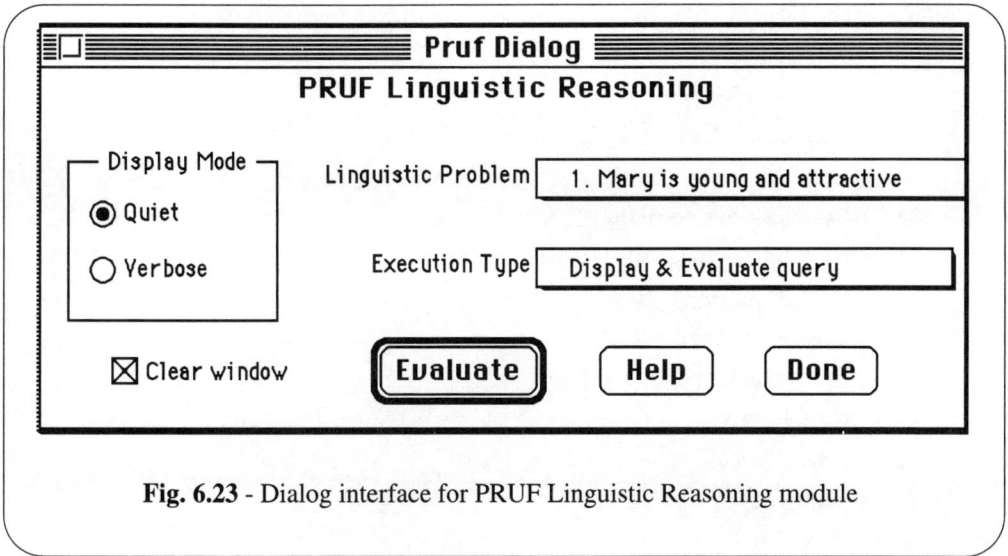

Fig. 6.23 - Dialog interface for PRUF Linguistic Reasoning module

The following elementary knowledge base is the basis of all the PRUF style queries which can be explored.

```
set (agedom (0 120) )
set (womendom (Mary Sally Liz Joy Anne Jean Jane Elspeth Janet) )
set (probdom (0 1) )
(young [20:1, 40:0] agedom)
(attractive {Mary:0.8, Sally:0.3, Liz:0.5, Joy:0.9, Anne:1, Jean:0.7} womendom)
(most [0.5:0, 0.8:1] probdom)
(very [0.7:0, 1:1] probdom)
(fairly [0:0, 0.5:1] probdom)
((age Bruce 40))
((age Ted young))
((age Brian 32))
((age Jimmy 16))
((age John 25))
((age Jeff 30))
((age Mary 25))
((age Sally 43))
((age Liz 23))
((age Joy 27))
((age Anne 18))
((age Jean 30))
((age Jane 28))
```

((age Elspeth 18))

((age Janet 35))

((likes John Mary)) : (0.9 1)

((likes Bruce Anne)) : (1 1)

((likes Ted Liz)) : (0.9 1)

((likes Jeff Jane)) : (0 0.2)

((likes Jimmy Elspeth)) : (0.8 1)

((likes Brian Joy)) : (0.9 1)

((likes John Jane)) : (1 1)

((likes John Elspeth)) : (0.8 1)

((male John))

((male Bruce))

((male Ted))

((male Jeff))

((male Jimmy))

((male Brian))

((female Mary))

((female Sally))

((female Liz))

((female Joy))

((female Anne))

((female Jean))

((female Jane))

((female Elspeth))

((female Janet))

((likes_mostly_young_women (X) RELATION)

   (testscore_relation most ((age Y young) (female Y))

          are ((likes X Y)) by (X) RELATION))

There follows a set of 10 queries which may be invoked by selecting the appropriate Linguistic Problem popup menu entry, and clicking on the Evaluate button.

1. **'Mary is young and attractive'**

qs ((age Mary [20:1 40:0]) (quality Mary
   {Anne:1 Joy:0.9 Liz:0.5 Jean:0.7 Sally:0.3 Mary:0.8}))

((age Mary [20:1 40:0]) (quality Mary
   {Anne:1 Joy:0.9 Liz:0.5 Jeah:0.7 Sally:0.3 Mary:0.8})) : (0.6 0.6)

This first example is a very simple example of support logic programming with predicate 'quality' obtaining the support for Mary being attractive in the given fuzzy set.

2. **'most young women are attractive'**

wh (_Supp (test_score [0.5:0 0.8:1] ((age X [20:1 40:0]) (female X)) are ((quality
        X {Anne:1 Joy:0.9 Liz:0.5 Jean:0.7 Sally:0.3 Mary:0.8})) by () _Supp))

Cardinality of conjunction ((age W young) (female W)
                                            (quality W attractive)) is (2.96 2.96)
        where young is [20:1 40:0]
        and attractive is {Anne:1 Joy:0.9 Liz:0.5 Jean:0.7 Sally:0.3 Mary:0.8}
Cardinality of conditioning goals ((age W young) (female W)) is (5.6 5.6)
Sigma count fuzzy proportion (0.528571 0.528571) for ()
Overall test score for () is (0.0952381 0.0952381)

(0.0952381 0.0952381)

This second example illustrates a straightforward example of test score semantics. The number of women who are both young and attractive is computed as 2.96, whereas the number of women who are young is 5.6. The ratio 2.96/5.6 = 0.529 represents the fraction of young women who are attractive. In this instance, the ratio satisfies fuzzy quantifier 'most' to the degree 0.095. Note that the above output was obtained by selecting the "Verbose" Display Mode option prior to clicking on Evaluate.

3. **'most young men like mostly young women'**

wh (_Supp (likes_mostly_young_women (X) _Relation) (test_score [0.5:0 0.8:1]
        ((age X [20:1 40:0]) (male X)) are ((_Relation X)) by () _Supp))

Cardinality of conjunction ((likes John W) (age W [20:1 40:0]) (female W))
                                            by (John) is (2.075 2.35)
Cardinality of conditioning goals ((likes John W)) by (John) is (2.7 3)
Sigma count fuzzy proportion (0.768519 0.783333) for (John)
Overall test score for (John) is (0.895062 0.944444)
Cardinality of conjunction ((likes Bruce W) (age W [20:1 40:0]) (female W))
                                            by (Bruce) is (1 1)
Cardinality of conditioning goals ((likes Bruce W)) by (Bruce) is (1 1)
Sigma count fuzzy proportion (1 1) for (Bruce)

311

Overall test score for (Bruce) is (1 1)

Cardinality of conjunction ((likes Ted W) (age W [20:1 40:0]) (female W))

by (Ted) is (0.765 0.85)

Cardinality of conditioning goals ((likes Ted W)) by (Ted) is (0.9 1)

Sigma count fuzzy proportion (0.85 0.85) for (Ted)

Overall test score for (Ted) is (1 1)

Cardinality of conjunction ((likes Jeff W) (age W [20:1 40:0]) (female W))

by (Jeff) is (0 0.12)

Cardinality of conditioning goals ((likes Jeff W)) by (Jeff) is (0 0.2)

Sigma count fuzzy proportion (0 0.6) for (Jeff)

Overall test score for (Jeff) is (0 0.333333)

Cardinality of conjunction ((likes Jimmy W) (age W [20:1 40:0]) (female W))

by (Jimmy) is (0.8 1)

Cardinality of conditioning goals ((likes Jimmy W)) by (Jimmy) is (0.8 1)

Sigma count fuzzy proportion (1 1) for (Jimmy)

Overall test score for (Jimmy) is (1 1)

Cardinality of conjunction ((likes Brian W) (age W [20:1 40:0]) (female W))

by (Brian) is (0.585 0.65)

Cardinality of conditioning goals ((likes Brian W)) by (Brian) is (0.9 1)

Sigma count fuzzy proportion (0.65 0.65) for (Brian)

Overall test score for (Brian) is (0.5 0.5)

Cardinality of conjunction ((likes John W) (age W [20:1 40:0]) (female W))

by (John) is (2.075 2.35)

Cardinality of conditioning goals ((likes John W)) by (John) is (2.7 3)

Sigma count fuzzy proportion (0.768519 0.783333) for (John)

Overall test score for (John) is (0.895062 0.944444)

Cardinality of conjunction ((likes John W) (age W [20:1 40:0]) (female W))

by (John) is (2.075 2.35)

Cardinality of conditioning goals ((likes John W)) by (John) is (2.7 3)

Sigma count fuzzy proportion (0.768519 0.783333) for (John)

Overall test score for (John) is (0.895062 0.944444)

testscore_relation 'testrel' is defined as follows:

(testrel
    (John) : (0.895062 0.944444)
    (Bruce)
    (Ted)
    (Jeff) : (0 0.333333)

312

(Jimmy)

(Brian) : (0.5 0.5)

)

Cardinality of conjunction ((age M [20:1 40:0]) (male M) (testrel M))

is (2.3713 3.075)

Cardinality of conditioning goals ((age M [20:1 40:0]) (male M)) is (3.15 3.65)

Sigma count fuzzy proportion (0.752792 0.842466) for ()

Overall test score for () is (0.842641 1)

(0.842641 1)

no (more) solutions

This third example uses test score semantics twice. In the first place the relation called 'testrel' is generated to represent the degree to which each man M satisfies the proposition R: 'M likes mostly young women' - in other words R represents the relation: 'most of the women that M likes are young'. Then the proportion of young men who satisfy R is tested against 'most'. For example, the number of 'young women' that John likes is in the interval (2.075 2.35), and the number of 'women' that John likes is in the interval (2.7 3), so that the proportion of young women amongst those that John likes is in the interval (0.769 0.783). This proportion tested against most gives the interval (0.895 0.944) which is represented in the relation 'testrel' against the tuple (John). The overall degree to which the proposition 'young men are R' satisfies 'most' is given by the support interval (0.843 1). As in example 2, the above output was obtained by selecting the "Verbose" Display Mode option prior to clicking on Evaluate.

4. (a) 'Somewhat older than young'

? ((composing [20:1 40:0] (greater_than 0 10) A) (p Age is A) (pp))
Age is [0:0 10:1 120:1 120.012:0]

5. (b) 'Somewhat older than young'

? ((composing [20:1 40:0] (approx_equal 10 5) A) (p Age is A) (pp))
Age is [5:0 10:1 30:1 55:0]

Examples 4 and 5 above solve the same problem with alternative interpretations of the meaning of 'somewhat older'. In example 4. (a), the fuzzy set young is composed with the relation 'more or less older by greater than 10 years' (an upper limit of 120 years is assumed), whereas in example 5. (b), the relation is 'more or less older by approximately 10 years'.

6. **(a) 'Somewhat older than not young'**

? ((fcomp [20:1 40:0] COMP) (universe [20:1 40:0] UNIV _)
    (composing2 COMP UNIV (greater_than 0 10) A) (p Age is A) (pp))
Age is [20:0 50:1 120:1 120.012:0]

7. **(b) 'Somewhat older than not young'**

? ((fcomp [20:1 40:0] COMP) (universe [20:1 40:0] UNIV _)
    (composing2 COMP UNIV (approx_equal 10 5) A) (p Age is A) (pp))
Age is [25:0 50:1 120:1 120.012:0]

Examples 6 and 7 are the counterparts to examples 4 and 5 respectively for the proposition: 'Somewhat older than not young', where predicates 'fcomp' together with 'universe' compute the fuzzy set 'not young' as the complement of young.

8. **'very young'**

? ((tfm [0.7:0 1:1] [20:1 40:0] A) (p Age is A) (pp))
Age is [-0.012:0 0:1 20:1 26:0]

9. **'fairly young'**

? ((tfm [0:0 0.5:1] [20:1 40:0] A) (p Age is A) (pp))
Age is [-0.012:0 0:1 30:1 40:0]

10. **'most most'**

? ((tfm [0.5:0 0.8:1] [0.5:0 0.8:1] MM) (p Modifier is MM) (pp))
Modifier is [0.65:0 0.74:1 1:1 1.0001:0]

Examples 8, 9 and 10 are straightforward examples of truth function modification of fuzzy propositions by 'hedge' modifiers.

6.7.4 Extensions to Linguistic Processing

Each of the examples of linguistic reasoning modelled above involves the translation from a natural language statement into a suitable pseudo-natural language structural form, which is the basis of the relevant Fril query. For many problems, the rules of translation are simple, intuitive and readily mechanised. In such cases, the mechanisation can easily be implemented in Fril, for example using the built-in Definite Clause Grammar translation and interpretation facilities of the language. In more difficult cases where the syntactic sentence structure is not sufficient to determine a suitable parse so easily, a semantic approach such as that provided by the theory of Conceptual Graphs [Sowa (1984)] can be employed. A Conceptual Graph toolkit has been implemented in Fril and this was used in a commercial Expert Systems application which is described in Section 8.5.

As a simple example of linguistic processing, consider the following Definite Clause grammar fragment for deriving support for the test-score semantics goal from the linguistic statement 'most young women are attractive' considered in example 2 of Section 6.7.3 above:

```
((test_score_support  S) -->
        (quantifier  QUANT)
        (noun_phrase  W  ANTECEDENT)
        (verb_phrase  W  CONSEQUENT)
        (? ((test_score  QUANT  ANTECEDENT  are  CONSEQUENT  by  ()  S)) ))
((quantifier  QUANT) --> ((Q))  (? ((fuzzy_quantifier  Q  QUANT)) ))
((noun_phrase  W  (ADJGOAL  NOUNGOAL) ) -->
        (adjective  W  ADJGOAL)
        (noun  W  NOUNGOAL))
((noun_phrase  W  (ADJGOAL) ) -->
        (adjective  W  ADJGOAL))
((verb_phrase  W  CONSEQUENT) -->
        (verb)
        (noun_phrase  W  CONSEQUENT))
((adjective  W  (PRED  W  FUZZADJ) ) -->
        ((ADJ))
        (? ((fuzzy_adjective  ADJ  FUZZADJ) (get_pred  ADJ  PRED)) ))
((noun  W  (PRED  W) ) -->
        ((NOUN))
        (? ((get_root  NOUN  ROOT) (get_pred  ROOT  PRED)) ))
((verb) --> ((are)) )
```

((fuzzy_quantifier most most))

((fuzzy_adjective young young))

((fuzzy_adjective attractive attractive))

((get_root women woman))

((get_pred young age))

((get_pred attractive quality))

((get_pred woman female))

The following goal can then be called to derive the query corresponding to example 2:

? ((test_score_support S (most young women are attractive) ()) (pp S))

which displays the corresponding support (0.095 0.095) for the test-score semantics query. This example of linguistic processing has not been incorporated into the Demonstration module. Of course, the grammar fragment displayed above is targeted specifically to the given sentence, but it can be generalised to a wide variety of related sentences of similar form. Also the user interface for entering the required sentence could be made more natural and user friendly.

6.8 BIBLIOGRAPHY

Baldwin J.F, (1992), "Evidential Support Logic, Fril and Case Based Reasoning", to appear in Int J. Intelligent Systems.

Baldwin J.F, Pilsworth B.W, (1979), "A Model of Fuzzy Reasoning through Multi-valued logic and Set Theory", Int J. Man-Machine Studies **11**, pp 351-380.

Kosko B, (1992), Neural Networks and Fuzzy Systems - A Dynamical Systems Approach to Machine Intelligence, Prentice-Hall Int.

Pearl J, (1988), Probabilistic Reasoning in Intelligent Systems, Morgan Kaufmann.

Sowa J.F, (1984), Conceptual Structures - Information Processing in Mind and Machine, Addison Wesley.

Waltz D.L, (1990), "Memory based reasoning", in Eds. M.A. Arbib and A. Robinson, Natural and Artificial Parallel Computing, MIT Press.

Zadeh L.A, (1965), "Fuzzy Sets", Information and Control **8**, pp 338-353.

Zadeh L.A, (1978), "PRUF - A meaning representation language for natural languages", Int J. Man-Machine Stud. **10**, pp 395-460.

Zadeh L.A, (1992), "Knowledge Representation in Fuzzy Logic", in Eds Yager R.R, **Zadeh L.A**, An Introduction to Fuzzy Logic Applications in Intelligent Systems, Kluwer Academic Pubs.

CHAPTER 7

Intelligent Databases in Fril

7.1 INTRODUCTION

The idea of a database as a computer-based repository of information is relatively old in information technology terms. In the 1970's the advent of relational databases gave a sound theoretical basis to data handling, and this has led to a huge industry based on the management of information. More recently, deductive databases have become increasingly popular. In deductive databases, the explicit relational tables of data are augmented by logical statements (rules) which allow implicit information to be extracted. In both traditional and deductive databases, the world is represented by a crisp, logical model. There can be problems in the mapping between the real world and the formal model of the world embodied in the relational database. One aspect of this is the problem of deciding the meaning of a *NULL* value. In the relation shown in Fig. 7 - 1 there are two null values. The first is Mary's age - this information is unknown but there is definitely a value to be entered here. The second null value is Bill's qualification. This might be null because it is unknown, as with Mary's age. On the other hand it might be null because Bill has no qualification so that this column of the table is not applicable to him. Alternatively, he might have a qualification which does not conform to any of the permitted values for this column. The different possible interpretations of the null value have led to much research and debate within the database community.

Name	Age	Qualification	Job	Salary
John	33	Graduate	Manager	25000
Mary	null	PhD	Researcher	20000
Bill	42	null	Accountant	30000

Fig. 7 - 1
A relation with null values.

Another problem arises from the constraints imposed by the crisp model of the world that is assumed in designing a database system. In order to represent a real-world situation in a database, information must be known precisely and with complete certainty. In practice this leads to a degree of arbitrariness in classifications. For example let us suppose that we need to add a new employee, Fred, to the database shown in Fig. 7 - 1. Fred will spend 2 days a week as a researcher and the remaining 3 days as a manager; however, the

317

database requires the job to be classified as one of the three categories manager, researcher, or accountant. The problem of what to enter as Fred's job can be tackled by

(a) extending the category of jobs to include this mixed post,

(b) classifying Fred as a manager since that will occupy the larger part of his time

(c) entering a NULL value since the actual value is not in the allowed set.

Option (a) is probably the best to represent the information, but it involves changing the model of the world embodied in the database and would therefore be most difficult. Options (b) and (c) are easier to implement but are less satisfactory in representing the information. The ideal solution would be to enter a value which exactly reflected the information given; however, this is difficult within the relational model.

Similarly, in some cases it might be possible to provide partial information such as one of the following:

• Mary is either 28 or 29

• Mary is in her late twenties

• Mary is thought to be 29 although this is not known for certain

• Mary is thought to be in her late twenties (again, not known for certain)

This type of information is difficult to model in the relational database framework as it is imprecise, uncertain, or both. The information actually stored in the database is forced into precise and certain categories, even when this is not justified by the information known about the real world. A closely related problem is that "soft" queries are not permitted, e.g. one cannot use databases to answer questions such as

How many employees *nearing retirement age* earn *large salaries*

Which *small* companies are *highly profitable*

Where does water *considerably exceed* flood levels

In which *major towns* is pollution at *dangerous* levels

without giving arbitrary definitions of the terms in italics. For example, one answer to the last question could be obtained by defining major towns as those with a population of greater than 40000 and a dangerous level of pollution as being more than 1ppm of a particular toxic substance; defining the cutoff points at 39000 and 0.8ppm could lead to a very different answer. Clearly the possibility of considering other pollutants introduces still more uncertainty into the picture. From the logical point of view, it is necessary to define precise categories but this can lead to a discord between the real world and the world modelled in the database, as the terms used to describe the real world are naturally imprecise.

In order to deal with some of these problems, fuzzy databases have been suggested. In this chapter we examine how an uncertain deductive database can be implemented in Fril, looking at ways of representing and processing uncertain information within Fril. Additionally, we show how the idea of an uncertain deductive database can be extended to implement an intelligent manual or documentation system.

We adopt the standard relational database terminology, and consider a number of domains which are sets of entities relevant to the problem under consideration. For example, we might be interested in the sets of *cars, speeds,* and *fuel consumption,* given respectively by

car = {Rolls, Mini, Sierra, Citroen-2cv}

speed = {S | S ∈ $\mathbb{Z}$, 0 ≤ S ≤ 200} where $\mathbb{Z}$ is the set of integers

mpg = {M | M ∈ $\mathbb{Z}$, 0 ≤ M ≤ 100}

i.e. speed is a positive integer less than 200 and mpg (miles per gallon) is a positive integer less than 100. A relation is a subset of the Cartesian product of two or more such domains, e.g.

Top-speed ⊆ car × speed

such as the relation shown in Fig. 7 - 2.

We refer to the columns of a relational table as *attributes,* and the rows as *tuples.* There are a number of places where it may be necessary to manage uncertainty within the relational model. These are covered below.

7.2.1 Uncertainty in Attribute Values

Frequently the actual value of an attribute is not known precisely, but may be known approximately, as discussed in Section 7.1 where we have the information that Mary is in her late twenties without being able to give a precise value for her age. This can be modelled using a possibility distribution in Fril. We might adopt either of the definitions

(late-twenties {26:0.5 27:1 28:1 29:1 30:0.5})
(late-twenties [25:0 27:1 29:1 31:0])

depending on whether the domain of *age* is the discrete set of positive integers or the real line (see Fig. 7 - 3). Fril enables us to use either named or unnamed fuzzy sets. Thus

Top-speed	car	speed
	Rolls	125
	Sierra	105
	Mini	80
	Citroen-2cv	55

Fig. 7 - 2
The relation *Top-speed* in tabular form

rather than defining the named fuzzy set *late-twenties* as above, and using the fact

((age Mary late-twenties))

we could simply use the fact

((age Mary [25:0 27:1 29:1 31:0]))

If the underlying domain is not numerical, Fril fuzzy sets can still be used; e.g. we could define a fuzzy set of small cars:

(small-cars {mini:1 metro:0.9 escort:0.3})

Continuous fuzzy sets can be used in arithmetic expressions within Fril, so that if for example we have information about the ages of three employees represented by the facts:

((age John 33))
((age Mary [25:0 27:1 29:1 31:0]))
((age Bill 42))

and we wish to find the average age of all employees we could use the Fril rule

((average-age AV)
    (findall AGE ((age EMPLOYEE AGE)) AGELIST)
    (sumlist AGELIST TOTAL)
    (length AGELIST NUM)
    (times AV NUM TOTAL))

((sumlist (E) E))
((sumlist (X|T) TOT) (sumlist T TS) (sum X TS TOT))

with the definition of *length* given in Section 2.6.3. The first goal in the body of *average-age* binds *AGELIST* to (33 [25:0 27:1 29:1 31:0] 42), the list of ages in the database. The second goal in the body finds the total of these ages, the third goal counts the number of elements in the list, and the fourth goal divides the total by the number of elements to find the average. It would be more efficient to use a tail recursive predicate which combined finding the length of the list with finding the sum of elements in the list, since both predicates work through all elements of the list; for clarity, the two stages are shown separately.

In this case, the total is a fuzzy number [100:0 102:1 104:1 106:0] because of the uncertainty in Mary's age. The fuzzy number can be divided by 3 (the number of entries in the table) to give the average [33.3333:0 34:1 34.6667:1 35.3333:0] . Thus we can combine precisely known information with approximate information and derive a solution which is imprecise but is nevertheless useful for many purposes - e.g. if we needed to

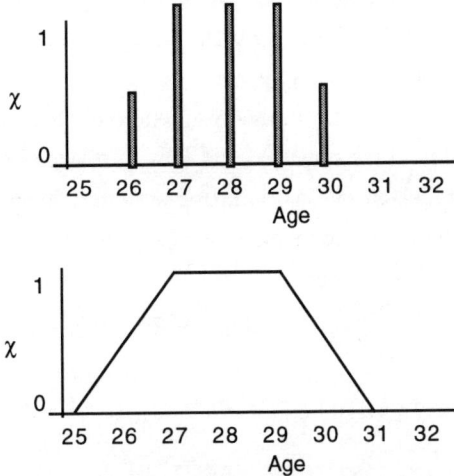

Fig. 7 - 3
The fuzzy set *late-twenties* represented as a subset of a discrete domain (top) and a continuous domain (bottom). In the latter case, membership values for points between vertices are obtained by interpolation

know whether the average age was below 40, we could answer the question with complete certainty.

Any number of attributes in a single tuple can be given in terms of possibility distributions. However, Fril only allows one semantic unification per inference step; i.e. during the unification of a goal with the head of a clause, only one semantic unification can be performed. This is for implementation reasons rather than theoretical reasons, since performing more than one semantic unification requires the construction of a cross-product space and the computation is time consuming; a single semantic unification, on the other hand, can be performed very quickly (see Section 3.7). The restriction does not prevent multiple unifications between variables and fuzzy sets; only multiple semantic unifications between fuzzy sets and other fuzzy sets, numbers, or constants are prevented.

7.2.2 Uncertainty in Relations

In logic programming, a relation between two or more objects is represented by a fact; the predicate names the relation, and the arguments name the objects which satisfy the relation. When there is no uncertainty about the attribute values or the relation that holds between them we can represent each tuple of the relation by a Fril fact. For convenience, Fril provides a specialised form of storage for large tables of facts, known as Fril relations. A Fril relation can be regarded as identical to a set of facts, with the following exceptions:
• all tuples must have the same number of arguments (arity)
• duplicate entries are not permitted in a relation. If a duplicate is added, its support is combined with the support for the existing tuple to give an updated support. By default,

the supports are combined by taking their intersection; however, this can be overridden to use any alternative combination method provided by the system or defined by the user.

• tuples should not contain variables. This is because a variable in the head of a fact is universally quantified (see Section 7.2.5 for further discussion of this point).

• tuples are not necessarily stored in the same order as they were added to the knowledge base. This is because Fril provides an internal indexing system to enable fast lookup of partially specified queries. Although some indexing is provided for ordinary Fril clauses, the indexing on relations is much more comprehensive and allows Fril to search only a subset of the tuples for a possible match. This provides an answer much more quickly than if the entire set of facts is searched.

The relation

$$\text{Top-speed} \subseteq \text{car} \times \text{speed}$$

is shown in Fig. 7 - 2. It can be represented in Fril by either of the following:

```
((Top-speed Rolls 125))
((Top-speed Sierra 105))
((Top-speed Mini 85))
((Top-speed Citroen-2cv 55))
```

or

```
(Top-speed
      (Rolls 125)
      (Sierra 105)
      (Mini 85)
      (Citroen-2cv 55))
```

Taking into consideration the restriction outlined above, these representations are equivalent and no knowledge of the underlying form is needed to query the knowledge base. Thus the query

```
?((Top-speed Mini S)(p S))
```

```
85
yes
```

would have the same response whichever representation was used to store the information in the knowledge base. The differences show up in the following situations:

• adding the fact

```
((Top-speed Mini 85))
```

322

Comfortable speed	car	speed	χ
	Sierra	85	1
	Sierra	50	0.7
	Sierra	105	0.8
	Mini	50	0.8
	Mini	80	0.1

Fig. 7 - 4
Some tuples from the fuzzy relation *Comfortable-speed* in tabular form

to either of the Fril definitions above. In the first case, the knowledge base would read

> ((Top-speed Rolls 125))
> ((Top-speed Sierra 105))
> ((Top-speed Mini 85))
> ((Top-speed Citroen-2cv 55))
> ((Top-speed Mini 85))

but in the second case it would be unchanged as this tuple is already present.

• adding the fact

> ((Top-speed Sierra X))

This would be added to the definitions in both instances; however, in the case of a Fril relation, a warning message would be printed.

• adding the fact

> ((Top-speed a b c))

This would be added to the definition in the first case, but rejected in the second case as it is of different arity to the other tuples in the relation.

• adding a rule such as

> ((Top-speed Sierra X) (Top-speed Rolls X))

i.e. the top speed of a Sierra is the same as that of a Rolls. This could not be added to the Fril relation as a Fril relation can only store sets of facts.

Fuzzy relations generalise ordinary relations by including a degree of membership for each tuple. Thus if we have the domains *car* and *speed* from above, we can define the relation

> Comfortable-speed $\subseteq_f$ car x speed

where for any given tuple there is no uncertainty in the attribute values, but there may be uncertainty as to how well a particular tuple satisfies the relation.

For example, we can say that travelling in a mini at 90 mph will definitely not be comfortable, but travelling in a mini at 50 mph is reasonably comfortable. Other tuples have different degrees of membership. There is no uncertainty here in the attribute values; the uncertainty is the degree to which any particular tuple satisfies the relation.

Fril models uncertainty in a relation by means of support pairs. This is more general than the membership value of a fuzzy relation, but by restricting ourselves to point values and choosing an appropriate calculus for queries, we can model fuzzy relations in Fril. Further discussion of the semantics of support pairs can be found in Chapter 3. Discrete fuzzy relations can be entered directly into Fril; continuous fuzzy relations can also be modelled but may require additional processing. Ways of implementing the additional processing are discussed in Section 7.2.6

It is possible to use Fril to combine uncertainty in attributes and in the relation holding between attributes, i.e. to have a fuzzy relation with a possibility distribution as one of its attributes. For example, the information that "Mary is strongly believed to be in her late twenties could be represented as

((age Mary [25:0 27:1 29:1 31:0])) : (0.8 1)

7.2.3 Conjunctive and Disjunctive Possibility Distributions

We must distinguish between the notions of *conjunctive* and *disjunctive* possibility distributions. A disjunctive possibility distribution represents a single valued attribute, where there is uncertainty in the actual value of that attribute. A conjunctive possibility distribution, on the other hand, represents a set-valued attribute, i.e. a summary of several single values. For example, consider the statement

John speaks {French:0.6, English:1, German:0.8}

If we interpret the possibility distribution conjunctively it could mean that John speaks three languages with varying degrees of fluency. On the other hand, we could interpret the clause as giving information on the language John is speaking at a particular instant. This is either English or French or German, with the memberships shown.

7.2.4 Representing Possibility Distributions in Fril

It is necessary to clarify what is modelled by a possibility distribution appearing in a Fril clause. Suppose we want to express the fact that travelling at speeds up to 60 mph in a mini will be comfortable, but that travelling above 70mph will definitely not be comfortable. If the domain of speed is restricted to positive integers less than 200, this could be expressed by a large number of facts:

((Comfortable-speed Mini 1)) : 1
((Comfortable-speed Mini 2)) : 1
.
.
((Comfortable-speed Mini 59)) : 1
((Comfortable-speed Mini 60)) : 1
((Comfortable-speed Mini 61)) : 0.9
.

$\cdot$
((Comfortable-speed Mini 65)) : 0.5

$\cdot$
((Comfortable-speed Mini 70)) : 0
((Comfortable-speed Mini 71)) : 0
etc

It is tempting to try to summarise these facts as follows:

(low-to-medium-speed [60:1 70:0])
((Comfortable-speed mini low-to-medium-speed))

This states that the pair *(Mini S)* satisfies the relation *Comfortable-speed* , where S is some particular value of the speed constrained by the possibility distribution *low-to-medium-speed*. It does not state that the relation holds for all values of S allowed by the possibility distribution. Possibility distributions in Fril are treated *disjunctively*. To make this clearer, consider the clause

((age Mary [25:0 27:1 29:1 31:0]))

which represents the fact that some person Mary is in her late twenties, i.e. that her age is some single value constrained by the possibility distribution. We can query the knowledge base

qs((age Mary 28))
((age Mary 28)) : (0 1)
no (more) solutions
yes

qs((age Mary 65))
((age Mary 65)): (0 0)
no (more) solutions
yes

These answers tell us that it is completely possible that Mary is aged 28, but that there is no necessary support for this as there is an equal possibility that she is (say) 28.2 or 28.7 or 29 etc. On the other hand it is known for sure that she is not 65. The presence of a possibility distribution represents a single tuple in the relation with an uncertain attribute value, not a collection of facts with every attribute value allowed by the possibility distribution. This is because of the non-commutative nature of semantic unification - the query

qs((age Mary 28))

causes the semantic unification of

(28 | [25:0 27:1 29:1 31:0])

which yields a support of (0 1). On the other hand, the unification of

([25:0 27:1 29:1 31:0] | 28)

yields a support of (1 1). In order to summarise the set of facts and use a fuzzy set conjunctively in the database, we need to reverse the semantic unification. We can do this by using a rule to represent the information:

((Comfortable-speed2 Mini SPEED)
   (poss_match [60:1 70:0] SPEED)) : ((1 1)(0 0))

where we use possibilistic semantic unification in case *SPEED* is bound to a fuzzy set rather than a point value. The support pair on this rule is an equivalence, so that it gives the same support to the head as to the body. This definition has the following behaviour:

qs((Comfortable-speed2 Mini 70))

((Comfortable-speed2 Mini 70)) : (0 0)
no (more) solutions
yes

qs((Comfortable-speed2 Mini 65))
((Comfortable-speed2 Mini 65)) : (.5 .5)
no (more) solutions
yes

qs((Comfortable-speed2 Mini 30))
((Comfortable-speed2 Mini 30)) : (1 1)
no (more) solutions
yes

This gives the desired behaviour. Since semantic unification on a cross-product space can be decomposed into a series of elementary semantic unifications, this approach can be used to summarise more than one attribute value.

7.2.5 Universal Quantification of Variables

A related problem arises when we wish to express a fact which is universally quantified over a limited domain. For example we could say that any journey in a Citroen 2CV is only slightly comfortable. An incorrect way of expressing this would be to use the clause

((Comfortable-speed Citroen-2cv SPEED)) : 0.2

where *SPEED* represents any speed. The problem with this representation is that the core

326

mechanism of Fril does not specify the domains on which a relation is defined. Thus the variable *SPEED* can be replaced by *any* value, not just those which are drawn from the relevant domain, and the query

qs((Comfortable-speed Citroen-2cv (list apples and pears)))

would be solved by matching with the clause above. We need to restrict the range of values which can be taken by the variable. One way to tackle this problem is to use a rule to check that the arguments are drawn from the appropriate domain:

```
((Comfortable-speed Citroen-2cv SPEED)
    (num SPEED)
    (less 0 SPEED)
    (less SPEED 200)) : ((0.2 0.2)(0 0))
```

This is no longer a simple statement of fact, but is a conditional relation. In this case, the conditions merely check that a particular attribute is of the correct form, but as we shall see later it is quite possible to have arbitrary conditions involving other relations.

This approach has the disadvantage that any clause using a universally quantified variable in this way must incorporate the code to check values. Alternatively we can leave the relation as it is but design a new querying mechanism which will automatically restrict the values that can be handled. This also allows greater sophistication to be built in to the query mechanism. For example, let us define the domains as follows:

```
((car Sierra))
((car Mini))
((car Rolls))
((car Citroen-2cv))
((speed S) (num S)(less 0 S)(less S 200))
((distance D) (num D)(less 0 D))
```

and specify the relation domains and tuples:

```
((relation Comfortable-speed (car speed)))
((Comfortable-speed    Sierra        80))
((Comfortable-speed    Sierra        70))
((Comfortable-speed    Sierra        30))
((Comfortable-speed    Sierra        105))  : 0.8
((Comfortable-speed    Mini          30))   : 0.7
((Comfortable-speed    Mini          70))   : 0.6
((Comfortable-speed    Mini          80))   : 0.6
((Comfortable-speed    Mini          85))   : 0.5
((Comfortable-speed    Citroen-2cv SPEED))  : 0.2
((Comfortable-speed    Rolls    SPEED))
```

We can query this database using the predicate *query* defined below. This takes a single goal and checks that all attributes are drawn from the relevant domains before finding the support for solutions to the query.

```
((query (PRED|ARGS))
    (verify-domains PRED ARGS)
    (supp_query ((PRED|ARGS)) (N P))
    (p (PRED|ARGS) : P)
    (pp)
    (fail))
((query X) (p no more solutions)(pp))

((verify-domains P ARGS)
    (relation P DOMAINS)                /* find the domains */
    (each-conforms ARGS DOMAINS))       /* check each argument */

((each-conforms () ()))
((each-conforms (ARG|RESTA) (DOMAIN|RESTD))
    (DOMAIN ARG)
    (each-conforms RESTA RESTD))
```

Then

        query (Comfortable-speed Citroen-2cv apple)

fails in *verify-domains* because *apple* does not conform to the domain *speed*. The code above is designed to handle ground queries, i.e. queries with all arguments instantiated. It will generate values if the argument corresponding to the type of *car* is left unspecified:

        query (Comfortable-speed CAR 70)

        (Comfortable-speed Sierra 70) : 1
        (Comfortable-speed Mini 70) : .6
        (Comfortable-speed Citroen-2cv 70) : .2
        (Comfortable-speed Rolls 70) : 1
        no more solutions
        yes

However the definition of *query* will not generate values for the continuous domain *speed*. It would be possible to extend the definition of the *speed* domain to cater for the case where the argument is an uninstantiated variable.

7.2.6 Modelling Continuous Relations

Fril provides a very straightforward way of representing discrete relations, i.e. relations in which each tuple is distinct. How could we represent a continuous relation, i.e. one that is defined for any value of one or more of its domains? One way of doing this is to summarise the set of facts using a continuous fuzzy set (i-type), as we saw in the example in Section 7.2.4 above. An alternative way is to interpolate between the known points of the relation. For example, the fuel-consumption of a car could be a relation

consumption $\subseteq$ car × speed × mpg

where the fuel consumption is only known at a limited number of speeds, e.g.

```
((fuel-consumption Sierra     55     33))
((fuel-consumption Sierra     85     28))
((fuel-consumption Sierra    105     24))
```

What happens if we wish to know the fuel consumption at a point outside this set, say 60mph? The relation should be defined for this value, but we obviously cannot store all possible tuples. One way to tackle this problem is to use an interpolation procedure to estimate the values at points in between those already known. Thus we could define

```
((consumption CAR SPEED MPG)
       (? ((estimate–consumption CAR SPEED EST)))
       (poss_match MPG EST))
((estimate–consumption CAR SPEED MPG)
       (findall (S M) ((fuel-consumption CAR S M)) L)
       (interpolate SPEED MPG L))
((interpolate SPEED MPG ((S MPG)|REST)) (less SPEED S)(!))
((interpolate SPEED MPG ((S MPG))) (!))
((interpolate SPEED MPG ((S1 M1) (S2 M2)|REST))
       (less S1 SPEED)
       (less SPEED S2)
       (!)
       (sum S1 S2mS1 S2)           % S2mS1 = S2-S1
       (sum SPEED S2mS S2)         % S2mS = S2-SPEED
       (sum M1 M2mM1 M2)           % M2mM1 = M2-M1
       (times M2mM1 S2mS T1)       % T1 = (M2-M1)*(S2-SPEED)
       (times T2 S2mS1 T1)         % T2 = (M2-M1)*(S2-SPEED)/(S2-S1)
       (sum MPG T2 M2))
((interpolate SPEED MPG (H|T))
       (interpolate SPEED MPG T))
```

Note that *estimate-consumption* is called by means of a query since it is a procedural piece of code, and we only require one solution to it. Also the *interpolate* routine assumes that the list of pairs *(speed mpg)* is ordered with increasing values of speed. In this case the assumption is valid because of the order in which *findall* obtains the solutions, but in general it would be necessary to sort the list of pairs. The interpolation algorithm is very straightforward, and simply takes a linear interpolation between the nearest speeds below and above; if the speed is out of the range of the known points, then the consumption is assumed to be equal to that of the nearest known speed.

We could have estimated a membership level for the interpolated value according to the distance of the nearest points, but this would probably be over-sophisticated for the present case.

7.2.7 Truth Functional Modification

Truth functional modification allows us to take a fuzzy relation and (for example) select tuples which satisfy that relation to a high degree, where high degree is defined as a fuzzy set on [0,1]. Let us define

(high-degree [0.5:0 1:1])

and consider the fuzzy relation *Comfortable-speed* defined in Section 7.2.5. The tuples that satisfy the relation *Comfortable-speed* to a high degree can be elicited by truth-functional modification of the relation using the predicate *tfm* defined as follows

```
((tfm MODIFIER REL)
    (supp_query (REL) (N P))
    (match MODIFIER N)) : ((1 1)(0 0))
```

This is executed by

qs((tfm high-degree (Comfortable-speed CAR 70)))

((tfm [.5:0 1:1] (Comfortable-speed Sierra 70))) : (1 1)
((tfm [.5:0 1:1] (Comfortable-speed Mini 70))) : (.2 .2)
((tfm [.5:0 1:1] (Comfortable-speed Citroen-2cv 70))) : (0 0)
((tfm [.5:0 1:1] (Comfortable-speed Rolls 70))) : (1 1)

where the degree to which the tuple *(Mini 70)* satisfies the relation is reduced by the truth-functional modifier *high-degree*. Other tuples belong to the relation either completely or not at all, and are unaffected by the truth functional modification. If necessary, the modified relation can be saved in the knowledge base using the *form-extension* program described in Section 7.3. Truth functional modification is discussed further in Section 3.8.2.

7.2.8 Uncertainty in Virtual Relations (Rules)

The examples in Sections 7.2.4 and 7.2.5 showed how a relation between attributes could be defined by means of a Fril rule. In these cases, the body of the rule was present to perform simple processing of attribute values, e.g. checking the domain. It is possible to use more sophisticated rules to define relations in Fril in terms of other relations. For example, consider the relation

Average-speed $\subseteq$ car × road × speed

which could represent the average speed obtained by a particular type of car on a given road. The domain *road* is given by

road = {motorway, dual-carriageway, a-road, b-road, unclassified}

On a motorway we assume speed is unrestricted, so that the average speed is simply the top speed of the car

((average-speed CAR motorway SPEED) (top-speed CAR SPEED))

On a dual carriageway, let us assume that the maximum speed is 80mph. However, the relation for *top-speed* shows that some cars are not capable of 80mph, and so we define the rule

((average-speed CAR dual-carriageway SPEED)
    (top-speed CAR TOPSPEED)
    (min TOPSPEED 80 SPEED))

which states that the average speed of a car on a dual carriageway is the smaller of 80 mph and the car's top speed. The complete definition for *average-speed* is

((average-speed CAR motorway SPEED)
    (top-speed CAR SPEED))
((average-speed CAR dual-carriageway SPEED)
    (top-speed CAR TOP) (min TOP 80 SPEED))
((average-speed CAR a-road SPEED)
    (top-speed CAR TOP) (min TOP 70 SPEED))
((average-speed CAR b-road 30))
((average-speed CAR unclassified 30))

with a suitable definition for *min*.

This uses the relation *top-speed* to define the relation *average-speed*. A more sophisticated form of rule defines a relation in terms of more than one other relations. Let us say that we wish to know which cars are suitable for a journey on a given class of road, with a high level of comfort (using truth functional modification as discussed in Section 7.2.7) and with a particular level of fuel economy such as medium consumption. We can define

(low–mpg [20:1 24:0])
(medium–mpg [22:0 26:1 32:1 34:0])
(high–mpg [30:0 34:1 42:1 45:0])
(very–high–mpg [40:0 44:1])
(any–mpg [100:1 110:0])

to represent the different levels of fuel economy. Then the virtual relation *suitable-for-journey* can be defined using the previously developed definitions for *average-speed*, *tfm*, *Comfortable-speed*, and *consumption:*. The predicate *query* is defined to use the operations: ((conjunction min)(conditional equiv)(combination max)) to simulate a fuzzy relational combination

```
((suitable-for-journey CAR ROAD COMFORT MPG)
        (average-speed CAR ROAD SPEED)
        (tfm COMFORT (Comfortable-speed CAR SPEED))
        (consumption CAR SPEED MPG))
```

This behaves as follows:

```
?((query  ((suitable-for-journey CAR a–road high any–mpg)) (L U))
        (p CAR : L)
        (pp)
        (fail))
```

```
Rolls : 1
Sierra : 1
Mini : 0.2
Citroen-2cv : 0
no
```

```
?((query  ((suitable-for–journey CAR b–road high very–high–mpg))(L U))
        (less 0 L)
        (p CAR : L)
        (pp)
        (fail))
```

```
Mini : 0.4
no
```

7.2.9 Using Mass Assignments to Represent Uncertain Attributes

So far we have considered the use of possibility distributions to represent uncertainty in attribute values, which is adequate for most cases. A more general representation can be obtained by using mass assignments as discussed in Chapter 3. If there is a domain defined for an attribute, the possibility distribution assumes that there is a sequence of nested subsets of this domain, and that each subset can be given a mass such that the masses sum to 1 for a normalised fuzzy set or less than 1 for a non-normalised fuzzy set. Using mass assignments allows us to represent the case where mass is given to non-nested sets. For example, assume there is uncertainty about the colour of a particular car.

One source of information suggested it was blue or blue/green and another that it was grey/blue. This could be represented by a mass assignment such as

{ {blue, grey} : 0.5 , {blue} : 0.1 {blue, green} : 0.4}

Because the sets are not nested, this cannot be expressed as a fuzzy set. Mass assignments are not fundamental data objects in Fril, but a database system written in Fril can easily be extended to deal with mass assignments. For example, in order to represent the mass assignment above we could adopt the list structure

((blue grey) 0.5 (blue) 0.1 (blue green) 0.4)

and use standard list processing techniques to deal with mass assignment operations.

To illustrate this, a simple program to form the join of two assignments is shown below. The program only handles cases in which there is a unique solution, and is written to illustrate the principles involved rather than with efficiency as a top priority. Parts of the program could be rewritten tail recursively, and the process of mapping *intersect*, *reverse*, etc. over lists could be accomplished more elegantly using meta-programming techniques; however this would be at the expense of clarity. The top level program is:

```
((ma_join M1 M2 MC)
          (combine M1 M2 M3 RC CC)
          (map_reverse CC CCR)
          (append CCR RC CONSTRAINTS)
          (assume_consistency M3)
          (process_constraints CONSTRAINTS)
          (simplify M3 MC))
```

assume_consistency <ma-list> takes a tableau represented as (l1 M1 l2 M2 ...) where l1, l2 are lists of labels and the masses are variables, and instantiates the mass associated with an empty set to zero

```
((assume_consistency () ))
((assume_consistency (() 0|R)) (assume_consistency R))
((assume_consistency (L M|R)) (assume_consistency R))
```

(process_constraints <clist>) takes a list of constraints of the form (mtot m1 m2 ... mn) where the m_i sum to mtot, the mass at the start of the list. If it is possible to find a constraint with a single variable in it, that variable can be instantiated to make the masses add up to the total. Otherwise, if it possible to delete a constraint containing no variables, check that the sum of the masses gives the correct total.

```
((process_constraints ()))
```

333

```
((process_constraints CONSTRAINTS)
        (delete (M|C)  CONSTRAINTS  NC)
        (listvars C  (ONEV) REST)
        (!)
        (sumlist  REST  R)
        (sum  ONEV  R M)
        (process_constraints  NC))

((process_constraints C)
        (delete (M|R) C NC)
        (listvars R () R)
        (sumlist R M)
        (process_constraints NC))
```

where standard definitions are used for for list processing predicates (see Chapter 2). The top-level predicate is *ma_join*, which expects the first two arguments to be mass assignments in the form given above. No error checking is included, and the result is returned in argument 3 . There are four distinct phases in the operation:

• create a 'tableau' in the same form as the mass assignments, but with the possibility of duplicate labels and with variables representing the masses. Constraints can be set up in the form

(total-mass m1 m2 ... mn)

corresponding to each row and column constraint. This is accomplished by the predicates *combine* and *map_reverse*.

		0.7 $\{a, b, c\}$	0.3 $\{b\}$
0.4	$\{a, b\}$	$\{a, b\}$ M11	$\{b\}$ M12
0.6	$\{a\}$	$\{a\}$ M21	$\{\}$ M22

Fig. 7 - 5
Example used in the program to combine two mass assignments

• assume that any empty set has an associated mass of zero. This is done in the predicate *assume_consistency* by instantiating the variable masses to 0. This predicate could be extended to allow incomplete mass assignments, if no solution is found using complete mass assignments.

• process the constraints one at a time, selecting any which contain zero or one variable for checking or instantiation of the variable as appropriate. A constraint is selected using the *delete* predicate, and checked to see whether it contains a single variable (*listvars* predicate). If so, the variable (corresponding to the mass in a cell) is instantiated to the value which satisfies the constraint. If the constraint does not contain a single variable, another constraint is selected.

• finally, merge cells of the tableau with the same label to give an overall mass assignment. This is a straightforward exercise in list processing.

For example, the intersection join of the assignments

((a b) 0.4 (a) 0.6) and ((a b c) 0.7 (b) 0.3)

is obtained by

?((ma_join ((a b) 0.4 (a) 0.6) ((a b c) 0.7 (b) 0.3) M)(p M))

((a b) 0.1 (b) 0.3 (a) 0.6 () 0)))
yes

The first stage in finding this result is to form a list representing the tableau:

((a b) M11 (b) M12 (a) M21 () M22)

and another list representing the constraints:

((0.7 M11 M21) (0.3 M12 M22) (0.4 M12 M11) (0.6 M21 M22))

where these are interpreted as "the first element is the sum of the remaining elements". The important part of this procedure is to form the constraints using the variables representing the mass in each cell of the tableau.

The next stage assigns a mass of zero to any cells with an empty set. After this stage we have the tableau

((a b) M11 (b) M12 (a) M21 () 0)

and the constraints:

((0.7 M11 M21) (0.3 M12 0) (0.4 M12 M11) (0.6 M21 0))

Now we can select constraints from this list. The program examines constraints until one is found to contain a single variable. That variable can be instantiated, e.g. in this case the second constraint is selected and *M12* is be given the value 0.3, leaving the constraint list

((0.7 M11 M21) (0.4 0.3 M11) (0.6 M21 0))

Next *M11* will be instantiated to 0.1 using the second constraint, leaving

((0.7 0.1 M21) (0.6 M21 0))

Finally *M21* will be instantiated to 0.6 using the first constraint, and the remaining constraint can be used to verify that the solution is consistent. There are a number of improvements that could be made to this program:

- checks for negative masses - the program simply instantiates variables to satisfy constraints, without ensuring that the values are reasonable
- split into a linear combination of independent mass assignments if there is not a unique solution
- allow non-zero mass for the empty set if it is not possible to find a complete solution

These extensions can be programmed easily in Fril, enabling the construction of a program that permits mass assignments to be used where there is uncertainty as to an attribute value. It is thus possible to represent attribute uncertainty using either possibility distributions or mass assignments. In order to use mass assignments, it is necessary to write an inference shell (i.e. an enhanced querying mechanism) incorporating code such as that shown above to handle the extended data types. If uncertainty in attributes is restricted to possibility distributions, standard Fril can be used, as the matching between fuzzy sets is performed automatically within Fril.

7.3 OPERATIONS ON RELATIONS IN FRIL

Relational database theory is frequently explained in terms of relational algebra - there is a small set of operations on relations which are "relationally complete", that is to say they allow any desired manipulation of the relations in the database. Typically, a set of relational operators would be *union*, *difference*, *Cartesian product*, *projection*, and *selection*. Other operations can be expressed in terms of these basic functions; e.g. intersection can be written using relational difference since

$$R1 \cap R2 = R1 - (R1 - R2)$$

where R1 and R2 are relations, $\cap$ denotes relational intersection and - denotes relational difference.

It is possible to express the operations of relational algebra in terms of relational calculus - the notations have equivalent power. There are two classes of relational calculus, known as tuple calculus and domain calculus. The former is expressed in terms of variables which represent entire tuples, and the latter uses a different variable for each argument within a tuple. Thus the union of two relations R1 and R2 could be expressed in the tuple calculus as

$$\left\{ t | R1(t) \vee R2(t) \right\}$$

i.e. the set of tuples t such that t satisfies R1 or t satisfies R2. The variable t denotes a fixed length tuple with components t[1], t[2], ... t[n] where n is the arity of the relation. Expressions in the tuple calculus can refer to the complete tuple or its components, using standard quantifiers from the predicate calculus and arithmetic comparison operators. For example, let us consider a relation R of arity 3. The expression

$$\left\{ (t[1], t[3]) | R(t) \wedge t[2] = 25 \right\}$$

selects the set of tuples satisfying the relation R where the value in the second column of the relation is equal to 25, and then projects the result onto the first and third columns. In relational algebra, the equivalent expression is

$$\text{project}_{A1,A3}(\text{select}_{A2=25}(R))$$

where A1, A2, A3 name the columns of the relation.

In the domain calculus, tuples are represented by expressions such as

$$R(x_1 x_2 \dots x_n)$$

where R is the name of a relation and x_i represents either a domain variable or a constant. Expressions in the domain calculus are similar to the tuple calculus, but domain variables such as x_i replace expressions of the form t[i]. Thus the expression

$$\left\{ (x_1, x_3) \mid R(x_1, 25, x_3) \right\}$$

performs the same selection and projection as the tuple calculus expression above. Evaluation of a domain calculus expression consists of computing the extension of the relation defined intensionally by the expression.

Since the operations of relational algebra can be expressed in any of the three notations, it is sufficient to show that we can use one of them to perform relational operations in Fril. The domain calculus notation is closest to Fril, and in this Section we show how relational operations can be implemented in Fril.

A Fril query can be interpreted as an expression in the domain calculus, specifying a relation to be computed. The query and the facts and rules in the knowledge base define a *search tree* (also known as an *and/or* tree) whose root node is the query (see also Chapters 2 and 4). The descendants of *or*-nodes are *and*-nodes, and vice versa. To illustrate this, consider a fuzzy database consisting of the relations *s1, r1, q1,* and *p1,* represented in Fril as follows:

```
((p1 X Y) (q1 X)(r1 X Y))
((q1 a)) : 0.85
((q1 Z) (s1 Z 1))
((r1 a a)) : .8
((r1 a b)) : .6
((r1 b a)) : 0
((r1 b b)) : .1
((s1 a 1)) : .7
((s1 a 2)) : .8
((s1 b 1)) : .4
((s1 b 2)) : 1
```

The query *(p1 A B)* defines the search tree shown in Fig. 7 - 6. There are four solutions to the query:

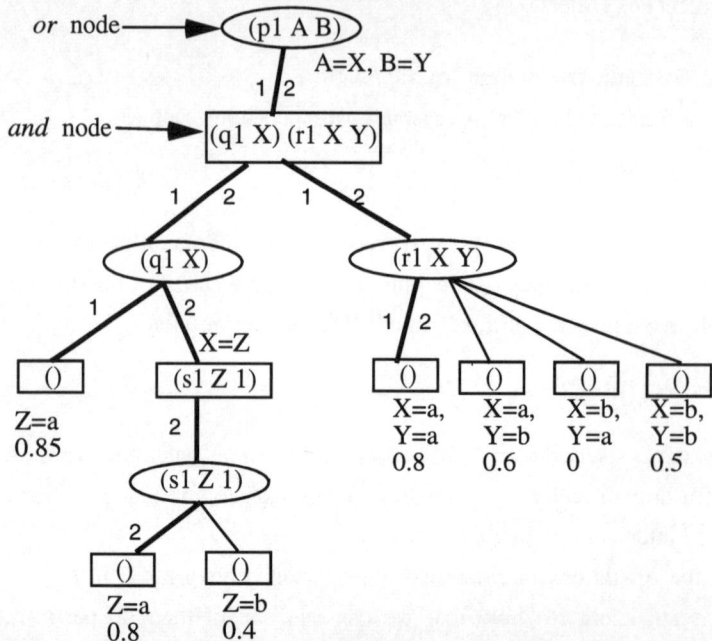

Fig. 7 - 6

An example of a search tree generated by a support logic program and query. The proof trees for the solution *(p1 a a)* are emboldened and labelled 1 and 2 respectively. Recall that a proof tree is a subtree of the search tree starting from the root node and containing every descendant of an *and* node and exactly one descendant of an *or*-node. The support for *(p1 a a)* is calculated from the supports associated with the *and*-nodes on the two proof paths

((p1 a a)) : 0.8
((p1 a b)) : 0.6
((p1 b a)) : 0
((p1 b b)) : 0.4

The first two solutions each have two proof trees; the third and fourth solution each have a single proof tree.

When Fril executes an ordinary logic program, it uses the standard Prolog strategy of depth first search with backtracking over the search tree to find a solution to the query, as discussed in Chapters 2 and 5. It is sufficient to find a single proof of the conclusion; if alternative proofs of the same conclusion are possible they are found only on backtracking, or ignored completely if backtracking does not occur. In contrast, when Fril is calculating the support for a conclusion it is necessary to find all ways of proving that conclusion. The support for a conclusion (an *or-node* of the search tree) is calculated from the supports for each descendant *and*-node using the conditional and combination rules. Similarly, the support for an *and*-node is calculated from the supports of its descendant *or*-nodes, using the conjunction rule.

Support logic execution computes the extension of the relation specified by the query. In order to do this, the extension of each constituent goal in the query must be found. This involves finding the extension of each goal in the body of each clause whose head matches the goal, which is the same as computing at each *or*-node in the proof tree a relation which is equivalent to the set of solutions to that goal. When all *or*-nodes corresponding to goals in the body of a clause have been converted to relations in this way, they can be combined to form a relation corresponding to the extension of the head of the clause. Although the answers provided by a *supp_query* are produced one at a time, internally the entire search tree has been examined in order to find all proof paths for that particular answer. Alternative solutions to the query are computed at the same time, and are there for the taking with little additional work required by the system.

In the search tree of Fig. 7 - 6, the lowest level *or*-node in the tree corresponds to the goal *(s1 Z 1)*. This is already in a form suitable for converting to a relation, since it only has leaf *and*-nodes below it. The relation thus obtained is

$$s1' \quad a \quad .7$$
$$b \quad .4$$

where the prime indicates that this is the extension of the relation specified by the predicate s1. Because of the use of equivalence as the conditional, this leads to the relation

$$q1'_2 \quad a \quad .7$$
$$b \quad .4$$

as the extension of the second clause for q1 (the subscript 2 indicates that this is derived from the second clause).

There is a single solution to the first clause for q1, hence the extension of q1, q1' is given by

$$q1' = q1'_1 \cup q1'_2$$

leading to

$$q1' \quad a \quad .85$$
$$b \quad .4$$

In a similar manner, the *or*-node *(r1 X Y)* is already in extensional form, as its descendants are all leaf nodes. The two relations can be joined to form p1', leading to

p1'	a	a	0.8
	a	b	0.6
	b	a	0.0
	b	b	0.4

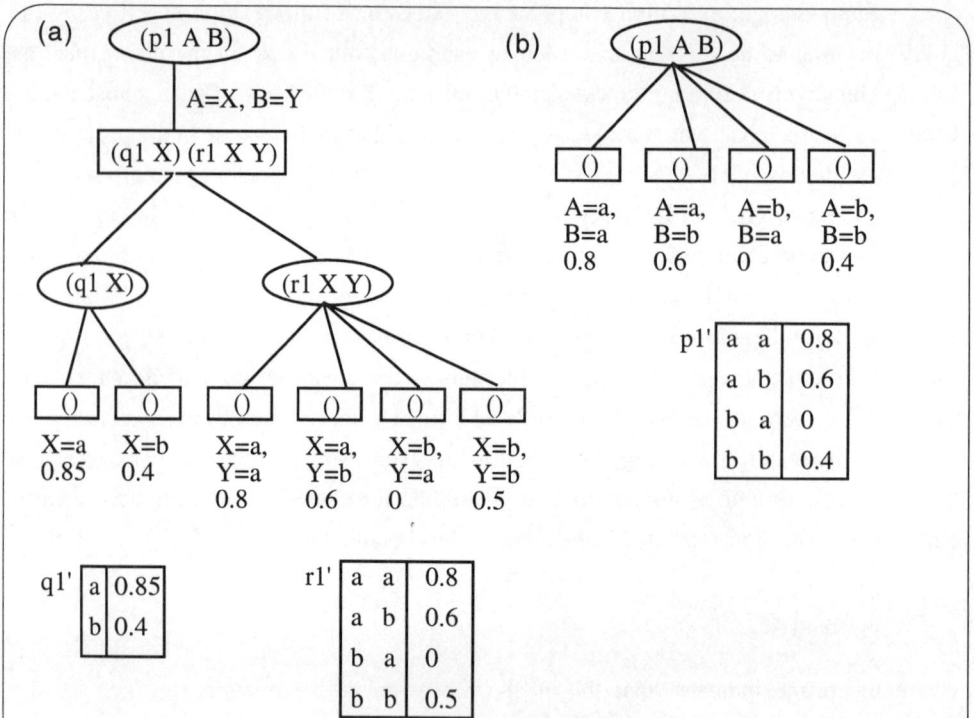

Fig. 7 - 7

The search tree of Fig. 7 - 6 is transformed into the extension of the query. First, the *or*-node *(q1 X)* is converted into relational form, as shown in (a). Next, the relations *q1* and *r1* can be combined to give the extension of the relation *p1*, as shown in (b)

This is illustrated by the search tree in Fig. 7 - 7. The relational operations to accomplish this query would be

$SELECT_{Y=1}$ from $S1'(X,Y) = REL1(X,Y)$

$PROJECT_X REL1(X,Y) = REL2(X)$

$REL2(X) \cup Q1'_1(X) = REL3(X)$

$JOIN_X REL3(X,) \& R1'(X,Y) = REL4(X,Y)$

To preserve consistency with ordinary logic programs in Fril, a depth-search strategy is used as far as possible when calculating supports. An intermediate relation is formed where necessary if there are multiple solutions to a goal, and all solutions are found before execution continues with the next goal. The intermediate relations are combined using tuple-by-tuple domain calculus expressions. If a goal contains no variables, it is never necessary to form an intermediate relation as there is only one support to be computed; however, it is still necessary to find all possible proof paths for that goal in order to calculate its support correctly.

The intermediate relations are temporary, and are discarded at the end of the computation, except for the relation corresponding to the top-level query which is retained until it is known that backtracking will not require further solutions. It is straightforward to save these solutions in a relation, if that is necessary. The built-in predicate *forall* is ideal for this purpose - the goal

    (forall (g1 g2 ... gn) (a1 a2 ... am))

will find all solutions to the list of goals *(g1 ... gn)* and for each solution it will execute the list of goals *(a1 a2 am)*. When used with the built-in predicate *addcl* a simple relation generator can be written:

    ((form-extension SPEC REL ARITY ARGS)
        (def_rel REL ARITY)
        (forall ((supp_query SPEC SUPP))
            ((addcl ((REL|ARGS)) : SUPP))))

This can be used to implement any relational operation, for example

    ((proj REL onto ATTRS to give NEW-REL)
        (length ATTRS ARITY)
        (form-extension REL NEW-REL ARITY ATTRS))

where *length* was defined in Chapter 2. To illustrate the use of this predicate, consider the relation *Top-speed* (see Fig. 7 - 2)

    (Top-speed
        (Rolls 125)
        (Sierra 105)
        (Mini 85)
        (Citroen-2cv 55))

We can project this relation onto its first attribute by the query

    ?((proj (Top-speed CAR SPEED) onto (CAR) to give rel1))
    yes

    list rel1
    (rel1
        (Rolls)
        (Sierra)
        (Mini)
        (Citroen-2cv))
    yes

	Bristol	Bath	Cam	Almonds-bury	Avon-mouth	Bradford--on-Avon	Gloucester
Bristol	1	.8	.4	.9	.7	.7	.2
Bath	.8	1	.3	.7	.5	.9	.2
Cam	.4	.3	1	.5	.1	.1	.7
Almondsbury	.9	.7	.5	1	.6	.6	.3
Avonmouth	.7	.5	.1	.6	1	.4	.1
Bradford-on-Avon	.7	.9	.1	.6	.4	1	.1
Gloucester	.2	.2	.7	.3	.1	.1	1

Fig. 7 - 8

The fuzzy relation *near* expressed in matrix form. The input to Fril would be as clauses or a relation; the matrix form is shown for brevity

This is also applicable to cases where the initial relation is a virtual relation, i.e. defined by a rule rather than by a series of explicit facts. For example

?((proj (suitable-for-journey CAR ROAD high any_mpg) onto (CAR) to give rel2))
    yes

list rel2

    (rel2
        (Rolls) : (1 1)
        (Sierra) : (1 1)
        (Mini) : (0.4 0.4)
        (Citroen-2cv) : (0 0)
)
    yes

Thus when implementing a relational database in Fril, it is more efficient to work in terms of the domain calculus. It is only necessary to save the extensional form of a relation if it is going to be required again later. If this is not the case, it makes no sense to go to the trouble of storing the relation permanently in Fril's knowledge base.

7.4 OPTIMISING QUERY EVALUATION - A PROBLEM GENERATOR

The support logic querying mechanism described in the previous section is crucially dependent on the order of execution of the goals. If we consider a set of relations defined on the domains

location =
    {Bristol, Gloucester, Bradford-on-Avon, Cam, Avonmouth, Almondsbury, Bath}
industry = {engineering, finance, chemicals, software, electronics, aerospace}
pop = $\{P \mid P \in \mathbb{Z}, 0 \le P \le 1000000\}$ where $\mathbb{Z}$ is the set of integers
employee-count = $\{E \mid E \in \mathbb{Z}, 0 \le E \le 200000\}$

population $\subseteq$ location × pop

near $\subseteq_f$ location × location

employment $\subseteq$ industry × location × employee-count

dependence $\subseteq_f$ industry × industry

These relations represent (invented) information on employment, population, and industrial links. In Fril we could express the relations as:

```
((population   Gloucester         300000))
((population   Cam                  6000))
((population   Bristol            550000))
((population   Bath               200000))
((population   Bradford-on-Avon    20000))
((population   Avonmouth           50000))
((population   Almondsbury         80000))


((employment engineering   Gloucester    10000))
((employment finance       Gloucester    20000))
((employment chemicals     Avonmouth      8000))
((employment software      Almondsbury    4000))
((employment electronics   Bristol       30000))
((employment finance       Bristol       40000))
((employment aerospace     Bristol       24000))
((employment software      Bristol       12000))


((dependence chemicals on engineering)) : 0.9
((dependence aerospace on engineering)) : 1
((dependence aerospace on software))    : 0.9
((dependence aerospace on electronics)) : 1
((dependence finance on software))      : 0.6


((near Bristol Bath)) : 0.8
...
etc.
```

Notice that we have added an extra argument to the clauses for *dependence*, in order to clarify the meaning. Let us also define the fuzzy sets

```
(small-pop [25000:1 30000:0])
(large-emp [15000:0 25000:1])
```

representing the concepts of *small* applied to the population of a town and *large* with respect to the number of employees in an industry, and consider the following queries expressed as virtual relations:

which towns have small populations and are near towns with large employers
>((query 1 L1)
>>(near L1 L2)
>>(population L1 small-pop)
>>(employment I L2 large-emp))

which large industries depend on nearby industries
>((query 2 I1)
>>(employment I1 L1 large-emp)
>>(dependence I1 on I2)
>>(employment I2 L2 ANY)
>>(near L1 L2))

which industries (any size) depend on nearby industries
>((query 3 I1)
>>(employment I1 L1 ANY1)
>>(dependence I1 on I2)
>>(employment I2 L2 ANY2)
>>(near L1 L2))

which locations near Almondsbury have industries that depend on industries located in Almondsbury
>((query 4 L)
>>(near L Almondsbury)
>>(employment I1 L ANY1)
>>(employment I2 Almondsbury ANY2)
>>(dependence I1 on I2))

In creating these virtual relations we have simply listed the conditions necessary to define the answer. No attention has been paid to the order in which the conditions will be evaluated. For the first query, we need to evaluate the conjunction of goals

(near L1 L2) (population L1 small-pop) (employment I L2 large-emp)

The order in which these goals are evaluated has a significant effect on the efficiency of the execution. The first goal has up to 49 possible solutions; the second goal has up to 7 possible solutions, and the third goal has up to 8 possible solutions. The actual values are dependent on the order in which the goals are evaluated, e.g. if the goal *(near X Y)* is executed last, the variables X and Y will both be instantiated and there will only be a single solution to the goal; on the other hand, if the goal is executed first the system will store all 49 solutions. What is at issue here is not the total number of solutions to the overall query (which must be the same irrespective of the evaluation order); rather, it is the size of the intermediate relations that must be computed. Since an intermediate relation is only computed by Fril when there is a non-ground goal (i.e. one containing variables) it is advantageous to evaluate goals with few solutions first in the hope that this will reduce or remove the need to store large intermediate relations.

Evaluating the goals in the order shown above requires the following temporary storage

(near L1 L2)	temporary relation with 49 tuples
(population L1 small-pop)	49 x lookup of ground goal (L1 is instantiated)
(employment I L2 large-emp)	49 x temp. relation with ≤4 tuples (L2 instantiated)

whereas leaving the goal *(near X Y)* until last requires

(population L1 small-pop)	temporary relation with 7 tuples
(employment I L2 large-emp)	temp. relation with 4 tuples (*I* is not required again)
(near L1 L2)	28 x lookup of a ground goal

The second option is clearly more efficient in terms of the intermediate storage required. Consideration of efficiency should also take into account whether any of the sets of facts are stored as Fril relations. A relation is almost always quicker for finding solutions, especially when some or all of the goal arguments are instantiated. The improvement in speed is more noticeable as the relation gets bigger, so that it would make sense to store *near* as a Fril relation.

Optimising the order in which goals are evaluated cannot be guaranteed to provide the optimum order, but useful heuristics can be applied which improve matters in the large majority of cases. As with many efficiency gains, the more analysis one is prepared to do, the greater is the guarantee of improved efficiency. Here, we outline a query optimiser that is relatively crude; suggestions for further gains are mentioned later.

The heuristics used rank the goals according to
• the number of arguments instantiated (the more the better)
• the cardinality of the relation in the database (the smaller the better)
• the number of variables uninstantiated (the smaller the better)

In relational algebra terms, these correspond to performing selections and projections as early as possible, working with smaller relations in preference to larger relations, and delaying joins as long as possible. We assume that the cardinality of each relation in the database is known, and that virtual relations are single rewrite rules so that the support for the head is equivalent to the support for the goals in the body, and an occurrence of the head can be replaced by the body. Additionally we assume that base relations are all ground (i.e. contain no variables) and thus will instantiate any variables in matching goals. The first stage in the optimisation process is to expand the query into its constituent base relations

```
((expand () ()))
((expand ((P|A)|R) ((P|A)|REXP))
      (negg negg cl ((P|A)))
      (!)
      (expand R REXP))
((expand ((P|A)|R) EXPANDED)
      (cl ((P|A)|BODY))
      (expand BODY EXPBODY)
      (expand R REXP)
      (append EXPBODY REXP EXPANDED))
```

In order to avoid unwanted bindings, the goal *(negg negg cl ((P|A)))* is used in the second clause. This succeeds wherever *(cl ((P|A)))* succeeds, but does not bind any variables. Since we only allow a single rule, it is not necessary to take this precaution in the third clause. The query *((query 1 X))* is expanded to

(near X L2)(population X small-pop)(industry I L2 large-emp)

This must be optimised according to the criteria above. In order to determine the first goal to be executed we must find the number of constants and variables in each goal, and the cardinality of the corresponding relation in the database. We assume that the latter information is determined at load time since it is static and may be expensive to compute repeatedly. The number of constants and variables in each goal is something that (potentially) changes each time we decide on a goal to be executed since the chosen goal may bind variables. It is possible to denote this flow of data using a graph representation; here we adopt the simpler approach of recalculating the call parameters each time. It is important to note that the query optimisation process must not bind any of the variables in the original query, but on the other hand it must be able to represent the fact that a variable has been bound for later goals. This is achieved by keeping a list of the variables which will be bound, and using *stricteq* to compare terms (*stricteq* is similar to *eq*, but does not instantiate any variables; i.e. it only succeeds if two terms are identical). The top level of the optimisation program is:

```
((optimise () () BOUND))
((optimise (FIRST|REST) (OPT|OPTREST) BND)
      (var_count FIRST 0 VC 0 CC BND)
      (optimum_goal FIRST VC CC REST OPT BND NEWBND)
      (deleteq OPT (FIRST|REST) REDUCED-QUERY)
      (optimise REDUCED-QUERY OPTREST NEWBND))
```

(optimise in out bindings) takes an input list of goals and variables that are already

bound, and tries to optimise the execution order. The variables and constants in the first goal are counted by *var_count*, and *optimum_goal* determines which goal should be executed next. This goal (OPT) is deleted from the list, and the optimisation continues recursively. *deleteq* is similar to the standard list processing predicate delete, but uses stricteq to determine equality of elements. The predicate *optimum_goal* takes the following arguments:

- CURR current best goal
- CC, VC its total of variables and constants
- the list of goals
- slot to return the best goal
- BOUND - the list of bound variables prior to this
- NEWBND - slot to return the updated list of bound vars (found by *extract_vars*)

Comparison is by means of *better_goal*, which encodes the heuristics discussed above.

```
((optimum_goal CURR  VC  CC () CURR  BOUND  NEWBND)
    (!)
    (extract_vars  CURR  BOUND NEWBND))
((optimum_goal CURR VC CC (NEXT|REST) BEST BOUND NEWBND)
    (var_count NEXT 0 NVC 0 NCC BOUND)
    (better_goal CURR VC CC NEXT NVC NCC BETTER BVC BCC)
    (optimum_goal BETTER BVC BCC REST BEST BOUND NEWBND))
```

The predicate *better_goal* compares goal G1, which contains V1 variables and C1 constants, with goal G2 containing V2 variables and C2 constants. The last three arguments are to return the best goal and its count of variables and constants. The comparison is on the basis of
(i) the number of constants (clauses 1 and 2)
(ii) the cardinality of the relations (clauses 3 and 4)
(iii) the number of variables (clauses 5 and 6)

```
((better_goal G1 V1 C1 G2 V2 C2 G1 V1 C1) (less C2 C1) (!))
((better_goal G1 V1 C1 G2 V2 C2 G2 V2 C2) (less C1 C2) (!))
((better_goal (P1|A1) V1 C (P2|A2) V2 C (P1|A1) V1 C)
    (cardinality P1 CARD1)
    (cardinality P2 CARD2)
    (less CARD1 CARD2)
    (!))
((better_goal (P1|A1) V1 C (P2|A2) V2 C (P2|A2) V2 C)
    (cardinality P1 CARD1)
    (cardinality P2 CARD2)
    (less CARD2 CARD1)
    (!))
((better_goal G1 V1 C1 G2 V2 C2 G1 V1 C1) (less V1 V2) (!))
((better_goal G1 V1 C1 G2 V2 C2 G2 V2 C2)))
```

Recall that the query *((query 1 X))* was expanded to

(near X L2)(population X small-pop)(industry I L2 large-emp)

After optimisation this is reordered as

(industry I L2 large-emp) (population X small-pop) (near X L2)

since the first two goals are equivalent as far as the selection criterion goes, but the *industry* relation has fewer tuples. The solutions with non-zero membership are:

(Cam) : 0.5
(Bradford-on-Avon) : 0.7

The second query is to find which large industries depend on nearby industries. The list of base relations to be queried is

(employment I1 L1 large-emp)
(dependence I1 on I2)
(employment I2 L2 _)
(near L1 L2)

which is found to be in optimum order already, giving the solutions:

(finance) : 0.6
(aerospace) : 0.9

Removal of the condition that the industry should be large changes the optimised order slightly:

(dependence I1 on I2)
(employment I2 L2 ANY2)
(employment I1 L1 ANY1)
(near L1 L2)

This is due to the additional term *on* in the relation *dependence*, which appears to be a selection operation from the optimiser's point of view. In fact this "selection" is no help in reducing the number of tuples to be considered, and more sophisticated processing would recognise that this particular argument is useless in partitioning the relation. The solutions are:

(chemicals) : 0.1
(aerospace) : 1
(finance) : 0.6

The final query is to determine which locations near Almondsbury depend on Almondsbury industries. This expands to the conjunction

    (near L Almondsbury)
    (employment I1 L ANY1)
    (employment I2 Almondsbury ANY2)
    (dependence I1 on I2)

and is optimised to give

    (employment I2 Almondsbury ANY2)
    (dependence I1 on I2)
    (employment I1 L ANY1)
    (near L Almondsbury)

with solutions

    (Bristol) : 0.9
    (Gloucester) : 0.3

More sophisticated optimisation could be obtained by analysing the relations to determine how effective the instantiation of any given argument is in reducing the number of tuples to be considered (see the remarks after example 2 above). Additionally, one could examine the overall query to determine any common sub-expressions which could be combined, and also perform more sophisticated analysis on the transmission of information by means of variable bindings.

7.5 AN INTELLIGENT DOCUMENTATION SYSTEM

Recent years have seen a degree of convergence between knowledge-based systems and database systems. Historically, a database has consisted of a large quantity of explicit data, with processing largely confined to the extraction or combination of components of the relational tables. Knowledge-based systems, on the other hand, are concerned with smaller quantities of explicit data but perform more extensive processing on that data to obtain results by an inference process. As we have seen above, the incorporation of probabilistic and possibilistic uncertainty introduces a new degree of flexibility and realism into the computer-based handling of information. The combination of uncertainty with knowledge-based inference and large-scale data storage opens up new possibilities in the management of complex information. One area that is currently in focus as a research topic is the idea of an intelligent manual. In this context, we take a broad interpretation of the word *manual* as a technical reference document containing structured information about a certain topic. The topic could be anything ranging from a description of a piece of hardware (specifications, diagrams, diagnostics, etc.) to a report on a complex engineering study (original aims, methods used, compromises, conclusions, open questions, etc.). Thus a manual is seen as a repository of a large body of technical knowledge. It is possible to take an electronic version of the manual and use it as the basis of a hypertext system, but this has a number of shortcomings:

- inference is left to the reader, e.g. if a manual states that *most widgets of type-A are likely to fail at high temperature* and that *contraptions of type-22 contain 7 widgets of type-A, which are critically important*, it is possible to deduce that a type-22 contraption should not be used at high temperature. In a simple example, the necessary inference is obvious, but a knowledge-based system can perform sophisticated inference involving many uncertainties.
- a related problem is that the conclusions are static - it is not possible to ask a question such as *what would the total cost of type-22 contraptions be if we used type-B widgets instead of type-A*. Such "what-if" capabilities are familiar in knowledge-based systems.
- hypertext systems enable navigation around the manual; they do not model information that is assumed as background knowledge, or not documented.

In this section we outline a knowledge-based system that has been used to model technical information contained in a report on safety assessment by the Swedish Nuclear Inspectorate, SKI. This report was chosen as a demonstrator, and initial stages of the work were sponsored by the CEC. The techniques developed for the knowledge-based system are widely applicable and are currently being used in a variety of other areas.

The safety assessment process requires a great deal of modelling, and there are many areas of uncertainty which must be resolved in a consistent and justifiable way. For instance, faced with the problem of modelling groundwater flow within a body of rock, there are several different *conceptual models* that can be used. The aim is to develop a mathematical model of the physical situation, so that predictions of behaviour can be made; however, in order to develop the mathematical model it is necessary to make certain simplifying assumptions about the physical system being studied. The set of assumptions is referred to as the *conceptual model* being used, and can range from a simple one-dimensional uniform flow model to more complex models such as representing the rock by a fractal network of discrete fractures. A conceptual model can only be partially validated by laboratory and/or field studies, leaving a degree of uncertainty as to whether the particular model is applicable to the geological formations at a particular site. Within each conceptual model, there are further areas of uncertainty - values may be measurable in isolation (e.g. diffusion coefficients), but such measurements may not give the exact value applicable to the site under consideration. Other parameters such as the actual rate of groundwater flow may be intrinsically unmeasurable, although they can be estimated by experts. Usually this uncertainty is treated using probability distributions and Monte Carlo simulation, i.e. the calculation is repeated with many combinations of values from the probability distributions.

If the underlying source of uncertainty is not random, it may be better to use fuzzy set theory and possibility theory to model some or all of the uncertain values. Several authors have proposed methods of incorporating fuzzy numbers into differential equations, although few have actually been applied to real problems. Shaw and Grindrod examined various methods proposed in the literature and found that none were satisfactory within the fuzzy framework, as additional assumptions were needed about the evolution of uncertainty. An alternative approach to the problem of fuzzy values in differential equations is to use a cellular automaton to solve the differential equation, and then fuzzify the automaton. In principle, it is possible to fuzzify any cellular automaton, and hence derive fuzzy solutions to the corresponding partial differential equation.

During and after the safety assessment process, the modelling approaches (including methods used to handle uncertainty), results, and conclusions must be documented. Once the project is complete, it can be a considerable task to trace back from the conclusions of the study to determine the key modelling decisions made in deriving a particular conclusion. The factors contributing to a conclusion can be of many forms, most of which involve uncertainty. It would be useful to have an automated system of storing, retrieving, and manipulating information within a technical project. Clearly such a system must be capable of representing and reasoning about the various uncertainties inherent in the performance assessment process. Ideally the system would be used during the course of a "live" project, but for demonstration purposes it is easier to start with a completed project and work backwards to model the information within it. The SKI Project-90 report was chosen mainly because one of its authors was available as an accessible expert.

The software on the demonstration disk is a considerably cut-down version of the full system. The intention is to illustrate the capabilities of Fril and the techniques used in developing the application, rather than to explain the technical content of the report or present a complete system. Much of the technical knowledge base has been omitted; however, it is hoped that there is sufficient material to convey the general principles. The Intelligent Manual framework is being actively developed in a number of projects.

7.5.1 Knowledge Representation

Knowledge-based systems are typically split into

(i) a knowledge base, incorporating specific information about the domain of interest. This can also include code for checking the validity of information added to the knowledge base, i.e. ensuring that attributes are drawn from the correct domain, etc. In the terms used earlier in this chapter, the knowledge base is a more general form of uncertain database.

(ii) an inference shell, which can make deductions from the knowledge base. The inference shell should be able to handle uncertainty, request additional information, and generally interact with the user. This can be viewed as an enhanced query language in database terms.

To this we add a third category, namely information presentation. It is standard practice to build computer systems with a window/mouse/menu-based interface, and Fril contains many features which enable a sophisticated interface to be constructed straightforwardly. As a general rule, it is important that the remainder of the system should not be dependent on details of the interface. This allows the knowledge-based modules to be embedded in a larger, overall system with its own interface.

One of the most important design decisions in any knowledge-based system is how to represent the knowledge. There are many methods proposed in the literature, with varying degrees of formality and rigour. It is important that knowledge should be represented in a form which does not rely on the system for its interpretation, i.e. it should be possible for a human who is conversant with the field to understand the knowledge base without having to understand any details of the program; at the same time, it is necessary to impose a degree of uniformity on the knowledge to enable automated processing. The knowledge representation adopted in this system is driven to some extent by the querying language. For non-expert users it is inconvenient to conform to a language such as Fril when adding information or posing queries to the database. Even in standard database systems using (say) SQL the user is required to know the form of the underlying relational tables. A possible solution to this is to develop a natural language interface to the database. This is a substantial project which removes the need for a user to be familiar with the underlying database structure, but at the same time adds several layers of complexity to the system as well as requiring considerable development effort. The approach adopted here steers a middle course between these two alternatives. The relations are expressed in a form which is close to natural language, known as *knowledge templates*. The querying mechanism is menu-driven and can only generate queries using the underlying knowledge templates; however, since these are in a form close to natural language they should be easily understandable.

To illustrate, the relation *average-speed* shown in Section 7.2.8 would be represented by the knowledge template

((template-for-average-speed is average-speed of car on road is speed))

where *car*, *road*, and *speed* are domain names which are used to restrict the arguments that can enter into the relation *average-speed*. Facts or rules defining this relation must provide arguments which conform to the appropriate domain. Of course, it is not necessary for the values to be crisp, as Fril can easily handle possibility distributions drawn from the appropriate domain. The system maintains a current focus of enquiry, so that if the current focus is *Mini* which belongs to the domain *car* then only questions relevant to that domain are presented, e.g. the user could ask for the *fuel-consumption of Mini, Top-speed of Mini, Average-speed of Mini,* etc. Once an option has been selected it must be translated into a query. This is accomplished by working through the knowledge template and inserting variables wherever a domain type is encountered. Thus, knowing that we are currently focussed on *Mini* which is of type *car*, the knowledge template *average-speed of car on road is speed* would yield the query *((average-speed of Mini on R is S))* with *R* and *S* respectively conforming to the types *road* and *speed*. The answers can be displayed in pseudo-natural language format, e.g.

Average-speed of Mini on motorway is 80

Since the knowledge templates are defined using an English-like syntax, this gives the appearance of natural language whilst actually constraining queries and solutions to use the exact form required by the knowledge base. The use of knowledge templates guarantees that the system can only contain meaningful data, e.g. the fact

((Average-speed of 80 on Mini is motorway))

would be rejected, as *80* is not a member of the domain *car*, *Mini* is a concept whose type is *car* not *road*, etc. Note that this only guarantees that data are meaningful, not that the data are necessarily true.

In modelling the SKI project, a number of key types and relations were extracted from the report, and used to define knowledge templates. For example, the type *Physical Effect* is used to represent any measurable processes or events that need to be considered in the system (for our purposes, this includes mechanical, thermal, chemical etc. processes). A physical effect has certain attributes, defined by its relations with other concept types, as shown in Fig. 7 - 9.

Use of knowledge templates makes it straightforward to ensure that only meaningful information is added to the system. It is of course rather more complex to validate the knowledge templates themselves, or changes to the knowledge templates, but this task can be automated. The knowledge templates force the

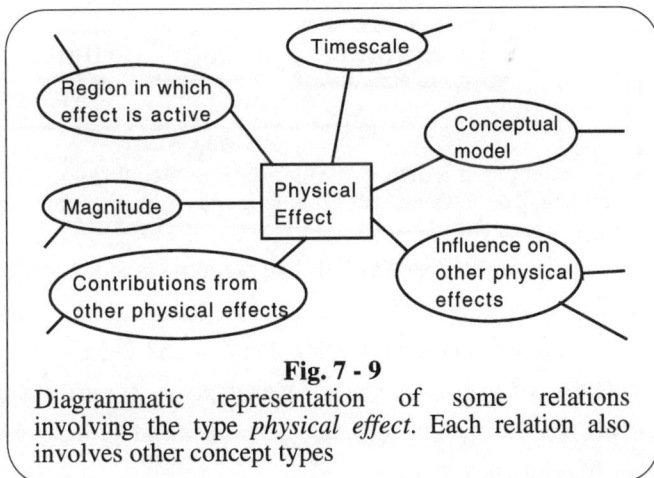

Fig. 7 - 9
Diagrammatic representation of some relations involving the type *physical effect*. Each relation also involves other concept types

353

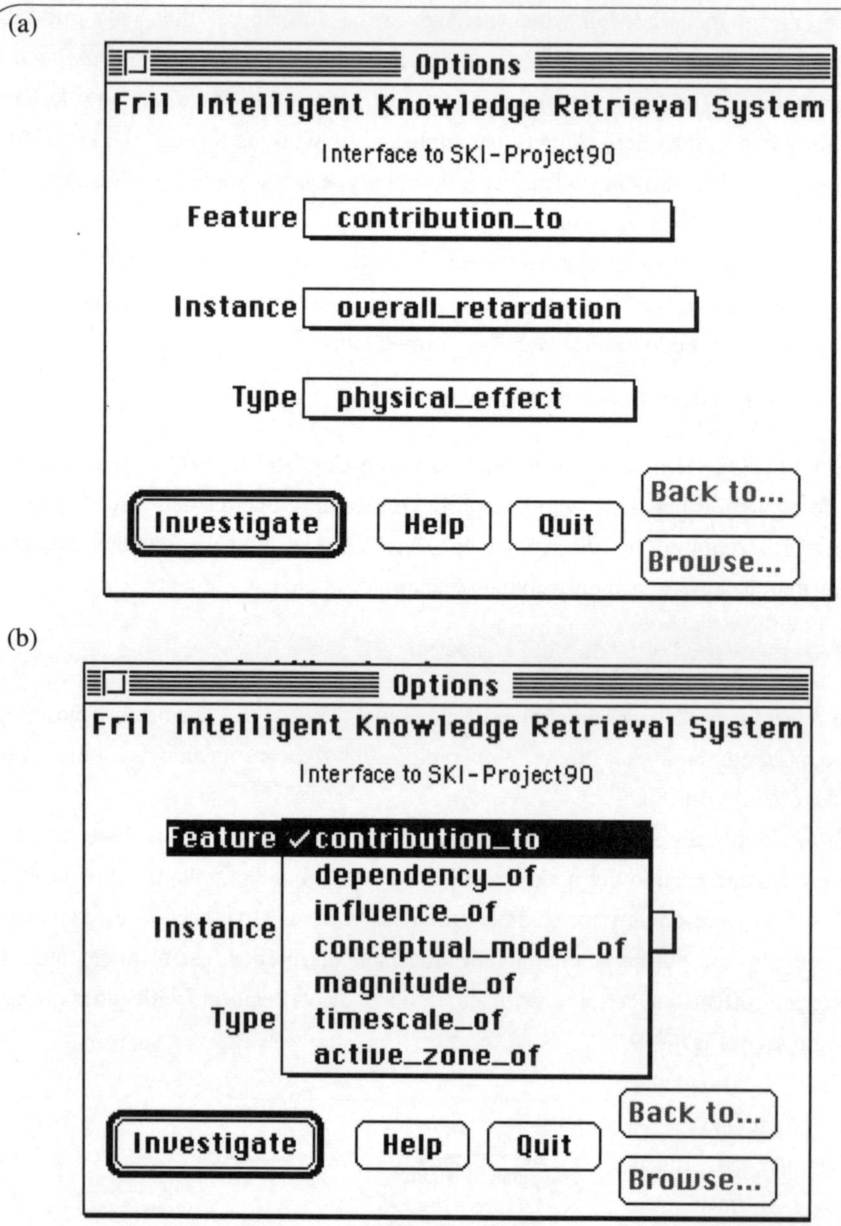

Options

Fril Intelligent Knowledge Retrieval System

Interface to SKI-Project90

Feature | contribution_to

Instance | overall_retardation

Type | physical_effect

[**Investigate**]   [Help]   [Quit]

[Back to...]

[Browse...]

(b)

Options

Fril Intelligent Knowledge Retrieval System

Interface to SKI-Project90

Feature ✓ contribution_to
dependency_of
influence_of
conceptual_model_of
magnitude_of
timescale_of
active_zone_of

Instance

Type

[**Investigate**]   [Help]   [Quit]

[Back to...]

[Browse...]

Fig. 7 - 10
An example of a dialog-driven user interface forming part of the intelligent manual system. The interface uses popup menus to select topics for investigation

information to take an English-like form, with added words such as *is, on,* etc. This is a fairly natural form, which makes the explanation of derived information much easier.

In addition to specifying domains and defining allowed relations that each concept may participate in, knowledge templates record the nature of the relations including
• whether the relation is unconditional (i.e. a set of facts or a Fril relation), conditional (a set of rules), or a mixture

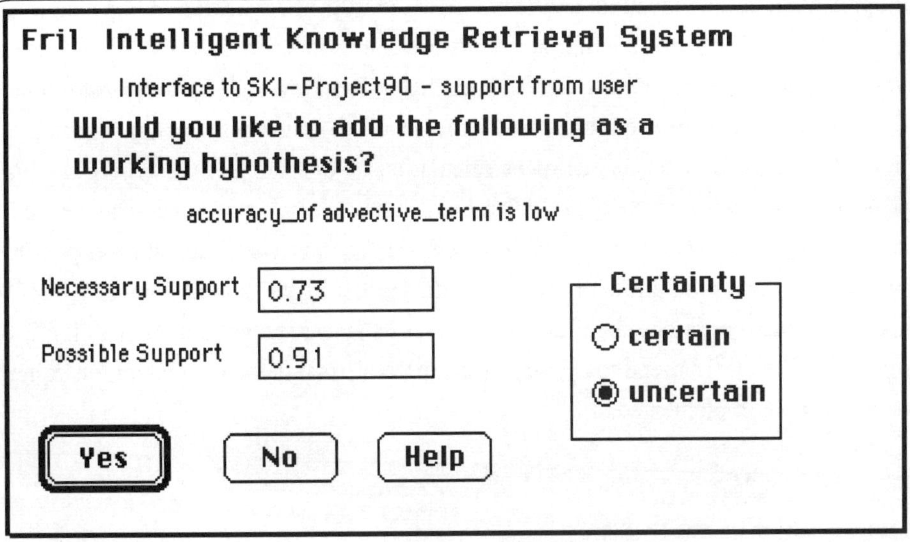

Fig. 7 - 11
The intelligent manual system refers to the user in cases where information defined by the knowledge templates to be "askable" is not found in the knowledge base. The required information can be adopted as a working hypothesis and used to derive answers in the normal way

• whether the relation is certain or can have uncertainty (a support pair) associated with it

• the calculus used to process uncertainty

• whether the user should be queried in the event of missing information

In the last case, information can be added to the knowledge base as a *Working Hypothesis* of *User*. This yields a "what if" mechanism, whereby the user can add information and test the consequences. The format and permitted values for the missing information can be obtained from the knowledge templates and specified domain values for the attributes involved. This process is illustrated in Fig. 7 - 11. Information supplied by the user may be certain or uncertain. In the case of uncertainty, a support pair may be used in the usual way to model the degree of truth of the working hypothesis.

Some concept types are defined as *evaluable*. This means they have associated procedures that can display information in a more sophisticated fashion than simply printing it out on the screen. For example, the type *Reference* is defined as evaluable, and participates in the relation *Reference_to Conceptual_Model* is *Reference*, e.g.

((reference_to advection_dispersion_model is ski90-4-176))

When information involving a *Reference* is found as a solution to a query, the system initially just presents the name of the document, section and page number. A request for further expansion is able to launch the application that created the document and display the appropriate section of text. (This facility is only available on platforms that support inter-application communication, and is not included in the demonstration copy supplied with this book.) With the appropriate hardware and software, this gives a powerful capability for information presentation and intelligent indexing of documents. Additionally, the mechanism can be used to provide an interface to "number-crunching" packages, such as those used in safety assessment calculations. For example, the type *Computer Code* is associated with a *Conceptual Model* which has a number of *Parameters*, each of which has a *Typical Value*. The *Computer Code* is defined as evaluable, and it is possible to run the associated program with values specified either by the default *Typical Value*, or by specific values chosen by the user. This further enhances the system by enabling it to acts as an intelligent front-end to existing software. Note that in the demonstration system this feature is not implemented.

7.5.2 Interacting with the System

At any time, the focus of attention is on a particular type (such as *physical-effect*) and an instance of that type (such as *groundwater-flow*). The questions relevant to that type are offered to the user (on the *Feature* pop-up menu in Fig. 7 - 10), and a query is generated when the *Investigate* button is clicked. This query can be optimised by a mechanism such as the one outlined in Section 7.4. All solutions to the query are found and displayed as shown in Fig. 7 - 12. Here the *contributions_to* the *overall_retardation* are found. The text 'Contribution to Overall Retardation' is derived from the knowledge template, and the answers found are displayed. The reasoning that led to any of the answers can be investigated by means of the *Explain* button, and the concepts arising from the answer (in this case the three additional topics *repository_retardation, near_field_retardation,* and *far_field_retardation*) are offered as candidates for further investigation. Alternatively, the *Back to* button allows the focus to switch to previously investigated topics. Thus a user can navigate through the knowledge base, investigating a sequence of topics and sub-topics before returning to a particular topic, as in a hypertext system. The use of knowledge templates ensures that the questions and answers are in a form which is close enough to natural language for a user to understand easily.

The explanation facility involves the system tracing back through the rules and facts used to derive a conclusion, and displaying this information. As the knowledge base contains English-like statements, this yields an understandable explanation. This is an important consequence of using knowledge templates to enforce an English-like structure on the information in the knowledge base. An example of an explanation is shown in Fig. 7 - 13. This illustrates a conclusion derived from two rules and a working hypothesis of the Ski Project-90 study. The information about extreme channelling is not present as a fact, but has been entered as a working hypothesis with a degree of support. The explanation also shows the propagation of support for the conclusion, which is

356

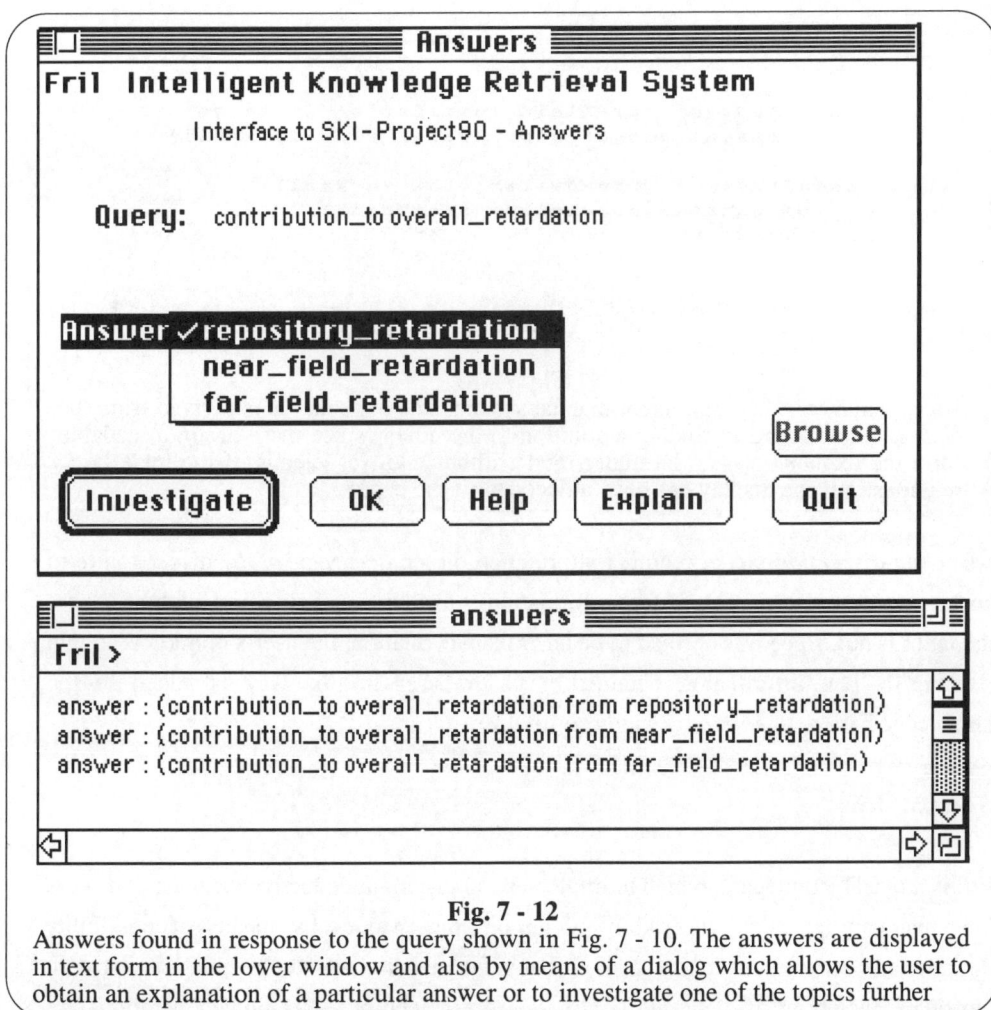

Fig. 7 - 12
Answers found in response to the query shown in Fig. 7 - 10. The answers are displayed in text form in the lower window and also by means of a dialog which allows the user to obtain an explanation of a particular answer or to investigate one of the topics further

straightforward in this case. Modules to elicit information and trace back through execution can be written easily in Fril, as illustrated by the systems programming examples in Chapter 5.

When the system requires information, it first looks for explicit facts and rules, then checks the working hypotheses, and finally (in some cases) asks the user for an opinion which can be stored as a working hypothesis of the user. For example, assume that the knowledge base contains the following:

((accuracy_of advection-dispersion-model is reasonable)
   (accuracy_of dispersion-term is high)
   (accuracy_of advective-term is low))
((working_hypothesis_of ski90 is accuracy_of dispersion-term is high))

plus an indication that *accuracy_of* is a relation that is askable, i.e. the user can be consulted in the case of missing information. Investigating the *accuracy_of* the

357

```
   answer : (magnitude_of far_field_retardation is large) with support
                                                           (0.8 1)

rule is(magnitude_of far_field_retardation is large)
        if(magnitude_of groundwater_flow is small)

rule is(magnitude_of groundwater_flow is small)
        if(extreme_channeling is absent)
   working hypothesis of ski90 is extreme_channeling is absent with
                                             support (0.8 0.9)

yielding solution (magnitude_of groundwater_flow is small) : (0.8 1)
yielding solution (magnitude_of far_field_retardation is large) :
                                                           (0.8 1)
```

Fig. 7 - 13

An explanation in the intelligent manual system. The explanation is derived from the facts and rules used in finding a solution to the query; since these are in a readable form the explanation can be understood without knowing details of the underlying relations (NB the display has been reduced to fit the page)

advection-dispersion-model requires information on the *accuracy_of the* dispersion term and the advective term. The former information is available as a working hypothesis, but the latter is not; since it is defined to be an "askable" relation, the user's opinion is sought (see Fig. 7 - 11). Information obtained from the user in this way is added to the knowledge base as a *working_hypothesis_of user*.

7.6 SUMMARY

Fril is an ideal language in which to implement an uncertain deductive database. The core language can represent uncertainty within attribute values by means of possibility distributions as well as fuzzy and probabilistic uncertainty in the relation between attributes, including discrete and continuous fuzzy relations. Relational operations are accomplished at the tuple level using standard Fril rules and compound queries.

It is a straightforward programming task to extend the Fril querying language so that additional forms of uncertainty can be handled, such as mass assignments. This can be accomplished by writing a "shell" (in expert systems parlance) to deal with the additional processing required. In database terms, such a shell is no more than an extension to the basic Fril query language. Many more features can be incorporated in the shell, such as a dialog-driven interface, facilities for explanation of answers to queries, and facilities for requesting additional information when appropriate. The idea of a data dictionary defining the forms of data allowed in the system has been extended to knowledge templates, giving a representation which is close to natural language. This aids readability of the knowledge base and facilitates explanation mechanisms.

The other major extension incorporated in the querying shell is the interface to other software which enables the knowledge base to function as an intelligent indexing and reference system, and as a front-end to other software packages, with the ability to explain the underlying model and supply reasonable values for input parameters.

7.7 BIBLIOGRAPHY

Baldwin J.F, Martin T.P, Zhou Y, (1993), "A Fril Knowledge Base for the Management of Uncertainty in Performance Assessment of Hazardous Waste Repositories", Proc. FUZZ-IEEE 93, pp 739-745.

Baldwin J.F, Martin T.P, Zhou Y, (1993), "Fuzzy Cellular Automata - a Practical Approach to Fuzzy Differential Equations", in Uncertainty in Knowledge-based Systems, Eds Bouchon-Meunier B, Yager R.R, Springer-Verlag.

Baldwin J.F, (1993), "Fuzzy and Probabilistic Databases with Automatic Reasoning", To be published.

Baldwin J.F, Martin T.P, (1993), "From Fuzzy Databases to an Intelligent Manual using Fril", J. Intelligent Systems **2,** pp 365-395.

Dubois D, Prade H, (1987), "On Several Definitions of the Differential of a Fuzzy Mapping", Fuzzy Sets and Systems **24,** pp 117-120.

Dubois D, Prade H, Testemale C, (1984), "Generalizing Database Relational Algebra for the treatment of Uncertain Information and Vague Queries", Information Sciences **34,** 2, pp 115-143.

Shaw W, Grindrod P, (1989), "Investigation of the potential of fuzzy sets and related approaches for treating uncertainties in radionuclide transfer predictions", CEC Report EUR 12499EN (DG XII).

Sowa, J.F, (1984), Conceptual Structures, Addison Wesley.

CHAPTER 8

Applications of Fril

8.1 INTRODUCTION

Since 1988, Fril has been used in a wide variety of applications both in industry and in academic institutions, in the UK and throughout the rest of the world. Examples of UK companies who have been using Fril in recent years are: SEMA Scientific, Royal Ordnance, Team Management Systems, BP Grangemouth, Admiralty Research Establishment ARE Portland, United Kingdom Atomic Energy Authority UKAEA Winfrith, Defence Research Agency Malvern, Cray Systems, INTERA Information Technologies, Reuters, and British Aerospace Bristol. Overseas companies using Fril include: Sanyo Electric and NRI & NCC in Japan, Defence Science and Technology Organisation DSTO in Australia and Saab Instruments in Sweden. Fril is also being used in academic institutions in the UK, and in other countries such as the USA (Cincinnati University), France (LAFORIA, CNRS Paris) and the City Polytechnic of Hong Kong.

In this final chapter we outline a selection of applications which have been developed in industry. Some of these have been developed as commercial applications from the outset. Others arose from collaborative work between industry and academic institutions - particularly the University of Bristol - such as the government sponsored Alvey Vision project "Object Identification from 2D images" and the IED/DTI project "QUINCE" on Software Cost Estimation. In another case a project was developed wholly at the University of Bristol and is now being commercially exploited by industry.

8.2 AIRCREW MODELLING

The Defence and Avionics Division of Cray Systems Ltd are using Fril to produce a modelling tool for representing the behaviour of aircrew in helicopter and fixed wing operations, work which is being carried out under contract RAEc/252 from the Flight Systems division at DRA, Farnborough. The tool is used to produce models of aircrew behaviour that can run within a simulation environment to aid the assessment of pilot workload on specific missions and examine the workload effects of various avionics and decision support aids in the cockpit. It will also be used in future to model aircraft in combat simulations.

The model represents the three fundamental tasks of the aircrew: data perception, situation assessment and decision about the actions to be taken. It also provides a mechanism for representing the memory characteristics of the aircrew. A fourth activity within the aircrew model evaluates the extent of any factors that may affect the performance of the aircrew, the so-called "affectors". These include physical affectors such as aircraft vibration, g-forces, temperature, cockpit pressure etc. and psychological affectors such as fear, work overload etc.

The behaviour and reasoning characteristics of the aircrew model, written in Fril , are accessed from an Ada simulation framework via C data structures and control routines. External events that occur within the simulation framework, and self-induced prompts to perform routine operations, are taken as input by the model to drive its reasoning and behaviour. The data perception task determines what instruments or other data the aircrew would examine as a result of the event and obtains that data, if available, from the simulation framework. The perceived data are passed on to the situation assessment task which determines the state of the aircraft within its current context and its ability to fulfil its mission. Using this perceived situation, the aircrew model decides what actions should be performed to optimise the success of the mission, addressing any outstanding problems.

The effects on the performance of the aircrew that arise from the affectors vary in type and intensity; examples are shorter memory, slower reasoning and tunnel vision. All conscious tasks are affected in some way by the affectors, but not necessarily in the same way. The aircrew modelling tool provides a mechanism for evaluating affectors and for altering the aircrew's behaviour according to the possible effects.

Fril lends itself ideally to the modelling of such a task by its ability to combine rule-based reasoning techniques with the qualitative analysis capabilities afforded by Support Logic and Fuzzy Sets. The uncertainty handling mechanism proves particularly useful in the evaluation of affectors and in representing the degree to which the resultant effects should be applied to the conscious tasks of the aircrew.

8.3 INTELLIGENT MANUAL SYSTEM

The University of Bristol under an EC contract with INTERA Information Technologies Ltd. are currently developing an Intelligent Manual System called SAFETIME (Safety Assessment in a Fril Environment for Technical Information Management and Encapsulation). This is an automated system of storing, retrieving and manipulating information within the performance assessment project SKI-90 which is concerned with the disposal of radiation waste.

In any country with a nuclear research programme, it is necessary to dispose of highly active waste in a safe and effective manner. One currently favoured approach to disposal is encasement of the waste in canisters which are then placed in an underground repository surrounded by additional barriers such as concrete. Clearly, in order to determine the safety of this process it is necessary to predict the performance of the repository, and this problem is the subject of considerable research. In principle, performance assessment should take account of all feasible processes and events affecting the repository, ranging from obvious possibilities such as leakage from canisters, transport of contamination through the rock mass, dilution of contamination, etc., through to less predictable events involving future climate and population patterns. Obviously any performance assessment cannot take into account all possible factors; however, it is necessary to provide a best estimate of the safety of a repository.

The performance assessment process requires a great deal of modelling, and there are many areas of uncertainty which must be resolved in a consistent and justifiable way. For instance, faced with the problem of modelling groundwater flow within a body of rock, there are several different conceptual models that can be used, ranging from a simple one-dimensional uniform flow model to more complex models such as the representation of rock by a fractal network of discrete fractures. There is a tradeoff between the resources available and the accuracy of results obtained, but even the most detailed conceptual models can only be validated by laboratory and/or field studies, leaving a degree of uncertainty as to whether the particular model is applicable to the geological formations at a particular site. Within each conceptual model there are further areas of uncertainty - for example, parameters such as diffusion coefficients may be measurable in isolation, but such measurements may not give the exact value applicable to the site under consideration. Other parameters such as the actual rate of groundwater flow may intrinsically not be measurable but nevertheless can be estimated by experts. Typically in past estimations of repository performance, uncertainty has been handled using probabilistic methods - indeed, some regulatory authorities almost require the use of probabilistic performance assessment by specifying conditions such as "less than one in one billion chance of failure". It is questionable whether classical probability is appropriate for all aspects of uncertainty in performance assessment, and more recent work in the field has investigated the use of fuzzy uncertainties.

During and after the performance assessment process, the modelling approaches (including methods for handling uncertainty), results and conclusions must be documented. Once the performance assessment is complete, it can be a considerable task to trace back from the conclusions of the study to determine the key modelling decisions made in deriving a particular conclusion. The factors contributing to a conclusion can be of many forms, most of which involve uncertainty. The Intelligent Manual System has been developed for storing, retrieving and manipulating information within a performance assessment project. Such a system must be capable or representing and reasoning about the various uncertainties inherent in the performance assessment process.

Ideally the system would be used during the course of a live performance assessment project. However, for demonstration purposes an approach has been adopted which starts with a completed project and works backwards to model the information within it. The system implemented encapsulates the knowledge within the far-field section of the SKI Project-90 report, and this was chosen mainly because one of its authors was available as an easily accessible expert.

8.4 VISION UNDERSTANDING

A government sponsored Alvey/SERC vision understanding project "Object Identification from two-dimensional images" involved a consortium of nine members including the Universities of Bristol and Reading and several industrial organisations including British Aerospace Sowerby Research Centre at Bristol, the Defence Research Agency at Malvern and Marconi Command and Control Systems at Frimley. The University of Bristol's particular involvement concerned the development of a computer system in Fril to interpret intermediate-level image data in terms of physical object labels. The project focussed on middle distance outdoor colour scenes. A digitised image was analysed and represented as a segmentation; that is, a set of putatively significant regions with associated luminous, chromatic, topological and geometric properties. The task was to obtain a labelling of these regions using a priori scene knowledge in the form of conceptual graphs and support logic techniques for combining low-level (data-based) and high-level (knowledge-based) evidence.

A Conceptual graph is a form of high level knowledge representation which is akin to the representations of semantic nets, frames and scripts, but with a much clearer and more mathematical semantics. Conceptual graph schemas were implemented in Fril and used to represent background knowledge and expectations about the types of concept that might be found in an image. Such schemas enabled the search for concepts to be guided by providing hypotheses to be tested. Support Logic programming provided the inference mechanism for combining various uncertainties and integrating evidence from different sources. Assigning a concept label to a region or a group of regions in an image consists of hypothesising a particular concept label on the basis of the knowledge in a schema and then evaluating the evidence for it using support logic programming inference with the low-level data. In addition to this top-down approach, a bottom-up method of identifying objects from the presence of particular features was investigated - for example, when looking for a car in an image, a relevant clue might be the semi-circular profile of the wheel housing.

On completion of this project further projects were set up with Marconi and DRA Malvern, to extend the Artificial Intelligence aspects of the work using Fril.

8.5 ADMINISTRATION OF MONEY MARKET SERVICES

Another application which involved the use of Conceptual Graphs for knowledge representation was an expert system called CAMES, which stands for "Client Administration Expert System". This application concerns the administration of money market services and was developed for commercial exploitation by Reuters Ltd in 1989. Reuters developed the system in Fril using a conceptual graph toolkit provided by Fril Systems Ltd.

Reuters is a blue chip company which supplies financial information to dealers, banks and brokers worldwide. This information is packaged up into various services which are delivered over a range of different terminals. These terminals are supplied by Reuters but the information is distributed via leased line, satellite, fibre optic cable and microwave links. Reuters also market complete trading room systems and interfaces to subscribers' in-house computers as well as services and equipment supplied by various competitors. The services and equipment are packaged up into products in a variety of ways according to various marketing and pricing policies. These are sold via a set of product codes which make up a price list.

Reuters maintains a record of all product codes that a subscriber has ordered, and also other information concerning permissions for services at the subscriber's site. When a subscriber wants extra services or equipment then an order is raised. Since many of the product codes package together a number of different services, there is usually more than one way in which extra services can be ordered. This might involve removing existing product codes and swapping in various other ones. This greatly adds to the complexity of any order. The task of getting the correct product mix for an order is in no way trivial, and it can involve many different price banding techniques as well as current marketing policies. There are two possible outcomes which follow from processing an order - that of installing or removing product codes from a subscriber's site. The department responsible for processing these orders is called Client Administration.

A Quality Assurance group is responsible for vetting orders after order entry. This involves checking all the orders on the order processing schedule, which is a very repetitive and laborious process. Quality assurance checks include: correct product mix, network terminations, correct permissioning, correct price banding and the relationship between orders. The knowledge-based system using conceptual graphs was motivated by the failure of traditional solutions, and the lack of flexibility of rule-based approaches due to the rapid propagation of rules, and the dependence on procedural coding for the validation process. Conceptual Graphs provided an effective level of expressiveness and flexibility for the problem requirements, which included: the system should have an easily maintainable structure so that updates made in any part of the system should not affect any other part unless new deductions or inferences follow directly by inheritance; the knowledge gathered for the system should be represented in a uniform and readily understandable form.

8.6 ORTHODONTIC EXPERT SYSTEM

An expert system for planning orthodontic treatment was originally developed at the University of Bristol in collaboration with practitioners at the Bristol Dental hospital. Recently this work was completed and the system is being commercially exploited by Team Management Systems Ltd.

Orthodontics typically concerns the management of growth and development of teeth to prevent or correct such problems as overcrowding or misalignment. The development of the expert system initially involved analysing the decision making processes used by orthodontists, in order to identify possible methods of emulating the process by computer. This resulted in a knowledge representation which used fuzzy sets since orthodontic reasoning routinely involves the manipulation of vague or uncertain concepts.

The manner in which the practitioner interacts with the expert system is fundamental to the system's effectiveness. The user interface has been developed to enable the practitioner easily to communicate the salient details regarding a patient. These details include aspects of the malocclusion which general practitioners could not be shown to assess in a reliable and consistent manner. Therefore, specific research was undertaken to identify methods which would improve the reliability of the data input.

The expert system has been tested extensively using a number of general dental practitioners entering a sample of cases. The system's recommendations have been shown to be comparable to the recommendations of a consultant orthodontist when assessed by peer review in a blind trial.

8.7 DESIGN AND ASSESSMENT OF COMPOSITE MATERIALS

A computer expert system called CODEX is currently being developed for the design and assessment of composite plates and struts. This is a collaborative project funded by the Science and Engineering Research Council, SERC, involving the Departments of Engineering Mathematics and Aerospace Engineering at the University of Bristol and the Civil Aircraft Division of Bristol Aerospace, Filton.

Due to the orthotropic macro-mechanical behaviour of advanced fibre-reinforced composite materials (FRMs) it is usual to bond together layers of material with the fibres in different orientations so that all-round strength is obtained. Optimisation of the amount of material with respect to weight, cost, stiffness, strength and other less quantifiable factors is central. The computer system has been implemented to aid users in the design of FRM plates and struts, and also to allow the assessment of the relative merits of previous designs based on such criteria.

A composite laminated plate is designed in a cyclical manner, where a netting analysis is employed to obtain an initial design, and heuristics are applied at successive stages to thicken layers of certain fibre orientations depending on the mode and direction of predicted failure. A composite strut is designed by optimising the dimensions of a given cross-sectional shape so that the buckling load is the same as the prescribed compressive load and structural failure loads for the different layers are not exceeded.

The plate or strut designs obtained can be compared by using a set of rules representing different design criteria. The relative importance of these rules can be set by the user, and an overall assessment for a design is derived using Support Logic programming.

8.8 SOFTWARE DEPENDABILITY AND RELATED APPLICATIONS

A research project concerning the assessment of software dependability was started at the University of Bristol in the mid 1980's in co-operation with SEMA Scientific. The research was in part inspired by Karl Popper's work on the dependability of scientific knowledge and by David Blockley's work at the University of Bristol, on the dependability and safety of civil engineering structures. The methodology of software dependability assessment was developed into a knowledge engineering tool using support logic programming in Fril.

The notion of software dependability was proposed as a way of thinking about the uncertainty in the properties and behaviour of software. Traditional software reliability models attempt to quantify the likelihood of software failure, but are very restrictive in application for several reasons: they do not make use of all the available evidence - for example, most models rely entirely on failure data gathered during testing, and few make use of any information regarding the processes used in the development of the software or knowledge of its structure; the models tend to be based on implausible assumptions - such as that each fault is removed immediately and perfectly, and each fault contributes equally to the unreliability of the software; the models treat uncertainty inappropriately and they cannot predict in advance how major functional changes will affect the overall reliability of a software system. On the other hand, formal methods which attempt to manage correct software implementations from specifications are constrained to produce correctness proofs for relatively small fragments of code and they do not address the significant problem of whether the specification follows from the requirements or whether any code produced is what the user wanted.

The software dependability assessment approach provides an abstract description of software and makes use of all the available evidence regarding both the software product itself and the processes used in its development. It is capable of dealing with both qualitative and quantitative evidence and provides a means whereby the risk involved in the development and use of software can be monitored and thus controlled. A prototype knowledge-based system provides rules for the assessment of software dependability by taking account of the means used in making and checking software. The support logic rules are based on concepts derived from a hierarchy of software attributes. For example, software is expressed in terms of product and process attributes; product is expressed in terms of object and use, whereas process is defined in terms of process profile, tools, personnel and machines; object is expressed in terms of form, scale, style and checkedness and so on. The software dependability assessment approach enables software to be treated at an appropriate level of abstraction. For example, the selection of formal methods and related tools for some safety-critical application may be highly desirable in itself, but it is only of use if it can be shown that the procedures and uses of such methods and tools have been applied with corresponding rigour and dependability and that such processes have been managed effectively.

Several projects have built upon the developments of this software dependability assessment model. For example, the United Kingdom Atomic Energy Authority UKAEA and SEMA Scientific developed an analogous model for the measurement of software diversity for fault tolerant software, and SEMA Scientific, UKAEA and the University of Bristol developed a prototype tool in Fril in the IED/DTI project "QUINCE: Quantifying Uncertainty for Software Cost Estimation". The QUINCE model used three complementary approaches to the estimation of software cost: an approach based on the intermediate COCOMO cost model; an analogy approach based on the comparison of Major Software Functions; and an approach based on bottom-up estimating using Work Breakdown structures. The prototype used a fuzzy set representation for the cost estimates and a method of aggregation for combining the estimates from the different approaches. The database of past projects was rather restricted at the time the project was completed, but with a more representative knowledge base of past projects, there would be considerable scope for extending and improving the estimation method using the evidential logic rule described in Chapters 4 and 6.

8.9 BIBLIOGRAPHY

Baldwin, J.F., Pilsworth, B.W. and Morton, S.K. (1987), "Object Identification from 2D images", Alvey project 007, SERC Final report.

Blockley, D.I. (1980), "The Nature of Structural Design and Safety", Ellis Horwood.

Burke, M.M. (1991), "Software Dependability Assessment", PhD thesis, University of Bristol.

Hufton, D. (1992), "The QUINCE Project: Final Management Report", DTI/IED report QUINCE/66.

Mackin, N. (1992), "Development of an Expert System for Planning Orthodontic Treatment", PhD thesis, University of Bristol.

Monk, M.R.M. and Swabey, M. "Simulation of Aircrew Behaviour for System Integration using Knowledge-Based Programming." In Proc. Modelling and Simulation: ESM93 (Lyons, France), Society for Computer Simulation, 459-463, (1993).

Popper, K.R. (1959), "The Logic of Scientific Discovery", Hutchinson of London.

Smith, B. (1990), "CAMES - Expert System Administration of Money Market Services", Conceptual Graphs Workshop, European Conference on AI.

Wu, C.M.L., Webber, J.P.H. and Morton, S.K. (1991), "A Knowledge Based Expert System for Laminated Composite Strut Design", The Aeronautical Journal of the Royal Aeronautical Society.

Index

373

379

Fril –
Fuzzy and Evidential Reasoning
in Artificial Intelligence

UNCERTAINTY THEORY IN ARTIFICIAL INTELLIGENCE SERIES

Series Editor: **Professor J. F. Baldwin,** *University of Bristol, UK*

Fril –
Fuzzy and Evidential Reasoning in Artificial Intelligence

J. F. Baldwin
T. P. Martin
B. W. Pilsworth
University of Bristol, UK

RESEARCH STUDIES PRESS LTD.
Taunton, Somerset, England

JOHN WILEY & SONS INC.
New York · Chichester · Toronto · Brisbane · Singapore

RESEARCH STUDIES PRESS LTD.
24 Belvedere Road, Taunton, Somerset, England TA1 1HD

Marketing and Distribution:

Australia and New Zealand:
Jacaranda Wiley Ltd.
GPO Box 859, Brisbane, Queensland 4001, Australia

Canada:
JOHN WILEY & SONS CANADA LIMITED
22 Worcester Road, Rexdale, Ontario, Canada

Europe, Africa, Middle East and Japan:
JOHN WILEY & SONS LIMITED
Baffins Lane, Chichester, West Sussex, England

North and South America:
JOHN WILEY & SONS INC.
605 Third Avenue, New York, NY 10158, USA

South East Asia:
JOHN WILEY & SONS (SEA) PTE LTD.
37 Jalan Pemimpin 05-04
Block B Union Industrial Building, Singapore 2057

Library of Congress Cataloging-in-Publication Data

Baldwin, J. F. (James Frederick), 1938–
    Fril, fuzzy and evidential reasoning in artificial intelligence /
J.F. Baldwin, T.P. Martin, B.W. Pilsworth.
      p.   cm. — (Uncertainty theory in artificial intelligence
series ; 1)
    Includes bibliographical references and index.
    ISBN 0-86380-159-5 (Research Studies Press). — ISBN 0-471-95523-X
(Wiley)
    1. Logic programming.   2. Fuzzy systems.   3. Artificial
intelligence.   I. Martin, T. P.   II. Pilsworth, B. W.   III. Title.
IV. Series
QA76.63.B35   1995
006.3'3—dc20
                                     94-37424
                                        CIP

British Library Cataloguing in Publication Data

A catalogue record for this book
is available from the British Library.

ISBN 0 86380 159 5 (Research Studies Press Ltd.)
ISBN 0 471 95523 X (John Wiley & Sons Inc.)

Printed in Great Britain by SRP Ltd., Exeter